MW00580546

Ōkagami, The Great Mirror

Michigan Classics in Japanese Studies
Number 4

Center for Japanese Studies
The University of Michigan

Ōkagami

The Great Mirror

Fujiwara Michinaga (966-1027) and His Times

A Study and Translation by Helen Craig McCullough

CENTER FOR JAPANESE STUDIES
THE UNIVERSITY OF MICHIGAN
ANN ARBOR, MICHIGAN

Copyright © 1980 by Princeton University Press
All Rights Reserved
Reprinted with the permission of Princeton University Press
Reprinted in 1991 by the Center for Japanese Studies,
108 Lane Hall, The University of Michigan,
Ann Arbor, MI, 48109

Library of Congress Cataloging-in-Publication Data

Ōkagami. English
    Okagami, the Great mirror : Fujiwara Michinaga (966–1027) and his times /
a study and translation by Helen Craig McCullough.
    p.   cm. — (Michigan classics in Japanese studies ; no. 4)
    Reprint. Originally published: Princeton : Princeton University Press,
1980.
    Includes bibliographical references and index.
    ISBN 0–939512–50–5
    1. Ōkagami. 2. Japan — History — Heian period, 794–1185.
I. McCullough, Helen Craig. II. Series.
[DS856.03813 1991]
952'.01—dc20   90–21410
                                                                          CIP

The paper used in this publication meets the requirements
of the ANSI Standard Z39.48–1984 (Permanence of Paper).
Printed in the United States of America

For Dundas Craig McCullough, who was in at the beginning

Contents

Translator's Preface

Unless new sources of information are unearthed, *The Great Mirror* (*Ōkagami*) will remain forever anonymous and undated. A few writers have accepted 1025, the narrative present of the text, as the approximate date of composition. Most others have assigned the work to the 100-year period between 1040 and 1140, with leading scholars clustering around the years 1085-1125. There are at least eighteen authorial candidates, ranging from the novelist Murasaki Shikibu (978?-1016?) to the poet Minamoto Tsunenobu (1016-1097). Modern opinions, all based on tenuous circumstantial evidence, favor various male aristocrats of the Fujiwara and Minamoto families, especially the latter. Hosaka Hiroshi, the author of the major *Ōkagami* study, *Ōkagami shinkō*, supports Minister of the Right Akifusa (1026-1094), an influential figure of the early *insei* period, who was a son of Minamoto Morofusa by Fujiwara Michinaga's daughter Sonshi. Matsumura Hiroji, the editor of the *Nihon koten bungaku taikei* text, agrees that Akifusa is as likely a candidate as any.

The *Nihon koten bungaku taikei* text, based on the Tomatsubon, is the one translated here. The Tomatsubon is the oldest known complete *Ōkagami* version, probably copied around the Bun'ei era (1264-1275). It consists of six scrolls, each in a different hand, the backs of which are covered with detailed annotations, known as the *uragaki*, or back writing. (The *uragaki*, printed as an appendix in the *Nihon koten bungaku taikei* edition, has not been included in the translation.) The Tomatsubon belongs to one of two main *Ōkagami* textual lines, that of the old texts (*kohon*), extant copies of which date from the medieval and Tokugawa periods. *Kohon* texts are ordinarily divided into either six scrolls (*maki*) or three booklets (*satsu*). Vulgate texts (*rufubon*), which make up the second main group, expand the *kohon* content with many minor additions and a few lengthy interpolations, most of which probably date from the late Heian period. They appear in Tokugawa-period printed editions, are usually divided into six or eight chapters, and were until recent times the best-known and most widely circulated *Ōkagami* texts. A *rufubon* of uncertain identity was printed by Satō Kyū in his valuable *Ōkagami shōkai* and translated in Joseph K. Yamagiwa, *The Ōkagami* (London, 1967), a pioneering work that can be said to have outlived its usefulness. Other modern printed editions have also reproduced *rufubon* texts, but the present tendency is to rely on *kohon*, especially the Tomatsubon, which might, therefore, properly be called a *rufubon*. Translations of major *rufubon* additions will be found in Appendix B. A minor textual line, the "different texts" (*ihon*), representing a separate tradition of accretion, survives in a few copies. It seems to have been of some importance in the Muromachi period.

The translation and introduction have benefited enormously from Hosaka's modern Japanese translation (based on the Tomatsubon), exhaustive research, and extensive commentary in *Ōkagami shinkō*. His discussion of *tamashii* has been particularly illuminating, although he should not be held responsible for the use I have made of it. I should also like to thank Edward Fowler and William McCullough for reading portions of the manuscript and making helpful comments and corrections; the Center for Japanese and Korean Studies of the University of California, Berkeley, for financial assistance; and Stanford University Press for permission to reproduce or adapt footnote material from *Tales of Ise* and *A Tale of Flowering Fortunes*.

Notes

1. In citations, *Ōkagami* means the *Nihon koten bungaku taikei* edition. Other editions are cited by editors' names.

2. In the translation, superscript figures in parentheses refer to Appendix B.

3. Readings for masculine personal names follow the *Nihon koten bungaku taikei* text—thus Fuyutsugi instead of the more familiar Fuyutsugu. Since Japanese (*kun*) readings of feminine personal names are usually impossible to establish for the Heian period, I have ordinarily used Sino-Japanese readings. Exceptions include Tokihime and names such as Mitsuko, recorded in three graphs, which are intended to be read phonetically.

4. Ages recorded in the translation are calculated in the Japanese manner, according to the number of calendar years during which the individual lived. Unless otherwise indicated by use of the notation *sai*, ages mentioned elsewhere are calculated in the Western manner.

5. The translation notes do not usually point out minor factual inaccuracies. Many authorial lapses can be detected by checking the text against Appendixes A and D, but the concerned reader is advised to consult Hosaka. On the general question of reliability, see the introduction, "Historicity."

6. The translation is complete except for the omission of cyclical dates.

Ōkagami, The Great Mirror

Introduction

The Question of Genre   For the western reader confronted with a book called *The Great Mirror*, the question that springs to mind is, "Mirror of what?" *A Mirrour for Magistrates, The Mirror of Alchemy, The Mirror of Salvation, Speculum Caritatis, The Mirrour of Mirth and Pleasant Conceits, The Mirrour of Good Manners, Speculum Historiale*—those and many similarly titled medieval and Renaissance works, as well as their innumerable modern successors, have led us to expect an immense variety of possible subjects. In China, on the other hand, the mirror image is closely associated with history. Ssu-ma Ch'ien (145?-86? B.C.) said, "One who lives in the present age and considers the ways of the past has a mirror wherein he may see that the two are not necessarily alike,"[1] and the idea of history as mirror, a source of guidance for ruler and minister, was one that informed the labors of most of the Grand Historian's successors, including Ssu-ma Kuang (1018-1086), the author of the famous *Comprehensive Mirror for Aid in Government (Tzu chih t'ung chien)*, a voluminous chronological account of Chinese history from 403 B.C. to A.D. 959. A Sinologue, aware of the extent of Japan's cultural debt to China, might be pardoned for assuming *The Great Mirror* to be still another Japanese imitation of a Chinese prototype.

The student of Japanese literature, while perhaps pausing briefly over Kūkai's ninth-century *Secret Treasury of Poetic Mirrors (Bunkyō hifuron)*, would recall that *The Great Mirror (Ōkagami)*, a late eleventh-century or twelfth-century work, does indeed belong to a genre called *rekishi monogatari* by modern scholars. Leaving aside for the moment the precise meaning of the term *rekishi monogatari*, we can say that it refers to a type of history *(rekishi)*, and that there is much in the content of *The Great Mirror* to support the classification. The book can be viewed as an account of the rise of an aristocratic family, the Fujiwara, from its seventh-century inception to its zenith in the career of its most conspicuously successful member, Michinaga (966-1027), who dominated the Court from 995 until his death, acting for many years as principal minister, and wielding de facto power, through marital and family connections, as the father-in-law of three Emperors, one Crown Prince, and one Retired Emperor; the grandfather of an

[1] Watson 1961, 1.493.

Emperor and a Crown Prince; and the father of a Regent. Furthermore, our author's main spokesman, an old raconteur called Yotsugi,
whose name itself can be taken to mean chronicle, says to his audience,
"Pay close attention, everyone. . . . [Y]ou should think, as you listen
to me, that you are hearing the *Chronicles of Japan*."[2]

Yotsugi also seems to be thinking of himself as a historian when—in
terms reminiscent of Lucian, who compares the historian's mind to a
mirror, "clear, gleaming-bright, accurately centered, displaying the
shape of things just as he receives them, free from distortion, false
colouring, and misrepresentation"[3]—he calls himself an old mirror,
"[which,] without concealment . . . reveals afresh the deeds of sovereigns, each in his turn."[4] As we shall see, however, *The Great Mirror*,
whatever else it may be, is no chronicle, despite the apparent symbolism of Yotsugi's name. Furthermore, it is hard to believe that it was
intended as a comprehensive history in any form, whether of Japan or
of the Fujiwara family. Important events, many of them intimately
connected with Fujiwara activities, are treated obliquely, barely mentioned, or omitted outright. There are only passing references to the
rebellions of Fujiwara Sumitomo and Taira Masakado (the two most
spectacular national events of the period between 850 and 1025, the
time span with which the book is primarily concerned); little or
nothing is said about the series of maneuvers by means of which the
Fujiwara destroyed other houses, secured the exile of influential non-
Fujiwara rivals, and prevented the accession of Princes born of non-
Fujiwara mothers; and the oldest extant *Ōkagami* manuscripts gloss
over or ignore some of the most striking manifestations of the power
struggle within the victorious Fujiwara ranks, notably the enmity between the brothers Kanemichi and Kaneie.[5] *The Great Mirror* is not
a Japanese version of the *Comprehensive Mirror for Aid in Government*, or of that other encyclopedic tome, the *Speculum Historiale* of
Vincent de Beauvais (1190-1264).

The author himself states at the outset, and repeats periodically, that
his primary concern is with Michinaga, and that such historical information as he presents is ancillary to his basic purpose, which is to describe and explain his protagonist's brilliant career. "I have only one
thing of importance on my mind," he says through Yotsugi, "and that
is to describe Lord Michinaga's unprecedented successes to all of you
here, clergy and laity of both sexes. It is a complicated subject, so I
shall have to discuss a fair number of Emperors, Empresses, ministers

[2] Translation, p. 86.   [3] Braudy 1970, p. 97.
[4] Translation, p. 86.   [5] See Appendix D.

of state, and senior nobles first. Then when I reach Michinaga himself, the most fortunate of all, you will understand just how everything came about."[6]

It would seem, therefore, that the book is the mirror of a man's life, a biography inspired by the same impulse to praise and edify that motivated Plutarch[7] and found later expression in such "mirror" works as *The Mirrour of True Nobility and Gentility, A Biography of the Renowned Nicolaus Claudius Fabricius Lord of Peiresk*, by Pierre Gassendi (1592-1655), and *The Mirrour of Vertue in Worldly Greatness, or The Life of Sir Thomas More, Knight*, by William Roper (1496-1578), to say nothing of a host of hagiographies, both western and eastern. But, although our author announces that Michinaga is his subject, he displays a persistent tendency to digress. "There is nothing I have not seen or heard," he says through Yotsugi, and again, "I do want to mention all the things I have especially admired."[8] The nervous reader comes to fear that he may intend to pass along the sum total of his experiences. Instead of drawing his account to a close at the end of the climactic section in which Michinaga and his immediate family at last become the focal point of attention, he suddenly whisks us back to the seventh century, remarking, "But I think people are inclined to believe that all the Fujiwara have been equally blessed, so I had better say a little more about some of the others."[9] Many seemingly irrelevant pages later, a member of the audience releases a flood of reminiscences about festival origins, elegant events during early reigns, miracles, poems, omens, and physiognomists' predictions by saying, "We are learning some fascinating things. What are your earliest memories? Won't you please give us a few?"[10] The entire final section of the book, amounting to about twenty percent of the total length, is made up of anecdotes that seem to have only the most tenuous connection with Michinaga. If we are to label the work a biography, we must do so with qualifications.

One is tempted to conclude that *The Great Mirror* is neither history nor biography, but a collection of traditional stories and anecdotes about historical figures, selected and ordered primarily, although not

---

[6] Translation, p. 68.

[7] "I began the writing of my 'Lives' for the sake of others, but I find that I am continuing the work and delighting in it now for my own sake also, using history as a mirror and endeavoring in a manner to fashion and adorn my life in conformity with the virtues therein depicted." *Plutarch's Lives*, 6.261. I am indebted to Ms. Claire Papapavlou for drawing this passage to my attention.

[8] Translation, pp. 87, 143.   [9] Translation, p. 199.

[10] Translation, p. 215.

exclusively, by the author's interest in the life and times of Michinaga. Certainly, its form and content can best be understood within the context of the role of the oral story in Japanese literary history.

The Oral Story   In all societies, anecdotes and related oral forms must be very nearly as old as speech itself, but in few have they contributed so extensively and persistently to the form and content of major literary works, and indeed of entire genres, as in Japan. Their present status in the west is low, and their connection with serious literature remote. They enjoyed, it is true, one period of high visibility in Europe, for reasons more practical than literary, and under circumstances similar to those that nurtured their Chinese and Japanese counterparts. Their prominence began in the late twelfth and early thirteenth centuries, when the rise of the preaching friars led to the proliferation of the exemplum, a brief tale related during a sermon for the edification and amusement of the congregation, and to the compilation of exemplum collections. Stories told by famous preachers, such as the French prelate Jacques de Vitry (ca. 1180 to ca. 1240), were brought together for the assistance of less gifted sermonizers, sometimes in abbreviated forms showing that they were intended for use as prompt books; and early collections in Latin, like those from Jacques de Vitry's *Sermones Vulgares* and the various versions of the misleadingly named *Gesta Romanorum* (Deeds of the Romans, late thirteenth century), were followed by vernacular collections, intended for the general reader as well as for the preacher.

As the story below shows, the typical exemplum marches straight ahead in a businesslike, matter-of-fact way, with few literary flourishes.

OF HANGING

Valerius tells us that a man named Paletinus one day burst into a flood of tears; and, calling his son and his neighbors around him, said, "Alas! alas! I have now growing in my garden a fatal tree, on which my poor first wife hung herself, then my second, and after that my third. Have I not therefore cause for the wretchedness I exhibit?" "Truly," said one who was called Arrius, "I marvel that you should weep at such an unusual instance of good fortune! Give me, I pray you, two or three sprigs of that gentle tree, which I will divide with my neighbors, and thereby afford every man an opportunity of indulging the laudable wishes of his spouse." Paletinus complied with his friend's request; and ever after found this remarkable tree the most productive part of his estate.

APPLICATION

My beloved, the tree is the cross of Christ. The man's three wives are, pride, lusts of the heart, and lusts of the eyes, which ought to be thus suspended and destroyed. He who solicited a part of the tree is any good Christian.[11]

Since the aim of the preacher was to entertain as well as to instruct, the exemplum ranged broadly over many kinds of subjects. A typical repertoire probably included biblical stories; pious tales; hagiographic stories; tales of visions and apparitions, of classical celebrities, and of historical events; legends; fables; incidents from the speaker's life; and farcical anecdotes.[12] As the story of the widower's tree suggests, many exampla were non-religious stories with superimposed allegorical interpretations. An increasing tendency toward secularization, especially of the farcical tales, eventually spelled the end of the form in the sixteenth century, after it had drawn the fire of prominent figures like Wycliffe, Erasmus, and Dante, the last of whom complained, "Now preachers make the congregation roar with quips and quirks, and so it laugh enough, their hoods swell, and they ask for nothing more."[13]

With the repudiation of the exemplum by its previous sponsors, the European anecdote reached a crossroads. Collections continued to appear, religious, secular, and mixed, but the rise of the romance and other prose forms relegated the short oral tale to permanent obscurity, and its influence on serious literature is seldom detectable except by specialists. Few who read *King Lear* are aware that its plot can be traced to one and one-half undistinguished pages in *Gesta Romanorum*.[14]

In Japan, on the other hand, stories of this type have bulked so large in literary history as to produce an important specialization called *setsuwa* studies. *Setsuwa* is a modern term embracing a number of sub-literary prose narrative forms—the anecdote, the legend, the folk tale, etc.—which have in common brevity, simple language, presumed factuality, emphasis on a single narrative motif, absence of description and psychological analysis, a tendency to move the action along by means of dialogue, subject-matter of an amazing, sad, frightening, humorous, or queer nature, and ultimately oral origins. Like the exemplum, the *setsuwa* frequently conveys a religious message, and the narrator often stresses the factuality of his account by providing concrete details about time and place, as in the story below.

[11] Swan 1905, p. 132.
[13] Dante 1970, p. 321 (29.115-117).
[12] Tubach 1957, p. 29ff.
[14] Swan 1905, pp. 30-32.

There was once a youth who lived in Shimoarashi Village, Izumi District, Izumi Province. I cannot tell you his name, but he was naturally perverse, refused to believe in karma, and made it a habit to hunt for eggs, which he cooked and ate.

In the Third Month of the sixth year of Tenpyō shōhō [754], an unknown soldier came to the youth's house. "The provincial officials wish to see you," he told him. Sure enough, there was a four-foot strip of wood [sic] at the soldier's waist, bearing an official summons. The youth set out with him, and presently they arrived at Yamatae Village. Then the soldier pushed the youth into a two-acre wheat field where the grain was two feet tall. When the boy looked at the field, he saw a sea of flame in which there was not even an inch of free space. Around and around he ran, shrieking, "It's hot! It's hot!"

One of the villagers had gone into the hills to collect firewood. Observing the youth running, falling, and shouting, he went down to try to pull him out. The youth struggled against him, but he got him outside the fence, mustering all his strength. The youth fell to the ground, motionless and silent. Then he came to his senses, stood up, and screamed in agony.

"My legs! My legs!"

"What is the matter with them?" asked the villager.

"A soldier came for me and pushed me into the fire so that my legs were cooked. There were mountains of flame in every direction. That was why I shouted and ran," the boy answered.

Rolling up the youth's trouser skirts, the villager saw that the skin on his legs was cooked to a jelly. Nothing was left but the bones. Within a day, the boy was dead.

This teaches us that hells actually exist. We must believe in karma. And we must not be like the crow, which loves its own young but devours the offspring of others. Human though he be, anyone who lacks compassion is the same as a crow. "Although there are differences of degree between men and beasts," says the *Nirvana Sutra*, "they are alike in prizing life and dreading death." It is of just such cases that the *Karma Sutra* says, "He who cooks eggs in this world will fall into the Hell of Hot Ashes after his death."[15]

Stories of this type, though not always specifically identified by scholars as *setsuwa*, appear in records of the origins and miraculous works of shrines and temples, in biographies of famous men like

[15] *Nihon ryōiki*, pp. 207-208 (2.10).

Shōtoku Taishi, and in collections describing rebirth in Amitābha's paradise (*ōjōden*). We also find *setsuwa*, both religious and secular, in headnotes to the compositions in poetic anthologies; in miscellanies like *Tsurezuregusa*; in the literary genres known as *uta monogatari* (poem tales), *rekishi monogatari*, and *gunki monogatari* (war tales); and, of course, in *setsuwa* collections (*setsuwashū*). Far more obviously than in the case of *King Lear*, a *setsuwa* often serves as the basis of a Nō play. And the influence of the form is apparent in the episodic, plotless structure of Japanese romances and novels, from the earliest times to the present. It is probably no exaggeration to say that there is scarcely a Japanese literary genre in which the short oral tale has not made its presence felt.

We cannot do more here than speculate briefly about the reasons for this rather remarkable state of affairs, this consistent preference for open-ended works amenable to accretions and deletions, and for presumed fact as opposed to fiction. The phenomenon may be related to the urge that has reduced Japanese poetry from *chōka* to *tanka* to *haikai*—to the apparent conviction, in other words, that the sole function of poetry is to serve as a vehicle for lyric expression, and that the briefest lyricism is the purest. A series of memorable prose vignettes, each appealing directly to one or more basic emotions, has seemingly been considered superior to the more cerebral, moralistic approach of an Austen, a George Eliot, or a James. In the case of war tales, in particular, there is also demonstrable influence from the ancient tradition of professional oral storytelling, which flourished throughout the pre-industrial era and is still far from dead. And there has undoubtedly been great influence from Chinese *setsuwa* collections and from Chinese ideas, both Confucian and Buddhist, concerning the function of literature.

As is well known, the art of oral storytelling has probably been more highly developed and longer-lived in China than in any other great cultural area. Some of the earliest of the Chinese professional storytellers were popular Buddhist preachers of the T'ang dynasty, who drew upon native history and mythology and the Buddhist canon for karma tales and other stories calculated to attract, entertain, and instruct listeners. Surviving performance records show that the preachers' recitals were sometimes illustrated by pictures, and that they frequently alternated prose and poetry in an effort to appeal to audiences. "Today, for your sake, this story has been proclaimed," one of their stories ends. "Tomorrow come early to hear the sutra."[16]

Such preachers inherited a tradition traced by the Chinese to Hui-

[16] Eoyang 1971, p. 87.

yüan (334-416), who is said to have been the first native monk to begin a religious service with karma stories.[17] As early as the third century, stories that must have been similar to those recited by Hui-yüan, as well as others with a purely secular orientation, had begun to be brought together by men of letters, primarily from written sources. A translated collection of *avadāna* stories[18] appeared around 223-253, as did indigenous collections of secular "strange tales"; and there is a surviving collection of miracle stories, based on the "Kannon Chapter" of the *Lotus Sutra*, which dates from the last half of the fourth century. It is useful for our purposes to note that the stories in collections of strange tales and miracle tales tended to be straightforward accounts of single incidents, couched in simple, non-allusive language; and also that there was mutual influence between them and Chinese biographies of eminent monks, which had begun to appear toward the end of the Six Dynasties period.[19] Possibly because the government prohibited public storytelling by Buddhist monks in the early Sung period, thus reducing the professional demand for anecdotes, the Buddhist miracle tale seems to have declined after reaching a peak in the T'ang dynasty, which saw the compilation of a huge 100-scroll anthology, *Fa yüan chu lin* (Forest of Pearls from the Garden of the Law), completed in 668 by the monk Tao-shih.[20]

Among the sources utilized for *Fa yüan chu lin* was a popular collection of karma stories, T'ang Lin's *Ming pao chi* (Records of Supernatural Retribution), compiled around 650, which is believed to have contained about eighty items. Like other collectors east and west, T'ang Lin went to considerable trouble to persuade readers of the authenticity of his tales by providing information about names, dates, and places, and by specifying his sources. Although no complete manuscript of his book survives, the oldest extant version, containing fifty-three stories, indicates that most of his sources were oral. They included "people of the neighborhood," local magistrates, people met during the author's official travels, an acupuncture doctor, relatives of the author or of people involved in the incidents, a caller who visited the author when he was ill, and a colleague who related the story to a group of officials, including the author, who were waiting to be admitted to the Imperial presence.

The *Ming pao chi* attributions, whether truthful or not, are unlikely to have been challenged by contemporary readers accustomed to the

[17] Nakamura 1973, p. 31.

[18] Stories about previous lives of the Buddha's contemporaries. For an example, see Gjertson 1975, p. 12.

[19] Gjertson 1975, pp. 37, 40.   [20] Gjertson 1975, p. 177.

"vast activity of amateur, casual storytelling which takes place in company."[21] Both from the west and from the east, moreover, there is ample evidence, if evidence were needed, that interest in such stories was not limited to the lower classes. "At night, after supper," says a *Gesta Romanorum* tale, set in a castle called Cathubica on the borders of the episcopal see of Ely, "as is usual in great families, during the winter, the household assembled around the hearth, and occupied the hour[s] in relating divers tales."[22] Structurally and thematically, the rainy-night yarns spun by Prince Genji's friends constitute one of the most important passages in *The Tale of Genji*, and *The Great Mirror* itself describes a rainy-night gathering in the Imperial presence at which "stories about frightening occurrences" were told.[23] T'ang Lin's last three attributions, in particular, suggest some of the kinds of sources *The Great Mirror* may have drawn upon.

It is safe to assume that *Ming pao chi* was not overlooked by T'ang preachers, or by Japanese monks who accompanied official missions to the continent in order to visit monasteries, study, and acquire books. By the early ninth century, at the latest, T'ang Lin's work had crossed the seas to Japan, where the four surviving manuscripts all remain, and where it contributed, both by example and by content, to the compilation of the oldest extant Japanese *setsuwa* collection, *Nihon ryōiki* (Miraculous Stories of Karmic Retribution in Japan).

Nihon ryōiki, compiled around 821 by an obscure Nara monk named Kyōkai, consists of 116 stories of Buddhist miracles, drawn, according to the author, from oral sources, and brought together to show that the kinds of events recorded in *Ming pao chi* were also happening in Japan. Eight of the 116 were in fact adapted from *Ming pao chi* itself, including the one about the boy who robbed nests.[24] That particular oriental examplum, like the others in *Nihon ryōiki*, was probably preserved by Kyōkai at least partly for the convenience of Buddhist preachers. Proselytization among the masses had been prohibited in the Nara period by the authorities, who complained that the monks were inducing people to abandon their responsibilities for the religious life,[25] but it is unlikely to have disappeared completely. In any case, such stories were useful for the Heian preachers who delivered sermons to aristocratic congregations or to groups made up of mixed social classes, and who, like their European counterparts, made active efforts to entertain and move their audiences.[26] Large collections of old stories,

21 Hanan 1973, p. 127.   22 Swan 1905, p. 332.   23 Translation, p. 194.
24 *Ming Pao chi* no. 37, translated in Gjertson 1975, pp. 377-379.
25 *Shoku nihongi*, 1.172-173, Tenth Day, Seventh Month, Yōrō 6 (722).
26 *Konjaku monogatari* speaks of a tenth-century preacher who "told stories

brought together in the twelfth and thirteenth centuries, strongly suggest that many Buddhist *setsuwa* were in circulation during the earlier part of the Heian period, both orally and in such compilations as *Sanbō ekotoba* (Illustrated Scrolls of the Three Treasures), *Jizō bosatsu reigenki* (Record of Miracles of the Bodhisattva Kṣitigarbha), and *Dainihon hokekyō kenki* (Record of *Lotus Sutra* Miracles in Japan), three other *setsuwa* collections that have happened to survive from the tenth and eleventh centuries.

Secular tales seem to have circulated with equal briskness, spread not only by Buddhist monks but also by other agents familiar throughout the world, such as old people, travelers, and professional storytellers.[27] The earliest dated mention of the famous *biwa hōshi* (lute monks), known for having carried *Heike monogatari* (Tales of the Heike) throughout Japan in the medieval period, comes in the diary of Michinaga's cousin Sanesuke, who reports in 985 that he has called one into his mansion to perform for him.[28] Murasaki Shikibu also refers to the *biwa hōshi*,[29] who seem, despite their name, to have been laymen dressed in clerical robes, and to have supported themselves by reciting poems, singing songs, and telling stories, often performing at temples in conjunction with the sermons of preachers. They were, no doubt, only one group among many.

To members of the upper classes who, like Sanesuke, summoned entertainers for private performances, attended religious functions at which monks related entertaining stories, and picked up anecdotes in the ordinary course of everyday life, it must have seemed natural to emulate Chinese literati by assembling unusual tales. No collections have been preserved from Michinaga's own day or before, but at least two eminent early Heian scholars, Miyoshi Kiyoyuki (847-918) and Ki no Haseo (fl. early tenth century), are known to have brought to-

---

amusingly and made people laugh," of another monk who was "good at telling stories," and of a third who moved the warrior Minamoto Mitsunaka (912-997) to tears and prevailed on him to take Buddhist vows; Sei Shōnagon describes a preacher playing up to a noble audience; and the diarist Fujiwara Munetada comments approvingly in 1112 on a sermon in which the congregation has been given "both flowers [entertainment] and fruit [doctrine]." *Konjaku monogatarishū*, 5.68 (28.7), 4.200 (20.35), 4.65-70 (19.4); Brower 1952, pp. 475-484; *Makura no sōshi* sec. 33, p. 75; Morris 1967, 1.35; *Chūyūki*, 4.180, Fifth Day, Eighth Month, Ten'ei 3 (1112). See also Kikuchi 1958, p. 49; Nagai 1966-1967, 1.90.

[27] Nagano 1969, p. 28.

[28] *Shōyūki*, Eighteenth Day, Seventh Month, Kanna 1. I rely for this reference on Tomikura (1958, p. 6) and Tamagami (1974-1976, 3.188), who have used a *Shōyūki* text unavailable to me.

[29] Seidensticker 1976, p. 255; *Genji monogatari*, 2.71.

gether tales about foxes, spirits, and immortals, and mystery stories, respectively. Aside from *Yamato monogatari* (Tales of Yamato, tenth century), which is assigned by some scholars to the *setsuwa* genre, the oldest extant secular collection is *Gōdanshō* (Excerpts from the Conversations of Ōe Masafusa), a work in six chapters, consisting of stories told by an eleventh-century scholar, Ōe Masafusa (1041-1111), to someone who probably recorded them between 1104 and 1108. *Gōdanshō* contains legends, stories about official ceremonies and other Court affairs, tales centering on poetry, on famous musical instruments, on Emperors and other prominent members of the aristocracy, and similar accounts, all jotted down in the kind of Japanized Chinese employed in the diaries of Heian gentlemen—doubtless because, like such diaries, it was intended primarily as a reference work.

For Heian Court society, which had reached its zenith in Michinaga's day, the twelfth century was a period of catastrophic decline, culminating in the transfer of power to the military class and the establishment of the Kamakura shogunate. Even during Michinaga's lifetime, reflective members of the Court circle like Murasaki Shikibu seem to have felt nostalgia for the reigns of earlier Emperors, during which the ambition of the house of Fujiwara had been kept within bounds; but the first quarter of the eleventh century had been, on the whole, a time when most members of the nobility viewed the present with complacent satisfaction, looked forward to the future, and considered the past musty and boring. The compilation of *Gōdanshō* was symptomatic of a new desire to preserve nostalgic memories of past greatness in the face of present distress, an attitude that found expression both in medieval literary works like *Heike monogatari* and *Tsurezuregusa* (Essays in Idleness) and in the growth of secret traditions and antiquarian activities of all kinds, including the collection of anecdotes about Court society and its concerns. By the middle of the twelfth century, there had appeared two more collections: *Chūgaishō* (Jottings by the Nakahara Senior Secretary) and *Fuke godan* (Stories and Discussions of Lord Fuke), which resembled *Gōdanshō* in that they recorded (in a terse, inelegant mixture of Chinese and Japanese) anecdotes and scraps of information about Court customs and usages, learned by the writer from a prominent man, in this case the Regent Fujiwara Tadazane (1078-1162), who was the source for both. Another work, *Shunrai zuinō* (Shunrai's Poetic Essentials), by the leading poet Minamoto Shunrai (1055?-1129), recorded gossipy bits about men of letters. And if some Japanese scholarly opinion is correct, it was probably at about this same time that the largest and most important of all *setsuwashū*, *Konjaku monogatari* (Tales of the Past), made its appearance, bringing together approximately 1,200 stories of all kinds, both religious and secular, from a wide variety of oral and written sources.

The period around the beginning of the twelfth century was, in short, a time when tale collecting was in the air, and when there was also a peculiar interest in preserving a record of past aristocratic glory. Compilations like *Gōdanshō*, *Chūgaishō*, *Fuke godan*, and *Shunrai zuinō* were clearly designed to be treated not as literary works but as references; and the huge *Konjaku* itself can be said to represent not only a desire to meet the practical needs of Buddhist preachers, who were beginning to reach out to the common people on an unprecedented scale, but also an urge toward preservation. *The Great Mirror*, different though it is from such works, is very much a product of the same age and spirit.

Rekishi Monogatari   Without wishing to deny the importance of *Tosa nikki* (Tosa Diary, ca. 935), Ki no Tsurayuki's pioneering literary diary, we may venture the generalization that every ambitious Heian writer regarded poetry as his proper medium. In view of the overwhelming Chinese-inspired prestige commanded by the art of verse, it is probably safe to assume that prose writers like Michitsuna's mother, Sei Shōnagon, and Murasaki Shikibu took up their brushes with no thought of winning literary immortality, but merely as a means of passing time or amusing others, or, in Murasaki's case, because of a creative urge too strong to be denied. The Confucian prejudice against fiction, in particular, seems to have been powerful enough to prevent any educated male from letting his name be associated with a romance, a novel, or any other out-and-out fabrication.

At the same time, many a courtier must have uttered a fervent mental assent when he read Murasaki's defense of fiction: "*The Chronicles of Japan* and the rest are a mere fragment of the whole truth. It is your romances [*monogatari*] that fill in the details."[30] The modern reader may have reservations about the surviving Heian romances, and he will also need to be aware, in using the Seidensticker translation, that romance is only one possible translation of *monogatari*, a word that makes no commitment as to truthfulness. In Heian usage, *monogatari* meant "telling something" in the colloquial language, as opposed to Chinese—an anecdote, a morsel of gossip, a story of whatever length or kind.[31] But to anyone who had read *The Tale of Genji*, the bald

[30] Seidensticker 1976, p. 437.

[31] Anecdotes and similar stories, now categorized as *setsuwa*, would thus have fallen into the same category as *The Tale of Genji*.

Chinese chronicles in the Six National Histories must have seemed woefully inadequate.

It is small wonder that an eleventh-century woman should have produced an unabashed imitation of Murasaki's language and literary technique, when—moved, perhaps, by the first stirrings of the new Zeitgeist—she set out to make a record of the life and times of the great Michinaga. That anonymous historian, the author of *Eiga monogatari* (A Tale of Flowering Fortunes, ca. mid-eleventh century), is conjectured by scholars to have been Akazome Emon, a lady-in-waiting to Michinaga's principal consort, Rinshi; and we may for convenience so identify her. Akazome's work is a chronological treatment of history in terms of family relationships, rivalries for official preferment and for favor in the Imperial harem, marriages, births, illnesses, deaths, poetry, music, dress, elegant entertainments, and the whole round of religious and secular activities characteristic of life at the Heian Court.

A modern reader is likely to feel that *Eiga monogatari* goes from one extreme to the other as a result of Akazome's desire to remedy the deficiencies of the laconic official histories. She "fills in the details" so relentlessly and uncritically that we are in danger of drowning in a sea of trivia. Akazome was no genius like Murasaki, but merely a rather ordinary, aging woman with time on her hands, a woman who knew Michinaga and his relatives intimately, enjoyed access to family records and other historical materials,[32] and possessed, in *The Tale of Genji*, a brilliant, exciting model for a new approach to historical writing. Nevertheless, her work, with all its faults, was important and original enough to necessitate the invention of a special literary genre, the *rekishi monogatari*, to accommodate it.

It will be seen that the term *rekishi monogatari*, although translatable as historical tale, is not to be equated with those popular western works of fiction in which authentic historical events and personages provide a context for the romantic adventures of imaginary characters. It means a special kind of *monogatari*, a story about historical persons and events, which is, in theory, at least, entirely factual except for minor authorial liberties; and it differs from the *setsuwa* in that it is by far the longer and more complex of the two—book-length, rather than a few lines or a few pages; that it is not traditional in nature but the creation of a single principal author; that it is based on written as well as oral sources; and that it is invariably recorded in colloquial Japanese.

Although we cannot prove that Akazome wrote *Eiga monogatari*, the predominantly feminine nature of the book's concerns makes it

---

[32] Akazome's husband was Ōe Masahira (952-1012), a prominent member of one of the Court's leading scholarly families.

reasonably certain that the author was a woman. Traditionally, however, historiography was a masculine occupation, in Japan as in China. Also, study of Chinese historical texts, particularly Ssu-ma Ch'ien's *Shih chi* (Records of the Historian), was part of the standard education of the male Japanese aristocrat, as contrasted with his female counterpart's concentration on Japanese poetry, music, and calligraphy. It is not surprising, therefore, that Japanese historiography yields only one significant example of history from a feminine brush, namely, *Eiga* itself. The future of the *rekishi monogatari*, as of other forms of history, lay in masculine hands.[33]

This brings us to our own author, the anonymous creator of *The Great Mirror*, which was to become the second and most distinguished representative of the *rekishi monogatari* genre. He seems to have lived toward the end of the eleventh century, or possibly somewhat later— during the period, at any rate, when *setsuwa* collections like *Gōdanshō* were coming into existence. The factual information he supplies shows that he had access to historical records, either official or family or both; the zest with which he tells a good story, whether or not it concerns Michinaga, points to the conclusion that he was one of the many Court nobles who enjoyed collecting anecdotes about their peers; and his demonstrable familiarity with *Eiga monogatari* suggests a motive for his undertaking.

In an era when books circulated only in manuscript, a long, dull work like *Eiga monogatari* was probably not well known, but Hosaka and others have shown that the *Ōkagami* author must have had it at his disposal. Comparison reveals, for instance, that Yotsugi's account of the resignation of Crown Prince Atsuakira is a skillful condensation of Akazome's version;[34] and linguistic similarities such as those in the passages below, where the two authors comment on the brevity of Michikane's tenure as Regent, are unlikely to be accidental.

Eiga monogatari: Sakizaki no tonobara, yagate yo o shirasetamawanu tagui wa aredo, kakaru yume wa mada mizu koso aritsure.
(In the past, [many] gentlemen [of his family] have failed to attain the regency, but nobody has ever [won it and then held it] for so fleeting and dreamlike an interval.)[35]

Ōkagami: Kono tonobara no mizō ni, yagate yo o shiroshimesanu tagui ōku owasuredo, mata araji kashi, yume no yō nite yami-

---

[33] For information about later *rekishi monogatari*, see McCullough and McCullough 1980, Introduction.

[34] Hosaka 1974, 2.362.   [35] *Eiga monogatari*, 1.150.

tamaeru wa. (Many gentlemen of his family have failed to attain the regency, but there has probably never been another who has [won it and then] lost it as though in a dream.)[36]

Since the *Ōkagami* author knew of *Eiga monogatari*, he must have found the work deficient as an account of Michinaga's career. The clue to his dissatisfaction appears early in *The Great Mirror*, in a passage that has already been quoted: "I have only one thing of importance on my mind, and that is to describe Lord Michinaga's unprecedented successes to all of you here, clergy and laity of both sexes. It is a complicated subject, so I shall have to discuss a fair number of Emperors, Empresses, ministers of state, and senior nobles first. Then when I reach Michinaga himself, the most fortunate of all, you will understand just how everything came about."

The shortcoming of Akazome's lengthy work is that it fails to tell us "just how everything came about"; it is purely descriptive. The *Ōkagami* author, looking back at the great days of the Fujiwara, feels the urge to explain how the family, and Michinaga in particular, rose to power. What techniques did they employ? What part did luck play? What kind of men were the successful Fujiwara leaders? If Akazome had been asked to explain "just how everything came about," she would probably have murmured something about the working of karma. Our author occasionally falls back on karma, but he also asks a modern historian's questions, which is one of the reasons why his book interests us as *Eiga* cannot.

If we are to think of *The Great Mirror* as a Japanese *Magnum Speculorum Exemplorum*, therefore, rather than as a history or a biography, we must recognize that its *setsuwa* have been brought together for a specific purpose, which is not religious instruction or the implicit advocacy of ethical theories (as in the case of the European exemplum collections, *Ming pao chi, Shih chi,* and *Plutarch's Lives*), but rather the examination of Michinaga's career and its significance. We may detect a reflection of the antiquarian spirit of the age in the author's determination to preserve stories, absent from *Eiga monogatari*, which seem to him to cast marginal light on his subject, as well as others which he considers simply too good to be consigned to oblivion.

The Great Mirror: Setting and Actors   Living in a society in which amateur and professional storytelling, both religious and secular, was

[36] *Ōkagami,* p. 196.

a part of everyday existence, the *Ōkagami* author hit on the expedient of presenting his narrative in the first person and making a Buddhist temple, the Urin'in, his setting. We have already noticed, in touching on the role of the *biwa hōshi* as *setsuwa* transmitters, that religious establishments, where preaching monks and lay entertainers came together, were among the storytelling centers of the Heian period. The Urin'in, a former Imperial villa pleasantly situated in a setting of woods and water, seems to have been a favorite destination for excursions on horseback during the cherry-blossom season, and to have attracted large crowds, made up of all social classes, to its great annual events, the enlightenment sermon in the Fifth Month and the perpetual Buddha recitations in the Eleventh. The "I" of the book, who gives us to understand that he is a member of Court society,[37] attends an enlightenment sermon in a year corresponding to 1025, and finds himself part of a large group waiting for the preacher. It is a perfect opportunity for the appearance of a storyteller, and one is introduced in the very first sentence—old Yotsugi, a man "of extraordinary and disturbing antiquity," who reveals a determined inclination to talk about the brilliant fortunes of Michinaga, "our present Novice Excellency." It is also the best possible time for such a disquisition, because Michinaga's life is soon to be shadowed by a series of sad events—the deaths of his daughters Kanshi and Kishi in the Seventh and Eighth Months of that same year, the retirement into Buddhist orders of his daughter Shōshi in 1026, and the deaths of his son Akinobu and his daughter Kenshi in 1027. And old Yotsugi is an ideal raconteur. His name, which can mean chronicle, is in itself a strong guarantee of his credibility, and although it is common for a storyteller to pretend to special knowledge,[38] his 190 years give him a unique advantage. "I am a remarkable old fellow," he boasts. "Wouldn't any honest soul feel embarrassed by comparison? . . . There is nothing I have not seen or heard. I think the things I am going to tell you will be new to many people." The members of the audience react with awed acceptance, "touching their foreheads and listening with fervor," when he instructs them to "think, as you listen to me, that you are hearing the *Chronicles of Japan*."[39]

The attitude of the crowd, taken in conjunction with the narrator's comment that Yotsugi and his two companions are people of "extraordinary and disturbing antiquity" (*reihito yori wa koyo nō toshioi, utatage naru [mono]*), calls to mind the emphasis placed in Japanese

[37] Translation, p. 214.
[38] Cf. the jongleur who says, "There are not many who can tell you this tale." Price 1975, "The Capture of Orange," p. 93.
[39] Translation, p. 86.

folk culture "upon mysterious visitors and upon members of outcast groups who travel from place to place as magico-religious beggars and reciters."[40] We feel, on the one hand, that Yotsugi has something in common with the latter group, and, on the other, that he may be a quasi-divine mysterious visitor, a *marebito*. The idea that old people possess superior wisdom, often accompanied by supernatural powers, is, of course, common in traditional societies. Plutarch reports that Alexander selected the site for the city that was to bear his name on the basis of advice received from a man "with very hoary locks and of a venerable aspect," who appeared to him in a dream;[41] and characters in myths, legends, and folk tales are constantly encountering aged men and women who supply them with magic objects, help them accomplish impossible tasks, answer riddles, explain enigmatic happenings, or predict their futures, as the old woman does for Tokihime in *The Great Mirror*.[42]

Indigenous Japanese divinities (*kami*) appear with remarkable frequency in the guise of white-haired old people. We find them in *Takasago, Hakurakuten, Chikubushima, Awaji,* and many other Nō plays; in *setsuwa* collections; and in other written and oral literature of all kinds, including *The Great Mirror*. Yanagita Kunio has observed that such deities usually turn out to be associated with water, as in the well-known case of the Sumiyoshi gods; that it was once customary in parts of northeastern Japan to refer to floods as "white hair waters"; and that there is still a tendency among his countrymen to seek a hidden meaning in premature white hair (for example, by calling it "lucky white hair"), which, in his view, may be traceable to a feeling that such people were in touch with the gods.[43] However that may be, the connection between old age and the supernatural seems to have been a powerful one, and we are probably justified in concluding that the author has it in mind, at least subconsciously, when he calls Yotsugi *utatage*, a word that might be translated as eerie.

There are also indications that Yotsugi's credibility is reinforced for the Urin'in congregation by association with Buddhism, a not surprising state of affairs, in view of the Shintō-Buddhist accommodation that was itself ancient by the time *The Great Mirror* was written. Not only is Yotsugi telling his story at a Buddhist temple, but he is a surrogate for the tardy preacher, who will edify and regale the crowd with anecdotes of his own when he arrives. Shigeki, the other old raconteur, likens Yotsugi to the famous Buddhist layman Vimalakīrti; and Yotsugi implicitly compares himself to Śākyamuni when he says, "They tell

---

[40] Hori 1963, p. 76.
[42] Translation, p. 164.

[41] *Plutarch's Lives*, 7.299.
[43] Yanagita 1962-1971, 8.428-429.

us that the Buddha began by expounding other sutras when he wanted
to explain the *Lotus*, which is why his sermons are called the teachings
of the five periods. That is how it is with me, too; I need to 'expound
other sutras' in order to describe Michinaga's successes."[44]

If Yotsugi's statement be considered faintly blasphemous, we may
note the existence of a *Konjaku monogatari* story in which the Buddha
appears as an old mackerel seller,[45] a somewhat comic association,
which reminds us again of the connection between the divine and
those lowly members of society who eke out a precarious existence by
begging, entertaining, and putting people in touch with the other
world; and which prepares us for the discovery of still another facet
of Yotsugi's personality. In addition to playing a dual role as a trans-
mitter of important information, drawing upon the prestige of two
sets of religious beliefs, he functions as an entertainer. Like any good
lecturer, he usually manages to hold our interest while discussing serious matters, and in that sense is an entertainer throughout, inspiring
the narrator to remark at one point, "One could not help feeling that
the most extravagant praise would have been inadequate."[46] But there
are also times when he is a simple, ingenuous old man, regarded by the
narrator with a superior smile; and others when he puts on the come-
dian's mask, telling about a dog that seems to have achieved buddhahood, describing how he and his wife have joked about finding a
young replacement for her, or rambling on, tongue in cheek, about
his courtship and early married life. Such jests must have been part of
the stock in trade of many of the entertainers who worked the crowds
at religious events like the Urin'in enlightenment sermons. Furthermore, there must have been few in old Yotsugi's audience who were
unaware that he bore a name reminiscent of the main performer in a
famous *sarugaku* piece.[47]

Sarugaku, an ancestor of Nō, seems to have taken two forms during
the Heian period: a serious dramatic presentation of religious subjects,
performed under temple auspices; and a medley of dance, comic singing and miming, juggling, and acrobatics, performed by independent
entertainers as an adjunct to festivals and similar events.[48] It is not clear
how the two merged with one another, and with other types of dramatic presentation, to form Nō, but at some juncture, according to

---

[44] Translation, p. 68.
[45] *Konjaku monogatarishū*, 3.139-140 (12.7). Translation in Brower 1952, pp.
393-395.
[46] Translation, p. 200.
[47] This has been pointed out by many scholars. See Hosaka 1974, 1.91.
[48] O'Neill 1958, pp. 4-5.

the dramatist Zeami (1364?-1443), three *sarugaku*, known as the ceremonial three pieces (*shiki sanban*), were singled out as particularly
sacred symbolic representations of the threefold body of the Buddha—
the *dharma-kāya*, the *saṃbhoga-kāya*, and the *nirmāṇa-kāya*. Each
consisted primarily of a dance performed by an old man, and the name
of the second was "Yo[na]tsumi no Okina" (Old Yotsumi).[49]

Yotsugi's name and character can thus be seen as conveying a mod-
estly complex symbolism. At one level he represents the historian, at
another he is cloaked in supernatural authority, and at a third he functions as an entertainer. As each role contrasts with the other two, so
there are internal contrasts. In the second role he stands for the indigenous gods, on the one hand, and for Buddhism, on the other. In the
third he is at once amateur and professional, at once spiritual and profane, at once dignified and comic: amateur because the author presents him as such, professional because of the traits he shares with
shrine and temple entertainers, spiritual and dignified because of his
connection with the *shiki sanban*, profane and comic because of the
mannerisms and humorous anecdotes associating him with the secular
sarugaku tradition.

The contrasts extend to the old man's relationship with the second
raconteur, Shigeki. We may note here, in anticipation of later consideration of *The Great Mirror*'s structure, that the work gives the
impression of having run away with the author. It develops a single
theme up to and including the formal biographical treatment of Michinaga, but then becomes, in effect, a *setsuwa* collection, not unstruc-
tured, but imperfectly integrated with what precedes it, which will be
referred to for convenience as Part One. Concentrating for the moment on Part One, we may hazard the guess that the author's original
plan gave Shigeki almost nothing to do. It is Yotsugi who tells the
whole story; Shigeki merely helps to introduce him to the audience
and encourages him from time to time. Shigeki himself impresses us as
a rather simpleminded nonentity, by no means comparable to his remarkable companion.

When the author decided to add Part Two—the sections ordinarily
identified as "Tales of the Fujiwara Family" and "Tales of the Past"—
it apparently did not occur to him at first to change his method of presentation. Yotsugi's monologue continues throughout "Tales of the
Fujiwara Family" and into "Tales of the Past," punctuated only by
an occasional comment from Shigeki or someone else. Early in "Tales

---

[49] Sometimes written with the graphs used for Yotsugi. Zeami 1961, p. 371;
O'Neill 1958, p. 70.

of the Past," however, Shigeki breaks in: "I won't give you as many details as Yotsugi," he says, "but . . . I have vivid recollections of certain occurrences when Emperors Uda and Daigo abdicated."[50]

He proceeds to relate a series of short anecdotes dealing with matters of taste, poetry, pleasant traits in the great, and so forth—the kind of topics we associate with *Makura no sōshi* (The Pillow Book), *Genji monogatari*, and other works by Court ladies, as contrasted with the more political, masculine interests of Yotsugi—and, in so doing, belatedly takes on a personality. In spite of his low social status, he is an old fellow with cultivated tastes, a humble counterpart, in this respect at least, of the ideal Heian noble depicted in *The Tale of Genji*. That the *Genji* ideal was not the only one in the Heian period, and that the *Ōkagami* author, through Yotsugi, reserves his highest praise for another, is a suggestion that will be advanced later. We shall merely note here that the author, mistaken though his decision to add Part Two may have been, redeems it somewhat by bringing Shigeki to the fore as a foil to Yotsugi, and by introducing a comparatively high proportion of dialogue between the two, which helps to unify his narrative.

In the first sentence of Part One, the author introduces four of his five speakers: Yotsugi, Shigeki, Shigeki's ancient wife, who makes a single brief appearance in "Tales of the Past," and the narrator, the "I" of *The Great Mirror*, whose remarks are addressed exclusively to the reader. The fifth is a member of the congregation, described in the Preface as "a man of about thirty . . . an attendant from a noble household, by the look of him,"[51] who, "bent on taking part in the conversation," makes his way to a spot near the old people after they begin to chat.

In the oldest *Ōkagami* texts (*kohon*), the attendant interrupts Yotsugi with an occasional question or a polite suggestion that he may have got his facts wrong. In "Tales of the Past," for instance, Yotsugi tells a story about a courtier whose career in the bureaucracy had stagnated until, at the age of fifty, he recited a poem at Iwashimizu Shrine and secured a promotion through divine intervention. "I seem to remember hearing that old story in the streets," the attendant says. "It is supposed to have happened at Kamo Shrine." "I won't argue the point," Yotsugi answers. "It was a long time ago; I may be mistaken." The attendant ends the exchange by saying, "It is true about Moroki's career. He became a Consultant at the age of fifty-six."[52]

In addition to brief episodes of that nature, the *kohon* texts contain a long passage in which the attendant questions Yotsugi's version of

[50] Translation, p. 217.   [51] Translation, p. 66.
[52] Translation, p. 225.

one of the most important events described in *The Great Mirror*, the sudden resignation of a Crown Prince who was only indirectly related to Michinaga, and his replacement by Michinaga's grandson, the future Emperor Go-Suzaku. Yotsugi has merely said, "For some reason the Prince began to feel unhappy. . . . His mind dwelt on the freedom he had enjoyed as an ordinary Prince, and he gradually persuaded himself that nothing would delight him more than to escape the restraints of his ceremonious existence. . . . Michinaga's extraordinary karma must have had something to do with [his] decision to resign."[53] The attendant presents a much more circumstantial account of the affair, making it clear that pressure from Michinaga has forced the Prince to step down.

In the vulgate texts (*rufubon*), the attendant speaks up again at another important juncture, the end of the biography devoted to Kanemichi, the brother of Michinaga's father, Kaneie. The power struggle between Kanemichi and Kaneie was one of the most notorious in the history of the Fujiwara family,[54] but Yotsugi barely mentions it in the *kohon* texts. "Kanemichi had a harsh nature," he says. "It was cruel of him to strip Kaneie of his office and rank with no justification at all— Kaneie, who was such a wonderful man that his descendants are still enjoying boundless success today."[55] If we are correct in assuming the *rufubon* additions to be the work of a later hand or hands, the original author was content to echo the sentiments of *Eiga monogatari*, which blames Kanemichi for all that happens between the brothers, and which ends its account of their relationship with the comment, "It was a pity that [Kanemichi] had chosen to inflict such a harsh blow on his brother when so little time was left to him on earth."[56] In the *rufubon*, however, the attendant interrupts to present Kanemichi's side of the story.

According to my information, Kaneie's demotion was only natural. I have the details from the lips of my grandfather, who served for years in Kanemichi's mansion. Because of rivalry over ranks and offices, the two brothers had been on bad terms for a long time when Kanemichi was stricken by his fatal illness. As the crisis drew near, the Regent's people heard outriders off to the east. Someone reported that Kaneie was approaching.

"Even though we have been estranged during all these years, he wants to see me before I die," Kanemichi thought. He saw to it that all the unsightly objects near him were cleared away, ordered his bed to be tidied, and waited impatiently for his brother's ar-

[53] Translation, pp. 118, 119.
[55] Translation, p. 157.
[54] See Appendix D, p. 347.
[56] *Eiga monogatari*, 1.77.

rival, only to learn that Kaneie had gone on past toward the Imperial Palace. He was speechless with mortification, and his attendants must also have felt foolish.

"I was going to talk to him about resigning in his favor," Kanemichi said to himself. "It is just because he is that kind of person
that I have never been able to get along with him."[57]

The interpolation, which occurs immediately before the introduction of a new topic, contains no indication of Yotsugi's reaction to the
attendant's statement. After the latter's long speech about the Crown
Prince in the *kohon* texts, however, the old man shows himself willing to accept correction in a friendly spirit. He offers no rebuttal,
and when the attendant says, "It was all so sudden that I wonder how
the Prince rewarded [the Imperial messenger who came to give him a
courtesy title after his resignation]," he responds, "Lord Michinaga
would have taken care of it. He wouldn't have lost any time after
matters had reached that stage."[58] The relationship between the two
remains amicable throughout, and Yotsugi makes his attitude explicit
near the end of the book.

"If I have rambled on today, it was only because you, sir, have
seemed to find our conversation unusual and interesting, and because you have joined us to such splendid effect. Much more
might be said; indeed, I could go on and on. But please send a pack
horse for me if you should really want to hear it all. I'll scramble
onto his back and pay you a visit. As a matter of fact, I would like
very much to call on you and receive the benefit of your learning,
because I have never in all my years met anyone capable of answering me as you do. Although you look young enough to be
my grandson's grandson, your comments show how much you
know. I think you must be in the habit of reading ancient diaries,
which is a most refined pursuit, far beyond the education of a
humble fellow like me. . . . Old as I am to be a pupil, I would be
very pleased if I might resolve some of my doubts by asking you
questions."[59]

The role of the attendant, then, is not to provide dramatic con-
frontations. Nor does the author intend to intrigue the reader by offering him a choice between equally plausible versions of the same event,

---

[57] Appendix B (14).   [58] Translation, p. 123.
[59] Translation, p. 234.

as Browning does in "The Ring and the Book" and Akutagawa in "Yabu no naka" (In the Grove). The attendant's statements set the record straight, and Yotsugi's willingness to accept correction authenticates the old man's devotion to accuracy and reinforces the audience's conviction that he is, as he claims, a veritable national history. Leaving aside for the present the attendant's significance within the context of the author's avowed intention to look behind the scenes at Fujiwara power, we may say that the youth, like each of the other four characters, makes a contribution to *The Great Mirror* as a work of literature.

Japanese scholars, in search of a precedent for *The Great Mirror*'s five speakers, have suggested that the author may have received a hint from the rainy-night conversation (*shinasadame*) in *The Tale of Genji*.[60] If so, we might argue that this is one area in which a relatively minor writer has improved on a distinguished model. Two of the four participants in the *shinasadame*, Hidari no Uma no Kami and Tō Shikibu no Jō, are shadowy figures who appear nowhere else in the book. The other two, Prince Genji and Tō no Chūjō, are central characters, but Genji, in particular, plays a passive role in this episode, and there is nothing in Tō no Chūjō's speech and actions to distinguish him from Uma no Kami and Shikibu no Jō, who, in turn, are virtual twins. Any of Uma no Kami's speeches might equally well have been attributed to Shikibu no Jō. Nor is there any discernible reason for setting the stage with four characters; there might as well have been three, five, or some other number. Murasaki's purpose is apparently to present different types of women in order to prepare the reader for later developments, and she does not seem overly concerned about her mouthpieces. Each of the five *Ōkagami* characters, on the other hand, stands out as an individual and performs a distinct function.

The narrator is an alert, observant fellow who sets the stage, brings the old people vividly before our eyes with his comments on their actions and appearance, and, as narrators are wont to do, tells us what to think: "He really had no business discussing such matters," "He was acting a bit too authoritative," "[It was a] rather theatrical and pretentious prelude."

Yotsugi, as befits a principal raconteur, seems very close to a professional storyteller, boasting, wiping his eyes and blowing his nose, lowering his voice to a whisper, raising his eyes, acting the clown, and holding up his skirts to show how muddy they are. His yellow fan, with its nine black persimmon-wood ribs, is in constant play. Now he

[60] Matsumura 1961, p. 26.

gives it a triumphant flourish, now he fans himself with a complacent smirk, now he hides his face behind it. The narrator, observing his antics, occasionally indulges in a patronizing smile, but he never strays far from the conviction that this is no ordinary mortal, and that what he says is not to be taken lightly. He tells us at the outset that there is something "extraordinary and disturbing" about all three of the old people; and, as we have seen, there is indeed much in Yotsugi to support the belief that he is associated with the supernatural on more than one level. The few corrections made by the attendant only strengthen the feeling that this seemingly simple old man verges eerily on the omniscient. The narrator calls him smug, theatrical, and pretentious, laughs at him, feels sorry for him, gets exasperated, but always comes back to the fact that his "extraordinary narrative" and "amazing memory" cannot be shrugged off. He sums up his basic attitude at the end of the book: "It was amazing, and a little frightening, to listen to him. Was there anything he didn't know?" Yotsugi is our guarantee of *The Great Mirror*'s credibility.

Shigeki represents the non-political, aesthetic side of Heian aristocratic life, demonstrating interests and tastes similar to those reflected in the poetic anthologies and the writings of Court ladies. He has a penchant for the touching anecdote—a lady's distress when men from the Imperial Palace dig up her prized plum tree, the loneliness of a neglected consort, the unhappiness of an Emperor who abdicates against his will—and he tends to treat his topics in the style of the *uta monogatari*, making one or more poems the focal point of a brief, well-told tale. It is perhaps worth noting that the *Ōkagami* author, whose lack of interest in the natural environment contrasts strikingly with the attitude of feminine writers like Sei Shōnagon and Murasaki Shikibu, puts one of his rare descriptions of scenery into Shigeki's mouth.

After they entered the hunting grounds, the Imperial falcon Shirashō came swooping down to the phoenix on top of His Majesty's litter, holding a bird in its talons. The sun was sinking toward the rim of the hills, and the autumn leaves on the slopes resembled a brocade mantle in the brilliant shafts of light. The falcon was pure white, the pheasant dark blue. And yes—a light snow sifted down as the raptor stood with outstretched wings. For me the moment captured the full charm of the season, and I was sure there had never been so marvelous a sight.[61]

[61] Translation, p. 218.

The lone episode devoted to Shigeki's wife constitutes a distinct *sarugaku* touch. The reader is reminded of those comic skits, still presented in conjunction with religious festivals in Japan, in which one of the characters is a round-faced old peasant woman. The author probably intends no witticism when he has Shigeki's wife say, "I have been married to Shigeki ever since my girlhood, so I'm afraid I haven't had any interesting experiences,"[62] but it is clear that she is presented as a contrast to her husband, just as Shigeki himself, the gentle aesthete, contrasts with the more flamboyant and politically oriented Yotsugi. Whereas Shigeki is a connoisseur of poetry, his wife is too stupid to remember the name of Nakatsukasa, one of the most famous poets of the day, in whose company she has travelled all the way from Michinoku to the capital. When pressed, she barely manages to reconstruct a single composition by the distinguished lady, faltering out the lines, the narrator tells us, "with a lack of assurance that was a far cry from Shigeki's fluency."

The brief interlude ends when Shigeki says, "Do you mean you can't remember who [the author of that poem] was? How could anyone forget a thing like that? Her one redeeming feature is that she has a wonderful head for practical matters. That's why I can't divorce her." His jocular comment, with its overtones of affectionate contempt, reminds us that women, in the masculine world of the *setsuwa*, are not always viewed through the sympathetic eyes of a Murasaki Shikibu, but, rather, are often treated as they are in the folk anecdotes of Europe, in which, as Stith Thompson points out, "perhaps [through the influence of] fabliaux and novelle with their medieval bias against women, the woman usually appears as wicked, overbearing, and faithless, or at best unutterably stupid."[63]

Ōkagami and Shih chi   Having assembled a cast—the narrator, the three old people, and the attendant—the author was faced with the problem of combining his *setsuwa* hoard with other materials in the manner that would best accomplish his goal of explaining Michinaga's success. Every modern discussion of *The Great Mirror* makes the point that he rejected the chronicle form (which had been employed by all previous Japanese histories, including *Eiga monogatari*) in favor of the Chinese annals-biography (*kiden*) structure, of which *Shih chi* is the first and greatest example. We should bear in mind, however, that that analysis applies only to what we have called Part One, that the

---

[62] Translation, p. 224.   [63] Thompson 1977, p. 209.

treatment is broadly chronological within each of the two main sections of that part, i.e., the annals and the biographies; and that the resemblance to *Shih chi* is only superficial.

Ssu-ma Ch'ien's masterpiece, which had been known in Japan since the Nara period, seems to have been one of the two established Chinese classics with which the average Heian noble was best acquainted, the other being *Wen hsüan* (Anthology of Literature, sixth century). It is a comprehensive work in 130 chapters, covering the course of Chinese history from remote antiquity until about 99 B.C., and organized into five major sections, as follows.

1. Basic Annals (12 chapters). The main record of events from the earliest times through successive kings and dynasties to Han Wu Ti (r. 141-87 B.C.).

2. Chronological Tables (10 chapters). Information about princely houses, princes, and high officials, presented in graph form.

3. Treatises (8 chapters). Eight essays on subjects unsuited to chronological treatment, such as rites, music, religion, rivers and canals, and economic affairs.

4. Hereditary Houses (30 chapters). Records of Chou states.

5. Biographies (70 chapters). Biographies of outstanding men, classified into categories (good officials, harsh officials, assassin-retainers, etc.); also a few brief essays on foreign peoples and countries.

The Great Mirror is also divisible into five sections.[64]

1. Preface. Meeting of the characters at the Urin'in; preliminary conversation.

2. Imperial Annals. Accounts of the reigns of fourteen Emperors, covering the years 850 to 1025.

3. Biographies. Biographies of twenty Fujiwara ministers of state.

4. Tales of the Fujiwara Family. A brief survey of Fujiwara leaders from Kamatari on, followed by anecdotes about Fujiwara shrines and temples, a list of Fujiwara fathers of Empresses and grandfathers of Emperors, and more stories about Fujiwara temples, culminating in a discussion centering on the Hōjōji, founded by Michinaga.

---

[64] The description below applies to the *kohon* texts. The vulgate texts contain an addendum at the end, some seven pages long, which is stated to be "a continuation of the story about Yotsugi's dream, set down by the Master of the Empress's Household" in a year corresponding to 1119. It deals primarily with Princess Teishi, the daughter of Emperor Sanjō and Michinaga's daughter Kenshi. Printed in Tachibana 1974, pp. 426-433. For a note on textual lines, see the. Translator's Preface.

5. Tales of the Past. *Setsuwa* dealing with festival origins, poems and poets, elegant events, Emperors of the past, members of the Minamoto family, Buddhist preachers, strange happenings, etc.

In *Shih chi*, annals and biographies together account for 82 of the work's 130 chapters; in a modern printed edition of *The Great Mirror*, they occupy 186 of 251 pages. The major portions of both works, therefore, can be said to conform to a single design. Both also devote more space to biographies than to annals—70 chapters, as opposed to 12, for *Shih chi*; approximately 162 pages, as opposed to 17, for *The Great Mirror*. Both are written in a good colloquial style with an eye for literary effect; both make illumination of character a major concern; and both rely heavily on the use of anecdote, including dialogue.

When the two are inspected carefully, however, it can be seen that the similarities do not extend very far. The Basic Annals are the core of *Shih chi*, incomparably more detailed than their skimpy *Ōkagami* counterparts. As a Japanese writer has put it, in *Shih chi* the Emperor is the sun and the biographees are the planets; in *The Great Mirror* Michinaga is the sun.[65] And there are no *Ōkagami* equivalents for the other three *Shih chi* categories—the Chronological Tables, the Treatises, and the Hereditary Houses.

Far more important than formal discrepancies is the matter of authorial motive and its relationship to content and tone. Ssu-ma Ch'ien adopts the orthodox Confucian approach, which attaches supreme importance to the ability to profit from the lessons of political history. The Grand Historian's interest focuses on the moral quality of men and deeds—on showing that a bad man like Ch'in Shih Huang Ti cannot establish a lasting dynasty, on identifying the kind of man a ruler should use, on judging character, and the like. His anecdotes are selected accordingly, and his biographies typically end with a personal moral assessment, such as the one he supplies for a joint essay on two eminent officials: "The Grand Historian remarks: Chang Shih-chih knew how to define a worthy man and to uphold the law without toadying to the will of the emperor, while Feng T'ang's discussions of the way to be a general—ah! they too have a flavor about them."[66]

The *Ōkagami* author wishes to commemorate and illuminate one man's career. And it is not moral considerations that engage his attention when he tries to explain Michinaga's success. Given the right set of circumstances, he implies, there is no reason why the descendants of a Ch'in Shih Huang Ti should not prosper forever. Success is a mat-

[65] Takeda Taijun, quoted in Matsumura 1961, p. 102.
[66] Watson 1961, 1.542.

ter of luck, of personality, and especially of having the right family connections.

Japanese society has traditionally held the individual to a fixed position within a group. To put it in Parsonian terms, ascription has been more important than achievement, particularly in stable periods like the Heian. At the Heian Court, there were two significant groupings, the great families and Court society as a whole; and the fundamental determinants of the individual's position in the latter were his birth and his family's position vis-à-vis other noble houses. Marital and blood relationships within the Imperial family were consequently of vital importance, and our author's main concern in his annals is to clarify the history and extent of the intermarriage between the Imperial line and the Fujiwara, with emphasis on the Northern House, to which Michinaga belonged. A detailed history of each reign would have been irrelevant to his purpose.

Imperial Annals   Beginning his annals with Emperor Montoku (the Fujiwara grandson whose reign signalled the start of the Northern House's ascendancy), the author shows that of the fourteen sovereigns from that Emperor to Go-Ichijō, who occupied the throne in 1025, all but three—Kōkō, Uda, and Daigo—were born of Northern House mothers. In every case, this is indicated by an initial statement concerning the Emperor's parentage. The purpose of the annals is made even more explicit by the other kinds of information supplied. The Emperor himself usually receives short shrift. Except in the two cases of Kazan and Sanjō, almost nothing is said about him or about his activities beyond a listing of important dates in his life, and he frequently receives less space than his mother. The three non-Northern House mothers are ignored after the initial mention, as are four others—Anshi, Kaishi, Chōshi, and Shōshi—who figure later in the biographies, but we are given basic biographical data about all the others, and in some cases they become the subjects of anecdotes.

The anecdotes about Emperors in the biographies and in Part Two ("Tales of the Fujiwara Family" and "Tales of the Past") show that the author did not limit himself to dry recitals of facts and dates for lack of material. Rather, he seems to have conceived of this initial section as a repository for essential background information, a first important statement about Michinaga's success, and an implicit criticism of *Eiga monogatari*, which had begun its coverage only with the reign of Uda. Anecdotes are irrelevant in the annals, and it may have been against his better judgment that he included a few.

Biographies   It would be difficult to argue that *The Great Mirror* annals are in any way comparable to those in *Shih chi*. The biographies, which adopt the anecdotal method, seem at first glance to be much closer to Ssu-ma Ch'ien's work, but the resemblance is more apparent than real. Whereas *Shih chi* deals with many men from many walks of life and many families, our author has restricted himself to twenty ministers of state, beginning with Emperor Montoku's grandfather, Fuyutsugi,[67] the founder of the fortunes of the Northern House. All twenty are members of the Northern House, nineteen are descendants of Fuyutsugi by a single wife, Mitsuko, and the last fifteen are descendants of Nagara, one of Fuyutsugi's sons. The basic arrangement is by succession from father to son: Fuyutsugi (1)—Nagara (4)—Mototsune (5)—Tadahira (8)—Morosuke (12)—Kaneie (17)—Michinaga (20), with selected brothers filling the remaining niches. Examination reveals the care with which the author has shaped his materials.

By the beginning of the Heian period, the dominant position established by the first two Fujiwara leaders, Kamatari and Fuhito, had been lost, owing to the early deaths of Fuhito's four sons (including Fusasaki, the founder of the Northern House), and to the involvement of family members in two unsuccessful plots. It was Michinaga's ancestor Fuyutsugi who earned the trust of Emperor Saga (r. 809-823), married his daughter to Saga's son, became the grandfather of the future Emperor Montoku, and thus started the Northern House on its upward path. It is natural, therefore, that the biographical section should begin with a brief acknowledgment of Fuyutsugi's accomplishments.

Fuyutsugi's son Yoshifusa, the brother of Michinaga's ancestor Nagara, becomes the second biographee because of his conspicuous contributions to the family fortunes. It was in his day that the rival Tomo, Tachibana, and Ki families were crushed, and it was he who became the first subject to serve as Chancellor and as Regent. The author gives us a brief factual account of his career, followed by an anecdote in which he skillfully sums up the minister's success and the satisfaction it afforded him.

Of his many poems, one in particular lets us guess how much satisfaction his accomplishments gave him. He recited it when he saw a vase of cherry blossoms standing in front of his daughter, the Somedono Empress.

| Toshi fureba | The years have passed |
| Yowai wa oinu | And I am old— |

[67] Better known as Fuyutsugu. See the Translator's Preface.

Shika wa aredo   But though it be thus,
Hana o shi mireba   The sight of the blossoms
Monoomoi mo nashi.   Makes me content.

Of course, he was using "blossoms" to mean the Empress.[68]

What the author wants us to keep in mind, however, is that Nagara's line was the only one to flourish for generation after generation, even though others helped the family to rise. "What a shame that a man as lucky as Yoshifusa should not have had any sons!" he says by way of conclusion. "His older brother, Middle Counselor Nagara, must have felt hurt when Yoshifusa rose so high above him . . . but it is Nagara's descendants who prosper today, so he has come out far ahead in the long run."[69] He seems to have included Nagara's brother Yoshimi, the third biographee, specifically to underline this point. Although *Sandai jitsuroku*, the official history of the period, devotes considerable space to Yoshimi, depicting him as a model statesman with an exemplary character, *The Great Mirror* dismisses him with the remark that his grandsons "ended ingloriously as officials of Fifth Rank."

Nagara, who became a minister of state only posthumously, is important not for his accomplishments but as Michinaga's ancestor, and the author hurries through his meager biography in order to arrive at that of his son, Mototsune, a major figure who receives as much space as all four of his predecessors combined.

Somewhat to the reader's surprise, the three pages[70] devoted to Mototsune contain no information about the machinations by which he assisted in the destruction of rival families, the maneuvers he employed to protect his position when Emperor Yōzei abdicated, and the pressure he exerted on Emperor Uda. Passing over such omissions for the moment, we note that his biography, like most of the others, begins by listing both his father and his mother. It also mentions his daughter at the very outset, stating that she was Emperor Daigo's Empress and the mother of Emperors Suzaku and Murakami. These important genealogical details are followed by facts and dates pertinent to Mototsune's official career, and by anecdotes about him, the longest of which touches on his intimacy with his cousin, Prince Tokiyasu (the future Emperor Kōkō), his admiration for the Prince, and his support for the Prince's candidacy when a successor was being sought for Emperor Yōzei. The author's reason for including this *setsuwa*, which constitutes the core of the biography, is probably to be sought in his final

[68] Translation, p. 91.   [69] *Ibid.*
[70] Here and below, references are to the *Nihon koten bungaku taikei* edition.

comment about it: "Emperor Kōkō's descendants have reigned a long time, and Mototsune's have continued to advise and assist them. I cannot help feeling that the two must have exchanged pledges in a former life." The biography draws to a close with information about Mototsune's sons.

The structure of Mototsune's biography is fairly typical of the author's method. Almost invariably, there is initial identification of both parents, followed immediately by information about the subject's career. Anecdotes centering on the subject frequently come next, as they do here. The focus then usually shifts to the subject's descendants, who may be assigned much more space than the subject himself. At least one daughter is almost always discussed before any son. (Mototsune's is atypical in that there is mention of the daughter even before the subject's mother is named.) Needless to say, the priority enjoyed by the ladies derives from the fact that daughters of successful ministers married into the Imperial family. There is considerable attention to other marriages as well, both of daughters and of sons, and to their issue. Much such information is relevant to the author's theme, and the remainder, which is likely to strike an American reader as superfluous, was no doubt welcome and interesting to members of an ascriptive, birth-oriented society. Writers like Alexander Carlyle, a Scottish divine of the eighteenth century, seem to have found an equally receptive audience for such tidbits as, "[He] Married Lady Frances Erskine, one of the Daughters of the Earl of Buchan, a Lively little Deform'd Woman, very Religious and a Great Breeder. There Children were no way Distinguish'd, except the Eldest Daughter Fanny who was very Beautifull, and became the Wife of Sir [William] Baird."[71]

The most conspicuous departure from the model occurs in Tokihira's biography, the sixth longest in *The Great Mirror*, which follows Mototsune's. The reader will wonder why the author chose to devote half his space to Sugawara Michizane, rather than to Tokihira and his descendants, and why, if he wished to focus on Michizane's exile, he refrained from describing the Fujiwara activities responsible for it, particularly those of Tokihira. It is obvious that he was led into a digression by his fondness for a good story and his sympathy for Michizane, who has traditionally been regarded as a tragic figure comparable to Minamoto Yoshitsune, and who, like Yoshitsune, seems to have been the subject of innumerable anecdotes.[72] But there is a purpose behind his discussion of the exile—namely, to show how Michizane

[71] Carlyle 1973, p. 11.
[72] Hosaka 1974, 2.237. For some of the ramifications of the Yoshitsune legend, see McCullough 1966.

happened to turn into an angry spirit, and thus to explain why the line founded by Tokihira, Mototsune's oldest son, failed to prosper. A lengthy passage in the second part of the biography describes the deaths of Tokihira and a number of his immediate descendants (all of whom, we are led to believe, perished prematurely), and the author comments, through Yotsugi, "People say Tokihira's descendants died out because of the terrible sin he committed."

After that remark, Yotsugi continues, "No doubt they are right, but it seems a great pity." He proceeds to tell three stories that cast light on different facets of Tokihira's character. We may question the authenticity of the second, in particular, which sounds suspiciously like an attempt to connect a great man's name with a specimen of that hoary staple of folk literature, the fart anecdote, but all three are important because they probably show how Tokihira appeared to his contemporaries, and because they tell us something about the traits of character admired by our author, a subject to be discussed later.

The seventh biography, one of the shortest in the book, is that of Mototsune's second son, Nakahira, who, we are informed, had no children. The author's reason for including Nakahira seems to have been twofold. First, he reminds us that birth is not enough to assure success, that a minister of state cannot have prosperous descendants unless he sires offspring. This is another way of saying that the ambitious man needs to have luck on his side, like Michinaga's great-grandfather Tadahira, who was blessed with one older brother whose family came under the shadow of a curse and with another who produced no children. Second, by telling a story about the relationship between Nakahira and Tadahira, he adds a dimension to the latter's character, which, as presented in the next short biography, Tadahira's own, seems designed to show that this ancestor of Michinaga is no ordinary man: he has been born after a seven-month gestation period, he can outface a demon, and he is on speaking terms with goddesses.

With the ninth biography, that of Tadahira's oldest son, Saneyori, we come to the generation of Michinaga's grandfather. It might be noted that here, as elsewhere, subjects are not necessarily treated in order of birth. Of the three biographees in this generation, it is Saneyori, the oldest son, who receives priority. He is followed by his own son, Yoritada, after which the order is Morotada (Tadahira's fifth son) and Morosuke (Tadahira's second son), an arrangement that makes it possible to proceed directly from father to son (Morosuke to Koremasa) in advancing to the next main-line generation.

In the biographies of Saneyori and Yoritada (eleven pages in all), we are introduced to the Ononomiya line of the Northern House, founded by Saneyori, which has as its prominent members Saneyori, Yoritada, Sanesuke (grandson and adoptive son of Saneyori), Kintō (son of Yoritada), and the famous calligrapher Sukemasa (grandson of Saneyori). Aside from Sukemasa, who is described as lazy, these are all men of exemplary conduct and many virtues, but it is not their line that triumphs in the internal power struggle, even though both Saneyori and Yoritada serve as Regents. The basic difficulty is probably that neither succeeds in becoming the grandfather of an Emperor, but the author also implies, through his choice of anecdotes, that members of the Ononomiya line lack vital personal qualities possessed by Michinaga.

Morotada's biography, the fourth longest in the book, devotes little space to the minister himself. The initial focus is on his daughter Hōshi, a favorite Imperial consort, whose only son proves to be feebleminded, and who cannot compete for position with Morosuke's powerful daughter Anshi. Hōshi's brother Naritoki and his daughter Seishi are then introduced to pave the way for the lengthy discussion, mentioned earlier, of the resignation of Seishi's son, Crown Prince Atsuakira, barely three months after the death of the Prince's father, Retired Emperor Sanjō; and there is a final anecdote about Naritoki's second daughter, the estranged wife of Prince Atsumichi, who falls on hard times and successfully petitions Michinaga for help.

We shall return to the question of why the author should have devoted the bulk of this biography to Michinaga's campaign against Prince Atsuakira, while at the same time saying not a word about the pressure from Michinaga that had already forced Sanjō to abdicate, or about the harassment of Seishi to which Sanesuke's diary attests. For the present, we may note an apparent attempt to stress a more amiable side of Michinaga's character. The attendant says, "Once Michinaga had forced Koichijōin to resign, he took him as a son-in-law and showered him with so many attentions that everyone said his cordiality was more than enough to make the former Crown Prince forget his troubles." And the only conceivable reason for including the anecdote about Naritoki's second daughter is to send the reader off with a mental picture of the great man, interrupted at his prayers, shocked by the lady's unconventional action, but generous, sympathetic, and unwilling to commit "the cruelty of wounding her with harsh words."[73]

In the next biography, that of Michinaga's grandfather Morosuke, the initial focus is on Empress Anshi. The anecdotes in which Anshi figures demonstrate all the main facets of her character, but it is perhaps significant that the author takes occasion not once but twice to illustrate the lengths to which she was willing to go in support of her

[73] Translation, pp. 124, 125.

brothers, and the influence she was able to exert on their behalf.[74] This strong-willed and fecund woman probably did as much as any man to promote the fortunes of the Northern House. Of the two future Emperors to whom she gave birth, the first, Reizei, suffered from a mental disorder; and it was consequently deemed necessary to restore the regency (which had lapsed during the reign of his late father, Emperor Murakami) when the boy succeeded to the throne at the age of seventeen. From Reizei's reign on, the position of Morosuke's descendants was so secure that it was never again possible, either during the period of our interest or for centuries thereafter, for even the most mature and competent Emperor to dispense with a Regent or the de facto equivalent—a circumstance of which we are reminded by the author. "It is precisely because of Emperor Reizei that the Fujiwara lords still flourish. 'If it hadn't been for him,' Michinaga once said, 'we would be officials of Fourth and Fifth Rank now, serving as outriders for the great and running their errands.' "[75]

The other principal object of attention in this lengthy biography is Morosuke, who figures at the end in a series of four anecdotes. As in Tokihira's case, at least one of the stories is probably spurious,[76] but the point to notice is that the author is again drawing a portrait of a man who has succeeded in political life. Morosuke is favored by fortune, he has a strong, decisive personality, and, like his father, Tadahira, he is something more than human. In discussing Emperor Reizei's Purification, Yotsugi says, "The stubbornness of the evil spirits caused great concern, but the Emperor seemed the very epitome of elegance during the Great Thanksgiving Purification procession. People said it was because Morosuke's ghost rode with him in the Imperial litter, embracing him from behind. Since Morosuke seemed superhuman in life, it is quite possible that his spirit guarded the Emperor after his death."[77]

Another long biography follows, that of Morosuke's oldest son, Koremasa, who, however, occupies the author's attention for less than two pages. Approximately four and two pages, respectively, are devoted to two of the minister's sons, Yoshitaka and Yoshichika, and most of the remaining fifteen or so are filled with anecdotes about two of his grandsons—the calligrapher Yukinari and Emperor Kazan, the last of whom was the son of Emperor Reizei and, like him, mentally unstable. Yoshitaka's section is essentially a digression, centering on the young man's extreme piety and rebirth in the Pure Land, such as one

---

[74] The point is made again in Kinsue's biography and a third time in the vulgate texts. See Appendix B, (11).

[75] Translation, p. 138.   [76] See below, p. 59.

[77] Translation, p. 138.

might expect to find in an *ōjōden*. The one devoted to Yoshitaka's son Yukinari, which follows, begins with a trio of anecdotes, pertinent to the author's main concerns of looking with a searching eye at Fujiwara power and examining the various sides of Michinaga's character, the latter both directly and by comparison and contrast. Two stories about Yukinari's resourcefulness and ingenuity, which can also be shown to be closely connected to *The Great Mirror*'s theme, are bracketed by an amusing exposé of Yukinari's deficiencies as a student of poetry, on the one hand, and, on the other, by a witty remark the calligrapher is alleged to have made, very much in the vein of the stories that fill old European jest books, such as this one from the sixteenth-century *Tales and Quick Answers*: "There was a poor man on a time the which unto thieves that broke into his house one night, he said in this wise: 'Sirs, I marvel that ye think to find anything here by night, for I ensure you I can find nothing when it is broad day.' "[78]

Yoshichika, one of two outsiders who controlled the government until Kaneie manipulated Kazan into abdicating, appears primarily in connection with his Imperial nephew, whose personality is explored in a series of anecdotes at the end of the biography. It is typical of the author's method that he provides a balanced account of the Emperor's strengths and weaknesses, and also that he singles out examples of Kazan's ingenuity for special praise. We are dealing here with a viewpoint very different from that of Akazome Emon, whose lengthy account of Kazan's activities tends to concentrate on affairs of the heart and their consequences.

Perhaps the most interesting feature of the next biography, which is devoted to Michinaga's uncle Kanemichi and his family, is that its five vulgate interpolations occupy more space than do those of all the other *Ōkagami* sections combined.[79] We have already touched on one of the five, involving the political struggle between Kanemichi and Kaneie.[80] A second explains the circumstances under which Kanemichi became Regent, a third consists of a short comment, quoted below, a fourth provides a long list of offices held by Kanemichi, and a fifth contains an entertaining digression on the second marriage of Kanemichi's son Asateru.

In the *kohon* texts Kanemichi's is one of the shortest *Ōkagami* biographies, revealing little of its subject except that he was handsome and disagreeable. There is an anecdote praising Asateru's ingenuity, and there is a good deal of factual information concerning Kanemichi's oldest son, Akimitsu, and his family. Well situated by birth to compete

[78] Zall 1963, p. 304.   [79] Appendix B, (10)-(14).
[80] See p. 23.

with his cousins (Kaneie's sons), Akimitsu married two daughters into the Imperial family—the first, Genshi, to Emperor Ichijō, and the second, Enshi, to Prince Atsuakira, who later became Crown Prince—but there is no evidence that he ever made an active effort to best Michinaga and his brothers in the competition at Court. Rather, he seems to have been a man of mediocre abilities who managed to rise to high office by keeping on the good side of Michinaga after the latter's assumption of power.[81] Within months of his appointment as Minister of the Left, such hopes as he may have entertained at the advanced age of seventy-three were dashed by Prince Atsuakira's resignation, marriage to Michinaga's daughter Kanshi, and subsequent estrangement from Enshi. *Eiga monogatari* describes Akimitsu's woes and those of Enshi at sympathetic length, and the short *rufubon* interpolation mentioned above says, "[Enshi] has turned into a frightful spirit, haunting people in concert with her father. Her persecution of Koichijōin's wife never ceases."[82]

As Hosaka points out, it is characteristic of the author that he makes no overt connection between Michinaga's ambition and Akimitsu's difficulties, contenting himself with bringing the matter to the reader's attention by a noncommittal remark: "[Akimitsu] died at the age of seventy-eight or so about five years ago. He is known as the Evil Spirit Minister of the Left, an unpleasant nickname. I suppose there must be some justification for it."[83]

Two more of Michinaga's many uncles, Tamemitsu and Kinsue, are the subjects of the fifteenth and sixteenth biographies, which together cover only about six pages. The sad story of Tamemitsu's daughter Kishi, Emperor Kazan's favorite consort, who died during the course of a pregnancy, receives extended treatment in *Eiga monogatari*. Akazome attributes the emotionally unstable Emperor's abdication to grief over her loss, but the *Ōkagami* author, who avoids such subjects, remarks only, "One of the daughters, Kishi, was Emperor Kazan's favorite consort until she died." Having already offered his own version of the abdication in Kazan's annals (where he lays the responsibility on the doorstep of Kaneie and Michikane), he provides here only a few statements of genealogical interest and an anecdote about the rivalry between two of Tamemitsu's sons, Sanenobu and Tadanobu.

The story is colorful. Sanenobu, after suffering the humiliation of seeing his younger brother win an office to which both had aspired, takes to his bed and dies "with his fingers piercing the backs of his

---

81 Hosaka 1974, 2.599.
82 McCullough and McCullough 1980, Chapter 13; Appendix B, (12).
83 Hosaka 1974, 2,600; translation, p. 155.

hands." But we may wonder why the author, if he wished to describe an example of sibling rivalry within the Northern House, did not choose to deal with the much more important case of Kanemichi and Kaneie. An apparent reluctance to dwell on the shortcomings of the Fujiwara leaders was doubtless a factor, but it might also be noted that in this instance, as elsewhere, he seems to be using tangential figures to refine his characterization of Michinaga, who is presented as adamant in his refusal to promote an unqualified man.[84]

Kinsue's biography, which at first glance seems a collection of digressions, is also more relevant than it would appear, because the author, in depicting this figurehead Chancellor as a mild, ineffectual old man who dotes on his grandson, implicitly contrasts him with the kind of man who wields real power.

The next short biography, which is Kaneie's, consists mainly of anecdotes about the minister himself (in which the contrast between the great Fujiwara leaders and men like Kinsue is further underlined), and about different aspects of his son Michinaga's character.

The remaining three biographies are those of Michinaga and two of his older brothers, Michitaka and Michikane. Michitaka's, the second longest in *The Great Mirror*, contains a number of digressions, but concentrates on the characters of the subject's two most prominent sons, Korechika and Takaie, the first of whom was Michinaga's principal rival. Michikane's is short, probably because none of his sons achieved prominence. Michinaga's, appropriately, is the longest of the twenty.

The first section of Michinaga's biography seems designed to illustrate the part played by luck in the great man's career. Successive deaths, most of them caused by the epidemic of 995, removed seniors who would otherwise have blocked his advance, and his one remaining rival by virtue of birth, Korechika, happened to lack political ability. "If Korechika had had better sense," Yotsugi says, "it would have been natural for him to inherit the regency, because the Emperor had already commanded him to head the government during his father's illness. But the Court chose Michikane after Michitaka's death, unwilling to entrust affairs of state to someone with the mind of a child."

The author then obliquely calls attention to the significance of Michinaga's marital alliances. The minister's principal wife, Rinshi, was a daughter of one of the leading members of the Minamoto family. She inherited the great Tsuchimikado Mansion, and, in further testament to her husband's good luck, produced a brood of attractive and intelligent children. His second wife, Meishi, whom he was able to

---

[84] Hosaka 1974, 2.641, makes essentially the same point.

marry through the assistance of his sister Senshi (the girl's guardian), contributed another Minamoto alliance; another valuable property, the Takamatsu Mansion; and more children. Rinshi's four daughters, in particular, were of the utmost importance to their father's career, because it was they whom Michinaga married off to three successive Emperors and a Crown Prince, thereby achieving the very pinnacle of worldly success. "No other minister of state has ever been able to make three of his daughters Empresses at the same time," says Yotsugi. "We may indeed call Michinaga the supreme ruler of the land."[85] At the banquet held in celebration of the third daughter's elevation, Michinaga expressed his elation in verse.[86]

Kono yo o ba	No waning
Waga yo to zo omou	In the glory
Mochizuki no	Of the full moon—
Kaketaru koto no	This world
Nashi to omoeba.	Is indeed my world.

Marrying a daughter to an Emperor, or even making one an Empress, was not in itself a guarantee of success. Male Imperial grandchildren were necessary, and in that respect Michinaga was again fortunate. As the author has frequent occasion to point out, his luck never seemed to fail. "Winds may rage and rains may fall day after day, but the skies will clear and the ground will dry out two or three days before he plans anything."[87]

The final section of the biography discusses Michinaga's personal qualities—the accomplishments, appearance, and traits of character which, the author implies, have combined with luck and family connections to bring about his triumphs. We shall return to that subject after completing our survey of *The Great Mirror*'s structure.

Tales of the Fujiwara Family   As has been indicated, Part Two is peripheral to the book's main subject. On first reading it seems a grab bag of miscellaneous stories, but further examination suggests that "Tales of the Fujiwara Family" and "Tales of the Past" may have been intended to supplement the biographies and annals, respectively, and that both were put together according to the rather mechanical prin-

---

85 Translation, p. 191.
86 *Shōyūki*, 5.55, Sixteenth Day, Tenth Month, Kannin 2 (1018).
87 Translation, p. 208.

ciples of association and progression known to us through structural studies of the Imperial poetic anthologies.[88]

The resemblance to the poetic anthologies is closer in "Tales of the Past" than in "Tales of the Fujiwara Family," which follows an A-B-A-B pattern. After an introductory passage, "Tales of the Fujiwara Family" presents brief discussions, in order of birth, of all of Michinaga's direct ancestors from Kamatari down, presumably because the author feared that the biographies had not made the line of descent clear. The family's hereditary shrines and temples are next discussed in the order of their founding—partly, perhaps, because divine assistance might have been considered second in importance only to genealogy as a source of power and prestige, and also because, conversely, the prestige of the institutions was a reflection of the family's power. "You can see that Yamashinadera is an awesome and holy temple," Yotsugi says. "Even the worst outrage is condoned if the temple is involved; people simply dismiss it as 'Yamashina propriety.' It merely goes to show what an incomparable position the house of Fujiwara enjoys."[89]

Next there is a list of Fujwara leaders paralleling the earlier one, but this time showing men who were fathers of Empresses and grandfathers of Emperors. Its purpose is obviously to provide a perspective for appreciation of Michinaga's unique achievements. "Of all our many Fujiwara ministers of state, only Michinaga has made three daughters Empresses at the same time," Yotsugi repeats. "Furthermore, he is the father of a Regent Minister of the Left, a Palace Minister, two Major Counselors, and a Middle Counselor. That is the truth! Compare him with anyone! He stands alone and unrivaled in Japan."[90]

The last of the four sections returns to the subject of Fujiwara religious establishments, the object being, as in the case of the third, to single out Michinaga for special praise. As Yamashinadera symbolizes the primacy of the Fujiwara among Court families, so Michinaga's Hōjōji, the focus of a long discussion and several anecdotes, represents Michinaga's preeminent position within the family.

Tales of the Past   "Tales of the Past" gets under way with anecdotes from Yotsugi about the origins of two religious festivals, inaugurated respectively by Emperors Uda and Suzaku. A link is thus

---

[88] On linking in poetic anthologies, see Konishi 1958. The technique can also be observed in *setsuwa* collections and other prose works.
[89] Translation, p. 205.   [90] Translation, p. 206.

established between the religious topics at the end of "Tales of the
Fujiwara Family" and the first major *setsuwa* cluster in this section of
Part Two, in which Shigeki tells stories about Emperors in the order
of their reigns. Shigeki's anecdotes are tied together both chronologi-
cally and by topical association, since almost all of them deal with
poetry, music, dance, and similar elegant subjects.

When Yotsugi returns to the center of the stage, he tells some
transitional stories, ending with one in which equal attention is devoted
to Emperor Murakami and two members of the Imperially descended
house of Minamoto. A cluster of Minamoto stories follows, ending
with a tearful scene involving Retired Emperor En'yū and Minamoto
Tokinaka, which is tonally linked to a reminiscence about an eloquent
preacher who "made everyone in the huge congregation choke up."
There follows a group of stories on the theme of wit and resourcefulness, with the clever individual a preacher in the first and a dancing
master in the last. Dancing constitutes a link with a *setsuwa* describing
Empress Shōshi's visit to the Fujiwara shrine at Ōharano, a flamboyant
exhibition of Michinaga's power, for which "the dancers were young
gentlemen from good families."

The Ōharano story can be read as hinting at disaffection on the part
of Palace Minister Kinsue, who "annoyed Michinaga by turning back
at Nishishichijō," unlike the complaisant Minister of the Right, Akimitsu, who "went all the way to the shrine and was rewarded with a
horse." If such an implication was intended, it might be regarded as a
link to the next anecdote, which concerns preparations for another
great event in Fujiwara history, the accession audience for Kaneie's
grandson, Emperor Ichijō. On the surface, Kaneie is praised for showing how to deal with the discovery of a gory animal head on the
throne, but it is possible to interpret the story as a covert reference
to the existence of a hostile faction. Since Yotsugi introduces the throne
incident with the comment that he is changing the subject, the author
may, however, simply wish to show, as he does in the next episode,
that seeming omens are not always what we take them to be. "Dreams
and other portents that we consider lucky sometimes fail to amount
to anything, and suspicious occurrences may presage good fortune,"
the old man says.[91]

There is some dialogue at this point, followed by a few final anecdotes, which are integrated in the same manner. Several of them concern Emperors, and the arrangement is again chronological, with topical linking.

[91] Translation, p. 234.

Tamashii   Of the stories in "Tales of the Past," the ones depicting resourcefulness are especially noteworthy, because praise of that quality is a recurrent motif in *The Great Mirror*. Sometimes the praise is explicit, as when the author introduces a pair of *setsuwa* with the comment, "Yukinari's resourcefulness and ingenuity show up in even the most trifling matters" (*sukoshi itaranu koto ni mo, ontamashii no fukaku owashite rōrōjū shinashitamaikeru onkonjō nite*).[92] The word *tamashii*, which is used here with an honorific prefix, covers a fairly wide range of related meanings in *The Great Mirror*, including wit, presence of mind, ingenuity, and the ability to cope with practical problems. In the first of the two anecdotes about Yukinari, the young Emperor Go-Ichijō calls on his courtiers for some new toys. Most of them bring in expensive gold and silver curiosities, but Yukinari demonstrates his *tamashii*, and captures the Imperial fancy, with a simple spinning top. In Morosuke's biography, the minister's sons are called resourceful (*tamashii fukaku*) when they solve the problem of a potential Minamoto Imperial father-in-law by shouldering aside Prince Tamehira, Minamoto Takaakira's son-in-law, in favor of the Prince's younger brother, the future Emperor En'yū, when the office of Crown Prince falls vacant.[93] Similarly, a famous preacher says that one of his rivals, Seihan, "has *tamashii*" when the latter, officiating at a memorial service for a dog, intones, "We may be sure the spirit of the deceased is barking on a lotus pedestal at this very moment."[94]

The same quality is praised elsewhere without explicit use of the word *tamashii*. Another preacher is called *chie fukaku* (witty, clever) when, in the course of a funeral prayer for Emperor Yōzei, who had exceeded the Buddha's life span of eighty years by living to eighty-one, he says, "He was the elder brother of Śākyamuni by one year."[95] Similarly, the fart anecdote mentioned earlier, which illustrates a facet of Tokihira's character—his propensity to "forget all about decorum once he began to laugh"—can also be interpreted as showing how a resourceful underling manipulates a superior.

Tamashii transcends class and is unrelated to aesthetic considerations, which are sometimes thought of as dominating every aspect of Heian Court life. On the one hand, it can appear in an obscure official's crude breach of decorum; on the other, it can take the form of a great noble's graceful gesture, as when a spoiled child refuses to perform a

---

[92] *Ōkagami*, p. 143; Hosaka 1974, 2.532; Translation, p. 147.
[93] *Ōkagami*, p. 119; Hosaka 1974, 2.427; Translation, p. 130.
[94] *Ōkagami*, p. 271; Hosaka 1974, 3.544; Translation, p. 231.
[95] *Ōkagami*, p. 43; Translation, p. 72.

dance and his uncle, Michitaka, saves the day by mounting the platform, drawing the boy to his side, and dancing with him.[96] Michitaka
demonstrates *tamashii* in another way when, after having fallen into a
drunken stupor while en route from one Kamo Shrine to the other, he
shows himself "perfectly prepared for that very contingency" by producing grooming aids at his destination, "tidying himself, and stepping
down, composed and fresh."[97]

Closely allied in meaning to *tamashii* is *yamatodamashii* (or *yamatogokoro*), "Japanese *tamashii.*" *Yamatodamashii's* locus classicus is in
The Tale of Genji, where Genji, who has imposed a strict academic
regimen on his young son, Yūgiri, says to the boy, "It is when there
is a fund of Chinese learning that the Japanese spirit is respected by the
world."[98] In the recent past, *yamatodamashii* has meant a quasi-mystic,
uniquely Japanese quality of purity and heroic self-sacrifice, symbol-
ized by the evanescent beauty of the cherry blossom, shining for a
moment in the morning sun before it falls. As modern dictionaries
point out, however, the term was used in the Heian period to contrast
native qualities with acquired Chinese learning. Japanese abilities (or
Japanese spirit, in the conventional translation used by Seidensticker)
meant wit, shrewdness, decisiveness, common sense, and the ability to
get things done. On the basis of evidence in *The Great Mirror*, one
can argue, as Hosaka has done, that it also implied tenacity and courage.[99]

It would appear that *tamashii/yamatodamashii* was regarded as a
masculine attribute of prime importance, especially for a statesman. Tō
no Chūjō seems to speak from that point of view when he tells Yūgiri
that too much learning is not a good thing, and so does the dying Korechika when, in *Eiga monogatari*, he says to his son, "Since you have
tamashii, I do not believe that [my death] will end your career."[100]
Similarly, when Tadazane's father complains to the scholar Ōe Masafusa that the boy is failing to acquire a proper Chinese education, Masafusa replies, "Whether a Regent is learned or not, he can rule as long
as he has plenty of *yamatodamashii.*"[101]

---

[96] Translation, p. 181.   [97] Translation, p. 169.

[98] Seidensticker 1976, p. 362; *Genji monogatari*, 2.277. *Zae o moto to shite koso,
yamatodamashii no yo ni mochiiraruru kata mo tsuyō haberame.*

[99] Hosaka 1974, 3.275-276.

[100] Seidensticker 1976, p. 367; *Genji monogatari*, 2.289; *Eiga monogatari*, 1.290.

[101] *Chūgaishō*, p. 884. Lest Masafusa be accused of disingenuousness, it might be
noted that he had an impeccable precedent in *Shih chi*, which says, "To be wise
only in knowledge but lack the resoluteness to act is to meet disaster in every
undertaking. . . . Better a wasp bent on stinging than a hesitant tiger." Watson
1961, 1.227.

Genji's attitude in the matter of Yūgiri's education resembles that of the early Heian Emperors, who did everything possible to foster the Confucian ideal of the scholar-bureaucrat, not only through genuine admiration for Chinese culture but also as a weapon against the hereditary principle. Tō no Chūjō, as one might expect from *The Tale of Genji*'s leading Fujiwara, stands in the opposite camp. Chinese learning, with its egalitarian, anti-ascriptive implications, recommended itself to those whose main hope of advancement lay in the examination system, but it was of limited utility to men whose birth placed them automatically in the upper echelons, where further progress depended not on passing examinations but on skill in social and political relations. For a member of the Northern House, in particular, the ability to survive internal challenges on the practical, day-to-day level was essential.

This aspect of Heian life is virtually ignored in *The Tale of Genji*, *Eiga monogatari*, and other works by female writers, who are notable for their lack of interest in politics. In view of our author's announced aim, it is not surprising that his own attitude is very different. Anecdote after anecdote points up some aspect of *tamashii*, either explicitly or by contrastive implication. To show why Korechika could not compete successfully with Michinaga, a whole series of stories illustrates the younger man's lack of judgment and his inability to rise to a challenge; to show how Yukinari managed to prosper after another branch of the family came to power, the author talks not about the calligrapher's skill with the brush but about his agile mind; to show why Takaie survived the wreck of Korechika's fortunes, we are given repeated instances of his good judgment, qualities of leadership, and independence. Takaie is one of only two people of whom *The Great Mirror* uses the highly laudatory term *yamatodamashii*.[102]

Since the author presents *tamashii* as the key to political success, it is incumbent upon him to demonstrate it in Michinaga, which he does repeatedly, both in Michinaga's biography and elsewhere. For instance, Crown Prince Atsuakira's resignation, attributed to karma by Yotsugi, is shown by the attendant to have resulted from a shrewdly calculated campaign on the minister's part, culminating in quick, decisive action to keep the Prince from changing his mind. Significantly, neither Yotsugi nor the attendant passes judgment on the morality of Michinaga's behavior; he is simply represented as resolving a difficult situation to his own advantage.

Other cases in point are the ingenious means Michinaga employs to obtain evidence of his sister's adultery and his skillful use of psycho-

---

[102] Actually *yamatogokoro* in Takaie's case. The other is Tokihira. *Ōkagami*, pp. 79, 192; Translation, pp. 102, 177.

logical pressure in the archery contest with Korechika.[103] It should be noticed that there is no independent confirmation of either story, and that the authenticity of others in the same vein is even more suspect. In Michinaga's biography, Kaneie laments the inability of his three sons to match their cousin Kintō's accomplishments, "[They] can't even get close enough to tread on his shadow," he says. Michinaga offers a self-confident retort, "I may not tread on his shadow, but I'll walk all over his face," thus contrasting with his older brothers, who, "speechless with embarrassment," tacitly admit their inferiority.[104] As Hosaka has remarked, this seems a bit too pat to be convincing.[105]

Similarly, we probably should not accept the famous rainy-night test of courage, which consisted of lonely trips to different parts of the Palace grounds by the three brothers, with the older two disgracing themselves and Michinaga amazing everyone by his presence of mind and coolness. The story has not been preserved elsewhere; both Michitaka and Michikane had reached a level in the bureaucracy at which their participation in such an exercise would have been considered unsuitable; and there is no independent evidence that Michinaga was known for his bravery, either in Kazan's reign or later.[106] But the author seems to have been determined to persuade us, even at the expense of accuracy, that Michinaga possessed *tamashii* in all its ramifications. He goes to considerable lengths elsewhere to work in another illustration of his protagonist's willingness to confront supernatural phenomena, a trait that must have been highly valued in a spirit-fearing society, and one that is also attributed to Tokihira, Morosuke, and Kaneie.[107]

As has been suggested, the author's attitude toward Michinaga's political activities is morally neutral. He is like the chronicler of the Icelandic *Egil's Saga*, who passes no judgment when Earl Arnvid ambushes a departing guest, or like the authors of *Nihon shoki*, who complacently describe the early instance of *yamatodamashii* in which Emperor Jinmu arranges to have his drunken banquet guests murdered.[108] The question in his mind is not whether Michinaga is good, but whether he is able. His frame of reference is not Plutarch's or Ssu-ma Ch'ien's, but that of a heroic age. We are reminded of how the Serbo-Croatian hero Marko Kraljević cuts off a swordsmith's arm, thus mak-

---

[103] Translation, pp. 164, 197.   [104] Translation, p. 193.
[105] Hosaka 1974, 3.267.
[106] *Ōkagami*, p. 478, s.n. 19; Hosaka 1974, 3.276.
[107] See p. 57 below.
[108] Pálsson and Edwards 1978, p. 193; Aston 1956, pp. 123-124. See also Hallberg 1962, p. 31.

ing sure that the man will never again forge a blade as good as the one he has made Marko.[109] Just as the bard, in the song "Marko and Musa," describes Marko's subsequent gift to the smith of 100 ducats, "for to nourish thee the days of thy life," so our author thinks fit to tell us, with no apparent justification, how Michinaga "showered [Koichijōin] with so many attentions that everyone said his cordiality was more than enough to make the former Crown Prince forget his troubles."[110] Generosity, an essential attribute of leadership in heroic societies, receives a good deal of attention in *The Great Mirror*, which consistently depicts men like Tadahira, Morosuke, and, especially, Michinaga as expansive, magnanimous, and open-hearted.

In rounding out his description of Michinaga, the author states that he was handsome and a good poet. The Heian love of beauty and esteem for poetry are so well documented that we are prepared to have both attributes singled out for comment. For readers of *The Tale of Genji*, what is less expected is the equal attention devoted to Michinaga's skill as a rider and archer.

Masculine sports, of which we hear almost nothing from feminine authors, flourished in the early Heian period and were still popular in Michinaga's day. Wrestling was one, as is attested by the *Ōkagami* anecdote in which Narihira and the future Emperor Uda figure as contestants; by the well-known, if apocryphal, story of the match between two courtiers, Tomo Yoshio and Ki no Natora, to decide the identity of the next Crown Prince; and by the importance of the annual wrestling festival in the Court calendar.[111] That hawking was another is known from such sources as *The Great Mirror* itself; *Montoku jitsuroku*, which comments, in an obituary of a courtier who died in 854, "He was no scholar but he loved hawks and dogs"; and *The Tale of Genji*, where Murasaki says that Kashiwagi's favorite grooms and falconers seemed lost after his death.[112] A third was archery. Murasaki Shikibu says of Ukifune's stepfather, who "could not have been called a man of low estate," that "he cared little for flute and koto, but he was an expert archer," and we find a tale in *Uji shūi monogatari* about a guards officer who practiced until he could shoot out a pirate's eye with a tiny arrow "quite unlike the proper ones used in fighting."[113]

---

[109] Low 1922, p. 128; Lord 1954, p. 115.

[110] Translation, p. 124; Hosaka 1974, 2.397-398.

[111] Appendix B, (3); *Genkō shakusho*, p. 190; Ury 1970, p. 295; McCullough and McCullough 1980, s.n. 33.

[112] *Montoku jitsuroku*, p. 95, Second Day, Fourth Month, Saikō 1 (854); Seidensticker 1976, p. 651; McCullough 1968, p. 250, n. 2.

[113] Seidensticker 1976, p. 937; Mills 1970, pp. 423-424.

Court archery contests, in which the participants were men of good family, are frequently mentioned in works of the mid-Heian period. Finally, riding was a skill necessary for participation in the annual shrine and festival races, and in Imperial progresses and the like; and Michinaga is not the only Fujiwara leader who has come down in history as an expert in the management of mettlesome horses.[114]

Tamashii and the Genji *Ideal*   It is easy to form the impression, from *The Tale of Genji, Makura no sōshi,* and similar works, that none of the values and customs of Japan's heroic age had survived the early years of the Heian period, except among the provincial warrior class— that the assimilation of Chinese culture had produced a new kind of civilized man, an ideal to which every courtier aspired: a connoisseur and practitioner of poetry, music, painting, calligraphy, and the lesser arts, and a devotee of beauty in all its aspects; in person and dress flawlessly handsome and elegant; in character and behavior unfailingly sensitive and considerate. A hasty reading of *The Tale of Genji* can lead us to conclude that the book's protagonist was such a man. Actually, Genji is far too complex a blend of virtues and flaws, far too human, to serve as an abstract model in the realm of character and conduct. It is rather his supposed son Kaoru who conforms to the ideal in every important respect—conforms so implacably, so almost ridiculously, as to suggest that Genji may have taken on a life of his own as his history unfolded, developing into a character very different from Murasaki's original conception, and that the author was determined to keep a tight rein on her new protagonist. This time, she seems to be saying, I shall create the kind of man every woman dreams about. There will be no occasion for jealous agonizing, no sense of insecurity.

Kaoru is likely to impress the western reader as a considerable diminution of the Shining Prince—the fading fragrance, perhaps, of the effulgent rose. It is not that he lacks Genji's talents. "Name me another young gentleman," Tamakazura says, "who has such a wide variety of talents and accomplishments."[115] Nor is he inferior in appearance or grace. We are told that "his good looks had always been somewhat intimidating" to Nakanokimi, and that "no one could more gracefully do honor" to an occasion such as a wedding.[116] He also possesses a good measure of Genji's famous attractiveness to women. "Such a fine young gentleman. . . ," says one of Ōigimi's ladies. "He's exactly

---

[114] Another is Uchimaro, who tames a vicious beast when an ill-natured Prince orders him to ride it. *Konjaku monogatarishū,* 4.230-231 (22.4).

[115] Seidensticker 1976, p. 758.   [116] Seidensticker 1976, pp. 877, 903.

what every woman has always asked for."[117] Tamakazura's "susceptible young women" pronounce him unique, "ladies who [have] a glimpse of him [seem] to make careers of deceiving themselves," and the romantic author of *Sarashina nikki* (Sarashina Diary), reading *The Tale of Genji* as a young girl, does not hesitate to bracket him with Genji as a Prince Charming: "I fancied that, when I grew up, I would surely become a great beauty with long flowing hair like Yūgao, who was loved by the Shining Prince, or like Ukifune, who was wooed by the Captain of Uji," she says.[118]

Murasaki, as though in reaction against Genji's self-indulgence and impulsiveness, the source of so much sorrow to the women in his life, has made Kaoru a bit of a prig, preternaturally self-controlled, aloof, and dignified. Kaoru is free of Genji's faults and foibles, but he also lacks his warmth, his vitality, and much of his charm. He is all yin and no yang, the sort of hero who does not appeal to western taste. For Murasaki and her feminine readers, however, he seems to have represented the ultimate daydream, the grand figure, standing at the very pinnacle of society, whose most conspicuous trait was consideration for the feelings of others. Genji, who calls himself "weak and indecisive by nature,"[119] is in actuality quite willing and able to get his way in most things, regardless of the consequences to others, but gentle, conscientious Kaoru, with his inconvenient empathy in crucial human relationships, is paralyzed by his refusal to inflict pain. No lady need fear that she will suffer at his hands, as, for example, the author of *Kagerō nikki* (Gossamer Journal) is shown to have suffered in real life at Kaneie's.

It is reasonably clear that Murasaki disapproves of Genji when he fails to live up to her ideal, that she accepts Kaoru's indecisiveness as the inevitable concomitant of honorable impulses, and that she finds little to admire, aside from physical charm, in the clever, unscrupulous Niou, who may be regarded as the second of the two half-Genjis in the Uji chapters—Genji shorn of his virtues, as Kaoru is Genji divested of his faults. But we may wonder whether the female view of what constituted ideal masculine attributes was necessarily the male view. There were undoubtedly broad areas of agreement. Thanks to the prestige of Chinese example and to Imperial sponsorship, mastery of polite accomplishments and attention to the arts were universally recognized as essential attributes of the man of breeding. The sexes also agreed in attaching more weight to male physical beauty than has been

[117] Seidensticker 1976, p. 834.
[118] Seidensticker 1976, pp. 754, 741; Morris 1971, pp. 56-57.
[119] Seidensticker 1976, p. 80.

common in other societies. And in the composition of poetry, at least, it was considered important to demonstrate sensitivity to the moods of nature and to the pathos inherent in the passing of time. In the *Ōkagami* author's eyes, however, accomplishments and physical graces are less important than character; and, further, there is much more of Niou than of Kaoru in the kind of man he admires. We must therefore ask ourselves whether or not he represents masculine opinion in general.

Careful study of Court nobles' diaries and other non-literary sources would be necessary in order to reach a firm conclusion, but an affirmative response is suggested by anecdotes preserved in *The Great Mirror*, in other works of the eleventh and twelfth centuries, and in later *setsuwa* collections, some of which have already been cited. Although *Konjaku monogatari* may perhaps date from the Kamakura period, most of its stories are much older, and it is therefore relevant to point out that it includes tales told from the same point of view as those in *The Great Mirror*. The one below, for example, demonstrates a desire to endow Emperor Uda with courage, which does not appear to have been one of his virtues.[120]

Long ago there was an estate called the Kawaranoin, built by Minister of the Left Tōru to serve as his residence. Its lake, which had been shaped to resemble Shiogama Bay in Mutsu Province, was full to overflowing with salt water, and in every other respect it was the most splendid and interesting establishment imaginable. Now it happened that the estate was presented to Retired Emperor Uda by one of Tōru's descendants after the minister's death. His Majesty took up residence there, and his son, Emperor Daigo, paid him magnificent visits from time to time.

One night around midnight, a storeroom door opened in the west wing while the Retired Emperor was in residence. His Majesty sensed a presence, looked over, and saw a man in full daytime Court attire with sword and baton, bowing respectfully about twelve feet away.

"Who are you?" His Majesty asked.

"I am the old man who owns this house."

"Tōru?"

"Yes."

"What are you doing here?"

120 *Konjaku monogatarishū*, 4.480-481 (27.2).

"It is my house, so I live here. If you will forgive me for saying so, having you on the premises makes things rather cramped. I really don't know how to manage."

"This is preposterous!" His Majesty shouted. "Do you think I would deprive anyone of his home? I am here only because your descendant gave me the property. Being a spirit is no excuse for being unreasonable." The spirit disappeared in an instant and was never seen again.

They say people praised the Retired Emperor to the skies when the story leaked out. "He is not like an ordinary human," everyone agreed. "Nobody else could have confronted Tōru's spirit so fearlessly."

As is well known, Konjaku monogatari contains a whole chapter dealing with the exploits of famous Minamoto and Taira warriors, some performed in the capital (as when Minamoto Yorimitsu [d. 1021] makes a difficult shot and is rewarded by the Crown Prince), others in the provinces.[121] It is significant that such tales were considered worthy of preservation by aristocratic and monkish compilers. Obviously, we are dealing with attitudes and interests very different from those of feminine writers like Murasaki Shikibu. Shortly after the middle of the eleventh century—probably during the regency of Michinaga's son Yorimichi—an anonymous member of the Court circle wrote Mutsu waki (A Tale of Mutsu), a short account in Chinese of a military campaign conducted by the warrior Minamoto Yoriyoshi in northern Japan, using Yoriyoshi's official reports and "stories presently current" as his sources.[122] The work can be read as an early statement of what was later to be characterized as the medieval warrior code, which attached supreme importance to personal and family honor and demanded loyalty, bravery, and self-sacrifice of its adherents. It is true that certain elements in the code were alien to the spirit of the Heian Court, and also that the Mutsu waki author's primary concern was probably to praise and encourage service to the throne, rather than to analyze character, but it seems unlikely that the anecdotes in the chronicle would have been set down with such relish and wealth of detail by an unsympathetic or indifferent brush. Yoriyoshi wins approbation not only because he upholds Imperial authority but also because of the kind of man he is—a peerless archer, a kind and generous lord, and an

---

[121] The Crown Prince was the future Emperor Sanjō. Konjaku monogatarishū, 4.381-382 (25.6). The chapter has been translated in Wilson 1973.
[122] Translated in McCullough 1965.

inspiring leader whose deeds of valor are such as are performed "but once in a generation."[123]

At first glance, it may seem that the differences between the warrior Yoriyoshi and the Court noble Michinaga are so great as to reduce any resemblances to insignificance. What they have in common, however, if our author is to be trusted, is the vital quality of *tamashii*. Both are men who know how to get things done. Neither is hampered by Chinese notions, by sentimental worries about the pathos of things, or by the kinds of misgivings that immobilize a Kaoru. Both are, in fact, very little different from Emperor Jinmu and other swashbucklers in the *Nihon shoki* legends, and, in many respects, very much like successful men of affairs in all societies.

It is unlikely that so useful a quality as *tamashii* was ever relegated to the ash heap in the practical masculine world of everyday Court life, even during the ninth-century peak of Chinese influence. On the contrary, it seems reasonable to suppose that a typically Japanese accommodation was reached with the imported notions of which we are so conscious in a book like *The Tale of Genji*—that, as the *Ōkagami* author tells us, the ideal man was the one who, like Michinaga, combined in himself the best of both worlds. We should probably see *Mutsu waki* and the *Konjaku* stories not as isolated precursors of the medieval war tales, not as sporadic gestures in the direction of an entirely new set of values, but rather as witnesses, preserved by chance, to the existence of a very old point of view, held in the Heian period as in the remote past, concerning worldly success and the qualities necessary to achieve it. It is true that a reputation as a poet or musician was much more important to a Court noble than to a warrior (although we are reminded of the story of how Tadanori, one of the Taira generals in the Genpei War, risked his life to have his poems considered for an Imperial anthology).[124] But one of the principal themes in *The Great Mirror* is that proficiency in the arts, no matter how great, does not in itself assure success, even for a man of the highest birth. It is for that reason, the author tells us, that Michinaga, who has *tamashii*, can "walk on the face" of his gifted cousin Kintō. Similarly, Yukinari's *tamashii* enables him to outstrip others in the competition for office, even though he is shown to be laughably ignorant of poetic tradition.[125] The ambitious Heian noble would doubtless have preferred not to have to choose between polite accomplishments and *tamashii*. But if choice were necessary, one need merely contrast the disappoint-

---

[123] McCullough 1965, p. 203.
[124] Kitagawa and Tsuchida 1975, p. 438.
[125] Translation, p. 146.

ing careers of the Ononomiya lords with the brilliant success enjoyed by Kaneie, a boorish, arrogant man who scoffed at religion, wrote an "astonishingly bad" hand,[126] and was in general the very antithesis of the *Genji* hero. The *Genji* attributes without *tamashii* were likely to lead at best to personal frustration, as with Kaoru, and at worst to ridicule, as in the case of the cultivated man in the *Uji shūi monogatari* story below, who makes a fool of himself because he lacks common sense.[127]

There was once a Retired Emperor's household official called the Tosa Secretary Michikiyo, a man who was forever composing poetry, reciting passages from *Genji* and *Sagoromo*, and seeking out cherry blossoms and moonlight to admire. Since everyone knew of his refined tastes, the Gotokudaiji Minister of the Left invited him to a flower-viewing party at the Ninnaji. Greatly pleased, Michikiyo set out promptly in his broken-down carriage. As he was riding along, he noticed a party of two or three vehicles behind him. Never dreaming that it might be anybody but the minister, he rolled up his rear blind and beckoned with his open fan, shouting, "What's the matter back there? Hurry up!" But the other person turned out to be His Lordship the Regent. One of the great man's Escorts saw the beckoning fan, galloped up, and ripped off Michikiyo's blind; and Michikiyo, struck all of a heap, fell forward and lost his cap. People said he was a pathetic sight. May we call this refined gentleman a bit of a fool?

The Great Mirror and the Critical Spirit   If the interpretation suggested above is correct, the *Ōkagami* author has a very simple purpose, which is, as Yotsugi states it to be, to explain Michinaga's success, and which he attempts to achieve by considering his protagonist's ancestry, his marital connections, the part played in his career by luck (or karma), and, especially, his personal attributes, as compared and contrasted with those of potential rivals. Many Japanese scholars, however, have seen the author as a revisionist, dedicated to exposing *Eiga monogatari* as an uncritical, misleading account of the Fujiwara rise to power, and to showing the truth about the methods employed to crush other families, the pressures exerted against the throne, the fierce internecine strife, and so forth. The argument can best be discussed in connection

[126] Seidensticker 1964, p. 33.
[127] *Uji shūi monogatari*, pp. 419-420 (no. 190).

with two other problems: the basis on which materials were selected
by the author, and the reliability of *The Great Mirror* as history.

As Appendix D shows, the first half of the Heian period was one in
which few political events of moment ruffled the placid surface of
Court life. The incidents that caused the greatest stir were the ouster
of Crown Prince Tsunesada and his replacement by the future Emperor Montoku (842), the designation of the future Emperor Seiwa,
rather than Prince Koretaka, as Crown Prince (850), the Ōtenmon incident (866), the deposition of Emperor Yōzei and his replacement by
Emperor Kokō (884), the *akō* controversy (887-888), the banishment
of Sugawara Michizane (901), the Anna incident (969), the unexpected abdication of Emperor Kazan (986), the banishment of Korechika
and Takaie (996), and the resignation of Crown Prince Atsuakira
(1017).

A crusader against the evils of Fujiwara domination could have been
expected to examine all of those events at length, because all illustrate
the frequently unscrupulous means by which members of the family
won and exercised power. Our author, however, has been extremely
selective. He passes over Prince Tsunesada's deposition without a
word,[128] says of the second succession dispute only, "I believe [Em-
peror Seiwa] was the one who competed with Prince Koretaka for the
heir apparency," and ignores the Ōtenmon incident. The accession of
Kokō, which can be said to show Mototsune in a good light, receives
considerable attention, but the *akō* controversy, in which Mototsune
humiliates Emperor Uda, is not mentioned. The detailed treatment of
Michizane's banishment avoids discussion of the events leading to the
minister's fall, or of its causes. The author merely speculates that it
may have been ordained by fate and, many pages later, adds a comment, "People say Tokihira's descendants died out because of the
terrible sin he committed, but it seems a great pity," which is followed
by a series of anecdotes in praise of Tokihira.

The Anna incident is treated with curious ambiguity. The author
states the situation in a forthright manner. "Power would have shifted
to Takaakira's family if Prince Tamehira had become Emperor, and
the Genji would have been the ones to prosper, so the Prince's resourceful uncles solved the problem by making his younger brother
the heir apparent, even though it was contrary to the natural order of
things (*hidō*)."[129] But in calling the uncles resourceful (*tamashii fukaku*), he gives us the impression that he is not so much censuring

[128] There is a brief allusion to the subject in a *rufubon* addition. See Appendix
B, (1).
[129] Translation, p. 129.

their violation of the natural order of things as commenting favorably on their ability to cope with a threatening situation, and he proceeds to hint that the Prince was a man of questionable judgment who might not have made a very good Emperor anyway. "Prince Tamehira refused to let his misfortunes discourage him. In his last years, he married off his daughter Enshi to Emperor Kazan (Emperor Reizei's son, the Prince's nephew), and went in and out of the Palace all the time. He came in for some sharp criticism from people who thought he should have been more discreet."[130] Of the wreck of Takaakira's fortunes, Yotsugi says only, "I don't know what Takaakira thought about it all. Anyway, some dreadful and heart-rending events took place. This does not do justice to the subject, but it is too presumptuous for humble folk to talk about such things in public; I am going to have to stop. Bringing up old stories is a bad habit of mine."[131]

The abdication of Emperor Kazan is handled in a somewhat similar fashion. Those familiar with the *Eiga monogatari* account, which presents the Emperor as having been motivated solely by grief at the loss of his favorite consort, may feel at first that our author is indeed revealing the seamy side of Fujiwara power. Michikane, backed by his father, Kaneie, is the evil genius who works the mentally disturbed Emperor up to the point of burning his bridges and then deserts him.

After the Emperor reached Hanayamadera and cut off his hair, Michikane spoke up. "I must leave you now. I want to let my father see me as my old self one last time, and I also have to tell him about my decision to become a monk. But I'll come back."

Tears filled the Emperor's eyes. "You have deceived me, haven't you?" he said. It was a pitiful scene. As far as I can make out, Michikane had been encouraging him for a long time by swearing to serve as his faithful disciple. What a terrible way to act![132]

In evaluating the author's attitude, however, we should notice that he later goes to considerable trouble to show that Emperor Kazan was not fit to rule. It is also likely that he is implicitly comparing Michikane with his brother Michinaga, to Michinaga's advantage, when he says, "What a terrible way to act!" Michikane demonstrates *tamashii* in his manipulation of Kazan, but his subsequent betrayal reveals his lack of the truly great man's magnanimity. Michinaga uses a different kind of *tamashii* against Koichijōin, one in which no deception is in-

---

130 Translation, p. 130.   131 *Ibid.*
132 Translation, p. 81.

volved, and he treats the former Crown Prince in the handsomest possible manner after he gets his way. That this is the author's real point is suggested by his apparent distortion of the facts in his treatment of both Kazan's abdication and Koichijōin's resignation. As Hosaka points out, the motives for Kazan's abdication are probably to be discovered by combining the *Ōkagami* account with the one in *Eiga monogatari*, which is supported by the existence of a number of Imperial poems of grief.[133] It has also been shown that Michinaga's solicitous treatment of Koichijōin after the Prince's marriage to Kanshi is a figment of the author's imagination—or at least that there is no known evidence to support his statement.[134] Both the abdication and the resignation seem, in short, to have been introduced in order to cast favorable light on Michinaga's character, even though many scholars have cited their inclusion as a prime example of the author's critical spirit.

Korechika's banishment, which is attributed to "the incident involving Retired Emperor Kazan,"[135] elicits a vague hint about a man's exile not always being his own fault, but there is no attempt to explore Michinaga's role in the matter. Rather, Yotsugi's expression of sympathy is followed immediately by an anecdote illustrating Korechika's lack of *tamashii*, at the end of which the old man remarks, "The whole affair was most undignified. It was not Korechika's fault, to be sure, but others said he might have been spared such humiliations if his social activities and general behavior had shown more discretion."[136]

Some observers detect a critical spirit in the stories of rivalry for office between Koremasa and Asahira, and between the brothers Sanenobu and Tadanobu, which they regard as exposés of the Fujiwara family's bitter internal struggles after the destruction of its competitors. We may feel, it is true, that the author is aware of the implications when he brings up such a story, even though he declines to pursue them. Perhaps he is inviting us, both in these two cases and in others, to look below the surface and draw our own conclusions, just as he must have done when, composing a *waka* in the contemporary fashion, he selected imagery and diction calculated to create the prized effect called *yojō* (overtones). But if his primary concern here was to call attention to internal discord, we must wonder why he failed to discuss the most famous case of all, that of the enmity between Kanemichi and Kaneie. He hints at it, but we must turn to the *rufubon* for particulars.[137] We are led to conclude that family quarrels interested him

---

[133] Hosaka 1974, 1.106-107. [134] See n. 110.
[135] Translation, p. 171. [136] Translation, p. 172.
[137] Translation, pp. 157, 163; Appendix B, (14).

only when they could be shown to have a bearing on his principal concern, Michinaga and his career. While there seems to be no such relationship in the case of Kanemichi and Kaneie, the story of Koremasa and Asahira is really a footnote to the section dealing with Yukinari, its function being to explain why an angry spirit should wish to attack the calligrapher. And that information, in turn, paves the way for an anecdote in which Michinaga demonstrates his bravery by interrogating the ghost when it appears in search of Yukinari.[138] Similarly, as was mentioned earlier, the story about Sanenobu and Tadanobu brings Michinaga to the fore as a wise and firm administrator, who places competence before birth in making appointments.

One last alleged example of the critical spirit should be noticed—the conversation between Yotsugi and Shigeki on the subject of forced labor at Michinaga's great temple, the Hōjōji. The passage runs as follows.[139]

"People seem to be doing a lot of complaining nowadays about Michinaga's incessant demands for laborers to work on his temple," said [Shigeki]. "Haven't you heard about it?"

"Yes, it is true, he does issue a call every two or three days," Yotsugi answered. "But when you go, it's not bad. If a man bears in mind that he is being called on to help build an earthly paradise, he will be glad to go if he can, and he will hope for rebirth as a shrub or tree at the Buddha Hall. Right-thinking people ought to be anxious to contribute their services. I have never evaded a summons, because I know I will never have such an opportunity again. And when a man does go, there is nothing bad about it at all. They are always handing out food and wine, and sometimes we get fruit and other dainties, which have been brought in as offerings. For workers who keep going back, there are even presents of clothing. So it seems that the lower classes scramble to join the levies."

"Yes, that's right," Shigeki said. "But I have thought of an even better plan for myself. In all my long life, I have never been forced to wear rags or suffer from lack of food or drink, but if a time should come when I was unable to put my hands on such necessities, I would look for three pieces of paper on which to write Michinaga a petition. And in the petition I would say, 'I was a page in the late Chancellor Tadahira's day. Now that I am old and destitute, I look to you as my lord because you are his descendant. I hope you will grant me a few things.' I know he wouldn't refuse

---

[138] Translation, p. 146.   [139] Translation, p. 209.

me some trifles, so I feel as secure of them as though they were in
my storeroom."

Perhaps we should look for *yojō* in what seems on the surface to be
an attempt to justify, rather than to condemn. But if a critical spirit is
present, either here or in the instances considered above, it is surely
very timid and retiring. If the author had wished to dwell on the questionable side of Michinaga's activities and character, he could scarcely
have resisted the temptation to utter a word or two of condemnation
in the course of the long Koichijōin episode, or to investigate the full
story of Korechika's banishment, or to touch, at least, on Michinaga's
harsh treatment of Teishi, Seishi, and Emperor Sanjō, concerning
which he says nothing.[140]
    The natural inference seems to be that the author is speaking the
truth when he says through Yotsugi, "I have only one thing of importance on my mind, and that is to describe Lord Michinaga's unprecedented successes." His basic attitude, far from being censorious,
is very nearly as adulatory as that of Akazome Emon. The difference
between *Eiga monogatari* and *Ōkagami* is not that one praises and the
other blames, but that one describes and the other explains.

Historicity   Having acquired some notion of the criteria governing the author's selection of materials, we must ask, before ending this
survey, whether what he has chosen to give us is reliable. Comparison
of the translation with Appendixes A and D will reveal many minor
factual errors, most of which are probably inadvertent. Tadahira is incorrectly said to have been seventy-one (*sai*), rather than seventy, at
the time of his death; Shōshi, who did not receive the title Jōtōmon'in until 1026, is referred to by that name once in the text, even
though the narrative present is 1025; Nakahira was twenty years behind
Tadahira in becoming a minister of state, rather than thirty; it seems to
have been Yoshifusa, not Tadahira, who secured a promotion for the
Munakata goddesses, and so forth. Other factual errors are probably
to be interpreted as authorial liberties, taken for dramatic effect or to
underscore a point, as when the *sake*-loving Michitaka is depicted as
worrying on his deathbed about whether he will meet his two dead
drinking companions in Paradise, even though one of the two, Naritoki,
is actually still alive; or when Michinaga is said to have appointed
Koichijōin's new household staff at the time of the Prince's resignation,
rather than nineteen days later, the date listed in reliable sources.

[140] See Appendix D.

Such inaccuracies do not seriously impair the value of *The Great Mirror*, nor does the inclusion of an occasional anecdote which reports a supernatural occurrence or bears the earmark of a traditional oral tale—the fart anecdote in Tokihira's biography, for example, or the story of Morosuke's encounter with the demon procession, which seems to belong to the same line as a *Konjaku monogatari* tale in which a young nobleman, meeting the same procession, is saved by a copy of the *Sonshō Dhāraṇī*, sewn into the collar of his robe by his nurse.[141] Of more concern is the authenticity of the vast bulk of the anecdotes used by the author to build up his picture of the Fujiwara leaders, and of Michinaga in particular. To what extent can we trust them?

In the first place, it must be said that almost none seem to derive from relatively trustworthy sources like diaries and official chronicles. There are a certain number of identical or related stories in *Yamato monogatari*, headnotes to poetic anthologies, *Eiga monogatari, Sanbō ekotoba*, and other sources, many of which are themselves of uncertain reliability, but most of the author's materials of this type appear for the first time in our work.[142] We can probably assume, in the light of what we know about *setsuwa* and their transmission, that the author's role was primarily that of a collector, and that most of his stories came from people who were persuaded of their authenticity. At the same time, we cannot ignore the likelihood that a number of them are outright inventions. In one case, that of the alleged rivalry between Koremasa and Asahira, the evidence seems quite clear. Although the author attributes the supposed feud, and the consequent unrest of Asahira's spirit, to Koremasa's wily maneuver to gain an appointment as Head Chamberlain at Asahira's expense, reliable records show that the two men were both appointed to Head Chamberlain positions in the same month of the same year. Furthermore, Koremasa could hardly have been responsible for Asahira's traumatic death, since he predeceased him by two years.[143] It is, of course, possible that the author has merely reworked an authentic story about ill feeling between the two, or that he has devised an explanation for a current belief in the hostility of Asahira's spirit toward Koremasa's descendants. As noted earlier, his real focus is not on the feud itself, but on Michinaga's confrontation of the angry spirit. Nevertheless, the episode constitutes a rather disquieting illustration of his carelessness with facts and/or willingness

[141] *Konjaku monogatarishū*, 3.335-337 (14.42); translated in Brower 1952, pp. 437-440.
[142] For a table collating *The Great Mirror*'s *setsuwa* with related stories in other works, see Tachibana 1974, pp. 449-479.
[143] Hosaka 1974, 1.112.

to improvise, especially when it is viewed in conjunction with the other doubtful stories about Michinaga noticed earlier.[144] Furthermore, when we compare his admiring treatment of Tadahira with the negative appraisal of modern Japanese historians, who dismiss the Chancellor as an amiable nonentity,[145] we cannot help wondering if we are being deliberately misled, and, if so, whether the much more detailed picture of Michinaga is similarly distorted.

It is obvious that *The Great Mirror* must be read with caution. With all respect to Yotsugi, it is not as reliable as the six national histories (*Nihongi*). But if we are to interpret *Nihongi* in the narrower sense of *Nihon shoki*, the old man's claim is not wholly unreasonable. Well over half of *Nihon shoki* consists of traditional stories about semi-legendary figures, selected, to be sure, with an eye to political expediency, but probably representative of what was believed to be the truth about the characters and actions of the Emperors and others described. In the same way, our author has collected and preserved stories about Michinaga and the other Fujiwara leaders, selecting and presenting them in such a way as to advance a point of view, but probably not doing violence to perceived truth. He does not, after all, invent stories claiming that Tadahira was a great statesman, but merely suggests that he was a man in touch with supernatural powers, and thus a fit ancestor for Michinaga. His portrayal of Kaneie coincides perfectly with the presumably authentic description in *Kagerō nikki*, the diary of Kaneie's wife; and there is no basic conflict between his Michinaga and the one we encounter in *Makura no sōshi*, in *Eiga monogatari*, and in the diaries of Sanesuke and Murasaki Shikibu. The same may be said of the members of the Ononomiya family and other figures. As far as can be determined, the author's perception of them was essentially that of their contemporaries and his own, as revealed in diaries, *setsuwa* collections, and other sources. We may suspect that he endowed Michinaga with an undeserved measure of physical courage, and we may regret a certain lack of forthrightness, but it would be difficult to accuse him of deliberate, systematic deception. Although it is seldom possible to authenticate a given anecdote, he seems, for the most part, to be reporting what he believes to be the truth.

If we must read *The Great Mirror* with caution, then, we must also read it with an appreciation of its virtues. As the narrator reminds us, Yotsugi's narrative is not to be taken lightly. Quite apart from its sheer entertainment value, which is considerable, the book remains the

[144] See above, pp. 45-46.   [145] Appendix D, p. 344.

best study ever done of Michinaga. Its treatment of the sources of Fujiwara power is still useful and instructive. And its author, in bringing to our attention the differences between masculine and feminine conceptions of the ideal Heian courtier, suggests to us that it may be time to re-assess our opinions on that subject.

THE GREAT MIRROR
Translation

CHAPTER ONE

Preface

It happened recently that I attended an enlightenment sermon at the Urin'in,[1] where I witnessed an encounter between three people of extraordinary and disturbing antiquity—two graybeards and a crone, who had, it seemed, sat down in the same place by chance. How strange that such a trio should have come together! As I stared, they laughed and exchanged glances.

"For years now, I have been wanting to meet someone from the old days with whom to discuss what has been going on in the world, and especially to talk about the fortunes of our present Novice Excellency,"[2] one of the old men said. "This happy meeting reconciles me to the thought of dying. A person feels stuffed when he can't get things off his chest. No wonder the man of old dug a hole and talked into it when he had a piece of news to pass along.[3] It's delightful to see you. Tell me, what is your age?

"I don't know," said the other, "but I am the Ōinumaro who acted as page to the late Chancellor, Lord Tadahira, when he was a Chamberlain Lesser Captain.[4] You are the famous Ōyake no Yotsugi who served

---

[1] See Appendix A for identification of persons and places. Enlightenment sermons (*bōdaikō*), delivered by a Buddhist preacher who used the *Lotus Sutra* as a text, were designed to assure rebirth in Amitābha's Pure Land. The ones at the Urin'in took place annually in the Fifth Month. Hosaka 1974, 2.18.

[2] *Tadaima no nyūdō denka*. Fujiwara Michinaga, probably so called to distinguish him from his father, Kaneie. Novice (*nyūdō*) was a courtesy title for an official of Third or higher rank who had taken the tonsure; Excellency (*denka*), a term of respect applied to Princes and Regents. For general information concerning Court ranks and titles, see McCullough and McCullough 1980, Appendix A.

[3] Possibly an allusion to Ovid's story of the barber who discovered King Midas's jackass ears when the monarch's turban was removed: "Saw, dared not tell, and wanted to, and could not/ keep matters to himself . . . and so he dug a hole/ deep in the ground, and went and whispered in it/ what kind of ears King Midas had." Translation from Ovid 1955, p. 265. *Samguk yusa*, a Buddhist-oriented Korean history of the late thirteenth or early fourteenth century, contains an adaptation of the anecdote, which may have entered a Buddhist text and travelled via Central Asia and China to Korea, and ultimately to Japan. *Ōkagami*, p. 437, s.n. 4; Hosaka 1974, 2.20-21.

[4] Conjectured to have been around 895—i.e., 130 years before 1025, the *Ōkagami* narrative present. If Shigeki was 180 (*sai*) in 1025, as the author indicates

the Empress Mother in that reign, aren't you? You must be much older than I am. You were a man of twenty-five or twenty-six when I was only a boy."

"Yes, yes," Yotsugi agreed. "That's right. What is your name?"

"Lord Tadahira asked about my surname when I went through the capping ceremony[5] at his mansion. I answered, 'Natsuyama,' and he named me Shigeki on the spot."

It was an astonishing dialogue. All the intelligent members of the congregation were watching from their seats or edging closer. A man of about thirty made his way to a nearby spot—an attendant from a noble household, by the look of him. "Really, now, you old people are saying some interesting things, but who is going to believe you?" he asked.

The two men looked at one another, laughing scornfully.

"You say you don't remember how old you are," said the attendant, fixing his eyes on the one who called himself Shigeki. "I wonder if this old gentleman might know?"

"Of course," said Yotsugi. "I turned 190 this year,[6] which makes Shigeki 180; it's just that he is too modest to say so. I was born on the Fifteenth of the First Month in the year of Emperor Seiwa's abdication [876], so I have seen the reigns of thirteen sovereigns. That's not a bad age, is it? People may not think I am telling the truth, but I had a father who served a young university student, and it was a case of 'humble but near the capital.'[7] He lerned to read and write, and he recorded my birthdate on a set of swaddling clothes, which has survived to this day. It was the *hinoe saru* year."[8] He made it all sound perfectly natural.

---

below, he was far too old to act as a page in 895. The vulgate texts give his age as 140. Hosaka 1974, 2.21.

[5] *Genpuku*, a ritual in which a boy formally became an adult. The central act was the ceremonious placing of a man's cap on his head. McCullough and McCullough 1980, s.n. 13.

[6] In 1025, a man born in 876 would have been 150 (*sai*), the age attributed to Yotsugi in the vulgate texts. For discussion of this and other inconsistencies concerning the old men's ages, see *Ōkagami*, p. 438, s.n. 6; and Hosaka 1974, 2.33. As Hosaka points out, the author seems to have been interested not in stressing the specific ages of his raconteurs but in presenting them as old enough to give first-hand accounts of the events described.

[7] Presumably a proverb to the effect that even humble folk pick up city ways and city accomplishments—in this case, literacy—when exposed to life in the capital.

[8] Like others of the ten stems and twelve branches, *hinoe* and *saru* occur in combination at sixty-year intervals; 876 was in fact a *hinoe saru* year. For information about the sexagenary cycle, see Webb and Ryan 1963, pp. 23-25.

The attendant turned to the other old man.

"I should still like to ask your age," he said. "Do you know your birth year? If so, we can easily calculate it."

"I was not reared by my own parents," Shigeki said. "Somebody else took care of me until I was twelve or thirteen. My foster father never mentioned my exact age. He just said, 'I didn't have a family, but once I happened to take along ten strings of my own money when my master sent me to market. I met a woman carrying a pretty baby, and she said to me, "I'm looking for someone to take this child. He is my tenth. His father was forty when he was born, and furthermore he even arrived in the Fifth Month.[9] I want to get rid of him." I traded my coins for him and took him home. When I asked about the family's name, the mother said it was Natsuyama.' I entered Lord Tadahira's service when I was thirteen."

"Well, well, I can't tell you how glad I am to meet you," said Yotsugi. "A buddha must have answered my prayers. Nowadays we are always hearing about sermons in some place or other, but I usually don't bother to go. It's a good thing I decided to attend this one. Is the lady someone you married in the old days?"

"No," Shigeki answered. "My first wife died young; I married this one afterwards. How about you?"

"My first wife and I are still living together. She got ready to come with me today, but she suffers from malaria, and it turned out to be one of her bad days, so she had to give it up." They seemed to be weeping, but their eyes were dry.[10]

Time passed while we waited for the preacher. We were all feeling bored when old Yotsugi spoke up again. "Well, since there's nothing else to do, what do you say? Shall I give you a story about the old days to let these people know what things were like?"

"By all means! That would be splendid," said Shigeki. "Do talk to us. I'll speak up once in a while if I have anything to add."

It looked as though they were eager to talk, and I for one longed to hear them. Many others in the crowd were probably determined to catch every word too, but I was struck most of all by the attitude of the attendant, who seemed bent on taking part in the conversation.

"The world is a fascinating place," said Yotsugi. "Yet it is only the old who have learned to understand it a little. In ancient times, wise sovereigns sought out the oldest men and women in the country, asked

---

[9] It was believed that a child born when his father was forty would grow up to be a patricide, and that one born in the Fifth Month would harm his parents.

[10] It is not uncommon for old people to lose the ability to shed tears.

them how various kinds of laws had worked in the past, and governed accordingly. The aged deserve your respect; don't look down on them, young people!" I watched in amusement as he gave a complacent cackle and hid his face behind his fan, which was made of yellow paper with nine black persimmon-wood ribs.

"I have only one thing of importance on my mind," he went on, "and that is to describe Lord Michinaga's unprecedented successes to all of you here, clergy and laity of both sexes. It is a complicated subject, so I shall have to discuss a fair number of Emperors, Empresses, ministers of state, and senior nobles first. Then when I reach Michinaga himself, the most fortunate of all, you will understand just how everything came about. They tell us that the Buddha began by expounding other sutras when he wanted to explain the *Lotus*, which is why his sermons are called the teachings of the five periods.[11] That is how it is with me, too; I need to 'expound other sutras' in order to describe Michinaga's successes."

In spite of this rather theatrical and pretentious prelude, I wondered whether he would have anything worthwhile to say, but he continued in a most impressive vein.

"I suppose you youngsters nowadays think every Regent, minister of state, and senior noble in history has been very much like Michinaga. That is far from true. Of course, they have all been descendants of the same ancestor and members of the same family,[12] but the family has

[11] In the *Lotus Sutra*, Śākyamuni explains that buddhahood is the only goal of Buddhism, and that his earlier preaching of other goals has been designed to encourage the weak and prepare them for the truth. The basic point is illustrated with a wealth of parables, and merit is repeatedly promised to all who revere and propagate the sutra. See Hurvitz 1976, pp. x-xv, for a convenient summary of the contents of this famous and immensely influential scripture, which was devoutly worshipped by Michinaga and his family. According to Tendai doctrine, the Buddha's fifty-year teaching career was divided into five periods: (1) three seven-day periods, immediately following his enlightenment, during which he preached the contents of the *Avataṃsaka Sutra*; (2) twelve years of preaching Hīnayāna scriptures in the Deer Park; (3) eight years of preaching a combination of Mahāyāna and Hīnayāna doctrines (the vaipulya period); (4) twenty-two years of preaching the *prajñā* (wisdom) sutras; (5) eight years of preaching the *Lotus* and, in a day and a night, the *Nirvana Sutra*. Soothill and Hodous 1937, p. 119b.

[12] Members of other families actually received 42 of the 105 ministerial appointments made between 645 and 1025. From 899 on, however, the only non-Fujiwara ministers were Minamoto who were closely related to the Imperial house. By about the same time, every senior noble (kugyō, a term used of Consultants and holders of the three highest Court ranks) was either a Fujiwara or a Minamoto.

produced many different kinds of people in the process of branching out.

"The first Japanese sovereign after the seven divine generations was Emperor Jinmu; and there have been sixty-eight Emperors from Emperor Jinmu to our present ruler. I ought to discuss each of them in turn, from Emperor Jinmu on, but that would take us far back into unfamiliar history, so I had better confine myself to the recent past.

"There was an Emperor called Montoku. From that Emperor to the present, there have been fourteen reigns. To put it in terms of years, 176 have elapsed since the accession of Emperor Montoku in the third year of Kashō [850]. Awesome as it is to speak the names of those august sovereigns . . . ."

And he went on to tell the following story.

Imperial Annals

THE FIFTY-FIFTH REIGN
EMPEROR MONTOKU

Emperor Montoku was the first son of Emperor Ninmyō. His mother, Senior Grand Empress Junshi, was a daughter of Minister of the Left Fuyutsugi, who was posthumously granted Senior First Rank with the title of Chancellor.

Emperor Montoku was born in the Eighth Month of the fourth year of Tenchō [827]. He was bright and a good judge of character. He performed the capping ceremony on the Twenty-Sixth of the Second Month in the ninth year of Jōwa [842], and became heir apparent on the Fourth of the Eighth Month in the same year, when he was sixteen.[1][13] He ascended the throne on the Twenty-First of the Third Month in the third year of Kashō [850], when he was twenty-four, and reigned for eight years.

The Emperor's mother gave birth to him in her nineteenth year. She attained Imperial rank at the age of forty-two, in the Fourth Month of the third year of Kashō [850]; rose to the status of Empress in the first year of Saikō [854]; received the sacramental waters as a nun on the Twenty-Ninth of the Second Month in the third year of Jōgan [861]; and became Grand Empress on the Seventh of the First Month in the sixth year of Jōgan [864]. She is called the Gojō Empress. It was her residence about which Middle Captain Narihira composed the poem in *Tales of Ise*, "Would that he might fall asleep every night"—and also "The spring of old."[14]

---

[13] Superscript figures in parentheses refer to translations in Appendix B.

[14] *Tales of Ise* (*Ise monogatari*) is an anonymous tenth-century collection of anecdotes centering on poetry. "Once when the former Empress was living in eastern Gojō, a certain lady occupied the west wing of her mansion. Quite without intending it, a man fell deeply in love with the lady and began to visit her, but around the Tenth of the First Month she moved away without a word, and although he learned where she had gone, it was not a place where ordinary people could come and go. He could do no more than brood over the wretchedness of life. Poignant memories of the past drew him back to her old apartments when the plum blossoms were at their height in the next First Month. . . . He composed this poem: *Tsuki ya aranu/ haru ya mukashi no/ haru naranu/ waga mi hitotsu wa/ moto no mi ni shite.* (Is not the moon the same? The spring the spring of old? Only this body of mine is the same body. . . .) . . . Once a man

THE FIFTY-SIXTH REIGN
EMPEROR SEIWA

The next sovereign, Emperor Seiwa, was Emperor Montoku's fourth son. His mother, Grand Empress Meishi, was Chancellor Yoshifusa's daughter. The Emperor was born in the Koichijō residence of his maternal grandfather, Yoshifusa, on the Twenty-Fifth of the Third Month in the third year of Kashō [850], which is to say on the fifth day of his father's reign—a happy and auspicious season.

Emperor Seiwa was a man of splendid character and appearance. I believe he was the one who competed with Prince Koretaka for the heir apparency. He became Crown Prince very quickly—on the Twenty-Fifth of the Eleventh Month in the year of his birth—and ascended the throne at the age of nine, on the Twenty-Seventh of the Eighth Month in the second year of Ten'an [858]. He performed the capping ceremony at fifteen, on the First of the First Month in the sixth year of Jōgan [864], abdicated at the Somedono Palace after a reign of eighteen years, on the Twenty-Ninth of the Eleventh Month in the eighteenth year of Jōgan [876], and entered holy orders on the Eighth of the Fifth Month in the third year of Gangyō [879]. He is called the Mizunoo Emperor. The members of today's warrior house of Minamoto are his descendants. Need I say that they serve as guardians of the Court!

Emperor Seiwa's mother gave birth to him in her twenty-third year. She rose to the position of Empress on the Seventh of the First Month in the sixth year of Jōgan [864], and enjoyed Imperial status for forty-one years. She is called the Somedono Empress.

The Imperial Exorcist[15] during that reign was Great Teacher Chishō.[2] He returned from China in the second year of Ten'an [858].

---

was paying secret visits to a lady in the eastern Gojō area. He had no wish to be observed, so he could not enter through the gate, but came and went through a broken place in the earthen wall where some children had been playing. The spot was not much frequented, but his repeated use of it became known to the house's owner, who posted a night guard there. The man, when he came, was obliged to go home without having seen the lady. He composed this poem: *Hito shirenu/ waga kayoiji no/ sekimori wa/ yoiyoi goto ni/ uchi mo nenanamu.* (Would that he might fall asleep every night—this guard at the secret place where I come and go.)" *Ise monogatari*, secs. 4-5; translation after McCullough 1968, pp. 71-72. The certain lady is said to have been Junshi's niece Kōshi, who later married the future Emperor Seiwa.

¹⁵ *Gojisō*, a Shingon or Tendai monk who guarded the Imperial person by reciting prayers at night in the Seiryōden.

THE FIFTY-SEVENTH REIGN
EMPEROR YŌZEI

The next ruler was Emperor Yōzei, the oldest son of Emperor Seiwa. His mother was Grand Empress Kōshi, a daughter of Provisional Middle Counselor Nagara, who was posthumously promoted to the office of Chancellor with Senior First Rank.

Emperor Yōzei was born in the Somedono Palace on the Sixteenth of the Twelfth Month in the tenth year of Jōgan [868]. He became Crown Prince during his second year, on the First of the Second Month in the eleventh year of Jōgan [869]; ascended the throne at the age of nine, on the Twenty-Ninth of the Eleventh Month in the eighteenth year of Jōgan [876]; performed the capping ceremony at the age of fifteen, on the Second of the First Month in the sixth year of Gangyō [882]; and reigned for eight years, after which he abdicated and went to live at the Nijō Palace. Since he was eighty-one when he died sixty-five years later, the supplication at the Buddhist services on his behalf said, "He was the elder brother of Śākyamuni by one year."[16] That was a witty conceit, but someone was told later in a dream, "His Majesty is suffering in the next world because he was called the Buddha's senior."

Emperor Yōzei's mother was nine years older than Emperor Seiwa. She gave birth to him at the age of twenty-seven. She received the title of Empress at the age of thirty-six, in the First Month of the sixth year of Gangyō [882], and rose to the rank of Grand Empress at the age of forty-one, on the Seventh of the First Month in the same year. It is not clear to me how she happened to marry Emperor Seiwa, because she was the girl whom the Ariwara Middle Captain carried off and hid while she was still living a sheltered life at home. Her older brothers, Minister of State Mototsune and Major Counselor Kunitsune, who must have been very young at the time, went to fetch her back, and Narihira composed the poem, ". . . my beloved spouse is hidden here, and so am I."[17] (Much later the Middle Captain recalled those

---

[16] Śākyamuni is said to have died at the age of eighty.

[17] "*Musahino wa/ kyō wa na yaki so/ wakakusa no/ tsuma mo komoreri/ ware mo komoreri.* (Do not set fire today to Musashi Plain, for my beloved spouse is hidden here, and so am I.)" The poem is actually an anonymous composition, attributed in *Ise monogatari* to a girl, abducted by her lover, who addresses their pursuers as the latter prepare to smoke them out. As Hosaka 1974 suggests, 2.69, the author, who undoubtedly knew better, has probably made Narihira the author in order to link episode and poem in the reader's mind with an *Ise* story about Narihira's abduction of Kōshi (sec. 6). *Ise monogatari*, sec. 12; *Kokinshū* 17, with Kasugano for Musashino. Translation after McCullough 1968, p. 78.

events in his poem, "What happened long ago in the age of the gods.")[18]

Under the circumstances, it would seem that Kōshi probably did not become an Imperial consort in the manner usual for carefully reared young girls. I suppose the Emperor must have met her when she visited the Somedono Empress, from whom she was inseparable.

It is presumptuous for a nobody like me to talk about such things, but they are all matters of common knowledge. Is there anybody nowadays who hasn't read the *Collection of Early and Modern Times*[19] and *Tales of Ise?*

People say the Middle Captain's poem, "Someone not unseen, nor yet quite seen,"[20] was also written during his affair with that lady. When we think of the poems he bequeathed to posterity, we can't help regarding him as an amazing gallant. Of course, the old times were more elegant and interesting than ours. (*This was said with a smile. He grew more and more impressive; I felt quite put to shame.*) She was the lady known as the Nijō Empress.

THE FIFTY-EIGHTH REIGN

EMPEROR KŌKŌ

The next ruler was Emperor Kōkō, Emperor Ninmyō's third son. His mother, Posthumous Grand Empress Takushi, was a daughter of Posthumous Chancellor Fusatsugi.

[18] "In the days when the Empress from the Second Ward [Kōshi] was still known as the Mother of the Crown Prince, she made a pilgrimage to the shrine of her ancestral deity. When presents were distributed to the people in her party, a certain elderly Bodyguards officer [Narihira] received his gift directly from her carriage. He composed this poem: *Ōhara ya/ Oshio no yama mo/ kyō koso wa/ kamiyo no koto mo/ omoiizurame.* (On this auspicious day, the divinity of Mount Oshio at Ōhara will surely remember what happened long ago in the age of the gods.) Perhaps she felt a pang of sorrow—but that is something we have no way of knowing." *Ise monogatari*, sec. 76; translation after McCullough 1968, pp. 120-121, which see for a discussion of the poem's possible levels of meaning. The poem also appears as *Kokinshū* 871.

[19] *Kokinshū*, the first Imperial poetic anthology, compiled ca. 905.

[20] "On the day of an archery meet at the riding grounds of the Bodyguards of the Right, a certain Middle Captain glimpsed a lady's face through the silk curtains of a carriage opposite him. He sent her this poem: *Mizu mo arazu/ mi mo senu hito no/ koishiku wa/ aya naku kyō ya/ nagamekurasan.* (Bewitched by someone not unseen nor yet quite seen, must I to no purpose spend this day lost in melancholy revery?)" *Ise monogatari*, sec. 99; *Kokinshū* 476. Translation from McCullough 1968, p. 137.

Emperor Kōkō was born at the Higashigojō Mansion in the seventh year of Tenchō [830], during the reign of Emperor Junna. He was granted Fourth Princely Rank at the age of seven, on the Seventh of the First Month in the third year of Jōwa [836], during the reign of his father, the Fukakusa Emperor. He became Minister of Central Affairs at twenty-one, in the First Month of the third year of Kashō [850]; advanced to Third Rank at twenty-two, on the Twenty-First of the Eleventh Month in the first year of Ninju [851]; assumed the additional office of governor of Kōzuke Province at thirty-five, on the Sixteenth of the First Month in the sixth year of Jōgan [864]; transferred to the post of Provisional Governor-General of the Dazaifu on the Thirteenth of the First Month in the eighth year of Jōgan [866]; advanced to Second Rank at forty, on the Seventh of the Second Month in the twelfth year of Jōgan [870]; became Minister of Ceremonial at forty-six, on the Twenty-Sixth of the Second Month in the eighteenth year of Jōgan [876]; advanced to First Rank at fifty-three, on the Seventh of the First Month in the sixth year of Gangyō [882]; assumed the additional office of Governor-General of the Dazaifu in the First Month of the eighth year of Gangyō [884]; and ascended the throne on the Fourth of the Second Month in the same year, at the age of fifty-five. He reigned for four years. He is called the Komatsu Emperor. I cannot say whether it is true, but I have heard that the Black Chamber next to the Fujitsubo Imperial Apartment was built during his reign.

THE FIFTY-NINTH REIGN
EMPEROR UDA

The next sovereign, the Teiji Emperor, was Emperor Kōkō's third son. His mother, the Grand Empress, was Princess Hanshi, a daughter of Prince Nakano, the Minister of Ceremonial of Second Rank, who was posthumously granted the title of Chancellor with First Rank.

Emperor Uda was born on the Fifth of the Fifth Month in the ninth year of Jōgan [867] and took the Minamoto surname at the age of eighteen, on the Thirteenth of the Fourth Month in the eighth year of Gangyō [884].[3] He became Crown Prince on the Twenty-Sixth of the Eighth Month in the third year of Ninna [887], succeeded promptly to the throne on the same day at the age of twenty-one, and reigned for ten years. The first Kamo Special Festival was held during his reign, on the Twenty-First of the Eleventh Month in the first year of

Kanpyō [889], with Middle Captain Tokihira as the Imperial Messenger.[4]

Emperor Uda became a monk on the Fourth of the Tenth Month in the first year of Shōtai [898]. Tachibana Yoshitoshi, a Hizen Secretary who had waited on him in the Courtiers' Hall, joined him in holy orders to serve as the sole companion of his religious practices. Once when the former sovereign was stopping at a place called Hine on the way to Kumano, Yoshitoshi recited, "That my home should thus appear in a travel-sleep dream at Hine."[21] It is only natural that those pathetic lines should still draw tears from our eyes.

It is hard to say how Emperor Uda happened to become a commoner; I don't remember much about it. His mother is known as the Tōin Empress.

People used to call the future sovereign the Princely Gentleman-in-Waiting, possibly because they were unaware that he had taken the Minamoto surname. While he was a courtier under Emperor Yōzei, he served as a dancer during Imperial visits to shrines.[22] He once passed in front of the Yōzeiin after his accession, and the Retired Emperor said, "Isn't the present Emperor one of my men?"[23] What monarch ever had a retainer like Emperor Uda!

THE SIXTIETH REIGN
EMPEROR DAIGO

The next sovereign, Emperor Daigo, was Emperor Uda's oldest son. His mother, Grand Empress Inshi, was a daughter of Palace Minister Takafuji.

Emperor Daigo was born on the Eighteenth of the First Month in the first year of Ninna [885]. He became Crown Prince at the age of nine, on the Fourteenth of the Fourth Month in the fifth year of Kan-

---

21 "*Furusato no/ tabine no yume ni/ mietsuru wa/ urami ya suramu/ mata to towaneba.* (That my home should thus appear in a travel-sleep dream at Hine: might they be angry with me because I have never returned?)" The poem, which puns on Hine and *tabine* (travel-sleep), reflects a contemporary belief that people who were thinking of one would appear in one's dreams. Yoshitoshi hints that his master's incessant travels are to blame if members of his household resent his prolonged absence. For an earlier version of this well-known anecdote, see *Yamato monogatari*, sec. 2, pp. 231-232; Tahara 1969, pp. 135-136.

22 A function routinely assigned to courtiers.

23 The vulgate texts continue, "He has no business riding past my house like that." Satō 1929, p. 45. Yōzei was unbalanced.

pyō [893]; performed the capping ceremony at eleven, on the Nineteenth of the First Month in the seventh year of Kanpyō [895]; and ascended the throne at thirteen, on the Third of the Seventh Month in the ninth year of Kanpyō [897]. On that very night, he suddenly emerged from the Bedchamber with the cap on his head and issued the proclamation. Some say he dressed himself, but I have no idea whether it is true or not.[24] At any rate, he reigned for thirty-three years.

That's right, it was during Emperor Daigo's reign that Middle Captain Korehira recited his poem when the rice cakes were brought into the Courtiers' Hall to celebrate the fiftieth day after the birth of a new Prince—I have forgotten whether it was Murakami or Suzaku. (*After making a show of searching his memory, he began to recite.*)

Hitotose ni	We shall behold
Koyoi kazouru	The light of the moon
Ima yori wa	For a hundred years
Momotose made no	From this night on which we count
Tsukikage o min.	Each day a year.[25]

His Majesty was graciously pleased to reply:

Iwaitsuru	If there be miraculous powers
Kotodama naraba	In your felicitations,
Momotose no	We shall indeed behold
Nochi mo tsukisenu	The moon undimmed
Tsuki o koso mime.	Even after a hundred years.

Emperor Daigo's collected poems are remarkably elegant. Even in that respect, he was an unusual man.

[24] Reliable sources indicate that Emperor Daigo performed the capping ceremony on the day of his accession in 897. (Hosaka 1974, 2.103, postulates an interpolation or corruption to account for the discrepancy.) He appears to have moved into the Seiryōden immediately after the ceremony, and to have come out that night, appropriately garbed, for the accession proclamation. The author's hints at haste and irregularity seem designed to suggest that Emperor Uda had been forced off the throne by the Fujiwara, presumably because they resented his patronage of Sugawara Michizane and his other efforts to curb their power.

[25] Moon is a metaphor for the Prince. As the text suggests, this poem and the Emperor's reply were actually composed on the 100th day after the birth of the future Emperor Murakami in 926, rather than on the fiftieth day. They appear as nos. 1052 and 1053 in the fourteenth Imperial anthology, *Gyokuyōshū*, where Korehira's reads: *Hi o toshi ni/ koyoi zo kauru/ ima yori ya/ momotose made no/ tsukikage mo mimu.*

THE SIXTY-FIRST REIGN
EMPEROR SUZAKU

The next sovereign, Emperor Daigo's eleventh son, is known as the Suzakuin Emperor. His mother, Grand Empress Onshi, was Chancellor Mototsune's fourth daughter.

His Majesty was born on the Twenty-Fourth of the Seventh Month in the first year of Enchō [923]. He became Crown Prince at the age of three, on the Twenty-First of the Tenth Month in the third year of Enchō [925]. He ascended the throne at eight, on the Twenty-Second of the Ninth Month in the eighth year of Enchō [930], performed the capping ceremony at fifteen, on the Fourth of the First Month in the seventh year of Jōhei [937], and reigned for sixteen years.[26]

THE SIXTY-SECOND REIGN
EMPEROR MURAKAMI

The next sovereign, Emperor Murakami, was Emperor Daigo's fourteenth son. He and Emperor Suzaku had the same mother.

Emperor Murakami was born in the Keihōbō on the Second of the Sixth Month in the fourth year of Enchō [926]. He performed the capping ceremony at the age of fifteen, on the Fifteenth of the Second Month in the third year of Tengyō [940]; became Crown Prince at nineteen, on the Twenty-Second of the Fourth Month in the seventh year of Tengyō [944]; ascended the throne at twenty-one, on the Thirteenth of the Fourth Month in the ninth year of Tengyō [946]; and reigned for twenty-one years.

Emperor Murakami's mother gave birth to Prince Yasuakira, the former Crown Prince, at the age of nineteen in the third year of Engi [903]. She was designated a Junior Consort by Imperial decree at the age of thirty-six, in the twentieth year of Engi [920]; gave birth to Emperor Suzaku in the twenty-third year of Engi [923]; and received Imperial status on the Twenty-Fifth of the intercalary Fourth Month in the same year, at the age of thirty-nine. (I wonder if the promotion

[26] In the *kohon* texts, the author devotes less space to Suzaku than to any other Emperor, probably because the two significant events of his reign, the revolts of Masakado and Sumitomo, were not directly connected with the story of the Fujiwara rise. Suzaku was a sickly man who failed to sire a son. For the well-known passage inserted at the end of this section in the vulgate texts, see Chapter 6, n. 8.

might have come during the month of the future Emperor's birth.)
Emperor Murakami was born when she was forty-one.

On the day of the lady's elevation to the rank of Empress, everyone
at her residence avoided mention of the former Crown Prince[27]—all
except a lady-in-waiting named Tayū no kimi, the daughter of the
Prince's nurse.[28] Tayū composed a poem.

Wabinureba	Bowed down by grief,
Ima wa to mono o	I had resolved
Omoedomo	To be moved no more—
Kokoro ni ninu wa	But tears, it seems,
Namida narikeri.	Are not like minds.

Again, on the day when people were leaving after the final Buddhist services, Tayū wrote:

Ima wa tote	In what villages
Miyama o izuru	Will they cry,
Hototogisu	Those cuckoos coming forth
Izure no sato ni	From the deep mountains,
Nakan to suran.	"Now that it is time"?

The month happened to be the Fifth.[29] It takes true elegance to compose poems so appropriate and moving that others will hand them on
for generations.

The former Crown Prince's mother was inconsolable after his death,
but she gave birth to Emperor Suzaku before the year was out, and
she also acquired the title of Empress, so her lot seems to have been
one of mingled sorrows and joys. She is the lady people mean when
they speak of the Senior Empress.[30]

[27] The Prince had died a month earlier. Mention of him would have been inauspicious.

[28] Tayū was actually the Prince's nurse. Hosaka 1974, 2.114.

[29] The Fifth Month was the one in which cuckoos traditionally emerged from
the mountains to sing near human habitations. The cuckoos in the poem represent the mourners, who leave the mountain temple where they have remained
during the forty-nine-day mourning period. Since the Prince had died on the
Twenty-First of the Third Month, the forty-ninth day would ordinarily have
fallen in the Fifth Month, as the author assumes was the case. In 923, however,
the calendar included an intercalary Fourth Month.

[30] *Ōkisaki*, an unofficial title.

THE SIXTY-THIRD REIGN
EMPEROR REIZEI

The next sovereign, Emperor Reizei, was Emperor Murakami's second son. His mother, Empress Anshi, was the oldest daughter of Lord Morosuke, the Minister of the Right.

Emperor Reizei was born on the Twenty-Fourth of the Fifth Month in the fourth year of Tenryaku [950], in the Gojō residence of Lord Arihira, who was then still vice-governor of Bizen with Junior Fifth Lower Rank. He became Crown Prince on the Twenty-Third of the Seventh Month in the same year, performed the capping ceremony at the age of fourteen, on the Twenty-Eighth of the Second Month in the third year of Ōwa [963]; and ascended the throne at eighteen, on the Twenty-Fifth of the Fifth Month in the fourth year of Kōhō [967]. He reigned for two years and died at the age of sixty-two, on the Twenty-Fourth of the Tenth Month in the eighth year of Kankō [1011]. Everyone said his death occurred at an awkward time, because it required the postponement of the Great Thanksgiving Services, which were supposed to take place after Emperor Sanjō's accession that year.

THE SIXTY-FOURTH REIGN
EMPEROR EN'YŪ

The next sovereign, Emperor En'yū, was Emperor Murakami's fifth son. He and Emperor Reizei had the same mother.

Emperor En'yū was born on the Second of the Third Month in the third year of Tentoku [959]. There were some unpleasant and scandalous happenings around the time when he became Crown Prince, but the story is so well known that I shall say no more.[31] He ascended the throne at the age of eleven, on the Thirteenth of the Eighth Month in the second year of Anna [969]; performed the capping ceremony at fourteen, on the Third of the First Month in the third year of Tenroku [972]; and reigned for fifteen years.

Empress Anshi gave birth to Emperor Reizei and this Emperor in two successive years, when she was twenty-three and twenty-four.[32]

---

[31] A reference to the Anna incident of 969. See Appendix D.

[32] Reizei was born in 950, when his mother was twenty-three; En'yū, nine years later.

What an incomparable karma! I have heard that her maternal grandfather, Fujiwara Tsunekuni, who had served as governor of Izumo with Junior Fifth Lower Rank, was posthumously elevated to the Third Rank through her intercession. Even though Tsunekuni was already dead, it was a great honor for him. She was the lady called the Middle Empress. His Majesty's grief is said to have been most affecting when she died after the birth of the Tenth Princess. Some of you have probably read the *Diary of Emperor Murakami*. It seems a pitiful and moving case, even to a humble fellow like me who has only heard vague rumors about his feelings. The Princess she left behind was none other than the Great Kamo Virgin.

THE SIXTY-FIFTH REIGN
EMPEROR KAZAN

The next sovereign, Emperor Kazan, was Emperor Reizei's oldest son. His mother, who is known as Posthumous Empress Kaishi, was Chancellor Koremasa's oldest daughter.

Emperor Kazan was born on the Twenty-Sixth of the Tenth Month in the first year of Anna [968], at his maternal grandfather's Ichijō residence, which I believe may have been what is now the Sesonji. (It was the date of Emperor Reizei's Thanksgiving Purification.)[33] He became Crown Prince at the age of two, on the Thirteenth of the Eighth Month in the second year of Anna [969]; performed the capping ceremony at fifteen, on the Nineteenth of the Second Month in the fifth year of Tengen [982]; and ascended the throne at seventeen, on the Twenty-Eighth of the Eighth Month in the second year of Eikan [984]. And to be sure, it was when he was nineteen, on the night of the Twenty-Second of the Sixth Month in the second year of Kanna [986], that he stole away without a word to become a monk at Hanayamadera—a shocking affair. He reigned for two years and lived twenty-two years longer.

A pathetic thing happened on the night of his abdication. As he was about to leave through the Fujitsubo Apartment's side door, he noticed the late moon flooding the surroundings with light.

---

[33] The Thanksgiving (*daijōsai*) was a harvest ritual performed by a new Emperor, ordinarily in the first or second Eleventh Month of his reign. The most important of its many preliminary events was the Imperial Purification (*gokei*), which took place beside the Kamo River late in the Tenth Month. McCullough and McCullough 1980, s.n. 18.

"It looks so bright," he said. "What shall I do?"

Michikane urged him forward. "There is no reason why you should stop now. The Necklace and Sword have already been transferred," he said. He had personally delivered the Imperial Regalia to the Crown Prince while the Emperor was still in the Palace, so he knew it would never do for His Majesty to go back.

While the Emperor hesitated, not wanting to venture into the light, some drifting clouds dimmed the moon's radiance. "I shall be able to take the vows after all," he thought. But as he stepped forward he remembered a note from the Kokiden Consort, something he had saved and read over and over.

"Wait a minute," he said, starting back to fetch it.

"You mustn't think about things like that any more," said Michikane, pretending to weep. "Some obstacle is certain to come up if you don't take advantage of this opportunity."

Michikane got the Emperor out through Tsuchimikado Gate and took him toward the east. As they were passing Seimei's house, they heard the diviner clap his hands and utter an exclamation. "The heavens foretold His Majesty's abdication, and now it seems to have happened. I shall have to report to the throne. Get my carriage ready," he said. Even though it was the Emperor's own idea to become a monk, those words must have cost him a pang.

"One of you spirits had better go on ahead to the Palace," Seimei said. And they tell me that an invisible person pushed open the door and answered, "It looks as though His Majesty has just passed the house." (He may have seen the Emperor's retreating figure. Seimei's residence was at the intersection of Tsuchimikado and Machiguchi, so it was on the way.)

After the Emperor reached Hanayamadera and cut off his hair, Michikane spoke up. "I must leave you now. I want to let my father see me as my old self one last time, and I also have to tell him about my decision to become a monk. But I'll come back."

Tears filled the Emperor's eyes. "You have deceived me, haven't you?" he said. It was a pitiful scene. As far as I can make out, Michikane had been encouraging him for a long time by swearing to serve as his faithful disciple. What a terrible way to act!

To guard against the possibility that Michikane might actually take the tonsure, Kaneie had arranged for prominent Genji warriors to go with him—sensible men well along in years. They seem to have kept out of sight while the Emperor and Michikane were still in the city, and then to have come out into the open and joined them somewhere near the Kamo River. They guarded Michikane at the temple with their hands on twelve-inch daggers, just to make sure that nobody would force him to cut off his hair.

THE SIXTY-SIXTH REIGN
EMPEROR ICHIJŌ

The next sovereign, Emperor Ichijō, was the first son of Emperor En'yū. His mother, Empress Senshi, was Chancellor Kaneie's second daughter.

Emperor Ichijō was born in Kaneie's Higashisanjō residence on the First of the Sixth Month in the third year of Tengen [980]. He became Crown Prince at the age of five, on the Twenty-Eighth of the Eighth Month in the second year of Eikan [984]; ascended the throne at seven, on the Twenty-Third of the Sixth Month in the second year of Kanna [986]; and performed the capping ceremony at eleven, on the Fifth of the First Month in the second year of Eiso [990]. He reigned for twenty-five years.

His mother, who gave birth to him in her nineteenth year, is known as the Higashisanjō Imperial Lady. Her mother was a daughter of Fujiwara Nakamasa, the governor of Settsu.

THE SIXTY-SEVENTH REIGN
EMPEROR SANJŌ

The next sovereign, Emperor Sanjō, was the second son of Retired Emperor Reizei. His mother, Chancellor Kaneie's oldest daughter, is known as Posthumous Empress Chōshi.

Emperor Sanjō was born on the Third of the First Month in the first year of Jōgen [976]. He became Crown Prince on the Sixteenth of the Seventh Month in the second year of Kanna [986]; performed the capping ceremony at the age of eleven on the same day; and ascended the throne at thirty-six, on the Thirteenth of the Sixth Month in the eighth year of Kankō [1011]. He reigned for five years.

It was a great tragedy that this Emperor was troubled by failing vision after his abdication. His eyes looked normal, and so it was hard to believe that he was blind. His eyeballs were as clear as anybody's. Furthermore, there were times when he saw quite well. For instance, he once said, "I can see the cords on the bamboo blinds." On another occasion, Princess Teishi came to the palace with a nurse called Ben.

The nurse was wearing a comb on the left side of her head, and His Majesty said to her, "Why are you wearing your comb in that odd way?" The Emperor was devoted to Princess Teishi. It was pitiful to watch him grope for her abundant hair, saying in a tremulous voice, "It hurts me so much not to be able to see those beautiful tresses."

Whenever the Princess visited him, he gave her a handsome memento. One time she went home with the deed to the Sanjōin. "What a clever Princess!" Michinaga joked. "Most children would have thought it was an old scrap of paper and thrown it away, but you brought it home." "How he talks!" the nurses laughed.

Emperor Sanjō also gave the Princess the Reizeiin, but Michinaga returned it. "The Reizeiin has always been Imperial property," he said. "It would be improper for it to pass into private hands; let it stay where it is." So the Reizeiin, like the Suzakuin, will probably be kept in the Imperial family.

His Majesty tried all kinds of ineffectual cures for his eyes. It was a sad case. In an effort to combat the nervous disorder from which he suffered so dreadfully, the doctors advised him to pour cold water over his head in midwinter.[34] The icy deluge made him tremble violently and change color, and I have heard that the witnesses all felt great sympathy and distress. He was also taking medicine for his ailment—a potion called the elixir of immortality. Some people said, "Anyone who drinks the elixir of immortality is bound to develop that kind of eye trouble," but as a matter of fact the blindness was caused by the spirit of a Chaplain[35] named Kanzan, who announced through a medium, "I sit on the former Emperor's head and cover his eyes with my wings. When I beat my wings he sees a little."

The Emperor's main reason for abdicating was that he wanted to make a pilgrimage to the Enryakuji Central Hall.[36] He did so, but nothing came of it in spite of his great sacrifice. What a tragedy! Even though he might not have been healed on the spot, surely there should

[34] "Nervous disorder" translates *kaze*, thought to have been a general term for a wide range of disorders which were predominantly ailments of the nervous system—lung, liver, and stomach trouble, paralysis, epilepsy, etc. McCullough and McCullough 1980, Chapter 1, n. 68.

[35] *Gubu*. Probably an abbreviation of *naigubu*, Palace Chaplain. The ten Palace Chaplains at the Heian Court performed religious functions in the Palace precincts, including night duty at the Seiryōden, played leading roles in the annual Suvarṇaprabhāsa services, and otherwise labored to protect the state.

[36] In order to pray for his eyes to be healed. The principal object of worship at the Central Hall was the Healing Buddha Yakushi.

have been some improvement. It was rumored that a goblin from
Mount Hiei was persecuting him.

His Majesty also made a retreat to Uzumasa, where he lodged under
a coffered ceiling, in quarters extending from the sacred image to the
eastern eavechamber.

Emperor Sanjō was the very image of Kaneie when he wore a soft
hat. He was an engaging, gentle person, much loved by all. "After a
sovereign has placed the comb of farewell in an Ise Virgin's hair, the
two refrain from looking at one another, but for some reason Emperor
Sanjō turned his head in her direction. I wondered about it," Michinaga is supposed to have said.[37]

THE SIXTY-EIGHTH REIGN
EMPEROR GO-ICHIJŌ

Emperor Sanjō was succeeded by the present sovereign, who is Emperor Ichijō's second son. His Majesty's mother, Grand Empress Shōshi, is the oldest daughter of His Lordship the Novice. I am sure you
know all about him, but I want to continue with my plan of discussing
each Emperor.

Emperor Go-Ichijō was born at the Tsuchimikado Mansion on the
Eleventh of the Ninth Month in the fifth year of Kankō [1008]. He
became Crown Prince at the age of four, on the Thirteenth of the
Sixth Month in the eighth year of Kankō [1011]; ascended the throne
at nine, on the Twenty-Ninth of the First Month in the fifth year of
Chōwa [1016], and performed the capping ceremony when he was
eleven, on the Third of the First Month in the second year of Kannin
[1018]. This is the second year of Manju [1025], so it would seem that
he has been reigning for ten years.

Although His Majesty is an Emperor like any other, he enjoys
unique security because of the many people who stand behind him.
His grandfather is Michinaga, who looks after us all like a father, even
though he has entered holy orders; his oldest uncle is Yorimichi, who
rules the nation as Regent and Minister of the Left; his next uncle is
Norimichi, the Palace Minister and Major Captain in the Bodyguards
of the Left; and his other uncles include Yorimune, who is a Major

---

[37] The departing Virgin was Princess Tōshi, one of Emperor Sanjō's daughters.
Michinaga suggests that the Emperor's unorthodox behavior was a bad omen,
heralding his later misfortunes. For the Ise Virgin, see McCullough and McCullough 1980, s.n. 25.

Counselor and heads the Crown Prince's Household; Yoshinobu, the Provisional Master of the Empress's Household; and Nagaie, a Middle Counselor. In any era, even the greatest sovereign can be overthrown if enough of his subjects oppose him, and so His Majesty is fortunate indeed to enjoy the support of every influential figure in the land.

When Emperor Ichijō fell ill, he said, "I ought to make my oldest son Crown Prince, but he lacks powerful friends. What can I do? I shall have to nominate the Second Prince." (His second son was the Prince who is now Emperor.) He was quite right.

"You may wonder why I have talked about all these reigns," [Yotsugi said], "but how can I explain Michinaga's success without discussing the Emperors and Empresses who made it possible? A garden tree won't grow and bear fruit unless we feed its roots and take good care of it. That is why I thought I ought to give you a history of the throne before discussing the ministers of state."

"You mustn't apologize," Shigeki interrupted enthusiastically. "It has been splendid! Your descriptions of all those Emperors have been just like reflections in a mirror. Now that you are going to tell us about the ministers too, I feel like a man witnessing a glorious sunrise after years in the dark. My wife's mirror at home is terribly cloudy, and we never get around to polishing it, so she keeps it in her comb box, and we have learned to manage with nothing better. When I listen to you, I feel as I do when I catch a glimpse of my face in a bright, shiny mirror—it's embarrassing to see what I really look like, but the reflection is amazingly true to life. This is a wonderful experience for me! It's bound to add ten or twenty years to my life."

Shigeki's raptures struck the rest of us as rather comical, but Yotsugi's extraordinary narrative was hard to dismiss, and everyone continued to pay close attention.

"Listen to this," Shigeki said. "I've thought up a poem."

"Excellent! Let us hear it," Yotsugi said. Shigeki recited bashfully:

Akirakeki	Now that I have chanced upon
Kagami ni aeba	This clear mirror,
Suginishi mo	I can see the past,
Ima yukusue no	The present,
Koto mo miekeri.	And what is to come.

Much impressed, Yotsugi mumbled phrases under his breath and came out with a reply.

Suberagi no   The old mirror!
Ato mo tsugitsugi   Without concealment,
Kakure naku   It reveals afresh
Arata ni miyuru   The deeds of sovereigns,
Furukagami ka mo.   Each in his turn.

"Do you feel as though you were facing a stylish flower-shaped mirror in an inlaid lacquer box?" he asked. "No, such trinkets make a fine glitter, but they tarnish before you know it. I am a plain old-fashioned mirror from a bygone age, made of good white metal that stays clear without being polished." It would have been amusing to capture his complacent smile in a painting. His self-praise put one off a bit, but there was no denying the interest and novelty of his story.

"Enough of trivialities," he said. "I am going to discuss serious matters now. Pay close attention, everyone. Just as you must look on today's exposition of holy writ as an aid to enlightenment, so you should think, as you listen to me, that you are hearing the *Chronicles of Japan*."[38]

"We have heard plenty of sutra expositions and sermons, but nobody has ever told us such marvelous things," said the monks and laymen. Ancient nuns and monks touched their hands to their foreheads and sat listening with pious fervor.

"I am a remarkable old fellow. Wouldn't any honest soul feel embarrassed by comparison? I am an old man who has kept his eyes open and remembered every single thing. But of all the things I have seen and heard, Lord Michinaga's situation is what stands out. Whether we inquire about the past or look at the present, Michinaga is just like the dharma of the One Vehicle: there is 'not a second, not a third.'[39] His success is beyond comparison or calculation. What a magnificent career! It is no easy matter to go through life without problems, even for a Chancellor or Regent. The holy writings and sacred teachings say, 'There are many baby fish, but it is hard for them to reach maturity; there are trees called mangoes, but it is hard for them to bear ripe fruit.'[40] That is exactly how it is with this matchless lord; he is

[38] *Nihongi*. Another name for *Nihon shoki*. the first of the *rikkokushi* (six official Chinese-language chronicles), but here probably a general reference to all six. Hosaka 1974, 2.176.

[39] "One Vehicle" is a term used in the *Lotus Sutra* to identify the teachings that lead to enlightenment. "There is no other vehicle, not a second, not a third." Hurvitz 1976, p. 30.

[40] Said by *Ōkagami uragaki*, item 51, p. 308, to be a quotation from the *Nirvana*

unique among the ministers of state and senior nobles of the nation. Who can hope to equal his good fortune in the future? It is not something that happens very often.

"Listen quietly, everyone. There is nothing I have not seen or heard. I think the things I am going to tell you will be new to many people."

All who were present paid close attention. "It is not for us to say anything at all," they agreed.

There have been ministers of state in all the reigns since the founding of our country (*Yotsugi said*). I can remember each of them—everyone who has served as Minister of the Left, Minister of the Right, Palace Minister, or Chancellor. From the founding of the state until the present, there have been thirty Ministers of the Left, fifty-seven Ministers of the Right, and twelve Palace Ministers. In the days of the early Emperors, a Chancellor was not lightly appointed; the occupants of the office were usually grandfathers or uncles of Emperors. Many grandfathers, uncles, and other male relatives looked after Emperors while serving as ministers of state or counselors, and a number of men seem to have been honored posthumously with the title of Chancellor. I believe there have been approximately seven such cases. But that office was difficult to attain, and few held it during their lifetimes.

I think it may have been during the reign of the Emperor known as Kōtoku, the thirty-seventh[41] in Emperor Jinmu's line, that the Court first established the eight ministries, the civil posts, and the offices of Minister of the Left, Minister of the Right, and Palace Minister. The Minister of the Left was Abe no Kurahashimaro, and the Minister of the Right was Soga Yamada no Ishikawamaro, Empress Genmei's grandfather. I have heard that Ishikawamaro became Minister of the Right in the first year of Emperor Kōtoku's reign, and that he was killed in the fifth year by the Crown Prince. That is a very old story. The Palace Minister was Nakatomi Kamako. Since there were no era names yet, I can't give you the dates. The thirty-ninth sovereign, Emperor Tenji, appointed the first Chancellor—his younger brother,[42]

Sutra. It is not to be found in extant versions of the sutra, but does appear, in slightly different form, in *Ōjō yōshū* and other Buddhist texts. *Ōjō yōshū*, p. 45c; Hosaka 1974, 2.177.

[41] Thirty-sixth, according to the modern method of calculation, which excludes Empress Jingū.

[42] *Ototo no miko*, taken by Hosaka 1974, 2.185, to mean younger son. In any case, the author confuses Emperor Tenji's brother, Prince Ōama (later Emperor

Prince Ōtomo, who assumed office in a First Month and succeeded to
the throne on the Twenty-Fifth of the Twelfth Month in the same
year. He is known as Emperor Tenmu. He reigned for fifteen years.
Another Chancellor—Prince Takechi, a son of Emperor Tenmu—was
appointed by Empress Jitō, the forty-first sovereign in the line established by Emperor Jinmu. Of those two Chancellors, one soon became
Emperor and the other, Prince Takechi, died in office.[43] For a long
time after that, no further appointment was made. The *Personnel
Code*[44] says, "Mediocre men are not to be appointed to the office of
Chancellor. If there is no suitable candidate, the position is to remain
vacant." This makes it seem that the office is no ordinary one.

During the reign of the forty-second sovereign, Emperor Monmu,
an era name was selected. The year became known as the first of Taihō
[701].

Late in the reign of Emperor Montoku, on the Nineteenth of the
Second Month in the fourth year of Saikō [857], the title of Chancellor
was conferred on the Emperor's uncle, Minister of the Left Fujiwara
Yoshifusa of Junior First Rank. He was fifty-four. Yoshifusa was also
the first subject to serve as Regent. From his day to that of the present
Kan'in Minister of State, there have been eleven successive Chancellors.
If we add the earlier cases of Prince Ōtomo and Prince Takechi, we see
that a total of thirteen persons have held the office. Men who have
become Chancellors are always given posthumous names. However,
Prince Ōtomo became an Emperor very soon, so he lacks one, and I am
not sure about Prince Takechi. Also, a Chancellor does not receive a
posthumous name if he has taken religious vows, which was true of two
of the eleven.[45] I intend to tell you all about those eleven Chancellors
in the order of their succession.

Since they tell us to "scoop up the water and investigate the source,"[46]
I ought to begin with Kamatari, but that would be going too far back.
I have no wish to slight anybody, but it could be that you would not
understand me. Also there would be so many things to talk about that
the preacher might come, and it would be a pity to have to leave off

---

Tenmu), with Tenji's son, Prince Ōtomo (Emperor Kōbun). See Appendix A,
Kōbun and Tenmu.

[43] The translation emends the text, which reads, "As regards these two Chancellors, [they] soon became Emperor[s]. Prince Takechi died while he was still
Chancellor."

[44] *Shikiinryō*, a part of the Yōrō Code. See *Ryō no gige*, p. 30.

[45] Kaneie and Michinaga.

[46] Probably a popular saying: To understand everything about a river, we must
not only sample the waters downstream but also trace out the source.

in the middle. So since I began my account of the sovereigns with the reign of Emperor Montoku, I shall start with that Emperor's grandfather, the one we call Fujisashi—in other words, with Minister of State Fuyutsugi, Kamatari's descendant in the sixth generation. But of all those ministers, Michinaga is the one who stands out.

CHAPTER TWO

Minister of the Left Fuyutsugi

Fuyutsugi was Minister of State Uchimaro's third son. His mother was a daughter of Asukabe Natomaro of Senior Sixth Upper Rank. He was a senior noble for sixteen years and a minister of state for six. Because he was Emperor Montoku's grandfather, he was posthumously granted the title of Chancellor on the Seventeenth of the Seventh Month in the third year of Kashō [850]. He is called the Kan'in Minister of State.

This minister is said to have been the father of eleven sons, but it is hard to keep them[1] straight. I know very little about them, except that Emperor Montoku's mother, Posthumous Chancellor Nagara, Chancellor Yoshifusa, and Minister of the Right Yoshimi all had the same mother.

CHANCELLOR YOSHIFUSA
(Chūjinkō)

Minister of the Left Fuyutsugi's second son, Yoshifusa, became Chancellor on the Nineteenth of the Second Month in the first year of Ten'an [857], and attained Junior First Rank at the age of fifty-four on the Nineteenth of the Fourth Month in the same year. Since Emperor Seiwa was his grandson, he was named *sesshō* by Imperial edict in the year of that sovereign's accession, with annual offices and ranks.[2] His title was changed to *kanpaku* in the eighth year of Jōgan [866], when he was sixty-three. He has been known since his death by the posthumous name Chūjinkō. He is also called the Shirakawa Minister of State and the Somedono Minister of State.

---

[1] "Them" follows Hosaka 1974, 2.194, in emending *on[na]gotachi* (daughters) to *mikotachi* (sons), which appears here in some texts. According to *Sonpi bunmyaku*, 1.40-45, Fuyutsugi had eight sons and two daughters.

[2] For *sesshō*, see Appendix D, n. 3. Emperor Seiwa ascended the throne at the age of eight. Recipients of annual offices and ranks (*nenkan* and *nenkyū*) enjoyed the privilege of naming appointees to offices and/or ranks and pocketing all or most of the attendant perquisites. McCullough and McCullough 1980, s.n.

Yoshifusa was the uncle of Emperor Montoku, the father of Senior Grand Empress Meishi, and the grandfather of Emperor Seiwa. He rose to the office of Chancellor, enjoyed the same treatment as the three classes of Empresses,[3] received annual ranks and offices, and served as Regent for fifteen years. He was a senior noble for about thirty years, a minister of state for twenty-five, and the first Fujiwara to act as Chancellor and Regent. We may well call him successful!

He was also a good poet. The *Collection of Early and Modern Times*, which refers to him as "the former Chancellor," seems to include a large number of his compositions.[4] Of his many poems, one in particular lets us guess how much satisfaction his accomplishments gave him. He recited it when he saw a vase of cherry blossoms standing in front of his daughter, the Somedono Empress.

Toshi fureba	The years have passed
Yowai wa oinu	And I am old—
Shika wa aredo	But though it be thus,
Hana o shi mireba	The sight of the blossoms
Monoomoi mo nashi.	Makes me content.

Of course, he was using "blossoms" to mean the Empress.[5]
Sosei composed these lines on the day when they buried Yoshifusa at Shirakawa:

Chi no namida	Tears of blood
Ochite zo tagitsu	Fall in torrents:
Shirakawa wa	White River, it seems,
Kimi ga yo made no	Was a name
Na ni koso arikere.	Doomed to pass with our lord.[6]

Everyone must know both of those poems. I had not intended to run on so, but I got carried away.

What a shame that a man as lucky as Yoshifusa should not have had

---

[3] Equality with the three (classes of) Empresses (*junsangū* or *jusangū*) was an economic privilege entitling the recipient to annual ranks and offices equivalent to those awarded the three categories of Empresses (Empress, Grand Empress, Senior Grand Empress)—i.e., to three annual offices and one annual rank.

[4] Actually only the one quoted below, *Toshi fureba* (*Kokinshū* 52).

[5] Indications of number are usually lacking in Japanese.

[6] "Tears of blood" is a common trope for tears of intense grief or indignation. Shirakawa means White River.

any sons! His older brother, Middle Counselor Nagara, must have felt hurt when Yoshifusa rose so high above him, and others seem to have wondered about it too, but it is Nagara's descendants who prosper today, so he has come out far ahead in the long run.

Minister of the Right Yoshimi

Fuyutsugi's fifth son, Yoshimi, had the same mother as Yoshifusa. He served as a minister of state for eleven years, and attained Senior First Rank posthumously. He is known as the Nishisanjō Minister of State. He commissioned Jōzō, the state temple monk,[7] to recite prayers for him, thereby enjoying the miraculous benefits we can secure through recitation of the *Thousand-Armed Dhāraṇī*.[8]

I know very little about his daughters, except that one of them was a Junior Consort during Emperor Seiwa's reign. His son, Major Counselor Tokitsura, had two boys of his own who ended ingloriously as officials of Fifth Rank—one was Assistant Director of the Bureau of Medicine and the other was Director of the Bureau of Grounds. I wonder if the reason for their poor showing might have been that Yoshimi moved ahead of his much older brother Nagara, whose descendants have prospered so gloriously.

Provisional Middle Counselor of Junior Second Rank and Commander of the Military Guards of the Right Nagara

Middle Counselor Nagara, Fuyutsugi's oldest son, was the full brother of Yoshifusa and Yoshimi. He was a senior noble for thirteen years. By reason of his having been Emperor Yōzei's grandfather, he was posthumously named Minister of the Left with Senior First Rank, an honor he received during the reign of that Emperor, in the First Month of the first year of Gangyō [877]. He was later granted the title of Chancellor. He is known as the Biwa Minister of State. Of his six sons, the most prominent was Minister of State Mototsune.

[7] *Jōgaku*, a term that originally indicated one of a fixed number of monks at a state institution. It was later used as an ecclesiastical title.

[8] *Senjū darani*, a Sanskrit chant extolling the merits of Thousand-Armed Kannon.

CHANCELLOR MOTOTSUNE
(Shōsenkō)

Minister of State Mototsune was Middle Counselor Nagara's third son. His daughter was Emperor Daigo's Empress, the Imperial mother of two sovereigns, Suzaku and Murakami. His mother, a daughter of Posthumous Chancellor Fusatsugi, was Imperial Dame[9] Otoharu of Posthumous Senior First Rank.

When Emperor Yōzei ascended the throne, Mototsune received an edict naming him *sesshō*. He was then forty-one years old. He became *kanpaku* during the reign of Emperor Uda, on the Twenty-First of the Eleventh Month in the third year of Ninna [887], and died at the age of fifty-six. His posthumous name is Shōsenkō. He was a senior noble for twenty-seven years, a minister of state for twenty years, and the ruler of the nation for something over ten years. People call him the Horikawa Minister of State.

Emperor Kōkō's mother and Mototsune's were sisters, and Mototsune had been intimate with the future sovereign ever since his childhood. Once there was a ministerial banquet—held, if I remember correctly, by Yoshifusa.[10] Imperial Princes always attended such affairs in the old days, so Prince Tokiyasu[11] was there. The attendants somehow forgot to give the guest of honor a pheasant drumstick, which is among the prescribed dishes; and one of them snatched up the Prince's and set it down in front of the other gentleman when he saw what had happened. What do you suppose went through the Prince's mind to make him quietly snuff out the oil lamp in front of him?[12] Mototsune, who was still a minor official, saw the whole thing from his seat in the rear. "He handled that well," he thought, and his admiration for the Prince increased.

Later there was a council of nobles to decide the question of Emperor Yōzei's abdication.[13] The very prominent Minister of the Left,

---

[9] [Kō]taifujin, also daibunin, a title of respect for an Emperor's mother who was a Dame (fujin or bunin: in the early Heian period, one of three categories of Imperial consort below the rank of Empress).

[10] Ministerial banquets (daikyō) were elaborate formal events, held annually by ministers of state during the New Year season, and by new ministers to celebrate their appointments.

[11] The future Emperor Kōkō. Name supplied by translator.

[12] His purpose was presumably to save the host embarrassment by concealing his loss.

[13] The Emperor was insane.

Lord Tōru, had set his heart on being Emperor. "Why do we need to argue?" he asked. "If you want someone in the immediate line of descent, how about me?"

"I have not heard of a precedent for the accession of a Prince who has taken a surname and served at Court as a subject," Mototsune said.

There was something to be said for Tōru's argument, but Mototsune's view prevailed, and Prince Tokiyasu ascended the throne. Emperor Kōkō's descendants have reigned a long time, and Mototsune's have continued to advise and assist them. I cannot help feeling that the two must have exchanged pledges in a former life.

On the night of Mototsune's burial at Fukakusayama, Bishop Shōen recited a poem.

Utsusemi wa	Gazing at his mortal frame—
Kara o mitsutsu mo	A cicada's cast-off husk—
Nagusametsu	I felt the pain less sharp.
Fukakusa no yama	O Mountains of Tall Grass:
Keburi dani tate.	Send up, at least, a plume of smoke.

Someone called Kantsuke Mineo composed these lines:

Fukakusa no	If you have hearts,
Nobe no sakura shi	O cherry trees
Kokoro araba	In Fukakusa's fields,
Kotoshi bakari wa	Bloom this year alone
Sumizome ni sake.	In charcoal hues.

Both poems are in the *Collection of Early and Modern Times.*

Mototsune lived in two houses, the Horikawain and the Kan'in. He used the first for formal functions on important occasions, and the second for periods of ritual seclusion.[14] People who were not on intimate terms with him did not go to the Kan'in, but he sometimes took close associates there. The Horikawain's excellent location permitted a most impressive disposition of his banquet guests' carriages. The equipage of the guest of honor would be drawn up on the east bank of the river, with the ox tethered to the ornamental knob of the bridgepost; and those of the other senior nobles would be on the west bank— an admirable arrangement. (I used to think there would never be

---

[14] *Monoimi*, undertaken in preparation for Shintō religious observances or as a precaution against anticipated inauspicious events. McCullough and McCullough 1980, s.n. 3.

another place where the principal guest's carriage could be kept separate, but the Horikawain has been put in the shade by the present Kayain. Of course, I thought the Reizeiin would always be the only mansion in the capital to cover four blocks and front on four main avenues. One by one, the old landmarks fall as time goes on.)

Mototsune was Emperor Yōzei's uncle. Furthermore, he became the equal of the three Empresses in status, with annual ranks and offices, during Emperor Uda's reign; and he was also the grandfather of Emperors Suzaku and Murakami. So I don't need to tell you that he enjoyed the very highest esteem. He had four sons. The oldest was Minister of the Left Tokihira, the second was Minister of the Left Nakahira, and the fourth was Chancellor Tadahira.

(Shigeki's expression changed. Letting his eyes sweep over the people in the rear, he said, "There! Tadahira was my revered lord, Teishinkō!" He fanned himself with an amusing air of pride.)

The third son, Kanehira, died without going beyond the office of Imperial Household Minister with Junior Third Rank, even though he might have been expected to rise much higher, especially since his mother was a daughter of Prince Tadayoshi, the Minister of Ceremonial. People call the three ministers the three Hiras.

MINISTER OF THE LEFT TOKIHIRA

Tokihira[15]

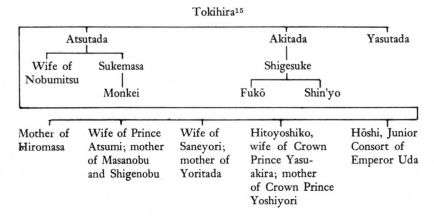

Atsutada			Akitada	Yasutada
Wife of Nobumitsu	Sukemasa		Shigesuke	
	Monkei		Fukō Shin'yo	

| Mother of Hiromasa | Wife of Prince Atsumi; mother of Masanobu and Shigenobu | Wife of Saneyori; mother of Yoritada | Hitoyoshiko, wife of Crown Prince Yasu-akira; mother of Crown Prince Yoshiyori | Hōshi, Junior Consort of Emperor Uda |

[15] With occasional minor modifications, genealogical tables follow *Sonpi bunmyaku*, which lists lay sons, clerical sons, and daughters in that order, from right to left. Listings within the three categories are by approximate order of birth, when known. Only principal descendants mentioned in the *Ōkagami* account are included.

Tokihira was Mototsune's oldest son. His mother was a daughter of Prince Saneyasu of Fourth Rank, the President of the Board of Censors.

Tokihira was Minister of the Left during the reign of Emperor Daigo, while he was still very young; and Sugawara Michizane was Minister of the Right. By command of the Emperor, who was only a boy at the time, Tokihira and Michizane governed the nation together: the Minister of the Left, who was about twenty-eight or twenty-nine, and the Minister of the Right, who was fifty-seven or fifty-eight. Now it happened that Michizane was a man of outstanding learning and judgment, whereas Tokihira was immature and not nearly so well educated. Quite naturally, His Majesty trusted and favored Michizane in a manner that became a constant source of chagrin for Tokihira. But in the end—perhaps because fate had ordained it—Michizane was overtaken by misfortune, and they banished him to Kyūshū on the Twenty-Fifth of the First Month in the fourth year of Shōtai [901], with the title of Provisional Governor-General of the Kyūshū Government Office.

Of Michizane's many children—the married daughters and the well-placed sons—all the sons were packed off to separate places of exile. The only ones from whom he was not parted were a little boy and girl, whose tears persuaded the authorities that it would do no harm to let them go with him. Since the Emperor's orders were exceedingly strict, the other sons were not even sent to the same general area.

Gazing with a heavy heart at the plum blossoms in his courtyard, Michizane composed a poem.

Kochi fukaba	Should an east wind blow,
Nioi okoseyo	Send me your fragrance,
Ume no hana	O blossoms of the plum:
Aruji nashi tote	Forget not the spring
Haru o wasuru na.	Because your master is gone.

He also sent a poem to Retired Emperor Uda:

Nagareyuku	Now that I have become
Ware wa mikuzu to	Drifting flotsam,
Narihatenu	Will not Your Majesty,
Kimi shigarami to	Act as a weir
Narite todomeyo.	To hold me back?

So bitterly did he feel his unjust punishment that he became a monk at Yamazaki. His melancholy increased as the capital receded into the distance.

Kimi ga sumu	Journeying ever onward,
Yado no kozue o	I looked back
Yukuyuku to	Until they disappeared—
Kakururu made mo	The treetops
Kaerimishi wa ya.	At the place where you dwell.

Again, having arrived in Harima Province, he spent the night at a place called Akashi post station, where the sight of the station master's sympathetic distress moved him to compose an affecting Chinese poem.

> Be not surprised, station master,
> That time brings change.
> Leaves flourish
> And then they fall,
> For such are the ways
> Of spring and autumn.

So he arrived in Tsukushi. On an evening when everything conspired to deepen his gloom, he noticed plumes of smoke here and there in the distance.

Yū sareba	Smoke rising at dusk
No ni mo yama ni mo	From field and hill—
Tatsu keburi	Is not your fuel
Nageki yori koso	This grief
Moemasarikere.	Burning in my heart?

Gazing at floating, drifting clouds:

Yama wakare	In spite of all,
Tobiyuku kumo no	Hope stirs unbidden
Kaerikuru	As I behold the return
Kage miru toki wa	Of clouds that had sailed
Nao tanomarenu.	Away from the hills.

"In spite of everything," he probably thought, "I refuse to believe that I shall never return to the capital."

He composed these lines on a bright moonlit night:

Umi narazu	The moon will illumine
Tataeru mizu no	A heart
Soko made ni	Clear to the bottom,
Kiyoki kokoro wa	Pure as brimming waters
Tsuki zo terasamu.	Deeper than the sea.

That was a clever poem. He must have meant that the moon and sun, at least, would bear witness to the purity of his heart.

(Not only was Yotsugi acquainted with political matters of great moment, but he reeled off Japanese and Chinese poems in so fluent and impressive a manner that the spectators were fascinated. Aware that even people of superior understanding had edged very close to watch and listen, he was spinning out his story like someone unravelling a skein. It was a rare sight! Shigeki sat enraptured, wiping away tears.)

Michizane kept the gates locked at the place where he stayed in Tsukushi. Although the Senior Assistant Governor-General's seat was far in the distance, he could see the roof tiles on its tall structures when his eyes strayed in that direction. Here is a Chinese poem, composed when he heard the bell of the neighboring Kannonji:

> I barely see the color of the Dazaifu tiles;
> I but hear the sound of the Kannonji bell.[16]

The scholars of old pronounced it superior to Po Chü-i's lines in the *Collected Works*:[17]

Propping up my pillow, I listen to the bell of I ai Temple:
Rolling up the blind, I gaze at the snow on Incense Burner Peak.

Observing chrysanthemums in bloom in Tsukushi on the Ninth of the Ninth Month, Michizane recalled a certain Chrysanthemum Banquet—an event held at the Imperial Palace while he was still in the capital, a year ago to the day.[18] The Emperor had heaped praises on his Chinese poem and given him a robe. Memories of the occasion flooded his mind as he gazed at the Imperial gift, which had accom-

---

[16] He lives in seclusion.

[17] [*Po shih*] *wen chi*, a collection of Po's poems. For the well-known quotation that follows, see *Pai shih chang ch'ing chi, chüan* 16, p. 21b.

[18] The Chrysanthemum Banquet (*kiku no en*), held on the Ninth of the Ninth Month, was one of the Five Banquets (*gosechie, gosekku*) of the Court calendar. McCullough and McCullough 1980, Chapter 8, n. 64.

panied him to Tsukushi; and he composed a Chinese poem that has been much admired:

Last year on this night, I served at the Seiryōden.
In my "Autumn Thoughts" poem, I spoke of secret anguish.
The garment His Majesty conferred is beside me now.
Holding it high, each day I worship the lingering scent.

Those poems are not mere scattered survivals. The many Chinese verses Michizane composed in Tsukushi have been recorded in a one-chapter work, the *Later Collection*,[19] and the Japanese poems he set down from time to time have also become known in the natural course of events. His melancholy fate moved me deeply when I was young, so I struck up a friendship with some impoverished university students and got them to teach me his poems by taking them bags and boxes of food. The lines have all slipped away, now that I am in my second childhood. Those are just a few that I remember.

(The audience interrupted with words of praise. "What literary tastes you had! People nowadays are not so eager to learn.")

One rainy day, when Michizane was staring off gloomily into space, he composed this poem:

Ame no shita	Is it because the rain
Kawakeru hodo no	Leaves nothing free of moisture?
Nakereba ya	I can find no way to dry
Kite shi nureginu	The drenched garments
Hiru yoshi mo naki.	I am compelled to wear.[20]

Michizane died while he was still in Tsukushi, and his spirit went to live at Kitano, where it caused an immense number of pine trees to spring up overnight. That place is the present Kitano Shrine, of which he is the god. It is even visited by Emperors, who seem to hold it in great awe. His dwelling in Tsukushi is an important temple called the Anrakuji, with an abbot and other officers appointed by the Court.

The Imperial Palace has been rebuilt several times after destructive fires. When the carpenters returned to work one morning during the reign of Emperor En'yū, they noticed a number of blackened places on some siding boards that had been planed smooth the day before.

---

[19] [*Kanke*] *goshū.*

[20] There is a pun on *nureginu*, which can mean both drenched robes and unjust accusations. The garments are wet with tears.

Upon climbing a ladder to investigate, they found a number of insect holes, eaten during the night in the shape of these words:

Tsukuru tomo   Though it be rebuilt,
Mata mo yakenan   It will burn again,
Sugawara ya   Until the boards fit snug,
Mune no itama no   Until the wound in Sugawara's heart
Awanu kagiri wa.   No longer gapes.[21]

It was rumored that the Kitano god was the author.

Michizane had died in Tsukushi at the age of fifty-nine, on the Twenty-Fifth of the Second Month in the third year of Engi [903]. Minister of the Left Tokihira died seven years later at the age of thirty-nine, on the Fourth of the Fourth Month in the ninth year of Engi [909], after having served as a minister of state for eleven years. He is called the Hon'in Minister of State.

Tokihira's daughter, the Junior Consort, also died, and so did his grandson the Crown Prince and his oldest son Yasutada, the Hachijō Major Captain.

Yasutada lived at Hachijō, so he used to have a long journey to the Palace. I can't say what he may have had in mind, but in the wintertime he used to toast one huge rice cake and two smaller ones, which he would carry pressed against his body like warming stones. When they cooled off, he would throw them to his carriage men, giving each of the small ones to a single person and breaking the big one in two. That was carrying foresight too far! People must have considered it odd even in those days, for otherwise the story would not have been handed down.

Yasutada offered all kinds of prayers when he fell ill. While he was having the *Healing Buddha Sutra* recited beside his pillow, the monks raised their voices and bellowed, ". . . *iwayuru Kubira daishō*," "He who is called the Divine Commander Kumbhīra." It seemed to him that someone was threatening to strangle him, and he perished of fright.[22] Even though the phrase was part of a sutra, it was chanted in a very strange manner, considering that the patient was possessed by a powerful spirit. It is all very well to attribute Yasutada's death to karma; words have a power of their own.

Death also claimed Yasutada's younger brother, Middle Counselor

---

[21] There are puns on *mune* (roof, heart) and *ita[ma]* (gaps between boards, pain).

[22] He mistakes *iwayuru Kubira*, "he who is called Kubira," for *ware o kubiru*, "strangle me." The someone was presumably the malignant spirit.

Atsutada, who was an accomplished poet and musician. After Atsutada was gone, whenever something happened to keep Hiromasa of Third Rank away from a Palace concert the Emperor would send messengers until he came. "We will have to cancel the music unless you join us," His Majesty would plead. The old men used to shake their heads. "This is the era of degeneracy,"[23] they would say. "When Atsutada was alive, neither His Majesty nor anybody else would have thought people would be so impressed by the musicianship of this Hiromasa!"

If we include a daughter of Tokihira who died, the former Crown Prince had three or four consorts. One of them, Chūjō no miyasudo-koro, later married Prince Shigeakira, the Minister of Ceremonial. She gave birth to the Virgin Consort and then died. She was a gentle lady who took the Crown Prince's death very hard. When someone told her Tayū had dreamed about the Prince, she sent the nurse a poem:

Toki no ma mo	Though the time was short,
Nagusametsuran	It must have eased the pain.
Kimi wa sa wa	How wretched am I,
Yume ni dani minu	Unable to behold him
Ware zo kanashiki.	Even in a dream!

Tayū's reply:

Koishisa no	Because I knew it
Nagusamubeku mo	To be a dream
Arazariki	Within a dream,
Yume no uchi ni mo	It could not assuage
Yume to mishikaba.	The longing in my heart.

If I am not mistaken, another of the Prince's consorts was Consultant Harukami's daughter. On the morning after the Prince first met the lady, he had his letter delivered by Middle Counselor Atsutada, who was then a Lesser Captain; and after the Prince's death she married Atsutada. Atsutada was head over heels in love with her, but one day he seemed struck by a premonition. "I come of a short-lived family," he told her. "I am sure to die before long. When I do, you'll probably marry Fuminori." Minister of Civil Affairs Fuminori was then a governor of Harima, serving as one of Atsutada's stewards.

"I can't conceive of such a thing," the lady answered.

[23] *Yo no sue.* It was believed in the Heian period that the world had entered the latter end of the dharma (*yo no sue, mappō*), a 10,000-year period of decline presaging the final disappearance of the Buddhist faith.

"My spirit will see you," he said. "It will be just as I have predicted." And that is exactly what has happened.

Of all Tokihira's sons, the only one who rose as high as Minister of the Right was Akitada, whose mother was a daughter of the Minamoto Major Counselor Noboru. Akitada served as Minister of the Right for six years, but (possibly for reasons of his own) he ignored the forms we expect a minister of state to observe, both on the public thoroughfares and in the privacy of his home. He usually dispensed with pairs of outriders on his journeys; and even on the rare occasions when he took them, there were only a few at the rear of the carriage. He got along without four carriage men, and his outriders' warning shouts were intermittent and subdued. Instead of having an elaborate basin for washing his hands, he kept a small tub and a little bail-handled pot on a shelf in a room adjoining the front stairway of his main hall. A servant filled the pot with hot water early in the morning, and he went to the room and washed his hands without any assistance. Nor did he dine ceremoniously from magnificent vessels. But in spite of such economies, he was unmistakably a great minister when he participated in state functions or signed official documents. It may have been because of his mode of life that he was the only member of his family to survive beyond the age of sixty. I might also mention that he held his ministerial banquet in a house that occupied only a quarter of a block. He is called the Tominokōji Minister of State.

I am sure the Kitano god's wrath was to blame for the fact that neither of Tokihira's other sons survived beyond his thirties or forties.

Bishop Shin'yo (the present Miidera abbot) and Bishop Fukō (the Yamashinadera provisional abbot) are sons of Akitada's son Shigesuke, the Assistant Commander of the Military Guards of the Right. They seem to be leading exemplary lives.

Among Atsutada's numerous sons, there was one whose name I don't recall—an Assistant Commander of the Military Guards, who took religious vows and was reborn as a buddha.[24] His son is Bishop Monkei of Iwakura. Atsutada's daughter married the Biwa Major Counselor.

People say Tokihira's descendants died out because of the terrible sin he committed. No doubt they are right, but it seems a great pity. He was a man who knew how to get things done. It was Emperor Daigo's policy to supervise social customs, but His Majesty could not seem to prevent extravagant display. One day Tokihira went to the Imperial Palace in flamboyant attire that violated all the rules. When

[24] The son was Sukemasa. News of his rebirth as a buddha in Amitābha's paradise was transmitted to others in dreams after his death. Hosaka 1974, 2.261.

he arrived at the Courtiers' Hall, the Emperor saw him through the window²⁵ and summoned a Chamberlain, scowling. "Even though the Minister of the Left is the grandest personage we have, it is inexcusable for him to come to Court in that costume just when I have issued strict prohibitions against extravagance. Order him to leave at once," he said.

The Chamberlain quaked as he delivered the message, but Tokihira rushed off with every sign of consternation, telling his Escorts not to clear the way. The outriders must have been amazed! He kept the Hon'in gates locked for a month, stayed inside his blinds, and turned away callers with the explanation that he had incurred the Imperial displeasure. The upshot of the matter was that extravagance ceased. I heard it whispered later that Tokihira had arranged the scene with the Emperor in order to make others obey the law.

Tokihira could never control himself when something funny happened. People say he would forget all about decorum once he began to laugh. There was an occasion on which he took an unreasonable position while sharing the reins of government with Michizane. What could Michizane do if the senior minister insisted on something? "I can't bring myself to agree," Michizane complained, "but he *is* the Minister of the Left, so I suppose we must accept it."

"Oh, there's nothing to worry about. I can find a way of stopping him," said one of the Recorders.

"It's no use. What can anyone do?" asked Michizane.

"Wait and see," said the Recorder.

Later on, while Tokihira was presenting his argument at the council chamber in a solemn, sonorous voice, the Recorder inserted a document into a holder and made a great show of presenting it to him with the proper ceremony. Just as he held it out, he released a fart. Tokihira roared with laughter. The paper eluded his shaking hand, and he gasped, "I can't do anything more today. Let the Minister of the Right take care of it." So Michizane disposed of the matter as he saw fit.

Michizane's spirit once became a thunder god and caused a frightful display of thunder and lightning. Just as it seemed that lightning was sure to strike the Seiryōden, Tokihira whipped out his sword. "Your office was lower than mine while you were alive. God or not, you ought to yield precedence to me in this world. How can it be any other way?" he shouted. People said the god quieted down when he uttered those words, glaring at the sky. But it was not Tokihira the

---

²⁵ A small aperture in the wall between the Courtiers' Hall and the Daytime Chamber.

man who made the thunder stop for a while. It ceased because Michizane knew we must all respect the hierarchy established by the Emperor, whose authority is supreme.

MINISTER OF THE LEFT NAKAHIRA

Nakahira, Mototsune's second son and Tokihira's uterine brother, served as a minister of state for thirteen years. He is called the Biwa Minister of the Left. He had no children.

It was Nakahira who composed these lines, which are preserved in the *Ise Collection*:[26]

Hanasusuki	You were the object,
Ware koso shita ni	O miscanthus,
Omoishika	Of my secret love:
Ho ni idete hito ni	Now ripened into plume,
Musubarenikeri.	You are bound to another.[27]

Nakahira was older than Tadahira, but he was thirty years behind him in becoming a minister of state.[28] When he finally received the appointment, Tadahira expressed his joy in verse:

Osoku toku	Whether early or late,
Tsui ni sakinuru	The plum blossoms
Ume no hana	Have come into flower.
Ta ga ueokishi	Who might he have been—
Tane ni ka aruramu.	The planter of the seed?[29]

Tadahira wore a spray of plum blossoms in his cap when the happy pair met. He must have found it an immense relief to assign the seat of honor at his eave-chamber banquet[30] to the brother he had pitied for so many years. How pleased they both must have felt! It was splendid for them to be on such excellent terms.

---

[26] *Iseshū*, the collected works of the poet Ise.

[27] *Kokinshū* 748. The poem alludes to an old practice of tying up tree branches, grasses, etc. as a charm to bind a pledge.

[28] Actually twenty by Japanese count.

[29] "We owe it all to our father."

[30] Held to celebrate his appointment as Chancellor in 936. A minister held his initial celebratory banquet in an eave chamber, and his subsequent annual banquets in his principal apartment (*moya*).

Nakahira was a truly honorable man. Everybody knows that, so I shall say no more.

CHANCELLOR TADAHIRA
(Teishinkō)

Tadahira was Mototsune's fourth son. He had the same mother as Tokihira and Nakahira. Imperial edicts named him *sesshō* on the Twenty-First of the Ninth Month in the eighth year of Enchō [930] and *kanpaku* in the Eleventh Month of the fourth year of Tengyō [941]. He was a senior noble for forty-two years, a minister of state for thirty-two, and the ruler of the nation for twenty. His posthumous name is Teishinkō. He is called the Koichijō Chancellor. He was the uncle of Emperors Suzaku and Murakami.

Tadahira had five sons. At the time of his death, he held the office of Chancellor; his oldest son, the Ononomiya Lord Saneyori, was Minister of the Left; and his second son, the Kujō Lord Morosuke, was Minister of the Right. The fourth son was Major Counselor Morouji, and the fifth was the Koichijō Lord Morotada, another Minister of the Left. It was wonderful that the four of them should have risen to such exalted positions, one after another. His daughter was a consort of the Crown Prince who died.

We can still see the paving stones south of Koichijō on Kageyuno-kōji, the street Tadahira's three ministerial sons always used when they visited him. In deference to the Munakata deities, the ministers would leave their carriages at either the Tōin or the Koshiro intersection; and I understand that the stones were laid to make it easier for them on rainy days.[31] People used to stay away from that block, but nowadays all kinds of common fellows go clattering past it with their horses and carriages. It seems sadly irreverent to those of us who remember earlier times. I never pass the mansion if I can help it. I had to make an exception today because of my backache, but I avoided the paving stones and stepped into some nasty deep mud on the south side. See how dirty I got? (*He pulled up his skirts for us to look at.*)

I have heard that Michinaga often says, "I would be happy to own anything that had belonged to one of my ancestors—anything, that is,

[31] The Munakata deities, three goddesses named Tagorihime, Tagitsuhime, and Ichikishimahime, were so called from their principal place of worship, Munakata District in what is now Fukuoka Prefecture, an ancient center of the Korea trade. They are still worshipped as protectors of commerce in branch shrines throughout Japan. Fuyutsugi is said to have installed them inside the grounds of the Koichijō Mansion in 795.

except the Koichijō Mansion. One wants a house for births and deaths. What good is place that has to be left at such times?[32] Besides, it would keep me on edge just to know that the goddesses were there." His feelings were natural enough.

The goddesses used to communicate directly with Tadahira. People say the minister persuaded the Emperor to raise their Court ranks because they said to him, "It hurts our feelings for you to have a higher rank than ours."

Tadahira once set out toward the council chamber to execute an Imperial command. (I can't remember who was reigning, but it must have been either Emperor Daigo or Emperor Suzaku.) He sensed a presence as he was passing behind the Shishinden curtain-dais, and then, to his amazement, something caught hold of his scabbard tip. His groping fingers touched a shaggy hand with long, knifelike nails, the sure sign of a demon. It was a horrifying moment, but he summoned up all his courage. "Who stops a man on his way to the council chamber with an Imperial decree?" he demanded. "You will regret it if you don't let go." He drew his sword and seized the hand, and the flustered demon released him and fled toward the northeast.[33] It must have happened at night.

Somehow it seems sadder and more sacrilegious to talk about Tadahira than about the others. (*His voice broke, and he blew his nose several times.*)

I don't know how it happened, but they say Tadahira was born after a seven-month gestation period. He died on the Eleventh of the Eighth Month in the third year of Tenryaku [949], and was posthumously promoted to Senior First Rank. His age was seventy-one.

CHANCELLOR SANEYORI
(Seishinkō)

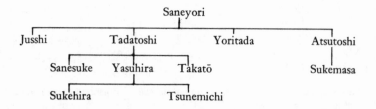

[32] To avoid defilement of the shrine.

[33] The direction of the Demon Lodge, in yin-yang lore one of the twenty-eight lodges in the celestial zone of the moon.

Tadahira's oldest son, Saneyori, was known as the Ononomiya Minister of State. His mother was a daughter of Emperor Uda. He served as a minister for twenty-seven years and, if I remember correctly, governed for about twenty years as Regent.[34] His posthumous name is Seishinkō.

Saneyori was a fine poet, many of whose compositions appear in the *Later Selection*.[35] He also excelled in all the other accomplishments, and his upright character is still cited as a model. He never went bareheaded into the Ononomiya main south chamber, from which the Inari cryptomeria trees were plainly visible, because he was unwilling to run the risk of letting the god see him improperly attired. He was a very circumspect man. If he happened to forget his cap, he would hastily cover his head with a sleeve.

Saneyori's daughter died after becoming a Junior Consort. I am not sure, but I think her death occurred during Emperor Murakami's reign. Lesser Captain Atsutoshi, who was Saneyori's son by one of Tokihira's daughters, also predeceased his father. While Saneyori was mourning him, a horse arrived from the east for the Captain, sent by someone who had not heard the news. Saneyori composed a poem:

Mada shiranu	Someone, it seems,
Hito mo arikeri	Had not yet heard.
Azumaji ni	Better for me had I, too,
Ware mo yukite zo	Journeyed to an eastern land
Sumubekarikeru.	And made it my home.

It was a sad affair. (*Yotsugi wiped his eyes.*)

Because Saneyori's childhood name was Ushikai, Ox Driver, members of his family say *ushitsuki*, Ox Attendant, when they want to refer to a real ox driver.

The famous calligrapher Sukemasa, the Senior Assistant Governor-General, was Atsutoshi's son. When Sukemasa started back toward the capital after finishing his tour of duty in Tsukushi, the weather took a turn for the worse at the harbor from which he was planning to cross to Iyo Province. The sea looked ominous, and a gale blew up. He prepared to leave when the wind and waves abated, only to see the storm return. Furthermore, the same thing happened day after day. In great perplexity, he consulted a diviner, all of whose investigations produced a single answer: a god had cast a spell over the weather.

[34] Saneyori was the senior minister from 949 on, but did not become Regent until 967, three years before his death.

[35] *Gosenshū*, the second Imperial poetic anthology, commissioned in 951.

What could it mean? It was not as though Sukemasa had been guilty of impiety. Then a dignified male figure appeared to the frightened traveler in a dream.

"It is I who have detained you by causing inclement weather every day," the apparition said. "All the shrines except mine have plaques, and so I must have one, too. An ordinary calligrapher would not suit me; it is you I want. I told myself to seize the opportunity when you arrived in the vicinity, and that is why I have kept you here."

"Who are you?" asked Sukemasa.

"I am the old man who lives at Mishima on the seashore,"[36] he answered. Sukemasa dreamed that he acceded in fear and trembling. Needless to say, he felt even more awe-stricken after waking up.

The weather for the passage to Iyo was as fine and calm as though there had been no storms day after day. Aided by a fair wind, the boat skimmed across the waves to its destination like a bird in flight. Sukemasa bathed several times in hot water, purified himself with scrupulous care, put on Court robes, inscribed the plaque in the presence of the god, summoned shrine officials to hang it, and then set out for home, having done everything according to form. That time, all the boats in his party reached the capital without the slightest mishap.

It is gratification enough even to have our fellow men praise and admire our work. We can imagine Sukemasa's elation when a god showed such eagerness for a specimen of his calligraphy! Thanks in large part to that incident, he has become known as Japan's greatest calligrapher.

The plaque at the Rokuharamitsuji was also inscribed by Sukemasa. That plaque and the one at Mishima are in the same hand.

Sukemasa was indolent by nature—a dawdler, if the truth be told. The late Middle Regent Michitaka, when he was building at Higashisanjō,[37] ordered some partitions decorated with paintings and poems, and it was Sukemasa whom he asked to inscribe the poems on the colored-paper squares. Everything would have been fine if Sukemasa had gone and done his work while the house was empty, but he failed to arrive until almost noon, by which time Michitaka was there waiting for him, attended by a company of senior nobles, courtiers, and others. The calligrapher was embarrassed, but the poems had to be written, so he scribbled them off. When he started to leave, Michitaka rewarded him with a woman's robe. Little as he wanted to take it, it was impossible to decline,[38] and he had to drape it over his shoulder and make his way out through the crowd.

[36] I.e., the god.   [37] Probably at the Higashisanjō Minaminoin.

[38] Michitaka, his second cousin, was treating him as an inferior to express his displeasure.

That humiliation was due entirely to Sukemasa's laziness. It would not have happened if he had gone to write the poems early in the morning while things were quiet. Such, at any rate, was the opinion of the witnesses, and so he himself believed. But there were those who criticized Michitaka. "It would have been all right to act that way if Sukemasa had been a professional calligrapher with no social standing," they said.

Sukemasa's daughter married her father's cousin Yasuhira, the Commander of the Right Gate Guards, and became the mother of Lord Tsunetō. She is a calligrapher of equal rank with her father in the woman's style. And Sukemasa's younger sister was the wife of Tamemitsu, the Hōjūji Minister of State. One of her daughters was the lady known as the Kokiden Consort during Emperor Kazan's reign, and another married Yoshichika, the Middle Counselor who became a monk. Tadanobu, Tamemitsu's son by Sukemasa's sister, is the Master of our present Empress's Household.

Saneyori's third son was Tadatoshi (Atsutoshi's full brother), who rose as high as Commander of the Gate Guards of the Right. Tadatoshi had three sons by a daughter of Masabun, the governor of Harima. The oldest, Takatō, died while serving as Senior Assistant Governor-General of the Dazaifu; and the second, Yasuhira, became a Middle Counselor and Commander of the Gate Guards of the Right. One of Yasuhira's sons is Tsunemichi, the present Commander of the Military Guards of the Right; another is the Gentleman-in-Waiting Consultant Sukehira, who is Provisional Master of the Grand Empress's Household.

One of Tadatoshi's sons was adopted by his grandfather, Saneyori, who named him Sanesuke and made him a great favorite. The Sane in his name comes from Saneyori's own name. He is the present Ononomiya Minister of the Right, a most exalted personage.

Grieved by his lack of a son, Sanesuke adopted his nephew, Consultant Sukehira. Later in his life, a Court attendant bore him the son who is now Palace Chaplain Ryōen. And a lady-in-waiting at his house has given birth to a daughter called Kaguyahime.[39] (The mother is the daughter of Consultant Yoritada's nurse.)[40]

[39] A nickname, implicitly comparing the girl to the beautiful maiden of that name in *Taketori monogatari* (The Tale of the Bamboo Cutter, translated in Keene 1956).

[40] Some *Ōkagami* texts have Yorisada (a son of Prince Tamehira), which is more likely to be correct. Kaguyahime's mother, as the daughter of Yorisada's nurse, would have been on intimate terms with both Yorisada and his sister Enshi (who, as the author notes below, was Sanesuke's principal wife), and would probably also have known Sanesuke well. Yorisada held the office of Consultant when he died in 1020. Satō 1929, p. 173.

Sanesuke's main wife, Princess Enshi, was a daughter of Prince Tamehira, the Minister of Ceremonial. She had been one of Emperor Kazan's consorts. Middle Captain Michinobu, who had fallen in love with her after the Emperor's retirement from lay life, sent her a poem when he heard of Sanesuke's visits.

Ureshiki wa	How deeply, I wonder,
Ika bakari ka wa	May your happiness be felt?
Omouramu	My misery seems to penetrate
Uki wa mi ni shimu	To the very marrow
Kokochi koso sure.	Of my bones.

The Princess married Sanesuke.

Kaguyahime has her own curtain-dais in the east chamber of the main Ononomiya building, where she is being educated with great care. I wonder what kind of husband fate holds in store for her.

Sanesuke is much richer than people realize. I imagine he owns all of the late Lord Saneyori's treasures and estates. The mansion he has erected is a splendid sight. Wings, a main hall, and galleries are common enough, but he also has a Buddha Hall to the southeast, three bays long on each of its four sides, with monks' quarters in all the corridors. The monks' bathhouse is furnished with two huge three-legged cauldrons, plastered with earth, under which fires are lighted every day. In the Buddha Hall itself, there are innumerable golden images, and the receptacles in front of them always contain thirty *koku* of rice.[41] People walk to the Buddha Hall from the front lake, following a path through a great park laid out to resemble a wild meadow, which is filled with trees and plants chosen for their seasonal flowers and autumn color— or else they can row across the lake. Those are the only ways of approaching it. Every one of the monks is either a distinguished scholar, a special sutra chanter,[42] or an expert in the mystic Shingon rites. Sanesuke gives them summer and winter vestments and sustenance allowances, and tells them to pray for the extinction of his sins, the growth of his virtues, and the safety of Her Ladyship his daughter.

The Ononomiya Mansion is kept in such beautiful repair that there is never a day when seven or eight carpenters are not busy there. The two places where one is certain to hear the sound of adzes are the Tōdaiji and the Ononomiya Mansion! Saneyori made no mistake when he singled out Sanesuke.

---

[41] One *koku* equals about 180 liters, or slightly under five bushels.

[42] *Jikyōja*, a monk who recited a set portion of a particular sutra, usually the *Lotus*, every day.

Oh, yes, Sanesuke has another son—Sukeyori, the present governor of Hōki. Sukeyori's mother was different from Kaguyahime's. I wonder who she might have been.

CHANCELLOR YORITADA
(Rengikō)

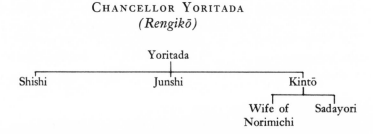

Yoritada was Saneyori's second son. He and Atsutoshi had the same mother, Tokihira's daughter. He served as a minister of state for nineteen years and as Regent for nine, scaling the very pinnacle of worldly success. He lived north of Sanjō and east of Nishinotōin, and so he is called the Sanjō Lord.[5]

After the accession of Emperor Ichijō, to whom he was not directly related, Yoritada gave up the regency and stayed in the Shijō Palace with his daughter Empress Junshi, retaining only the title of Chancellor.[43] The new Regent's grandson Takaie was putting on great airs in those days. Since he was the son-in-law of the Rokujō Lord Shigenobu, he was always travelling north on Nishinotōin.[44] Anyone else would have made a detour, but he rode his horse right past the Shijō Palace—and what could Yoritada do, much as he resented it? The Chancellor did confess to a certain curiosity about his appearance, and he peered out one day through the lattice window in the gallery north of his middle gate. The young gallant, his collar strings casually loose, was riding along on a mettlesome horse, escorted by twenty or thirty attendants who cleared the way with peremptory shouts; and he cast a glance inside the gate as he went past with taut reins, fanning himself haughtily. Yoritada was upset, but it would have made matters worse to complain. He simply said, "Takaie seems to have no consideration for other people's feelings."

There is no denying that Takaie was rude. His wife, Shigenobu's daughter, was Yoritada's granddaughter on the maternal side, so he

---

[43] Kaneie succeeded him as Regent.

[44] En route to the Imperial Palace from Rokujō, where Takaie's wife lived in her family home. For marriage customs in the Heian period, see McCullough 1967.

was just the same as a grandson to the Chancellor. He ought to have made a special effort to call and inquire after his health.

Even as Regent, Yoritada never went to the Imperial Palace in an informal cloak. If he had something to report, he put on full Court dress, except for the very formal outer trousers. Furthermore, he used to stay beside the Partition of the Annual Ceremonies[45] in the Courtiers' Hall, reporting and receiving orders through the appropriate Chamberlain. He never entered the Imperial presence unless His Majesty came to the Demon Room to call him in. I suppose the reason for his formality was that he was not closely related to the Emperor, even though he was the Regent.

Yoritada had two daughters and a son by a daughter of Prince Yoakira, the late Minister of Central Affairs. The older daughter, Junshi, became a Junior Consort during Emperor En'yū's reign, and was granted the title of Empress at the age of twenty-six, on the Eleventh of the Third Month in the fifth year of Tengen [982]. She bore no son. She was called the Shijō Empress, and was reputed to be exceptionally discreet and well informed. She never cut corners when it was a matter of pious deeds or prayers. Instead of dismissing the seasonal sutra recitations[46] as routine events, she saw to it that the twenty monks spent the four days in comfortable, well-appointed quarters; and she also provided them with baths and took great pains with their vegetarian fare. Furthermore, she made a point of personally presenting them with suitable gifts, to which she first made obeisance after having put on clean robes and purified herself.

It happened once that everyone in the capital was preparing delicacies for the Eshin Bishop, who had decided to travel around as a mendicant monk. Empress Junshi ordered a metalsmith to forge a beautiful rice bowl with a lid, but when she offered it to the Bishop he gave up his plan. The bowl was much too fine for a beggar, he said.

Yoritada's other daughter, Shishi, was a Junior Consort during Emperor Kazan's reign. She seems to be living in the Shijō Palace as a nun.

Lord Kintō, the present Inspector Major Counselor, is the uterine brother of the two Imperial ladies. He excels at poetry, possibly because he is Saneyori's grandson; and people regard him as a man of

---

[45] A silk screen, covered with minute inscriptions listing the major annual Court ceremonies and rituals. It stood at the main entrance to the Courtiers' Hall.

[46] At the Imperial Palace. Semiannual ceremonies, usually held in the Second and Eighth Months, at which the Ninnōgyō (Benevolent King Sutra), Daihannyakyō (Sutra of Great Wisdom), and other sacred writings were intoned. They lasted for three or four days.

the utmost elegance and refinement. Just now, he is distracted with grief because of the death of his daughter, Palace Minister Norimichi's wife, who passed away in the last First Month, after having given birth to several children over the years. His only son, Major Controller of the Left Sadayori, is one of the most discriminating of the younger courtiers, and a first-rate poet, too. The mother, Kintō's wife, is a high-born lady—a daughter of Emperor Murakami's ninth son by a daughter of the Tōnomine Novice, Lesser Captain Machiosa—so Norimichi's wife and Sadayori can claim an exalted lineage.

Just once, Lord Kintō was guilty of a thoughtless speech. When his younger sister, Junshi, first entered the Palace after having been elevated to Imperial rank, she passed the Higashisanjō Mansion on her way north along Tōin Avenue. Of course, Kaneie and Senshi were both in a state of unutterable chagrin.[47] Elated at being the older brother of an Empress, Kintō pulled up his horse, looked into the mansion's grounds, and said, "I wonder when the consort in there will receive Imperial rank." Kaneie and the rest of the family were outraged, but they consoled themselves with the thought that Senshi was the mother of a Prince. Outsiders considered the remark unfortunate.

When Emperor Ichijō ascended the throne, it was Senshi's turn to go to the Palace as a new Empress. On the day of her ceremonial entry, someone thrust out a fan from one of the ladies' carriages and called to Kintō, who had joined her entourage as Assistant Master.[48] "We would like a word with you," she said.

"What is it?" asked Kintō, approaching the carriage.

A lady called Shin no naishi put out her head. "Where is your sister, the Barren Empress?" she asked.

"She remembered that affair several years ago," Kintō said later. "I had already recognized my mistake; she was quite within her rights. I felt like shriveling up."

But Kintō was a man of great refinement, indispensable to the success of every event, so Naishi was the one people criticized, and nothing came of it.

Michinaga arranged a boating excursion on the Ōi River one year, setting aside one craft for guests who were skilled in the composition of Chinese verse, another for expert musicians, and a third for outstanding *waka* poets. When Kintō arrived, His Lordship sent someone to invite him to choose his own vessel.

[47] Because they felt that the promotion should have gone to Senshi, who was the mother of the Emperor's only child, the future Emperor Ichijō.

[48] *Kei no suke.* Conjectured to mean Assistant Master of Senshi's Household. The title she received was Grand Empress (*kōtaigō*).

."I would prefer the Japanese poetry boat," Kintō said. He composed this poem:

Ogurayama	Chill blows the gale
Arashi no kaze no	From Ogurayama
Samukereba	And Storm Mountain:
Momiji no nishiki	No man but wears a robe
Kinu hito zo naki.	Of autumn-leaf brocade.

Would anyone deny that he rose to the occasion?

"I ought to have picked the Chinese boat," Kintō is supposed to have said later. "Think what it would have done for my reputation if I had composed a Chinese poem as good as the Ogurayama *waka*! It was an unfortunate mistake. I let it go to my head when His Lordship asked me to choose my own company."

Few are fortunate enough to excel in anything at all. Even in antiquity, there was probably not another universal genius like Kintō.

Yoritada died on the Twenty-Sixth of the Sixth Month in the first year of Eiso [989], and was posthumously elevated to Senior First Rank. He is called Rengikō. I have already told you about his descendants.

MINISTER OF THE LEFT MOROTADA

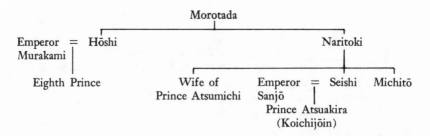

Tadahira's fifth son, the Koichijō Minister of State Morotada, was born of the same mother as Morosuke. He was a minister for three years. It was as a replacement for Takaakira, who went to Tsukushi, that he became Minister of the Left, and there were those who blamed his slanders for Takaakira's troubles. I wonder if there is any truth to the story that Takaakira's enmity caused his death, which occurred before the year was out.

His daughter Hōshi, Emperor Murakami's Sen'yōden Consort, was a lady of exceptional beauty and charm. Whenever she seated herself in a carriage to go to the Imperial Palace, the ends of her hair trailed all the way back to the inside pillar. They say a single strand from her head was enough to cover a sheet of Michinokuni paper,[49] and the corners of her eyes slanted downward bewitchingly. The Emperor, to whom she was very dear, is supposed to have addressed this poem to her:

Ikite no yo	Both in this world
Shinite no nochi no	And in the world
Nochi no yo mo	After death,
Hane o kawaseru	Let us be birds
Tori to narinan.	Who share a wing.

Her reply:

Aki ni naru	If only your heart,
Koto no ha dani mo	Unlike the leaves of autumn,
Kawarazuba	Might remain unchanged,
Ware mo kawaseru	I, too, would wish us to be
Eda to narinan.	A pair of fused branches.[50]

Having heard that Hōshi knew the *Collection of Early and Modern Times* by heart, the Emperor made up his mind to test her memory. He hid the book from sight, read off "The poetry of Japan," and continued with the first seventeen syllables of each poem, calling on her to supply the remainder; and she recited everything without a mistake—both the forewords and the poems.[51] When Morotada found out what was happening, he put on formal attire, cleansed his hands, ordered sutra readings at temples, and offered fervent prayers for his daughter's success.

It was hard to see how Hōshi could have been more of a favorite.

---

[49] A type of thick, white crepe paper, famous as a Michinoku product. Long hair was a principal criterion of feminine beauty.

[50] Both poems allude to Po Chü-i's "Song of Everlasting Sorrow," which describes the ill-starred love of Emperor Hsüan Tsung of China (685-762, r. 712-756) for his beautiful concubine, Yang Kuei-fei (719-756). Toward the end of Po's poem, Yang Kuei-fei compares herself and the Emperor to two birds sharing a single wing, and to two trees with a common branch. For a translation, see Payne 1947, p. 263.

[51] Vulgate texts of the anthology contain 1,111 poems, each with a foreword. "The poetry of Japan" is the first phrase in Tsurayuki's preface.

The Emperor even went to endless trouble to teach her to play the thirteen-stringed koto, upon which he performed with admirable skill. But, strangely enough, people said he rather lost interest in her after Empress Anshi's death. "Whenever I think of how Her Majesty detested the lady, I can't help pitying her and regretting my own behavior," he said.

Hōshi gave birth to a son known as the Eighth Prince—a handsome lad, but excessively slow-witted, or so it was rumored. When people talk about wise sovereigns, they are sure to name Yao and Shun for China, and Engi and Tenryaku for this country. Engi means Emperor Daigo and Tenryaku means Emperor Murakami. It was amazing that a son of Emperor Murakami and grandson of Morotada should have been such a simpleton.

Hōshi's older brother was Major Captain of the Left Naritoki, who died at the age of fifty-five, on the Twenty-Third of the Fourth Month in the first year of Chōtoku [995]. Naritoki was said to be even more fussy and cantankerous than his father. He was also very jealous of his reputation. He used to wait on the Emperor during Hōshi's koto lessons, and in due course he and others came to feel that he had heard enough to qualify as an expert, but he never condescended to play on ordinary occasions. Even when an important function was taking place, he waited to be begged, and then merely plucked out a simple tuning piece. Everyone said he was insufferably conceited. He also had a habit of leaving callers' gifts of food in the garden outside his main hall. He put them in his storehouse during the night and carted them out again to the garden the next morning, and so it went until new things came to replace them. It did smack a bit of putting on airs. He must have wanted visitors to think he was constantly being deluged with presents. (People said he claimed to be following an ancient custom.)

Naritoki considered himself clever when he did such things, but others laughed at him. He once persuaded his nephew, the Eighth Prince, to hold a banquet. Being a heavy drinker, he thought it would be amusing to make the guests drunk, so he gave the Prince careful instructions. "If any of the important senior nobles tries to leave early, detain him in a graceful manner. You might say, 'Do stay just a little longer.' "

Feeble-minded or not, this was an august Imperial Prince sponsoring a great affair, and throngs of gentlemen attended. It was quite like old times.[52] But it happened that the guests had to hurry off to an official function, which had been scheduled for the same date. As they were

---

[52] Princes were no longer holding such banquets in Emperor Murakami's day.

getting ready to leave, the Prince remembered, "Oh, yes! Naritoki told me to do something." He darted anxious glances at Naritoki, who responded with a wink; and then, brick-red and tongue-tied, his face contorted with anxiety, he began to clutch the guests' cloak sleeves so violently that he almost tore them. All the senior nobles exchanged glances, even the ones in the lowest seats. I suppose it was a struggle for them to keep straight faces, because they changed countenance and rushed off, pleading urgent business elsewhere. (Michinaga, who was still a young courtier, had been assigned to a remote seat where the view was not very good. I hear that he often describes the incident, which he seems to find most amusing. "All I could see was the half-smiles of the guests as they left," he says.) Naritoki, ashen-faced, wondered what had possessed him to encourage the Prince to give a banquet, much less try to teach him what to say.

Since people understood about the Prince, nobody blamed him, but Naritoki was not let off so easily. "He knew perfectly well the Prince had something wrong with him," everyone said. "There was no reason why the banquet had to be held. It was his fault that the boy made a spectacle of himself in front of all those gentlemen." The gossip must have been especially galling to Naritoki because of his previous reputation for prudence.

Naritoki's wife, a daughter of the Biwa Major Counselor Nobumitsu, was the mother of two daughters and two sons. One daughter, Seishi, was Emperor Sanjō's favorite consort while he was still heir apparent. She was called the Sen'yōden Consort. She bore four sons and two daughters to the future Emperor, who honored her with the title of Empress in the year following his accession, on the Twenty-Eighth of the Fourth Month in the first year of Chōwa [1012]. After Naritoki's death, the other daughter[53] became the wife of Prince Atsumichi, Emperor Reizei's fourth son, entirely on her own initiative. During the period of the marriage, a matter of two or three years, the Prince transferred his affections to Izumi Shikibu, and Naritoki's daughter, miserably unhappy, went back to Koichijō.[54] I heard not long ago that she had been living in shockingly reduced circumstances.

The person who has been a credit to Naritoki is Empress Seishi. When Emperor Sanjō abdicated, on the Twenty-Ninth of the First Month in the fifth year of Chōwa [1016], the Empress's oldest son, Prince Atsuakira, became the new Crown Prince at the age of twenty-

---

[53] Called Naka no kimi.

[54] Naritoki's Koichijō residence was also the home of Naka no kimi's grandmother, who had adopted the girl. Hosaka 1974, 2.354; McCullough and McCullough 1980, Chapter 4.

three. Everyone considered it a natural choice, but for some reason the Prince began to feel unhappy in the following year. His mind dwelt on the freedom he had enjoyed as an ordinary Prince, and he gradually persuaded himself that nothing would delight him more than to escape the restraints of his ceremonious existence. He unburdened himself to the Empress, but I need not tell you that she found the idea ridiculous. He was not to dream of resigning, she admonished him.

Not knowing what else to do, the Prince sent Michinaga a letter. Michinaga went to see him, and he told him everything. "I want to resign from this office so I can live in peace," he said.

"I could never, never agree to such a proposal," Michinaga answered. "Do you want to extinguish Emperor Sanjō's line? What a shocking, saddening notion! There is only one way to explain it: the angry spirits that used to haunt Emperor Reizei are putting ideas into your head.[55] You must remember that."

"Well, then, I suppose I'll have to become a monk. I've been thinking about it for a long time anyway," the Prince said.

"If you are ready to go that far, I can't argue with you," said Michinaga. "I'll speak to His Majesty."

The Prince felt happy for the first time.

You may imagine the emotions with which Grand Empress Shōshi greeted the news her father brought to the Imperial Palace. She probably would have liked to see Prince Atsuyasu become the next Crown Prince, but the situation was exactly the same as when Emperor Ichijō had said, "I can't make Atsuyasu the Crown Prince because he lacks influential male relatives. It must be Atsuhira." So the appointment fell to the Third Prince, who became heir apparent at the age of nine, on the Fifth of the Eighth Month in the first year of Kannin [1017].[(6)]

The new Crown Prince performed the capping ceremony at the age of eleven, on the Twenty-Eighth of the Eighth Month in the third year of Kannin [1019]. The former Crown Prince is now called Koichijōin.

What words could do justice to the good fortune of the present Crown Prince? People thought he would probably be nominated some day, but nobody expected it to happen so soon.

Koichijōin was the first person to relinquish the title of Crown Prince voluntarily. If I remember correctly, nine others have been forced to retire in the course of Japanese history.[56] One of them, the Priestly Crown Prince, has become known as the Posthumously Ap-

---

55 The wraiths of Motokata and his daughter.

56 Actually five: Princes Funado, Osabe, Sawara, Takaoka, and Tsunesada. See Appendix A. As Satō 1929, p. 210, suggests, nine is probably a scribal error for five, which it resembles in cursive script.

pointed Retired Emperor since his death. He is worshipped in every province, and I believe the Court recognizes his powers by sending part of the First Tribute to his tomb.[57]

Michinaga's extraordinary karma must have had something to do with Koichijōin's decision to resign—and Motokata's spirit probably played an even more important part.

"That sounds reasonable enough," the attendant interrupted, "but I have heard quite a different version of the affair. There are some facts I happen to know all about."

"That doesn't surprise me," Yotsugi said. "I would like nothing better than to hear what people have told you. It's a hobby of mine to listen to stories."

Encouraged by the old man's show of interest, the attendant began his tale.

To tell the truth, everything was fine as long as Retired Emperor Sanjō lived, but the Prince was not treated like a proper heir apparent after his father's death. No courtiers came to amuse him with poetry and music; nobody danced attendance on him. Oppressed by the monotony of his existence, he lapsed into nostalgic reveries about the happy past, growing quite dull and apathetic. As long as Retired Emperor Sanjō had lived, his courtiers had called on the Prince, and his messengers had streamed in and out, and so there had been many people going back and forth, and many sources of diversion. But there was a feeling of danger in the air after His Majesty's death. People were afraid even to use the avenue.[58] With prudence uppermost in everybody's mind, it was hard for the Prince's own household officials to go and wait on him—and you can imagine the thoughts that ran through the heads of the lower servants. The people from the Bureau of Grounds failed to arrive for the morning cleaning and gardening, and the plants ran wild. It was a disgraceful way for a Crown Prince to have to live.

On the rare occasions when callers did come, they passed along gossip. "According to what we hear, Michinaga and Shōshi are upset because Prince Atsunaga is still a plain Imperial Prince. 'What's going to happen if His Majesty has a son?' they say. 'If only we could make Atsunaga Crown Prince first!' It looks as though you are going to be

[57] In the Twelfth Month of each year, messengers were sent to the Imperial ancestral tombs with offerings of newly harvested rice and other tribute articles.
[58] In front of the Prince's house.

forced out." Some of the tales were probably false, but they bothered the already uneasy Prince, who must have felt that his present circumstances made it impossible to shrug them off. "Better to resign than to be deposed," he thought.

At the same time, there were rumors that Michinaga was going to offer Kanshi, his daughter by Lady Takamatsu, to the Prince as a consort, and that he intended to treat him handsomely in every respect. The stories, making the rounds in the usual way, filled Empress Seishi with joy, but the Prince thought, "Attractive as the prospect sounds, there will be even less chance of living as I please if I marry Kanshi. I can't go on as Crown Prince." He broached the subject to his mother, who was, of course, firmly opposed.

"It is out of the question," she said. "If it is true about Kanshi, you ought to go ahead and ask for her. But you must forget about resigning." She ordered prayers, convinced that a malevolent spirit was at work, while the Prince continued to turn the matter over in his mind.

News of the Prince's deliberations apparently leaked out, and Michinaga, hearing that he was planning to resign and ask for Kanshi, wondered how he ought to respond.

At last the Prince made up his mind. He seems to have told himself he would stand a better chance of getting Kanshi if he asked for her after his resignation, which was a bit of wishful thinking.[7] To the Empress he said not a word. His only thought was to let Michinaga know of his intentions. For want of a suitable confidant, he sent a Chamberlain with a message requesting the favor of a visit from Yoshinobu, the Provisional Master of the Empress's Household, whom he chose, I imagine, because he lived at the intersection of Shijōbōmon and Nishinotōin, close to the Prince's own house.[59] Yoshinobu, taken aback, asked why he was being summoned.

"I suppose His Highness wants a word with you," said the messenger.

"It must have something to do with the rumors," Yoshinobu guessed. "He can't intend to resign, so it must be about Kanshi." In any case, the matter was not one for him to handle alone.

"I realize that I ought to present myself immediately," he told the Chamberlain, "but I shall have to speak to my father first." He went off to see Michinaga.

Michinaga was also surprised. "What can he want?" he said. The same thought crossed his mind. "He must be going to ask for Kanshi,

59 Shijōbōmon is probably a mistake for Sanjōbōmon. It is likely that Prince Atsuakira was living with his consort, Enshi, at the Horikawa Mansion, which was immediately adjacent to Yoshinobu's residence, the Kan'in. Both establishments bordered Sanjōbōmon on the south. Hosaka 1974, 2.376.

and it would be awkward to turn him down. He could not very well be left in his present situation if she married him. On the other hand, they say he is thinking about resigning as Crown Prince. He would never go through with it if we made life pleasant for him."

"It would be out of the question to refuse to go, now that he has made a point of calling you in," he said. "You must listen to what he has to say."

It was getting dark by the time Yoshinobu reached the Prince's palace. To his annoyance, he saw Akimitsu's carriage and outriders at the guard station, but he could not very well go home, so he went into the Courtiers' Hall and asked a Chamberlain to announce him.

"I won't be able to deliver your message just now. The minister is with His Highness," the Chamberlain answered. Glancing about, Yoshinobu saw that the garden was overgrown. The hall itself was disgracefully shabby, not at all a fit room for a Crown Prince's residence.

When Akimitsu had gone, the Chamberlain announced Yoshinobu, and the Prince called him into the Dining Room. "Come right over here," His Highness said. "Since you are not in the habit of visiting me, it was an imposition to ask you to call, but there is something I need to let His Lordship know, and I have nobody of the right sort to use as a messenger. I thought I might ask you because your house is close to mine. Please say this to him for me:

" 'My present position is just what anyone would want, and I also have many qualms about upsetting an arrangement made by my late father, the Emperor, but I have thought it all over, and I feel that it would be a sin for me to go on like this. With such a long future ahead of His Majesty, there is no prospect of my succeeding to the throne. Furthermore, I might die at any time in this uncertain world. I wish, therefore, to resign and be free to visit holy places and undertake pious works whenever I please. It would humiliate me to be known simply as the Former Crown Prince;[60] I should like to have the same treatment as a Retired Emperor, with a palace name,[61] annual offices, and so forth. What do you say?' " Yoshinobu assented respectfully and withdrew.

The hour having grown late, Yoshinobu waited until early the next morning before going to Michinaga's house. His Lordship was dressing for the Imperial Palace, and the mansion buzzed with people, mostly gentlemen waiting to join the escort, but also many others hoping for a word with the great man as he left. Yoshinobu sat down by a shutter

[60] The title would suggest that he had been deposed.

[61] *Ingō*, an epithet (*gō*) ending in *in*, usually derived from a house or other place associated with the Retired Emperor or Empress so designated. Thus Sanjōin, rendered in the translation as Retired Emperor Sanjō.

in one of the corner rooms, intending to intercept his father on the way to the carriage; and presently Minister of Popular Affairs Toshi-kata went over to ask what he was doing there. There was no reason for secrecy where Toshikata was concerned.[62] Yoshinobu told him the news, adding, "I don't see how I can deliver the message with all those people around."

Toshikata looked dumbfounded. "This is a matter of the greatest importance. You must not hesitate to speak up," he said. "He will be surrounded once he gets to the Palace—completely beyond your reach."

Recognizing that he was right, Yoshinobu sought out Michinaga, who guessed his business and went with him to a corner room. "Did you visit the Crown Prince?" His Lordship asked.

I need not tell you what an impression it made when Yoshinobu repeated everything the Prince had said the night before. To force the Prince to resign, Michinaga had thought, would be too disrespectful to the Imperial house, but now, to his boundless delight, the Prince him-self had solved the problem. Shōshi's karma was nothing short of magnificent! What should the next step be, he asked Toshikata.

"Don't waste any time," Toshikata answered. "There is no need to have diviners pick an auspicious date. If you delay, he'll probably change his mind and decide to stay, and then where will you be?"

Michinaga agreed. Consulting the calendar, he saw that that very day was not inauspicious. The Regent, Yorimichi, who had happened onto the scene, urged, "Act now! Act now!"

"First of all, I must let Shōshi know," Michinaga said. He went to the Imperial Palace, where his daughter was in residence, and told her the news. Since she was a woman, I suppose it was an even bigger thrill for her. Then he went to see the Crown Prince, accompanied by his sons and the other senior nobles and courtiers who usually formed part of his retinue. It was a stately, imposing procession, and the Crown Prince, firm though his resolution was, must have greeted its approach nervously.

Since nobody ever visited the Prince, the curiosity of the uninformed had already been piqued by Yoshinobu's call on the preceding day. You may imagine the stupefaction with which the neighborhood greeted the roars of Michinaga's outriders and the immense size of his train, which would have seemed appropriate for a regental visit to Kamo Shrine. People of the better sort concluded, reasonably enough, that His Lordship must be going to talk to the Prince about Kanshi. Ig-

---

[62] Toshikata, Yoshinobu's uncle, was a close friend of the family.

norant common folk wondered in alarm if something might have happened to the Emperor, which was a shockingly inauspicious notion. Empress Seishi was as much in the dark as anybody else. Puzzled by the commotion at her son's residence, she sent someone to make inquiries, but Michinaga's men had blocked the route her ladies usually followed.[63]

Although the Prince had made up his mind to tell Michinaga all about his worries and misgivings, he found himself in a great state of agitation when the moment arrived. Could he say what he meant? I suppose he was overcome by timidity when the two met face to face, because he merely repeated his words of the day before. As a matter of fact, he was even briefer. Michinaga must have answered, "Very well, but what made you decide to do it?" or something of the sort. Moved in spite of himself by the Prince's pathetic air, he wiped away a tear or two as he said, "If you intend to resign, today is auspicious."

So Michinaga made the Prince a Retired Emperor. He proceeded at once with the decisions necessary for the new household to commence operations: all the Chamberlains and officials from the old household were kept on as Household Secretaries, and Yoshinobu, the new Superintendent, went down to perform an obeisance. When the arrangements were finished, he took his leave.

A touching thing happened while Michinaga was still with the Prince. One of Empress Seishi's ladies managed to make her way to the house, her clothing in a shocking state, and her whole body quivering with indignation. "What do you mean by shutting us out like that?" she cried. For all the attention she paid to Michinaga, he might not have been sitting there in broad view. "It was pitiful, but it did have its comic side," His Lordship said later.

I have not heard anything definite about the identity of the Imperial messenger.[64] It was all so sudden that I wonder how the Prince rewarded him.

(*"Lord Michinaga would have taken care of it," Yotsugi said. "He wouldn't have lost any time after matters had reached that stage."*)

There were those who shed furtive tears when the fire huts[65] and

---

[63] Seishi was probably living at the Sanjōin, about four blocks away.

[64] Sent to give the Prince his palace name, Koichijōin.

[65] Fire huts (*hitakiya*), used in the grounds of the Imperial Palace, were also a perquisite of Empresses, Crown Princes, Ise Virgins, and Imperial personages with palace names. They were small, portable structures where members of the Guards or other functionaries kept fires burning on dark nights. Scattered references indicate that their basic purpose was to provide illumination, but little else is known about them. It is not clear why the author depicts Koichijōin's as

guard stations were demolished. And it was easy to imagine the emotions of Empress Seishi and the Horikawa Consort Enshi, both of whom had cherished such high hopes for the Prince. People say Enshi recited a poem:

Kumoi made	How unforeseen
Tachinoborubeki	The fate of smoke
Keburi ka to	Destined, it had seemed,
Mieshi omoi no	To rise
Hoka ni mo aru ka na.	As high as the heavens.

I myself consider it improbable. Nobody is going to think about versifying at a time like that. It would have been natural to compose something later, but could those lines really have originated as people claim they did?

("There is something to what you say," old Yotsugi remarked, "but all the same, we hear about lots of people who have composed remarkable poems at moments of crisis, both in earlier times and in our own." He muttered something inaudible.)

Once Michinaga had forced Koichijōin to resign, he took him as a son-in-law and showered him with so many attentions that everyone said his cordiality was more than enough to make the former Crown Prince forget his troubles. When they served Koichijōin's dinner, Michinaga went to the Table Room and personally wiped the table and plates. He tasted all the food before it was presented,[66] carried it as far as the partition before entrusting it to the lady-in-waiting, and went along with it to the sitting room, issuing admonitions against carelessness. It is rather sad to think that that kind of thing apparently makes Koichijōin perfectly happy.

It is not true that Prince Atsuyasu, the late Minister of Ceremonial, was considered as a possible successor to Koichijōin. It might be differ-

---

having been dismantled, since he would presumably have been entitled to keep them. If the statement is correct, the explanation is possibly to be sought in the fact that the present passage departs from accounts of the resignation preserved in contemporary diaries, which show the Prince resigning on the Sixth of the Eighth Month in the first year of Kannin (1017) and receiving his palace name almost three weeks later, on the Twenty-Fifth. Or, as Hosaka suggests, the Prince may not have been granted all the privileges accorded a bona-fide Retired Emperor, who ordinarily played a significant political role. Hosaka 1974, 2.394; McCullough and McCullough 1980, Chapter 6, n. 21.

[66] As a routine precaution against poison.

ent if this were ancient history, but why should people spread false rumors about exalted personages who are still alive?

Anyway (*Yotsugi resumed*), Prince Atsuyasu was the late Retired Emperor Ichijō's oldest son. He succeeded Koichijōin as Minister of Ceremonial, after having served for a number of years as Governor-General of the Dazaifu. He grieved himself to death because of his second failure to be named Crown Prince, and his post was taken over by Prince Atsunori, who is Koichijōin's younger brother and Retired Emperor Sanjō's second son. Retired Emperor Sanjō's third son, Prince Atsuhira, is Minister of Central Affairs. The fourth son, Prince Moroakira, became a monk as a boy, and is now, it seems, the Ninnaji Archbishop's favorite disciple. One of the former Emperor's two daughters (the sisters of the Princes)[67] went to Ise as Virgin when her father ascended the throne. After returning, she outraged her ailing father by getting involved with Michimasa, the Wild Lord of Third Rank. The Retired Emperor saw to it that she took Buddhist vows, and presently she died. The other Princess is still alive.

Naritoki's daughter Seishi is our present Empress.[68] When Emperor Sanjō decided to give her Imperial status, he issued a decree making Naritoki a posthumous Chancellor, because there was no recent precedent for the elevation of a Major Counselor's daughter. She is a lucky lady! One of her brothers is the Gentleman-in-Waiting Novice; a second is Lord Michitō, the Treasury Minister; and a third is the Iyo Novice.

Naritoki's other daughter, Naka no kimi, is a pathetic figure. Someone seized an Ōmi estate she had inherited from her father, and there was nothing she could do about it. I suppose she felt too desperate to worry about appearances, because people say she went off on foot one night to register a complaint at Michinaga's Amitābha Hall. It was very late, and Michinaga, who had been praying and reciting sutras in front of the images, had begun to doze against an arm rest. To his surprise, he sensed a presence at the dog barricade.[69] A woman's soft voice

[67] Emperor Sanjō had three daughters, Tōshi, Shishi, and Teishi, but only the first two had the same mother as the Princes.

[68] *Kōgō.* The *kōgō* of a deceased or retired sovereign ordinarily retained her title until she died, entered religion, or was named Grand Empress (*kōtaigō*). McCullough and McCullough 1980, Appendix A. Seishi remained a *kōgō* until her death.

[69] *Inufusegi*, a low, latticed barrier separating the sanctuary from the outer portion of a Buddhist hall (so called from earlier barricades erected to keep dogs off the stairs of buildings).

seemed to be murmuring, "Excuse me." He wondered if his ears were playing tricks. The words came again; it was clear that someone was there.

"Who is it?" he asked doubtfully.

"Naritoki's daughter, come with a petition."

It was an appalling thing she had done, he thought, but it would be cruel to wound her with harsh words.

"What is it you want?" he asked.

"No doubt the affair is known to Your Lordship." She told him the whole story.

He felt sorry for her. "Yes, of course, everybody has heard about it," he said. "It is an extremely sad case, and I shall see that the guilty party is admonished at once. But you ought to have sent someone to speak for you instead of coming here like this. You had better get back home now."

"I kept telling myself it was wrong, but there was nobody to send, so I hoped you might feel sorry for me in spite of everything. Please don't think I was unaware of my presumptuousness. I can never thank you enough for the happiness your words have given me." She wept with clasped hands, and Michinaga found himself shedding tears of sympathy, much as he disapproved of her behavior.

A certain rude fellow laid hands on the lady as she made her way out through the guards at the Great South Gate.[70] Michinaga flared up when he learned about it, and the offender suffered from his displeasure for a long time.

Michinaga has ordered that the land in question is to belong to Naritoki's daughter in perpetuity, and that no complaints from others are ever to be entertained, so she holds it even more firmly than before. Isn't that wonderful! People said she did the right thing. "Anyone who has fallen that low can't worry about the proprieties. She deserves a lot of credit for speaking up." Still, that is not the kind of gossip a person welcomes.

The man who detained Naritoki's daughter at the gate was the father of Minamoto Masanari, a Senior Clerk of Fifth Rank in the Ministry of Ceremonial.

[70] The main gate of the Hōjōji.

CHAPTER THREE

Minister of the Right Morosuke

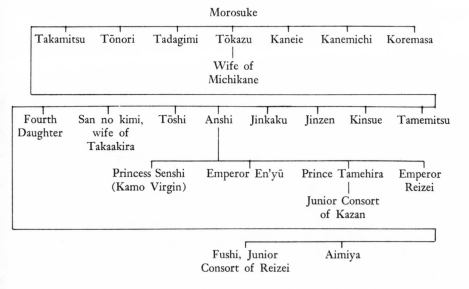

Morosuke was Tadahira's second son. His mother was a daughter of Minamoto Yoshiari, the Minister of the Right. He is known as the Kujō Lord. He was a senior noble for twenty-six years and a minister of state for fourteen. It was a great pity that he died leaving one grandson who was a Crown Prince and two others who were the reigning Emperor's fourth and fifth sons. Since he was still under sixty, he should have had a long future, and there must have been many things that he looked forward to. (*Although he had lowered his voice to a hoarse whisper,*[1] *he involuntarily struck his hands together and looked skyward.*)

Morosuke was the father of eleven sons and five or six daughters.[2] The oldest daughter, Anshi, became a Junior Consort during Emperor Murakami's reign, enjoying the highest position among that sover-

---

[1] To avoid a display of emotion.

[2] The correct figures are probably twelve and seven. See McCullough and McCullough 1980, s.n. 5, for a list.

eign's many consorts and ladies of the bedchamber. The Emperor seemed too much in awe of her to refuse even the most unreasonable demands, let alone such other favors as she might choose to ask. She was rumored to be hot-tempered and possessive, and not even the Emperor himself, it seemed, was able to escape the consequences of her jealousy. I don't know what might have happened beforehand, but there was a night when nobody opened the shutter after His Majesty rapped for admittance. "Go ask a lady-in-waiting why they don't open up," he told an attendant, a certain gentleman who was then a page. The page, searching high and low, found an open entrance at the end of a corridor, where he thought he detected a human presence. He went up and asked his question, only to be greeted by a peal of laughter. When he got back with his report, the Emperor laughed, too. "That's the way she is," he said, and went away. The page was the grandfather of Sukekuni, the former Iga provincial official.

The Fujitsubo and Kokiden Imperial Apartments are close together. It happened once that Hōshi was visiting the first while Empress Anshi was in the other. I suppose the Empress must have let her feelings run away with her, because she made a peephole in the partition and stole a look at her sweet, appealing rival. "No wonder he's crazy about that girl," she thought. Burning with resentment, she told a lady to throw over a pottery fragment—one just big enough to go through the hole. But as luck would have it, the Emperor had gone into the Fujitsubo Apartment. "No lady-in-waiting would act that way," His Majesty snapped, losing his usually excellent temper. "Koremasa, Kanemichi, and Kaneie[3] must have put her up to it." The three gentlemen were ordered to leave their duty posts in the Courtiers' Hall and place themselves under domiciliary confinement.

Anshi sent the Emperor a furious summons, which he disregarded, guessing what she wanted. She insisted that it was a matter of the utmost importance—he absolutely must come—and in the end he gave in. If he refused to relent, he realized, feeling mingled apprehension and pity, he would merely fuel her wrath.

"How could you do such a thing?" she burst out as soon as he appeared. "Even if one of my brothers were to commit a terrible crime, you ought to pardon him.[4] And to act like this when I am involved is too cruel and distressing. Call them back at once."

"How can I turn right around and pardon them? Think of the gossip," he said.

---

[3] Anshi's brothers.   [4] For my sake.

"You must not leave it like this."

"Oh, very well." He started off.

"If you go, you won't do it now. Recall them right here." She held onto his sleeve until he called a Chamberlain and ordered her brothers back to the Palace.

That was not an isolated case; there were many tales of similar incidents. Empress Anshi was generous and considerate by nature. She took great pains on behalf of the people in her service, treating each according to his or her status; and she was also kind to the Junior Consorts, exchanging poems with them and so forth. But how did she react when a lady made her intolerably jealous: that's the question. The scenes probably came when she felt goaded beyond endurance—especially considering what a beauty Hōshi was. It may be that character does not always govern conduct when affairs of the heart are involved. But I have no business commenting on such things.

Whenever there was a noteworthy event in the life of a courtier, lady-in-waiting, or minor female attendant, the Empress would give the matter her personal attention. And of course she showered all kinds of favors on her own brothers. She trusted each of the older ones like a daughter, and loved each of the younger ones like a mother. That was the kind of woman she was, so no wonder people found it hard to accept her death in the proper spirit of resignation. They carried the news by word of mouth to remote country areas, and everyone sorrowed and lamented. The Emperor consulted her in all affairs of state. She interceded whenever anything threatened to cause grief, recommended whatever promised to make people happy, and never repeated remarks that might have led to trouble if they had reached the Emperor's ears. Such rare qualities are exactly like prayers; I feel sure they will bring eternal prosperity to her descendants.

Anshi was the mother of Emperors Reizei and En'yū, of the Minister of Ceremonial Prince Tamehira, and of four Princesses[5]—an incomparable achievement. Almost all our recent Emperors, Crown Princes, and Regents have sprung from Morosuke's line. I have already talked about two of her sons in discussing the Emperors, so there is no need to repeat myself here.

Although Prince Tamehira ought to have succeeded Emperor Reizei as Crown Prince, he was passed over in favor of his younger brother, just because Minamoto Takaakira was his father-in-law. Some extraordinary things happened at the time.[6] Power would have shifted to

[5] Princesses Shōshi (948-951), Hoshi (953-992; Ise Virgin, 968-969), Shishi, and Senshi.

[6] A reference to the Anna incident of 969.

Takaakira's family if Prince Tamehira had become Emperor, and the Genji would have been the ones to prosper, so the Prince's resourceful uncles solved the problem by making his younger brother the heir apparent, even though it was contrary to the natural order of things. Nobody inside or outside the Palace had any way of knowing what they were up to. Everybody thought the nomination would go to Prince Tamehira, who was the next in order of birth. But all of a sudden, it seems, the youngest Prince's nurses were told to dress his hair. Then Kaneie put him into a carriage, and he entered the Palace by way of the north guard quarters.[7] You can imagine the feelings of those who had supported the rightful candidate. Prince Tamehira even had to stand beside the throne,[8] although plenty of other Princes were available in those days, and there were other roles he might have played. Those who witnessed the spectacle said it was pathetic.

I don't know what Takaakira thought about it all. Anyway, some dreadful and heart-rending events took place. This does not do justice to the subject, but it is too presumptuous for humble folk to talk about such things in public; I am going to have to stop. Bringing up old stories is a bad habit of mine.

Prince Tamehira refused to let his misfortunes discourage him. In his last years, he married off his daughter Enshi to Emperor Kazan (Emperor Reizei's son, the Prince's nephew), and went in and out of the Palace all the time. He came in for some sharp criticism from people who thought he should have been more discreet. Just the same, it seemed that he might realize his old ambition if his daughter produced an heir to the throne. Oddly enough, though, Emperor Kazan abdicated and Enshi became the wife of Lord Sanesuke, the present Ononomiya Minister of the Right. Middle Captain Michinobu, who had been sending her letters, composed these lines when she chose Sanesuke instead of him:

Ureshiki wa	How deeply, I wonder,
Ika bakari ka wa	May your happiness be felt?
Omouran	My misery seems to penetrate
Uki wa mi ni shimu	To the very marrow
Kokochi koso sure.	Of my bones.

That excellent poem is still praised today.

I neglected to mention the Day of the Rat excursion, the one time

[7] Situated at Sakuheimon Gate, the back entrance to the Imperial Residential Compound.

[8] During his younger brother's accession ceremony.

when it seemed Prince Tamehira had not lived in vain.[9] In comparison with his younger brothers, who were still small children, the Prince was quite grown up. Everyone liked him, and he was Emperor Murakami's special pet—so much so that His Majesty is supposed to have issued orders that day for the Prince's party to come into the Palace, where he personally inspected the hunting costumes worn by the senior nobles and courtiers in the entourage, as well as the horses and saddles. People said it was an unprecedented act. Even in the reign of a great man like Emperor Murakami, can anybody in an unfigured hunting robe really have entered the Inner Precincts—except, of course, members of the Palace Guards?[10]

What a spectacular procession it was! Do you suppose the sight-seers' carriages on upper Ōmiya Avenue left any vacant space at all? There has never been anything like it.

"It is usual enough for a procession to go along the great avenues," one of the gentlemen said, "but we paraded right past the Fujitsubo Imperial Apartment. The sleeves and skirts of indescribably beautiful dresses overflowed everywhere, and we knew perfectly well that the Emperor and Empress were watching together inside the blinds. We almost swooned."

Furthermore, ten carriage-loads of the Empress's ladies-in-waiting were drawn up in the avenue, with skirts and sleeves billowing out from behind their blinds, and the whole block was closed off. The Palace Guards and attendants who had been chosen as outriders were all young men from good families, and to the onlookers they seemed a splendid sight in their dazzling costumes, chasing people away just as they pleased, as though to say, "The world is ours today." (*It was astonishing to hear him recall every detail, even to the colors of the dresses in the carriages.*)

One of Empress Anshi's daughters died at a sadly early age.[11] Another, Princess Shishi, lived in Sanjō and was called the Nun Princess of First Rank. I believe it has something over ten years since her death. Princess Senshi, after whose birth the Empress died, is the

[9] A visit to Kitano in the Second Month of 964, when the Prince was twelve years old. Day of the Rat outings, which took place in the First or Second Month, involved gathering nutritious young greens, hawking, picnicking, and composing poetry. McCullough and McCullough 1980, s.n. 20.

[10] Unfigured hunting robes (*hōi*) were worn by minor functionaries of Sixth and lower ranks. The reference is probably to handlers of hawks, dogs, and horses. Inner Precincts translates *uchi*, which usually means the Imperial Residential Compound (Dairi), but here may refer to the Seiryōden grounds. For Palace Guards, see Appendix B, n. 11.

[11] Princess Shōshi (n. 5).

present Kamo Virgin.[12] Many Princesses have served as Virgin, but Princess Senshi's tenure has been remarkable for its length—a sign, in my opinion, that karma has ordained the prosperity of Morosuke's line.

Although earlier Virgins avoided words like buddha and sutra, Princess Senshi is such a devout Buddhist that she performs pious recitations every morning. To take an example close at hand, I am told that she sends offerings to this very temple whenever they have events like today's sermon. Since she has served the gods for so long, I can't help wondering how she could have developed such an interest in Buddhism. I have heard that on the day of the Kamo Festival[13] she once vowed to seek buddhahood for herself and for all the multitude assembled at Ichijō Avenue. That was going a little too far.

Concerned though the Princess may be with the life to come, she does not disregard worldly splendor. The utmost elegance and refinement distinguish all her arrangements for the ceremonies on the three days,[14] the ladies' carriages, and so forth. While the present Regent, Yorimichi, held the office of Assistant Commander of the Military Guards, he once served as an outrider in the Purification procession. The Virgin usually waits until after the return to her residence before

[12] Like the Ise Virgin, the Kamo Virgin was an unmarried Imperial Princess. Her principal function was to participate in the great annual Aoi Festival of Kamo Shrine. During the remainder of the year, she lived quietly in a Palace in the Fields at Murasakino, near the Arisugawa River north of the capital. It was usual to appoint a new Virgin at the beginning of each reign, but the custom was not observed in Senshi's case. See also McCullough and McCullough 1980, s.n. 25.

[13] Also called Aoi Festival, or simply "the festival"; the regular festival of Kamo Shrine, held on the middle Day of the Cock in the Fourth Month. It was one of the great religious and social events of the year, valued not so much for the actual rituals as for the magnificent procession, including the Virgin, an Imperial Messenger, and many lesser figures, which made its way from the Imperial Palace along Ichijō Avenue and so to the shrine. Of numerous preliminary events, the most important was the Virgin's Purification, mentioned in the next paragraph, which took place on the middle Day of the Horse, shortly before the festival, at a spot on the Kamo River previously selected by divination. The Virgin's return to Murasakino on the day after the festival was also a major spectacle. McCullough and McCullough 1980, s.n. 50.

[14] The Purification, the Yamashiro Festival, and the Kamo Festival proper. The Yamashiro, or provincial, Festival, appears to have been a relic of the period before the designation of the Kamo Festival as a national event. Supervised by officials of Yamashiro Province, of which Kamo Shrine was officially regarded as the premier Shintō institution, it took place at the shrine on the middle Day of the Monkey. Its main feature appears to have been the presentation of *aoi* and *katsura*, the two plants most closely associated with the Kamo Festival. Hosaka 1974, 2.441; Ishimura 1958, 1.227; n. 15 below.

rewarding members of the retinue, but young Yorimichi started straight home from the river. Caught off guard, the Princess solved the problem by calling him over for an audience and giving him her semiformal coat. When Michinaga heard about it, he said, "She handled it beautifully. It would not have done to let him go without a present, but it would have taken time to send for something, so she paid him a special courtesy. Someone with no taste wouldn't have thought of it."

While our present Emperor and Crown Prince were still ordinary Princes, Michinaga arranged for them to watch the Kamo procession. As the Virgin passed the viewing stand, His Lordship took both the boys onto his lap. "Look at these Princes," he called out. She thrust the edge of her red fan through the litter curtains. Michinaga and the others were struck with admiration. "What a considerate lady the Virgin is! If she hadn't given the signal, how would we have known whether she had seen them?"

The Virgin later sent Shōshi a poem:[15]

Hikari izuru	Now that I have beheld
Aoi no kage o	The shining young *aoi*,
Miteshi yori	Radiant as the emergent sun,
Toshi tsumikeru mo	I count my many years
Ureshikarikeri.	A blessing indeed.

The reply:

Morokazura	It was truly a mark of divine grace
Futaba nagara mo	That the *aoi*,
Kimi ni kaku	Though still a tender sprout,
Au hi ya kami no	Has thus encountered Your Ladyship
Yurushi naruran.	On the day of the double sprays.[16]

[15] The exchange actually took place between the Virgin and Michinaga. Hosaka 1974, 2.446. The Virgin's poem uses *aoi* as a metaphor for the Princes, punning on the last syllable and *hi*, sun, which is written with the same kana symbol. On the day of the Kamo procession, the houses along the way, the carriages and viewing stands, and the spectators were all decked with garlands of real and artificial flowers, leaves of the *katsura* tree (*Cercidiphyllum japonicum*), and especially the *aoi* leaves that gave the festival its popular name. The *aoi*, properly *futabaaoi* (*Asarum caulescens* Maxim), is a creeping, ivylike plant with attractive pairs of heart-shaped leaves growing directly from rooted horizontal stems—an appropriate metaphor for two young brothers.

[16] "Double sprays" translates *morokazura*, which can mean either *aoi* or a Kamo Festival decoration, made of *katsura* and *aoi* leaves, which was attached to blinds, worn on the head, etc. In the present poem, it functions in the second sense,

It is undoubtedly because this Virgin has found favor in the sight of the Kamo gods that she has flourished for five reigns.[17] Her gesture on the occasion I have just described won praise from everyone except Takaie, the former Governor-General of the Dazaifu. "The old fox knew how to flatter them," Takaie said. "It was disgusting."

Oh, yes, Empress Anshi's younger sister Tōshi married Prince Shige-akira, the Minister of Ceremonial, who was Emperor Murakami's brother. The Empress used to invite Tōshi to come and watch when-ever there was an interesting function, and the Prince's wife would slip into the Palace. One day the Emperor caught a glimpse of her, and her beauty swept him off his feet. He could not seem to put her out of his mind, he confessed to Anshi. Might it be possible to arrange a brief chat? The Empress sanctioned a meeting or two, of which she pre-tended ignorance, and from those beginnings there developed an inti-macy that could hardly have been to a wife's liking. It was bad enough to have to compete with strangers, much less one's own sister. But Her Majesty, ever considerate, made an awe-inspiring and impressive effort to protect Tōshi's reputation by concealing her unhappiness.

After the Empress's death,[18] Emperor Murakami installed Tōshi in the Palace as his favorite. She was called the Jōganden Principal Hand-maid. His partiality aroused jealous pangs in the other consorts and ladies of the bedchamber, but there was nothing they could do about it. "It's just another example of Morosuke's luck," people said.

Morosuke's third daughter married Minamoto Takaakira and died after giving birth. Takaakira thought it would be bad for the children to bring in a stranger as their stepmother, so he married Morosuke's fifth daughter, Aimiya. The fourth daughter died young. The sixth married Emperor Reizei while that sovereign was still Crown Prince. Such were Morosuke's daughters.

Of Morosuke's eleven sons, five became Chancellors.[19] What amazing good fortune! Among the others were Tadagimi, the Commander of the Military Guards of the Right; Kitano no sanmi Tōnori; Tōkazu, the Treasury Minister; and Lesser Captain Takamitsu, the Tōnomine Novice. Those who became monks were the Iimuro Provisional Arch-bishop and the present Zenrinji Archbishop. Although simply called

---

constituting an ornamental adjunct to *futaba*. The absence of number makes it possible to interpret *aoi* as referring to both boys.

[17] The translation follows the text in Satō 1929, p. 264, rather than the Tōmatsu text, which has "two reigns." *Ōkagami*, p. 124.

[18] The vulgate texts read, "after the deaths of the Empress and Prince Shige-akira."

[19] Koremasa, Kanemichi, Kaneie, Tamemitsu, and Kinsue.

monks, the last two have been the greatest wonder workers of our day. There is nobody inside or outside the Court who does not trust and revere them as though they were buddhas. Kitano no sanmi's sons are Masters of Discipline Jinku and Chōgen. Tōkazu's daughter was the wife of Michikane, the Awata Lord; Kanetaka, the present Commander of the Left Gate Guards, is her son.

Many moving and admirable things happened when one member of that illustrious family, Lesser Captain Takamitsu, embraced the religious life. If I may say so, I have heard that the Emperor himself was graciously pleased to send Takamitsu a letter, which must have shaken even so firm a resolve. His Majesty wrote:

Miyako yori	Better than in the capital
Kumo no ue made	Must be your life
Yama no i no	Beside Yokawa's clear waters
Yokawa no mizu wa	Flowing from mountain springs
Sumiyokaruran.	High in the clouds.

Takamitsu's reply:

Kokonoe no	Constant my yearning
Uchi nomi tsune ni	For the ninefold Palace:
Koishikute	Life is hard
Kumo no yaedatsu	In these mountains where soar
Yama wa sumiushi.	The eightfold clouds.

At first, Takamitsu stayed at Yokawa; later, he lived at Tōnomine.

Takamitsu's renunciation of the world was a deeply moving event. At the same time, we must remember that he did not become a monk until after the deaths of Morosuke and Anshi.[20] It was much more unusual and sad that Akinobu should have taken vows when he did, throwing away all his prospects just as his parents were beginning to prosper. I wonder if Akinobu might have been planning it for a long time. When he accompanied his brothers to the Enryakuji Central Hall on the night of the Fourteenth of the First Month,[21] he went to bed instead of offering prayers. The next morning before dawn, his brothers said, "Why are you lying there like that? Get up and say some prayers."

"I'll recite them all together in a little while," he said. His answer seemed ordinary enough at the time, but they remembered it after he

[20] Anshi was in fact still alive at the time.
[21] Of 1012. He became a monk two days later.

became a monk. "He must have been thinking about it all along," they said.

Nobody had thought of Akinobu as morose or peculiar. He was an unusually high-spirited, cheerful lad.

There was an occasion on which Morosuke encountered the demon procession.[22] I have not heard what the month was, but he lowered his carriage blinds late one night near the Nijō intersection, while he was traveling south from the Palace along Ōmiya Avenue. "Unyoke the ox and get the shafts down. Get the shafts down," he shouted. The puzzled attendants lowered the shafts, and the Escorts and outriders came up to investigate. Morosuke lowered his inner blinds with meticulous care and prostrated himself, baton in hand, as though paying someone every possible mark of respect.

"Don't put the carriage on the stand," he said. "You Escorts stand to the left and right of the shafts, as close to the yoke as you can, and make your warnings loud. You attendants keep shouting too. Outriders, stay close to the carriage." He began a fervent recitation of the *Sonshō Dhāraṇī*.[23] The ox had been led out of sight behind the carriage.

After about an hour Morosuke raised the blinds. "Hitch up now and go on," he said. His attendants were completely at sea.

I suppose he kept quiet about it until much later, and then spoke of it only in confidence to close friends, but a queer tale is bound to get out.

It happened that the Emperor held a *kōshin* party while Motokata's grandson was still the presumptive heir apparent.[24] Motokata was there, of course, along with Morosuke and many others, some of whom were playing backgammon. Empress Anshi was pregnant at the time with the future Emperor Reizei; and even without the portent I am about

---

[22] *Hyakki yagyō*. Made up of various kinds of ghosts and goblins; believed to travel through the city on specified nights.

[23] A magical incantation explaining the virtues of Sonshō (Skt. Vikīrṇa), a deity regarded as a manifestation of one of the five forms of the Buddha's wisdom. He was worshipped as a protector against evil.

[24] The calendar date known as *kōshin* recurred every sixty days, when the Day of the Elder Brother of Metal (*kanoe* or *kō*), one of the ten stems (*jikkan*), coincided with that of the Monkey (*saru* or *shin*), one of the twelve branches (*jūnishi*). According to Taoist doctrine, every human body contains three malevolent worms that never leave except on *kōshin* nights, when, after waiting for the host to fall asleep, they make a quick trip to heaven bearing reports of his misdeeds, with the aim of shortening his life. In imitation of the Chinese, who tried to circumvent the parasites by staying awake all night, the Heian nobility held *kōshin* vigils, whiling away the time with refreshments, games, stories, appropriate Buddhist prayers, and the composition of Chinese and Japanese poetry.

to describe, people were wondering what would happen if the child turned out to be a boy.

"I think I'll try my hand at backgammon tonight," Morosuke said. "Let a double six come up if Anshi is carrying a boy." He shook the dice as he spoke, and didn't a double six come up the very first time? All the guests exchanged glances and showered him with congratulations, and he himself considered it a wonderful omen, but Motokata looked pale and upset. Later, when Motokata returned to the world as an angry spirit, he said, "The minute I saw the double six on that *kōshin* night, I felt as though someone had driven a nail into my breast."

I wonder if Morosuke might have been different from ordinary men. He always got the things he wished for. But he did suffer one misfortune in his youth. He told people about a dream in which he had stood before Suzakumon Gate, with his left and right feet planted on West and East Ōmiya Avenues, facing north and holding the Imperial Palace in his embrace; and a saucy lady-in-waiting ruined everything by saying, "It must have been a strain on your crotch!" So he was never able to become Regent, even though his descendants have prospered in the manner I have described. The misinterpretation of that dream was probably also to blame for the unexpected troubles that beset some of his descendants—Korechika's banishment, for instance. "Even the most auspicious dream will fail to come true if the interpretation is bad," people have said since ancient times. You who are listening to me: never tell a dream in front of a thoughtless fool! But anyway, I don't think Morosuke's descendants are in any danger of losing their preeminence.

Now here is an interesting fact. Exalted as Morosuke was, he once paid a call on Ki no Tsurayuki. It made me realize the importance of poetry. Some kind of damage had befallen the fish box Morosuke was supposed to wear on the First of the First Month.[25] While it was being repaired, he went to see Tadahira, told him what had happened, and explained that his arrival at the Palace would be delayed. Much disturbed, the Chancellor brought out a favorite box of his own and gave it to him, formally attached to a pine bough. "I hope it will bring you my luck," he said. Morosuke would surely have been able to express

---

[25] For the Congratulation of the Emperor (*chōga*), a formal expression of homage at the beginning of the new year. The fish box (*gyotai*), worn as a belt ornament with Court dress, was a small, rectangular wooden object, covered with sharkskin and decorated with six gold or silver fish on the front and one on the back.

his gratitude in verse, but he went to Tsurayuki's home to ask him to
write something on his behalf. What an honor for the poet!

Fuku kaze ni	The fish in the pond
Kōri toketaru	Where blowing breezes
Ike no uo	Have melted the ice
Chiyo made matsu no	Will shelter forever
Kage ni kakuren.	In the shadow of the pine.[26]

It is easy to understand why Tsurayuki included the poem in his collected works.

For all of Morosuke's unparalleled prosperity, there was one thing
that caused him great unhappiness and disappointment, and that was
the future Emperor Reizei's mental instability.

*("But whenever people look for precedents, don't they always cite
that Emperor's reign?" said the attendant.)*

Yes, of course. It is precisely because of Emperor Reizei that the
Fujiwara lords still flourish.[27] "If it hadn't been for him," Michinaga
once said, "we would be officials of Fourth and Fifth Rank now, serving as outriders for the great and running their errands." I have heard
that Toshikata laughed and said, "I'd hate to have to look at attendants
of Fourth and Fifth Rank with figures like yours."

So it is natural that people should turn to Emperor Reizei's reign for
public and private precedents.

The stubbornness of the evil spirits caused great concern, but the
Emperor seemed the very epitome of elegance during the Great
Thanksgiving Purification procession. People said it was because Morosuke's ghost rode with him in the Imperial litter, embracing him from
behind. Since Morosuke seemed superhuman in life, it is quite possible
that his spirit guarded the Emperor after his death.

*("If so, he ought to have chased away Lord Motokata and the Court
Monk Kanzan," the attendant interposed.)*

The visitations of those spirits must have been caused by karma from
a previous existence. Emperor Reizei was a fine person, someone who
would have made an excellent ruler. Everyone considered it a tragic
case.

Six of Morosuke's children were the offspring of a daughter of
Tsunekuni, the governor of Musashi of Junior Fifth Upper Rank:

---

[26] Fish and pine are metaphors for Morosuke and Tadahira. Lines 1 and 2
(lines 2 and 3 of the translation) allude to the New Year season.

[27] Reizei's accession, followed two years later by that of the ten-year-old En'yū,
resulted in the institutionalization of the Fujiwara regency.

Anshi, Tōshi, Koremasa, Kanemichi, Kaneie, and Tadagimi. I wonder if that lady might have inspired the proverb, "If one is to have a child, let it be a girl." Of all Morosuke's sons by various ladies, five were Chancellors and three were Regents.[28]

CHANCELLOR KOREMASA
(Kentokukō)

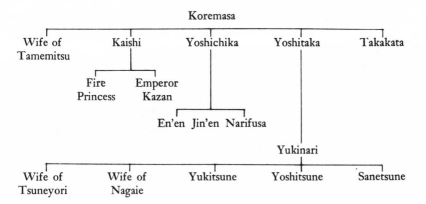

The Ichijō Regent Koremasa was Morosuke's oldest son. He compiled an excellent collection of his own poetry,[29] using the pseudonym Toyokage. He died very young, after having prospered as a minister of state for only three years—the result, people claimed, of his having disobeyed Morosuke's testament, but what else could he have done? Morosuke had left instructions for the family to restrict itself to absurdly simple funerals, and so Koremasa went ahead with the usual rites for his father, as was only proper. The best explanation I can think of is that he was too handsome and talented to live very long.

Koremasa composed splendid occasional poems. He sent these lines to a lady when he was on his way home after having served as Imperial Messenger to Kasuga:

Kureba toku	When darkness falls
Yukite kataran	I shall hasten to tell you
Au koto wa	Of my misery

[28] The Chancellors were Koremasa, Kanemichi, Kaneie, Tamemitsu, and Kinsue; the Regents, Koremasa, Kanemichi, and Kaneie.
[29] Known as *Toyokage[shū]* or *Ichijō sesshō goshū*.

Tōchi no sato no   Far distant from you
Sumiukarishi mo.   In Tōchi Village.

The lady's reply:

Au koto wa   That you should have lingered
Tōchi no sato ni   In far-off Tōchi Village
Hodo heshi mo   Means, I suppose,
Yoshino no yama to   That you found it as good
Omou nariken.   As the Yoshino Mountains.[30]

When Lesser Captain Sukenobu set out for Usa as an Imperial Messenger, Koremasa composed a farewell poem at the banquet in the mansion,[31] taking faded chrysanthemums as his topic:

Saba tōku   So you are going, they say,
Utsuroinu to ka   To distant places,
Kiku no hana   And what am I to do,
Orite miru dani   I who never see enough of you
Akanu kokoro o.   Even when you are here?[32]

As uncle of the Emperor, grandfather of the Crown Prince, and Regent, Koremasa could do exactly as he pleased. His tastes were uncommonly extravagant. When he was planning a ministerial banquet, he suddenly noticed that some of the interior walls in his main hall looked dingy, so he had his servants create a splendid white effect by covering them with Michinokuni paper. I wonder if an ordinary person would have thought of it. His house has now become the Sesonji, his family's temple. It is a moving reminder of old times to see the paper, still there, when I stop by on my way to some event like today's sermon. Everyone was sorry when Koremasa died before the age of fifty, with no chance to witness his family's later triumphs; it was just as sad, people said, as his father's untimely death.[33]

Koremasa had a good many sons and daughters. One of the latter, a Junior Consort during Emperor Reizei's reign, became the mother of

[30] There is a pun on Yoshino and *yoshi*, good.

[31] *Tono.* Presumably Koremasa's house. The vulgate texts have Tenjō[noma], Courtiers' Hall.

[32] Puns on *utsurou, kiku,* and *ori/oru* give the poem another meaning: "It saddens me even to break off a faded chrysanthemum and gaze at it—how much the worse to hear of your departure."

[33] The translation follows the vulgate texts. Satō 1929, p. 389.

Emperor Kazan and received the posthumous title of Empress.[34] The next two, who both married the Hōjūji Minister Tamemitsu, died one after the other. The ninth has entered holy orders since the death of her husband, who was Emperor Reizei's son, the President of the Board of Censors. She seems to be exceedingly pious. I understand that it was the fourth daughter who was once the wife of Tadagimi, the Commander of the Military Guards, and who later married Major Controller of the Right Munekata, the son of the Rokujō Minister of the Left Shigenobu.

The First Princess, Emperor Kazan's younger sister, died. The Second Princess became one of Emperor En'yū's consorts, after having served as Kamo Virgin during Emperor Reizei's reign. The Palace burned to the ground soon after her arrival, so people nicknamed her the Fire Princess. Later she went to the Palace two or three times and then died. The book called *Pictures of the Three Treasures*[35] was compiled for her to look at.

Koremasa had two fine sons by a daughter of Prince Yoakira—the Former and Later Lesser Captains Takakata and Yoshitaka, who both contracted smallpox during an epidemic in the second year of Ten'en [974], barely three years after their father's death. The Former Lesser Captain died in the morning and the Later Lesser Captain in the evening. We may imagine how their mother must have felt about losing two sons in one day. People say she was pitiful.

The handsome young Later Lesser Captain had been a devout Buddhist for years. Recognizing that the disease would prove fatal, he told his mother not to treat his body like an ordinary corpse. "I have set my heart on living a while longer to recite the *Lotus Sutra*," he said. "I shall be sure to come back." Then he intoned the "Expedient Devices Chapter"[36] and died.

His mother can hardly have forgotten his last wish, but I suppose she was so distraught that someone else took charge of affairs. Anyway, Yoshitaka's pillow was moved[37] and all sorts of other things were done according to custom, with the result that he was prevented from returning to life. He later appeared to his mother in a dream, chanting the words of a poem.

---

[34] The daughter was Kaishi.

[35] *Sanbō e[kotoba]*, 3 *maki*, compiled in 984 by Minamoto Tamenori. An illustrated collection of Buddhist tales, designed to serve as a religious handbook.

[36] Of the *Lotus Sutra*.

[37] In imitation of the manner in which Śākyamuni is said to have entered nirvana, the pillow of the deceased was oriented to the north, with the body facing west.

Shika bakari   When I had made
Chigirishi mono o   A pledge such as that,
Watarigawa   Ought you to have forgotten it
Kaeru hodo ni wa   In the time required to return
Wasurubeshi ya wa.   From the River of Crossings?[38]

We may imagine her remorse.

Somewhat later, a certain monk, known as Holy Teacher Gaen, encountered both brothers in a dream. Takakata, the older, was the picture of misery, but Yoshitaka seemed to be in high spirits.

"Why do you look so happy?" the Holy Teacher asked. "I think
your mother is grieving for you even more than for your brother."

Yoshitaka seemed mystified. He recited these lines:

Shigure to wa   What we here call showers
Hachisu no hana zo   Are but lotus blossoms
Chirimagau   Scattering in profusion.
Nani furusato ni   Why then should sleeves be wet
Tamoto nururan.   In my old home?

Later still, Sanesuke dreamed that he saw Yoshitaka standing under
a brilliant display of flowers. Since the two had been close friends, he
asked him, "What are you doing there? Where are you?" The reply
was a Chinese poem:

> Once we sealed our friendship
> Beneath the moon
> At P'eng lai Palace.[39]
> Now I take my pleasure
> Amid the breezes
> Of the Pure Land.

He must have been reborn in Amitābha's paradise. Even if he had
not said so in the dreams, there could have been no doubt about it.

Unlike most young noblemen, Yoshitaka avoided casual intimacies
with ladies-in-waiting at the Imperial Palace, or even desultory gossip,

---

[38] *Watarigawa*, also *sanzu no kawa*, "River of Three Crossings." A river in hell
forded by the soul on the seventh day after death. The worst sinners were required to use the most difficult crossing.

[39] A palace on P'eng lai, the legendary Chinese island of immortality in the
eastern seas; here a metaphor for the Imperial Palace.

but there was one occasion on which he did stop in at a gallery. (I am not sure just when it was.) He was such an unusual caller that the ladies were vastly intrigued. They chatted with him until he took his leave around midnight, and then sent someone to follow him, curious about his destination. As soon as he reached the other side of the north guard quarters, he began to chant the *Lotus Sutra* in a sonorous voice. He walked north along Ōmiya Avenue to the Sesonji, came to a halt under a flowering red plum tree in front of the east wing, and performed a long series of prostrations, facing the west and chanting, "May evil be eradicated. May good be created. May I be reborn in the Pure Land." All the ladies were moved when their man came back with his report.

It so happened that I was living on Ōmiya Avenue at the time. The chanting awakened me, and it sounded so holy that I got up and went outside. The sky was hazy under a bright moon. Yoshitaka was wearing smartly bloused purple trousers and a pure white cloak, with colored inner robes spilling out through his left sleeve opening.[40] His face, very white in the monlight, contrasted splendidly with his black hair. I trailed along behind, keeping him in sight, and witnessed his prostrations, which I found deeply affecting. His only attendant was a young boy.

A group of courtiers went on an excursion one day, making a great point of decking themselves out in elegant hunting robes. Yoshitaka arrived late, soberly attired in a brown tunic and lavender trousers over a set of white robes, and somehow managed to look much better than all of his companions with their elaborately contrived effects. As was his custom, he was murmuring the *Lotus Sutra* under his breath, tactfully concealing a sandalwood rosary studded with crystal beads. How rare it is for someone like him to devote a lifetime to the pursuit of enlightenment!

Although I am afraid of appearing repetitious, I do want to mention all the things I have especially admired, so let me just add this about Yoshitaka. I once saw something that made me think there would never be another man so handsome. It was when he had called at the home of Masanobu, the Ichijō Minister of the Left, after a heavy snowfall.

---

[40] The left sleeve of the cloak was split below the shoulder, with the two sections attached by a cord. In case of need, the wearer could extend his arm through the opening, which provided the freedom of a short sleeve. The design, said to have been introduced for the convenience of guards officers participating in archery contests, was imitated in the *kazami*, a ceremonial outer robe worn by young girls. For a picture of a *kazami*, see Rekisei Fukusō Bijutsu Kenkyūkai 1965, p. 70. See also Hosaka 1974, 2.511.

He broke off a snowy twig from a plum tree in front of the mansion and gave it a shake, and the white flakes scattered onto his robes, contrasting vividly with the blue lining of his reversed cloak sleeve. It was a wonderful sight.

Yoshitaka's older brother, the Former Lesser Captain, was also very handsome. As if in reaction to Yoshitaka's correctness, he tended to be somewhat rough and boisterous.

Yoshitaka's son by Minamoto Yasumitsu's daughter is Lord Yukinari, the present Gentleman-in-Waiting Major Counselor, who is famous as a calligrapher. Two of Yukinari's sons—Sanetsune, the present governor of Tajima, and Yoshitsune, the governor of Owari—are children of a daughter of Yasukiyo of Third Rank. Yukinari's principal consort has given birth to Lesser Captain Yukitsune. The calligrapher's daughter was married to Middle Counselor Nagaie, one of Michinaga's sons by Meishi, but she died. Another daughter is the wife of Tsuneyori, the present governor of Tanba. I believe there is also an oldest daughter.

Yukinari became a Head Chamberlain while he was still a junior courtier serving as vice-governor of Bingo—a most unusual turn of events.[41] Minamoto Toshikata, the previous holder of the office, was scheduled to become a senior noble, and he proposed Yukinari when Emperor Ichijō asked him to recommend a successor. "But should we pick someone who is only a junior courtier?" the Emperor asked. "Yukinari is not a man who can be ignored," Toshikata answered. "Your Majesty should not hesitate just because he is a junior courtier. He can be useful in many ways for a long time. The nation will be the worse for it if you overlook people like him. The sovereign who distinguishes between ability and mediocrity is the one whose officials work hard. In my opinion, it would be a great mistake to miss this opportunity to promote him." So it was only natural that Yukinari won the post.

It used to be customary to appoint a new Head Chamberlain on his predecessor's recommendation. A certain courtier, confident that he would be Toshikata's choice, presented himself at the Palace on the night when the appointment was to be announced. Happening to run

---

[41] Junior courtiers (*jige*) were gentlemen who were denied permission to enter the Courtiers' Hall, usually because their ranks were too low. The two Head Chamberlains (*kurōdo no tō*), on the other hand, occupied the highest seats in the hall, taking precedence over men of superior rank; and in the mid-Heian period they enjoyed substantial powers and responsibilities. Since their position was a stepping stone to a consultancy, it was one through which many prominent men passed in the early stages of their careers.

into Yukinari, he asked who he was. Yukinari gave his name. "I am here because I have been made Head Chamberlain," he explained. People say the other was too dumbfounded to move, and I can well believe it. It was a bolt from the blue.[8]

The members of that family have all made enemies in the Head Chamberlain competition. I wonder if Yukinari is any exception. Everyone knows the story about Koremasa and Middle Counselor Asahira, who were courtiers at the same time. Asahira was not Koremasa's social equal, but he had a good education and a high reputation, and the time came when he was eligible to serve as Head Chamberlain. Needless to say, Koremasa was also a potential candidate.

"It won't hurt your reputation if you fail to win the appointment," Asahira told Koremasa. "You can have it later, whenever you say the word. It will be a terrible blow to me if they pass me over this time, so please don't ask for it."

"All right, I won't," Koremasa said.

Asahira was delighted. But Koremasa must have changed his mind, because he went ahead and secured the post without a word to Asahira.[42]

"I never dreamed he would play such a trick on me," Asahira said. The two were no longer friends after that.

One day Asahira was rude to a man in Koremasa's service. "Whether he feels aggrieved or not, he has no business insulting us!" Koremasa said in a fury.

Asahira concluded that it might be wise to go to Koremasa and tell his side of the story. Now a member of the nobility, when he calls on a social superior, stays in the open until he is invited inside. Asahira's visit took place in the Sixth or Seventh Month, when the heat was almost intolerable. After sending someone to announce his arrival, he waited expectantly at the middle gate. The afternoon sun was so unbearable that he felt himself sickening. "Koremasa must intend to roast me alive," he thought. "I was a fool to come." Need I say that bitterness flooded his heart?

Twilight fell. Since there was no point in lingering, Asahira got to his feet, using his baton as a staff.[43] The wood snapped in two, which shows how upset he must have been. When he reached home, he swore to wipe out Koremasa's family. "I will never let a member of

---

[42] It appears, rather, that both men were appointed at the same time. Hosaka 1974, 2.528.

[43] The baton (*shaku*) was a narrow, slender, tapered wand about a foot long, usually made of wood. It was carried by both civil and military officials as an adjunct to the Court costume (*sokutai*).

that house lead a happy life, male or female. Anyone who sympathizes with them will feel my wrath too," he vowed. Then he died and became an angry spirit haunting Koremasa's descendants.

Yukinari is in an especially dangerous position because of his close relationship to Koremasa. Michinaga once dreamed that a man was standing behind the Shishinden, squarely in the path of anyone going to the Courtiers' Hall, with his face conveniently masked by the upper part of the door. "Who is it? Who is it?" His Lordship kept asking, until at last the other answered, "Asahira." Dream or no dream, it was a terrifying experience, but Michinaga mustered all his courage. "Why are you standing there like that?" he said. "I am waiting for Head Chamberlain Yukinari," came the reply. Then Michinaga woke up.

"Yukinari will be arriving early for the official function today.[44] I pity him if he meets Asahira's spirit," Michinaga thought. He scribbled a hasty note. "I have had a dream about you. Plead illness today. Stay in strict ritual seclusion, and don't let anything lure you to the Palace. I'll tell you about it when I see you." But Yukinari had left home before the messenger arrived.

A god or buddha must have had Yukinari's welfare at heart. Instead of following the usual route, he entered the Palace through Sakuheimon Gate and passed between the Fujitsubo and the Kōrōden in order to reach the Courtiers' Hall.

"What!" exclaimed Michinaga. "Didn't you get my letter? I dreamed Asahira was waiting for you in the Shishinden." Yukinari struck his hands together and left without a word, not even stopping to ask for details. He ordered prayers afterward, and stayed away from the Palace for a time.

Asahira's old residence is north of Sanjō and west of Nishinotōin. No member of Koremasa's family ever sets foot in it.

Although Yukinari excels at every art, his knowledge of poetry has occasionally seemed shaky. There was once talk of a poetry disputation in the Courtiers' Hall, and all the experts were formulating questions and answers and reviewing their stocks of poetic lore. Noticing that Yukinari had had nothing to say, a certain gentleman asked him, "What is your opinion of 'Flowers on the trees bloom at Naniwazu'?"[45] After earnest deliberation, Yukinari answered, "I've never heard of it." Everyone laughed and lost interest in the affair.

[44] Official functions were staged by members of the Chamberlains' Office.

[45] "*Naniwazu ni/ saku ya ko no hana/ fuyukomori/ ima wa harube to/ saku ya ko no hana.* (Flowers on the trees bloom at Naniwazu! They say, 'Now the winter yields to springtime!' Those flowers on the trees!)" The poem is discussed in the kana preface to the *Kokinshū* by Tsurayuki, who says, "The Nani-

Yukinari's resourcefulness and ingenuity show up in even the most trifling matters. When the Emperor was young, he commanded his courtiers to bring him some toys.[46] Most of the gentlemen racked their brains for elegant gold and silver baubles that might please him, but Yukinari's contribution was simply a top with a shaded purple string. "What is that funny-looking thing?" His Majesty asked. Yukinari told him its name. "Try making it go around," he suggested. "It's fun." The Emperor went to the Shishinden and gave the top a spin, and it twirled and twisted into every corner of the vast hall, capturing his fancy so completely that it became his constant companion. The other presents went into storage.

And then there was the time when the courtiers prepared folding fans for the Emperor. Most of their creations had ribs of gold lacquer, or of carved or inlaid silver, gold, aloeswood, or sandalwood; and their gorgeous paper surfaces were inscribed with unfamiliar Chinese and Japanese poems, or adorned with pictures of famous places mentioned in poetic handbooks. But Yukinari, with his usual flair, chose plain, tasteful lacquered ribs and yellow Chinese paper decorated with intriguingly faint pictures. On the front he wrote a Chinese song in elegant formal script, and on the back a few graceful cursive lines. The Emperor examined the fan many times and then treasured it carefully in his handbox. The others he forgot after a brief show of interest. Say what you will, nothing is better than a sovereign's approbation.

Yukinari was a great wit. On the day of the Kayain horse races, the drummer was Akimasa, the former Sanuki official.[47] Well-known though they were, I find it impossible to remember the names of the contestants in the individual events, but someone who should have won was declared the loser because Akimasa made a mistake in striking the drum. Still on horseback, the infuriated Escort[48] shouted over his shoulder, "He can't do anything right! To think people used to call him and Yukinari a good pair! No wonder Yukinari is the senior Major Counselor now, while he's only a stinking ex-governor of Sanuki—

---

wazu poem . . . and the Asakayama poem . . . are, as it were, the father and mother of poetry, the first lines we learn when we begin calligraphy practice." *Kokinshū*, pp. 94-95.

[46] Emperor Go-Ichijō, seventeen in 1025, had ascended the throne at the age of eight.

[47] Probably a reference to an event described in *Eiga monogatari* as having been held on the Nineteenth of the Ninth Month in 1024. McCullough and McCullough 1980, Chapter 23.

[48] Most jockeys were Escorts (*zuijin*) or Bodyguards attendants (*toneri*), presumably because they were among the best riders at Court. Hosaka 1974, 2.540.

an unemployed provincial official standing there beating a drum
wrong!" Yukinari laughed. "There was no need for him to link my
name to Akimasa's mistake," he said. "I'm very upset." Everyone considered the remark amusing, and it was widely repeated at the time.

Another of Koremasa's sons, Middle Counselor Yoshichika, was
uncle to the sovereign during Emperor Kazan's reign. (He was the
full brother of the two Lesser Captains.) He wielded great power
while Emperor Kazan was on the throne, but then the Emperor became a monk, and Yoshichika immediately made up his mind to join
him in holy orders. He followed him to Hanayama, took the vows a
day later, and lived at Iimuro with exemplary piety until his death.

Although not learned, Yoshichika was a man of excellent judgment,
well versed in Court usages. He and Controller Koreshige took charge
of the government during Emperor Kazan's reign, so you may imagine
the extent of his influence.

It was said of Emperor Kazan that he was inferior in private and
superior in public.[49] He once issued an order: "The winter Special
Festival ought not to drag on after dark.[50] Participants will kindly report during the Hour of the Dragon [7:00 a.m.-9:00 a.m.]." Just the
same, everyone thought, the ceremonies would never start before the
Hour of the Snake [9:00 a.m.-11:00 a.m.] or Horse [11:00 a.m.-
1:00 p.m.]. But the dancers found the Emperor standing there, attired
in full Court dress, when they came for their costumes. Michinaga,
who was one of them, apparently likes to tell the story, which is supposed to go something like this.

Michinaga and the rest assumed that the Emperor must want the
procession to pass along the avenues while it was still daylight. But a
very different notion had entered the mind of the sovereign, who had
always been passionately fond of horses. His Majesty issued orders for
the dancers' mounts to be led through the Kōrōden north passageway
to the Dining Room Court; and there the dancers were required to
dismount and be replaced by courtiers under the Imperial gaze. Everyone was aghast. By a stroke of luck, Middle Counselor Yoshichika arrived just as the Emperor had further dismayed the company by elect-
ing to go for a ride. The Emperor greeted him with a flushed and
guilty countenance, but it would merely have made matters worse to
halt the proceedings, so Yoshichika put on an animated air, tucked his

---

[49] I.e., his private life was undisciplined but his public activities were governed
by prudent advisers.

[50] The Kamo Special Festival, held in the Eleventh Month. See Appendix B,
(4).

jacket tail into his belt, and selected a mount. Around and around he circled in the tiny courtyard, putting the beast through all kinds of entertaining paces. The Emperor regained his color, stopped worrying, and lost himself in the spectacle.

Yoshichika's expression showed that he considered the Emperor's behavior shameful and pathetic. He was not entering into the wretched business like a sycophant. Everyone understood his feelings, which is why the story has been preserved. But there were those who said it was going too far for him to ride the horse.

There were other occurrences of the same kind. The Emperor's peculiarity manifested itself less on the surface than in his innermost nature, which made it all the more serious. That was why Toshikata once remarked, "Emperor Kazan's insanity was even harder to handle than Emperor Reizei's." Michinaga roared with laughter. "A most improper observation," he said.

People say it was Koreshige, a man of great good sense, who persuaded Yoshichika to become a monk. "You would merely invite humiliation by staying on at Court as an outsider," he told him. He was probably right, Yoshichika realized, so he stifled his misgivings and went ahead. Since his motivation was not purely religious, others wondered what kind of monk he would make, but he was a steady, deliberate gentleman, and he performed his pious duties faithfully for the rest of his life. His sons are the present Iimuro Bishop Jin'en, the Painter Holy Teacher En'en, and the Novice Middle Captain Narifusa. All three are the offspring of a daughter of Tamemasa, the governor of Bitchū. I believe Narifusa's daughter is married to Sadatsune. All of Koremasa's family seem to be short-lived for some reason.

After satisfying his desire to become a monk, Retired Emperor Kazan threw himself into the religious life with great fervor. There was no holy site that he failed to visit. At a place called Chisatonohama on the way to Kumano, he felt as though he might be coming down with an illness, so he stretched out with a beach stone for a pillow, not far from a spot where a salt-maker's fire was sending up a plume of smoke. How terribly alone he must have felt! He composed this poem:

Tabi no sora	Were the smoke from my pyre
Yowa no keburi to	To rise by night
Noborinaba	Into these travel skies,
Ama no moshiobi	Others might think it
Taku ka to ya min.	But a salt-maker's fire.

In the course of time, the former sovereign's pious exertions endowed him with impressive supernatural powers. It happened that he was at the Central Hall[51] on a night when some monks were comparing their skills. He put himself to the test with a silent prayer, and one of the company, who was already possessed by a guardian spirit,[52] found himself pulled to the front of the Imperial screen and frozen there. When His Majesty decided that enough time had passed, he let the fellow go leaping back to the colleagues who had been responsible for the original possession, and everyone realized that he had summoned a controlling spirit of his own.

It was natural that such a thing should have happened. Since the strength of a person's spiritual powers is influenced by his station in life, not even the most outstanding ascetic can hope to compete with a former Emperor. To the powers accumulated by obeying the Buddhist commandments in a previous existence, His Majesty had added the merit of renouncing the throne to become a monk, which meant that his virtue was beyond calculation. Can we suppose that so devout a man would have neglected his prayers? Angry spirits must have been to blame for his eccentricities.

As an example of his odd behavior, I might mention the figure he cut when he went to see his father, Retired Emperor Reizei, on the night of the disastrous fire at the Southern Palace. Emperor Reizei was sitting in a carriage at the Nijō-Machijiri intersection when Emperor Kazan came along on horseback, wearing a bamboo hat with an inset mirror on the back of his head, and personally asking everyone for news of his father.[53] Upon being directed to Emperor Reizei's carriage, he rode up to it, dismounted, and knelt meekly, with his arms folded and his whip dangling from his wrist. Who ever heard the like! Furthermore, the older Emperor was bawling out a sacred song inside the blinds. It was all very entertaining. Everyone burst out laughing when Akinobu quipped, "The flames are blazing up in the courtyard."[54]

---

[51] Believed by commentators to refer to a building at one of the three Kumano shrines. According to *Genpei seisuiki*, 1.64, Kazan visited Kumano three times. His name is linked especially to Nachi. Hosaka 1974, 2.555; Shimonaka 1941, 1.477.

[52] *Gohō* [*dōji*]. One of a group of spirits who manifested themselves as young boys and protected the dharma by guarding ascetics. As the author indicates below, the combined exertions of a group of monks had summoned the spirit.

[53] Instead of using an intermediary, as would have been proper for someone of his status.

[54] The speaker is presumably Takashina Akinobu, rather than Michinaga's son of the same name, who was twelve years old in 1006, the probable date of the fire.

And everyone must have noticed Retired Emperor Kazan the year he went to watch the Kamo Return. Having got himself involved in an unfortunate incident the day before,[55] he ought to have avoided public appearances, but there he sat with a crowd of cocksure monks behind his carriage, led by his favorite, the swaggering High Hat Raisei. The thing that interested me was his rosary, which consisted of a string of small oranges, interspersed with larger ones in place of the main beads.[56] It was inordinately long, and hung down outside the carriage blinds next to his trousers. Can there ever have been a spectacle to equal it?

While everybody was watching the Retired Emperor's carriage, the Imperial Police arrived at Murasakino, intent, it seemed, on arresting the pages responsible for the previous day's violence. Yukinari was still a young man at the time. He sent a runner to warn His Majesty, and the huge retinue scattered like spiders in a wind, leaving only the carriage men to escort their master as he drove off behind the carriages of the other spectators. I could not help feeling that it was both pathetic and wrong for a former sovereign to have to submit to such indignities.

The Retired Emperor was later subjected to police surveillance and other forms of harassment, all of which sadly besmirched his title. No wonder Toshikata said what he did! Just the same, though, his poems are great favorites because of their elegance. It is hard to believe anyone in his condition could have written, "I should like to go elsewhere to view the moon."[57] What a pity! He once gave Retired Emperor Reizei a bamboo shoot with a poem attached:

He alludes not only to the conflagration at the Southern Palace but also to the fact that the Retired Emperor's song, a *kagurauta* (sacred music song), suggests a Court *kagura* performance. There were bonfires in the courtyard on such occasions, and the first song presented was entitled "Niwabi" (Courtyard Fires). McCullough and McCullough 1980, s.n. 51.

[55] For reasons that apparently never entered the historical record, a carriage occupied by Kintō and Tadanobu had been subjected to "disorderly conduct" on the part of a large contingent of Kazan's underlings. *Shōyūki*, 2.32, Sixteenth Day, Fourth Month, Chōtoku 3 (997); Hosaka 1974, 2.563.

[56] Orange translates *tachibana*, which seems to have been a general term for any citrus tree that produced edible fruit. Koga 1971, p. 202, identifies the celebrated *tachibana* tree in front of the Shishinden as a cultivated variety of the bitter orange (*Citrus aurantium var. tachibana Makino*), prized not for its pear-shaped, bitter fruit, but for its aromatic rind and fragrant white blossoms.

[57] "*Kokoromi ni/ hoka no tsuki o mo/ mite shi ga na/ waga yado kara no/ aware naru ka to.* (Just as a test, I should like to go elsewhere to view the moon. Might this feeling of sadness be linked to my home?)"

Yo no naka ni	The bamboo shoot
Furu kai mo naki	Living to no avail
Take no ko wa	Presents to you
Waga hen toshi o	The years
Tatematsuru nari.	It has yet in store.[58]

The reply:

Toshi henuru	Were the bamboo required
Take no yowai o	To give back the years
Kaeshite mo	Through which it has passed,
Kono yo o nagaku	Still would it seek long life
Nasan to zo omou.	For the bamboo shoot.

The poems appear in Retired Emperor Kazan's collection, with the touching notation, "A gracious reply." There is something very affecting about his confused desire to wish his father a long life.

We can tell from the construction of his palace that the former sovereign was a remarkably ingenious man.[9] He had hit on the clever notion of equipping his carriage house with a slanting floor and a pair of large doors; and thus his men had only to open the doors, in case of emergency, for a fully equipped vehicle to come clattering out by itself.

His Majesty's personal belongings were indescribably beautiful. I once saw an inkstone box, presented by him for sutra recitations when the Sixth Prince lost consciousness, on which the artisan had depicted Peng lai Mountain and long-legged and long-armed men, superimposed in gold lacquer on a seashore design.[59] It was a truly splendid example of lacquer technique, use of gold, and edge ornamentation.

When he laid out his garden, he gave orders for the cherry trees to be planted beyond the middle gate. "Cherry blossoms are lovely," he said, "but the trees have graceless branches and ugly trunks. The crown is the only part worth looking at." Everyone was impressed by his resourcefulness. He also sowed wild pink seeds on top of his earthen

---

[58] Since the bamboo lives a long time, this is a wish for long life. The bamboo shoot is of course Emperor Kazan.

[59] The subject was probably suggested by the famous Rough Seas Partition (*araumi no sōji*) at the Imperial Palace. The picture on the partition displayed men with grotesquely elongated limbs, fishing on a rocky, wave-lashed shore, an allusion to a Chinese legend preserved in the *Shan hai ching*. For an illustration, see Hosaka 1974, 2.570.

walls, and presently a glorious burst of bloom encircled the palace, just as though someone had hung out Chinese brocades.

His Majesty was once invited by Michinaga to witness some horse races at the minister's house. It was only to have been expected that he would dress for the occasion, but his carriage was also incomparable. Even his shoes fascinated the spectators. I have heard that the man who fell heir to them took them around for others to admire.

His paintings were interesting, too. In representing the wheels of a speeding carriage, he used faint swirls of India ink, to which he added a few dark touches to suggest the size, the spokes, and so forth. That was the ideal technique. How can anyone tell how black the wheels are when a carriage is flying along? He once drew a picture of a man with bamboo-shoot bark on his fingers, pulling down his lower eyelids at a terrified, red-faced child. He also painted scenes in rich and poor houses. In every case, the beholder could only think in amazement, "That is exactly how it must have looked." Some of you have probably seen his work.

CHANCELLOR KANEMICHI
(Chūgikō)

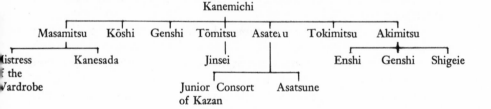

Kanemichi, Morosuke's second son, was called the Horikawa Regent. He served as Regent for six years.[10] I wonder if the lack of information about his mother might mean that she was the same lady as the one who gave birth to Koremasa.[11]

When Kanemichi performed the Putting On of the Trousers,[60] he went to pay his respects to his grandfather, Tadahira. Tadahira asked Tsurayuki to compose a poem to accompany the remembrance he gave the boy:

[60] *Hakamagi*, a *rite de passage* for noble children of both sexes. It was usually celebrated when the child was about two years old, but was sometimes delayed until he was five or six. McCullough and McCullough 1980, s.n. 35.

Koto ni idete   That it should wordlessly transmit
Kokoro no uchi ni   A divine message
Shiraruru wa   Straight to the heart—
Kami no sujinawa   Surely it is because
Nukeru narikeri.   A god has touched the strings.

The gift must have been a koto.[61]

How well I remember Kanemichi's fresh, radiant beauty! While he was living at the Horikawa Mansion, it happened that the plum tree beside the main hall was a brilliant mass of red on the day of the Special Reception.[62] As he was leaving for the Palace after the affair, he went and stood under the blossoms, broke off a spray to decorate his cap, and struck a brief, splendid dance pose.

Kanemichi's people used to provide a freshly killed pheasant to go with his bedtime wine. It would have been hard to capture a live bird at just the right moment, so they always brought one into the house early in the evening. During Naritō's first night there, while he still held Sixth Rank, he heard some curious thumps inside a shoe chest near his seat. A stealthy nudge to the lid in the dim light revealed a cock pheasant crouching inside. So the stories were true! He was scandalized. As soon as the household had gone to bed, he quietly removed the bird from the chest, put it in his bosom, and sent it clucking off among the Reizeiin hills.[63]

"It gave me great satisfaction," he said later. "I also felt very lucky."[64]

All the nobility kill living things, but nobody profits from that kind of behavior.

Kanemichi had a daughter, Kōshi, whose mother was a daughter of Prince Motohira, the Minister of Ceremonial. Kōshi entered the Imperial Palace during Emperor En'yū's reign, and came to be known as the Horikawa Empress. For some reason, Kanemichi chose not to treat her with parental affection when she was young; and so, being a bright girl, she was apparently very diligent about making pilgrimages

---

[61] There is a pun on *koto* (an instrument traditionally associated with oracular utterances) and words. On the one hand, the poet hints at the antiquity and value of the instrument, asserting that it was once played by a god; on another level, he is saying, "What you must realize, without my telling you, is that you are a god's descendant [and thus destined for a glorious future]."

[62] *Rinji* [*no*] *kyaku, rinjikaku,* a regental banquet for New Year callers of Third or higher rank, as distinguished from the *daikyō* for invited guests.

[63] Probably artificial hills in the estate's extensive gardens. The Reizeiin adjoined the Horikawa Mansion on the northwest.

[64] To have had an opportunity to acquire merit by releasing a living thing.

and offering prayers.[65] (I suppose the people who took care of her encouraged her.) My wife once saw her toiling up the Inari Hill. She was gazing toward the top with her veil pushed aside, and there was something uncommonly distinguished about her appearance—the shape of her waist where the trousers began, for instance.

As a result, perhaps, of such pious exertions, her father placed her in the Palace when she grew up, thus making it possible for her to occupy a most exalted position. Since he possessed no older daughter, he could not very well refuse to let her be Empress simply because she had failed to take his fancy.

Kanemichi's other daughter, Genshi, became a Principal Handmaid. She is still alive. I think people say she is married to the governor of Sanuki, who is one of the sons of the Rokujō Minister of the Left Shigenobu.

Kanemichi's oldest son, Akimitsu, became Minister of the Right on the Twenty-First of the Seventh Month in the second year of Chōtoku [996]. He died at the age of seventy-eight or so about five years ago. He is known as the Evil Spirit Minister of the Left, an unpleasant nickname. I suppose there must be some justification for it.[66]

Akimitsu married Emperor Murakami's fifth daughter, whose mother was the Hirohata Lady of the Bedchamber. She bore him a son and two daughters. The son, Lesser Captain Shigeie, was a fine, popular young man. He mingled in society for a while and then entered religion and died, possibly because he was not long for this world. One of the daughters, Genshi, is the lady who was called the Shōkyōden Consort during Emperor Ichijō's reign. She ended by marrying Consultant Yorisada, a son of Prince Tamehira, the Minister of Ceremonial, and apparently gave birth to a good many children. I am sure you are all well acquainted with the things that happened in those days.[67] She has become a nun since Yorisada's death.

[65] To win his love. An affair with the poet Hon'in no jijū seems to have led Kanemichi to neglect Kōshi's mother, Princess Shōshi, and, consequently, to lose interest in Kōshi herself, whom the Princess was probably rearing in her own home. It is also possible that Kanemichi preferred another consort, Prince Aria-kira's daughter, and her child, Asateru. (It should be noted, however, that sources disagree as to the mothers of Kanemichi's three principal children, Kōshi, Asa-teru, and Akimitsu. According to *Sonpi bunmyaku*, 1.55, Kōshi and Asateru were uterine siblings.) Hosaka 1974, 2.588, 591-592; McCullough and McCullough 1980, s.n. 24.

[66] Akimitsu was believed to have become an angry spirit to avenge Enshi's humiliation at the hands of Michinaga's daughter, described below.

[67] Genshi's bizarre false pregnancy during Emperor Ichijō's lifetime, and her later quarrels with her father over Yorisada, are discussed at some length in *Eiga monogatari*. See McCullough and McCullough 1980, Chapters 5 and 11.

The other daughter, Enshi, married Koichijōin while he was still Minister of Ceremonial. Akimitsu was overjoyed when his son-in-law was named heir apparent, but the Prince settled down with Meishi's daughter Kanshi after assuming his palace name. Often as his thoughts strayed to Enshi, it was in thought alone that he visited her; and she and Akimitsu grieved themselves to death. (They may have had some physical ailments too.) (12) Koichijōin has a number of children by her.

Kanemichi's second son, Asateru, was Empress Kōshi's half-brother. His mother was a daughter of Prince Ariakira, the War Minister. He was known as the Kan'in Major Captain. He was already a Middle Counselor while his older brother Akimitsu was still a Consultant,[68] which was a notable accomplishment; and in those days he was very popular and cut a great figure in society. He was the first one to think of having crystal notches on quiver arrows. Once he was accompanying the Emperor on a visit somewhere, and all his arrows glittered magnificently in the morning sunlight. Everyone is used to crystal notches nowadays, so nobody considers them remarkable.

After his father's death, this dashing gentleman lost his popularity, struggled against illness, and resigned as Major Captain. It was a great pity. Thereafter he was simply called the Inspector Major Counselor. He composed excellent poetry. He died in his forty-fifth year.

Asateru's wife was Prince Shigeakira's second daughter. (Her mother was the Jōganden Principal Handmaid Tōshi.) She gave birth to three sons, and to a beautiful daughter who entered the Palace during Emperor Kazan's reign. The Emperor seemed madly in love with the girl for about a month, but then something must have happened, because they stopped visiting one another, and things finally got so bad that they were not even exchanging notes. She went home in despair after another month or two. Was ever anything stranger? I wonder how it made her father and brothers feel to witness the misery of so charming a creature.

The oldest of Asateru's three sons by Prince Shigehira's daughter is the present Fujiwara Middle Counselor Asatsune. He seems to be very well thought of. The second and third sons—the Director of the Imperial Stables and the Lesser Captain—both took religious vows and died.[69] The Director's son is now the Master of the Right Capital Office. (13)

[68] Asateru became a Consultant in 974 and a Provisional Middle Counselor in the First Month of 975; Akimitsu was named Consultant in the Eleventh Month of 975 and Provisional Middle Counselor on the Twenty-Fourth of the Fourth Month in 977, the date on which Asateru was promoted to Provisional Major Counselor.

[69] The identities of the sons are uncertain. Hosaka 1974, 2.605. According to

Another of Kanemichi's sons, Treasury Minister Masamitsu, had a daughter by Minamoto Takaakira's second daughter—a lady who was once Mistress of the Wardrobe to Grand Empress Kenshi, and who is now married to Kinnobu, the Commander of the Military Guards of the Left. Masamitsu was also the father of a son called Kanesada, a former official in the Kōzuke provincial administration.

I almost forgot to mention two more of Kanemichi's sons—Tokimitsu, whom people used to call the North-Facing Middle Counselor or something of the sort, and Tōmitsu, the Master of the Right Capital Office. Tōmitsu's son is Master of Discipline Jinsei, the Ninnaji abbot. I think that must be all there is to say about Kanemichi's descendants.

Kanemichi had a harsh nature. It was cruel of him to strip Kaneie of his office and rank with no justification at all—Kaneie, who was such a wonderful man that his descendants are still enjoying boundless success today. The gods must have been furious! When Kaneie presented a long poem of distress to the reigning sovereign, Emperor En'yū, the reply was "Rice boats,"[70] so his unhappiness was short-lived.[14]

CHANCELLOR TAMEMITSU
(Kōtokukō)

Tamemitsu, Morosuke's ninth son, was a minister of state for seven years. He is called the Hōjūji Minister. He was the father of seven sons and five daughters. Two of the daughters were children of War Minister Sukemasa's younger sister, and the mother of the other three was Koremasa's daughter. The mothers of the sons were all different.

One of the daughters, Kishi, was Emperor Kazan's favorite consort until she died. Another, Yoshichika's wife, is also dead.

Sonpi bunmyaku, 1.52, the Director's son, mentioned in the following sentence, was named Morotsune.

[70] The Emperor promises to do what he can, warning that it will take time. His allusion is to *Kokinshu* 1092, an old Eastern song in which a girl puts off a suitor whom she intends to accept eventually: "*Mogamigawa/ noboreba kudaru/ inafune no/ ina ni wa arazu/ kono tsuki bakari.* (My answer is not 'No' ['No' is *ina*, like *inafune*, 'rice boats,' plying up and down the Mogami River]—just for this month. . . .)" Kamemichi deprived Kaneie of the highly prestigious office of Major Captain on the Eleventh of the Tenth Month in the second year of Jōgen (977). Kaneie did, however, retain his principal office, a major counselorship; and, contrary to the author's assertion, his rank. The enmity between the brothers, and the circumstances under which the demotion occurred, are described later in the vulgate texts. Appendix B, (14); Appendix D; *Nihon kiryaku*, 2.134-135; *Kugyō bunin*, 1.216.

The oldest son was Commander of the Left Gate Guards Sanenobu. He came to a shocking end, destroyed by hatred. Since it is common enough for gentlemen to suffer disappointment in the race for preferment, I suppose it was Sanenobu's karma that made his reaction so violent. He and his younger brother Tadanobu were both Consultants, but he must have been the less able and popular of the two, because he made it a point to see Tadanobu when he decided to try for a vacant middle counselorship. "Don't ask to be made Middle Counselor. I intend to apply," he said. "How could I go ahead of you?" Tadanobu answered. "I would never suggest such a thing, especially now that you have spoken to me about it."

Satisfied and reassured, Sanenobu may have felt it unnecessary to press his case, but in the meantime Michinaga said to Tadanobu, "Don't you want to ask for the Middle Counselor post?" Tadanobu's reply was half-hearted. "Sanenobu is applying, so I don't think I should." "Sanenobu won't be appointed. It will go to someone else if you don't take it." "It won't do any good for me to stand aside if Sanenobu isn't going to get it. I'd like to have it," Tadanobu said. Michinaga saw no reason to consider anyone else, and so Tadanobu became a Middle Counselor.

"Why did Tadanobu look me in the face and swear not to apply?" Sanenobu asked himself. "Why did he lie to me?" Burning with resentment, he took to his bed on the morning after the appointments ceremony, and stayed there, face down, clenching his fists and repeating, "Tadanobu and Michinaga tricked me." Not a morsel passed his lips. Presently he fell ill, and on the seventh day he died, with his fingers piercing the backs of his hands.

Sanenobu used to swill down huge amounts of wine. They say he vomited in his seat at the Regent's Special Reception one year, too drunk to stand up, and dirtied a Chinese screen painted by the famous Hirotaka. Tadanobu, the one who became a Middle Counselor, was a fine man with an excellent reputation.

Another of Tamemitsu's sons, Provisional Middle Captain Michinobu, was a good poet, admired for his refined tastes. He is dead now. Among the other sons are Commander of the Left Gate Guards Kinnobu, the Hōjūji Bishop, and Holy Teacher Yoshimitsu.

Oh, yes, Tamemitsu's third, fourth, and fifth daughters were the offspring of a daughter of Koremasa. The third daughter, Lady Takatsukasa, has become a nun. The fourth died after bearing a child to Michinaga in the days before he entered religion, and the fifth is in the service of the present Grand Empress.

So much for the family. I should add that Tamemitsu made the

Hōjūji into an imposing, magnificent temple. It was an impressive achievement for someone who was never a Regent.

Tamemitsu was an important figure, but his descendants have not amounted to much.

CHANCELLOR KINSUE
(Jingikō)

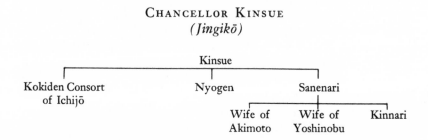

Kinsue, the present Kan'in Minister of State, is Morosuke's eleventh son. His mother was an Imperial Princess. His principal wife, the daughter of an Imperial Prince, became the mother of a daughter and two sons. The daughter, who is still living, was the Kokiden Consort during Emperor Ichijō's reign. One of the sons, the Samādhi Bishop Nyogen, has died; the other is Lord Sanenari, the present Commander of the Gate Guards of the Right. Sanenari has two daughters and a son by a daughter of Nobumasa, the governor of Harima. The older daughter is married to Yoshinobu, the present Provisional Master of the Empress's Household, and the younger to Middle Captain Akimoto, the son of Minamoto Toshikata, the Minister of Popular Affairs. The son has been adopted by his grandfather, Chancellor Kinsue, who has named him Kinnari. He is a Head Chamberlain and a great favorite at Court. Such are the members of Kinsue's family. None of his descendants has become an Emperor or Empress.

Kinsue's mother, the Fourth Princess, was the beloved daughter of Emperor Daigo. Controller Kintada composed this poem for one of her folding screens when she performed the Putting On of the Train:[71]

Yukiyarade
Yamaji kurashitsu
Hototogisu
Ima hitokoe no
Kikamahoshisa ni.

My journey interrupted,
I have spent the day
On this mountain path,
Hoping to hear again
The cuckoo's song.

[71] *Mogi*, a *rite de passage* for well-born girls, symbolizing the attainment of adulthood. McCullough and McCullough 1980, s.n. 56.

Many poems were composed for the occasion by Tsurayuki and other professionals, but everyone pronounced those lines a splendid achievement for someone like Kintada.[72]

The Fourth Princess was the younger sister of Emperors Suzaku and Murakami. While she was being carefully reared in the Imperial Palace, Morosuke persuaded one of her attendants to smuggle him into her rooms. The gossips were critical and Emperor Murakami was annoyed, but Morosuke escaped Imperial censure because of the high esteem in which the sovereign held him. One day, before people had begun to whisper about the affair or the Emperor had learned of it, a torrential rain began to pour down, accompanied by peals of thunder and flashes of lightning. The Princess was in the Palace, so His Majesty said, "The gentlemen in the Courtiers' Hall will please call on the Fourth Princess. She must be frightened." Everybody went except Saneyori, who muttered, "I'm not going. It's too dirty for me." The Emperor probably put two and two together later.

As I need hardly tell you, Morosuke showered the Princess with attentions after he moved her from the Palace to his mansion. Presently Lord Kinsue was conceived, and she began to feel miserable. "I shall never live through it," she kept saying to her husband. "Wait and see."

"I don't think I could last an instant if you were to die," he told her. "If I did, I would certainly become a monk. I would never take another wife. See for yourself when your spirit flits through the air."

The Princess must have felt skeptical, because she secretly filled a pair of little Chinese chests with caps and white silk socks for him, all sewn with her own hands. In the end she did die, so Kinsue's birthday is the anniversary of his mother's death. Morosuke wept whenever he saw the caps and socks, and he lived alone for the rest of his life.

Since Empress Anshi, Kinsue's older sister, was a lady with a strong sense of family, I need not say that she reared the motherless child. The boy stayed in the Palace and was always with the Emperor, who made a great fuss over him. He was treated exactly like the Imperial Princes; the only mark of distinction was that his dining table was an inch lower than theirs.

Kinsue's presence in the Palace excited criticism. Not even Imperial Princes lived there as children in the old days. Nevertheless, that was where he grew up, so he could not have been expected to act like an ordinary courtier. Then, too, he was young, and he unconsciously behaved as though among equals when he joined the Princes in their amusements. "Does Kinsue think he is just the same as we are? I wish he wouldn't," the future Emperor En'yū once sighed.

[72] Kintada's poetry was not considered good enough for inclusion in *Kokinshū*.

Now that Kinsue is an old man, he dotes on his grandson, Middle Captain Kinnari, refusing to go to the Palace unless he can take him along in his carriage. When official business detains Kinnari, Kinsue stands and waits for him at the Yubadono with his outriders shouting. Once an onlooker said to him, "Why are you standing there like that?" "I'm waiting for Inu,"[73] he answered.

Kinsue rode in the Crown Prince's carriage when the Muryōjuin Golden Hall was dedicated. All through the journey, he kept repeating, "Be sure to remember Kinnari." "It was touching, but a bit comical," His Highness said later. My niece's daughter, who works for the nurse Nakatsukasa, told me about it when she came to visit us.

People say Middle Captain Akimoto has a young son. On the Fiftieth Day, they took the baby to Shijō,[74] where Kinsue fed him the rice cakes. The child began to cry while his uncle,[75] Sanenari, was holding him.

"You don't usually fret. What's the matter?" asked Sanenari, jumping up and sitting down again in an effort to pacify him.

"It's natural for a baby to cry. You were the same way," Kinsue said.

All the important people who had come for the ceremony smiled. They say Lesser Captain Takakuni still laughs about it. I suppose we must call Kinsue old-fashioned.

Kinsue's childhood name was Miyaogimi.

[73] Inu (Dog) was presumably Kinnari's childhood name. Compare Inumiya, the name given one of the characters in *Utsubo monogatari*, and Inuki, one of young Murasaki's companions in *The Tale of Genji*. It has been suggested that the purpose of such names was to shield children from the attention of malignant forces, which might otherwise have claimed their lives. Hosaka 1974, 2.658.

[74] From the mother's home, Sanenari's house. The father, Akimoto, lived in the Shijō area. The Fiftieth Day (*ika*) was a celebration held on or about the fiftieth day after a birth. Using chopsticks, a male member of the family, usually the father or maternal grandfather, fed the baby from an assortment of fifty special rice cakes (*ika no mochii*), probably as a formal indication that its diet would thenceforth include solid food. The event, which took place at night, was accompanied by an elaborate banquet, at which the guests composed poems predicting a long life for the child.

[75] Corrected to grandfather in the vulgate texts.

CHAPTER FOUR

Chancellor Kaneie

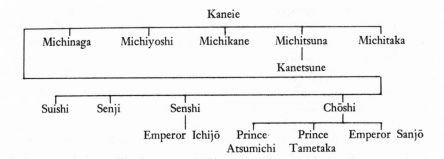

Kaneie, the Higashisanjō Minister of State, was Morosuke's third son. He had the same mother as Koremasa. He was the uncle of Emperors Reizei and En'yū, the grandfather of Emperors Ichijō and Sanjō, and the father of the Higashisanjō Imperial Lady and of Posthumous Empress Chōshi. He was a senior noble for twenty years, a minister of state for twelve, a Regent for five, and a Chancellor for two. The period of glory during which he governed the state lasted for five years. He entered holy orders, so he has no posthumous name.

Needless to say, Kaneie rode in a carriage as far as Sakuheimon Gate whenever he went to the Palace.[1] Even though it is no distance from the gate to the Seiryōden, he used to enter with his collar unfastened. That might not have been so bad, but he peeled off all his outer robes during the wrestling matches and sat there in front of the Emperor and the Crown Prince with nothing on but a shift.[2] I have never heard of anything so disrespectful! In his last years, after the death of his principal wife, he lived a bachelor's life at the Higashisanjō Mansion, where the west wing exactly duplicated the Seiryōden, furnishings and all. People called him presumptuous, and blamed arrogance for the brevity of his rule. I wonder if his karma prohibited him from acting like an Emperor. After all, he was only a subject.

[1] Special permission was required to ride in a carriage as far as the Middle Enclosure of the Greater Imperial Palace.

[2] Shift translates *asetori* (sweat absorber). For the annual wrestling matches (*sumai no sechi*), which took place in the Seventh Month, during the hottest season of the year, see McCullough and McCullough 1980, s.n. 33.

They tell me there were wonderful dream interpreters and shamanesses in those days. While the Horikawa Regent Kanemichi was at the peak of his power, Kaneie suffered the pain of being relieved of his official positions.[3] Meanwhile a certain person had a dream in which, to his amazement, swarms of arrows went speeding eastward from the Horikawa Mansion to land on the Higashisanjō Mansion. Coming from a quarter for which Kaneie had no liking, it seemed an ominous visitation, so the man reported it to Kaneie, who anxiously consulted a dream interpreter. "The dream was excellent," the interpreter said. "It shows that the government of the realm will pass to your house, and that all the people who now wait on Kanemichi will soon be coming to you." What he predicted was precisely what happened.

A remarkable shamaness was also active at the time, someone who was said to be a medium for the young Kamo deity.[4] People called her the reclining shamaness because she always spoke from a prone position. Kaneie called her into his mansion one day, asked some questions, and found the answers perfect. Since her statements about the present and past were accurate, he saw no reason to distrust her predictions—and, sure enough, first one and then another came true. On subsequent occasions, he received her in formal robes and cap, pillowing her head on his knees while he asked his questions; and not one of her prophecies proved to be wrong. Since she was allowed such close access to his person, she was more like a principal lady-in-waiting than an insignificant commoner.

People tried to persuade Kaneie to stay away from the Hokoin's eerie atmosphere, but he liked the house too well to pay any attention, and in no time he was dead. It was amusing, he said, to send one of his Escorts to Awataguchi, mounted on a horse from the stables, and to be able to pick out the man's figure far in the distance. He also used to leave his shutters raised in order to enjoy the view on moonlit nights. One night an invisible hand slammed all the shutters into position, throwing the attendants into great turmoil. Kaneie calmly drew the sword next to his pillow. "Who presumes to close the shutters I left up so I could look at the moon?" he demanded. "I won't tolerate this. You'll regret it if you don't raise them." And at once all the shutters went back up.

There were many such disturbing incidents. I suppose that may explain why the house was eventually made into a temple instead of being left to one of the sons.

[3] Kaneie appears to have lost only one office. See Appendix B, (14).

[4] *Kamo no wakamiya.* Thought to refer to a subsidiary shrine at the upper sanctuary. Hosaka 1974, 3.20.

Kaneie had four daughters and five sons. Two of the girls and three of the boys were the children of Tokihime, a daughter of Fujiwara Nakamasa, the governor of Settsu: Posthumous Empress Chōshi (the mother of Emperor Sanjō), the Imperial Lady Senshi, and the three ministers of state, Michitaka, Michikane, and Michinaga.

When Tokihime, the mother, was still a girl, something made her go out to Nijō Avenue to try her hand at evening divination.[5] It is hard to say what she may have had in mind. Anyway, a solitary white-haired old woman stopped and spoke to her in an offhand voice before going on her way. "What are you doing? Trying a little evening divination? All your wishes will be granted, and your prosperity will be greater and longer than this avenue." She was probably not human. My guess would be that she was delivering a supernatural message.

One of Kaneie's daughters was the person known as Senji in Grand Empress Senshi's day. Another was Suishi (the child of the Lady in the Wing Chamber), a pretty girl whom her doting father sent to live in the Imperial Palace as a Principal Handmaid when she was eleven years old. Even at that age, Suishi had a magnificent head of silky hair. It seemed natural to Kaneie to make her the Crown Prince's bed partner on the night of the Prince's capping ceremony;[6] and the Prince, who later became Emperor Sanjō, showed no displeasure with the arrangement.

The Crown Prince once dropped in at Suishi's apartments on a torrid summer day. He picked up a piece of ice from a dish and handed it to her. "Hold this a while. If you love me, don't put it down until I tell you to," he said. She held it until her skin turned blue. "I expected her to let go of it after a minute or two," the Prince said later. "I passed the point of being impressed. It made me feel queasy."

Presently there were shocked reports that Suishi was having an affair with the Consultant Minamoto Yorisada. She went off home, and the Crown Prince asked Michinaga to see whether there was any truth to certain rumors he had heard, which made it seem that she might be pregnant. "I'll go and find out," Michinaga answered. "Then I'll be back."

Startled by the unexpected visit, Suishi drew her curtain-stand closer, but Michinaga pushed it aside. She was looking even lovelier than usual,

[5] *Yūke*, a type of crossroads divination. One apparently stood at a crossroads in the evening, chanted a special poem three times, scattered rice, twanged a comb three times, and then asked a question of the first passerby, whose answer would furnish a clue to one's future. Hosaka 1974, 3.27.

[6] Suishi did not become Principal Handmaid until 987, a year after the Prince's capping. She did, however, join his harem in 989.

her showy beauty enhanced by cosmetics. "When I went to the Crown Prince's palace, he told me about some stories he had heard," Michinaga said. "I have come to see for myself, because it will be very sad for you if he believes false tales." He opened her robes and pinched one of her breasts—and didn't he get a stream of milk in the face? He left without a word.

Back at the Crown Prince's palace, Michinaga confirmed the stories and told the Prince what he had done. His Highness felt a twinge of pity—I suppose because he and Suishi had been together a long time and he had once loved her. According to someone who saw it all, Suishi shed floods of tears after Michinaga's departure, even though she knew it was her own fault.

Yorisada used to visit Suishi when she was in attendance on the Crown Prince. The talk spread until it reached the Prince's ears. "I toyed with the idea of having my Guards eject him, but gave it up when I thought of how Kaneie would grieve in the other world," His Highness said.

Yorisada's transgression prevented him from serving as a courtier during Emperor Sanjō's reign. He was a senior noble who was denied permission to enter the Courtiers' Hall. He became a courtier in the present reign, and died after having held the office of Superintendent of the Imperial Police.

Kaneie's oldest daughter, Chōshi, was the child of another lady.[7] As Emperor Reizei's consort, she gave birth to Emperor Sanjō, Prince Tametaka, and Prince Atsumichi. She was posthumously honored with the title of Empress when Emperor Sanjō ascended the throne.

Their grandfather Kaneie doted on the three Princes. Whenever there was some small social disturbance, or a thunderstorm or an earthquake, he would rush off to the Crown Prince's apartments. "You go to the Emperor. I'll stay here," he would tell the uncles and other gentlemen. He gave the Prince the famous belt named Cloud Shape,[8] and I am told that he personally used the tip of his dagger to inscribe "For the Crown Prince" on the back of the clasp. They say Princess Teishi of First Rank owns it now.

The Crown Prince's younger brothers were a little flighty. Prince Atsumichi and Izumi Shikibu shared a carriage in a most interesting way during the Kamo Return one year: the front blind was cut down the middle so it could be raised on the Prince's side and lowered on the lady's. Izumi's sleeves trailed out through the apertures, and her red

---

[7] Tokihime, as the author has stated above.

[8] Said to have been an heirloom in the regental house. Tachibana 1974, p. 257, n. 26.

trousers hung to the ground, emblazoned with wide red ritual seclusion signs. Everyone seemed to be looking at the two of them instead of watching the procession.

When Prince Tametaka was a long-haired little boy, the radiance of his beauty was beyond description. His capping ceremony made a great change for the worse.

Disapproving though they were of the Princes' frivolity, Kaneie's sons took great care of their nephews on important occasions. During Emperor Ichijō's reign, it happened that Prince Atsumichi arrived at a Palace Chinese poetry party in splendid style, accompanied by a throng of outriders and other distinguished gentlemen. While he was in the Imperial presence, his tight inner boots gave him so much pain that he appealed in desperation to Michinaga, who took him to the Demon Room, removed the boots, and restored his spirits.[9]

Chōshi's uterine sister, Senshi, was called the Umetsubo Consort during Emperor En'yū's reign. She gave birth to the Emperor's first son, who became Crown Prince at the age of five, ascended the throne at seven, and raised her to Imperial rank, with the title of Empress, on the Fifth of the Seventh Month in the second year of Kanna [986].[15]

Kaneie's oldest son, Michitaka, was Senshi's full brother. He became Regent while serving as Palace Minister.

The second son, Michitsuna, was the offspring of a daughter of Tomoyasu, the governor of Mutsu. He rose to the office of Major Counselor, with the added title of Major Captain of the Right. His mother, an accomplished poet, set down an account of the things that happened while Kaneie was visiting her, together with some poems from the same period. She named the work *Gossamer Journal*,[10] and allowed it to be made public. She once took her time about opening the gate when Kaneie came. After he had sent in a number of notes, she wrote this:

Nagekitsutsu	Do you know, I wonder,
Hitori nuru yo no	How long it seems
Akuru ma wa	Before night opens into day
Ika ni hisashiki	When one lies alone,
Mono to ka wa shiru.	Locked in misery.[11]

[9] Inner boots (*shitauzu*) were white silk substitutes for stockings, fastened at the top with a drawstring.

[10] *Kagerō no niki*, also *Kagerō nikki*. Translated by Edward Seidensticker as *The Gossamer Years*. For the poetic exchange recorded below, see Seidensticker 1964, p. 38.

[11] The poem puns on *akuru*, a form of *aku* (open, end). The *Kagerō nikki* passage indicates that Kaneie had not arrived until almost dawn.

Impressed by her cleverness, he replied:

Ge ni ya ge ni	True, true—
Fuyu no yo naranu	But though a wooden gate
Maki no to mo	Is not a winter night,
Osoku akuru wa	It too causes grief
Kurushikarikeri.	When it is slow to open.

That lady's son, Michitsuna, later became Mentor to the Crown Prince and was called His Lordship the Mentor. His health deteriorated, obliging him to resign both that office and his major captaincy.

Michitsuna lived with a sister of Michinaga's principal wife—the lady who gave birth to Consultant Middle Captain Kanetsune. I remember hearing that he died at the age of sixty-six.

Kaneie's third son was the Awata Lord Michikane.

The fourth son, by a different lady, was Michiyoshi, a Junior Assistant Minister in the Civil Affairs Ministry. People say he was so feeble-minded that he never appeared at Court to the day of his death.

The fifth son is Michinaga, our present Buddhist Novice.

Now I am going to tell you about Senshi's brothers, the three sons of Kaneie's consort Tokihime. Since Mototsune's sons were called the three Hiras,[12] one wonders if Kaneie's might have been called the three Michis, but I have never heard the expression. *(He smiled.)*

PALACE MINISTER MICHITAKA

Michitaka was Kaneie's oldest son. His mother was the same as Senshi's. I believe the prosperity he enjoyed as Regent must have lasted for about six years before he died in the year of the great epidemic.[13] The cause of his death, I must tell you, was not the pestilence but excessive consumption of alcohol. Although drinking is one of the masculine pleasures, intemperance can cause dreadful consequences.

Michitaka once drove out in a carriage with Naritoki and Asateru to witness the Kamo Return at Murasakino. The three of them were drinking from a crow-shaped flask that he favored on such occasions. It was all very entertaining, and they were soon so drunk that they raised the blinds at both ends of the carriage and sat with their bare heads exposed.

Michitaka always hated to let Naritoki and Asateru leave his house

[12] Tokihira, Nakahira, and Tadahira.

[13] 995. The disease was probably smallpox. McCullough and McCullough 1980, s.n. 57.

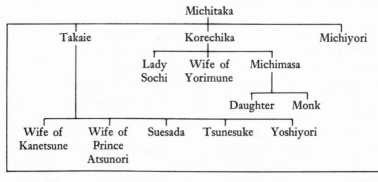

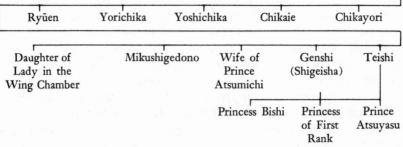

sober. It tickled him to see them helped, tipsy and disheveled, into carriages that had to be drawn all the way to the main steps. All things considered, he possessed the knack of sobering up with remarkable speed. During one of his official visits to Kamo Shrine,[14] the forewarned priests at the Lower Sanctuary provided a huge bowl for the customary three potations, but his thirst was not slaked until he had drained it seven or eight times. He proceeded to fall into a deep slumber on the way to the Upper Sanctuary, lying stretched out with his head pillowed on the back of the carriage. Michinaga, who had gone along as senior Major Counselor, was shocked to see no figure behind the blind when he happened to glance toward the carriage. (Night had fallen, making it possible to see inside by the light of the outriders' torches.) Presently they reached the sanctuary and unyoked the ox, with the Regent still fast asleep; and the outriders formed ranks and waited, afraid to wake him up.

Michinaga left his own carriage. Since they could not stand around forever, he went over to Michitaka's shafts, shouted, and beat on the wood with his fan, but Michitaka slept on. Michinaga moved closer,

---

[14] Prescribed for the Regent on the day before the Kamo Festival.

grabbed the bottom of his brother's trousers, and jerked him awake. Perfectly prepared for that very contingency, Michitaka took out a comb and hair stick,[15] tidied himself, and stepped down, composed and fresh. Who would have expected anybody that drunk to get up on the same night? He was no ordinary toper.

Michitaka never lost his love of wine. As he lay dying, his people turned his face toward the west, urging him to recite the name of Amitābha. "Will Naritoki and Asateru be there in the Pure Land?" he asked pathetically. His preoccupation with drinking reminds me of the man who remembered to call on the Three Treasures just as his head touched the edge of the hell cauldron.[16]

Michitaka was a fine-looking man. When Minamoto Toshikata came to his house as Head Chamberlain, bearing the Imperial edict authorizing Korechika to govern, Michitaka was too ill to put on full dress. Wearing an informal cloak, he crept outside the blinds on his knees, and there, unable to negotiate the threshold beam, he took up a woman's costume and draped it over Toshikata's shoulder according to form. It was a moving scene. Anyone else in such straits would have looked grotesque, but Michitaka seemed as dapper and aristocratic as ever. Toshikata is said to remark frequently, "I realized that beauty is never so indispensable as after one has fallen ill."

Michitaka had a number of sons and daughters by different ladies. His widow is Takashina Kishi, a daughter of Naritada, the governor of Yamato, who was called Kō nii in his last years. It was unseemly for Naritada to take precedence over Michinaga at the Shakuzenji dedication. Kishi is the mother of three sons and four daughters. The oldest daughter, Teishi, married Emperor Ichijō after His Majesty performed the capping ceremony at the age of eleven. I believe she must have been fifteen. She was granted Imperial rank on the First of the Sixth Month in the very same year, and people called her *chūgū*.

Teishi gave birth to a Prince and two Princesses after Michitaka's death. The older of the girls, who lives in Sanjō, is known as the Novice Princess of First Rank. The second died at the age of nine. The son, Prince Atsuyasu, died of a broken heart after repeated disappointments

---

[15] *Kōgai*, a long, narrow instrument, usually made of ivory or silver, which was employed as a hairdressing aid by both sexes. Its exact function is no longer understood.

[16] Boiling in fiery cauldrons was one of the punishments to which sinners were subjected in the Buddhist hells. *Ōjō yōshū*, p. 33b and passim. The reference here appears to be to a preachers' tale, not otherwise known today. See Hosaka 1974, 3.61-62, for similar stories in which sinners are saved from cauldrons at the last minute by invocations of the *Lotus Sutra* or Amitābha Buddha. The Three Treasures are the Buddha, the dharma, and the saṃgha.

—a sad end for a twenty-year-old. People would have been content with conventional regrets if he had been as flighty as Emperor Reizei's sons, but he was blessed with a splendid disposition and an exceptional talent for learning.

Michitaka's second daughter was known as Shigeisha while Emperor Sanjō was still Crown Prince. She led a gay life in those days, but she followed her father in death at the age of twenty-two or twenty-three.

As husband to his third daughter, Michitaka chose Prince Atsumichi, Emperor Reizei's fourth son. The relationship came to an end, and people said the lady was eking out a precarious existence somewhere in the vicinity of Ichijō Avenue. I don't know how true it is, but they say the Prince was alienated by his wife's unpredictable behavior. When guests came to the house, she was apt to roll up the blinds and stand there with her robes open at the breast, making the Prince blush with shame. The other gentlemen, equally disconcerted, would stare at the floor, uncertain whether to go or stay. "I used to sit there with my eyes averted, too embarrassed to move or think," the Prince said later.

On one occasion, when the Prince was composing Chinese poetry with a gathering of university students at the mansion, his wife pelted the guests with twenty or thirty *ryō* of gold dust, which she threw over the top of a folding screen.[17] The students considered her action inappropriate and unwelcome, but they scrambled for the gold to keep up appearances. I am told that they still say, "Giving us the gold was fine, but what an ugly scene!"

The Prince's wife also used to offer loud appraisals of the Chinese poems people recited.

Even the women in Naritada's family are learned. Kishi, the mother of Michitaka's daughters, is the lady everyone knows as Kō no naishi. Since she lacked authorization to enter the Seiryōden, she used to go to the Shishinden when there was an Imperial progress or festival banquet. She is a serious Chinese poet. She participated in Emperor Ichijō's Chinese poetry parties, and her compositions outshone the perfunctory efforts of certain gentlemen. People say that when His Majesty called for her on such occasions she would go and sit in the Two-Bay Room (which she entered by way of the Kokiden Imperial Apartment), rather than venture into the Table Room. That was old-fashioned of her, wasn't it?[18] They say it is bad for a woman to be too

---

[17] One large *ryō* (a unit of weight) of gold dust is said to have been worth about 10,000 yen; one small *ryō*, about 8,000 yen (as of ca. 1960). Hosaka 1974, 3.76.

[18] The Table Room was not supposed to be open to ladies who were denied

well educated, so I suppose that must be why she suffered such dreadful reverses later.[19]

Kishi's fourth daughter, Mikushigedono, was a great beauty. She acted as Prince Atsuyasu's foster mother until her untimely death.

Such were Michitaka's daughters by Kō no naishi. He also had one by the person called the Lady in the Wing Chamber—someone who is in the service of the present Grand Empress. There are said to be others, too.

Michitaka's oldest son was Ōchiyo, whose mother was a daughter of Morihito, the late governor of Iyo. The boy's grandfather, Kaneie, adopted him as his sixth son and called him Michiyori. After rising to the office of Major Counselor, Michiyori died on the Eleventh of the Sixth Month in the year of his father's death. I have heard that he was twenty-five. He seemed almost too handsome for this world—a figure from a painting, as it were—and his disposition was mild and affable, unlike those of his brothers. He was born of a different mother.

One of Empress Teishi's full brothers, the monk Ryūen, was made a Bishop when he was a little more than ten years old. He died at the age of thirty-six. Another, Kochiyo,[20] far outstripped his half-brother, Ōchiyo. Michitaka made him Palace Minister when he was twenty-one,[21] and then, in the first year of Chōtoku [995], which was the year of his own death, he dragged himself to the Palace, desperately ill, to advise the Emperor to put the boy in charge of the government. Having secured the edict, he took Buddhist vows, and everyone flocked to Korechika's house, hailing him as the Regent.[22] But the regency passed into the hands of Michikane, the Awata Lord, and Korechika was left grieving like a hunter whose falcon has escaped his grasp. The whole family was terribly upset.

The new Regent's tenure proved as fleeting as a dream. He died, and Korechika suffered the humiliation of watching Michinaga assume the reins of government on the Eleventh of the Fifth Month in that same year. In the next year, there was the incident involving Retired Emperor Kazan, which caused Korechika to be deprived of his office,

---

access to the Courtiers' Hall. Yotsugi implies that it was unnecessary for the Empress's mother to be so punctilious. It would appear that the Emperor was in the Daytime Chamber, which adjoined both the Table Room and the Two-Bay Room. The gentlemen in attendance were presumably in the Courtiers' Hall. See Figure 4.

[19] A reference to the downfall of Michitaka's family after his death.

[20] Korechika.   [21] In 994.

[22] Korechika had actually received *nairan* powers, rather than a formal regental appointment. For *nairan*, see Appendix B, n. 7.

stripped of his rank, and demoted to the position of Provisional Governor-General of the Dazaifu. He set out for Kyūshū on the Twenty-Fourth of the Fourth Month in the second year of Chōtoku [996], at the age of twenty-three. It was a very pathetic affair. A man's exile is not always entirely his own fault. Both in China and in this country, outstanding men have been subjected to Korechika's fate. Remember Sugawara Michizane. (*Yotsugi blew his nose in an affecting manner.*)

Korechika was simply too accomplished and learned for Japan; that's why such a thing happened to him. He was recalled during the celebrations after Prince Atsuyasu's birth. There was later an Imperial edict granting him the same treatment as a minister of state, and he went about in society in a rather inappropriate style, plagued by rumors of unfortunate incidents. There was an occasion, for instance, on which he entered the Middle Enclosure through Sakuheimon Gate and turned west. Michinaga also happened to have come to the Palace, and great numbers of his servants were jammed into the cramped space outside the Umetsubo east wall. Making a tremendous show of clearing everyone out of the way, Korechika's attendants sent the whole pack piling into the Umetsubo courtyard, much to His Lordship's surprise. The gentlemen inside hesitated to protest, even though they felt most indignant, but a certain Escort, pretending not to know who was passing, fell on the intruders and drove them all back outside. Korechika's attendants were inundated, and their corpulent master, unable to thread his way through the press, found himself squeezed against a window in the Tōkaden corridor. Despite his shouts, he was pinned to the spot by the mobs of servants who were still being chased into the narrow area, and it was some time before he made his escape. The whole affair was most undignified. It was not Korechika's fault, to be sure, but others said he might have been spared such humiliations if his social activities and general behavior had shown more discretion.

Michinaga took extraordinary precautions when he went to Kinbusen, having been warned on the way about possible trouble from Korechika; and the return trip was accomplished without incident. Korechika considered the rumors absurd, but he could not very well ignore them, so he went to see Michinaga. His host, chatting about the events of the trip, found his nervousness amusing and pathetic. "You and I haven't played backgammon together for a long time," he said. "I've missed our games. Let's have one today." He drew up a board and wiped it, and he and the rest of the company were touched by Korechika's expression of relief.

It would have been natural for Michinaga to display a certain coolness toward Korechika after having heard such stories, but his is a sympathetic nature. He always gives people the benefit of the doubt and treats them as friends.

Whenever Michinaga and Korechika settled down to gamble, they bared their torsos, bundled up their robes around their waists, and kept at it until midnight or beyond. Michinaga's people disapproved of the contests, because, they said, Korechika was a childish person who might stir up trouble.[23] Some remarkable and very tasteful stakes changed hands—magnificent antiques wagered by Korechika and interesting modern novelties by Michinaga. Even in those games, Korechika invariably went home the loser.

Korechika still hoped to recoup his fortunes through Prince Atsuyasu; and others at Court privately considered him someone to be cultivated and feared, regardless of his current difficulties. But he lost heart after the successive births of the present Emperor and Crown Prince, fell into a lingering illness, and died on the Twenty-Ninth of the First Month in the seventh year of Kankō [1010]. I have heard that he was thirty-seven years old.

The illness that eventually claimed his life caused him so little discomfort that he dismissed it for a time as bronchitis. When it began to seem serious, he summoned monks to offer prayers, only to find that no one would come.[24] In desperation, he sent Michimasa to Michinaga with a plea for help. It was late at night, after everyone had gone to bed. Heading straight for Michinaga's shutters, the boy cleared his throat. "Who is it?" Michinaga asked. Michimasa gave his name and explained the difficulty. "My father tried to begin some rituals, but there doesn't seem to be any Holy Teacher available. We would be grateful if you would speak to someone." "That's terrible! I had no idea he was sick. How is he getting along? Monks have no business acting that way," said Michinaga in great surprise. He proceeded to make detailed inquiries about the names of the monks who had turned the family down, and then he sent a certain Holy Teacher to Korechika's house.

Still, one might have expected Korechika's spirit to trouble Michinaga, because, as people have pointed out, there was bad feeling there. But I have heard of nothing to compare with the depredations of Major Counselor Motokata. Can spirits be weaker in this era of degeneracy? In my own opinion, Michinaga's power is simply too great to be overcome, but I suppose that may be a typical old man's exaggeration. (*Yotsugi was speaking in a solemn whisper.*)[25]

[23] Because he threw himself completely into the game.
[24] The monks were afraid of displeasing Michinaga.
[25] To avoid giving offense to Korechika's spirit.

Korechika had two daughters and a son by a daughter of the Minamoto Major Counselor Shigemitsu, all of whom grew up safely. He
reared the daughters with great care, hoping to make Empresses of
them, but his plans came to nothing. When he was near death, he
called the girls to his side and spoke to them in tears. "I have been a
faithful servant of the gods and buddhas for many years, and so I was
sure everything would come out right in the end, but now, it seems,
I am to die like a dog. I would have prayed for you to go first if I had
known what was to happen. It distresses me to think of how you may
have to live after my death. People will laugh at you." Still weeping,
he addressed his last words to his wife. "I will resent it in the other
world if you fail to keep up appearances."

Korechika's older daughter has married Meishi's son Yorimune, the
Master of the Crown Prince's Household, and is, I believe, the mother
of a good many children. There is certainly nothing wrong with that.
The other one has entered the service of Senior Grand Empress Shōshi,
where she is a respected attendant known as Lady Sochi—something
her father could never have dreamed of. It is sad, isn't it?

From the day of his birth on, the son, Michimasa, was the special
pet of his grandfather, who gave him presents whenever he invited him
to the mansion. Michitaka even spoiled the boy's nurses. I think I am
right in saying that Michimasa holds Third Rank nowadays. When
Korechika was on his deathbed, he said to him, weeping, "Never, never do anything shabby after my death. No matter how great your
need, don't disgrace me by handing out ill-considered name certifi-
cates.[26] Don't let the gossips say, 'Oh, Korechika was high and mighty
enough, but look at his son.' You'll simply have to become a monk if
it's too hard for you to make your way in the world."

Michimasa served as Assistant Master of the Household when our
present sovereign was Crown Prince—a very respectable post, which
was a source of considerable prestige for him. Somehow, though, he
failed even to become a Head Chamberlain when His Majesty ascended the throne; he merely received Third Rank as a reward for his
previous services, without so much as a middle captaincy. It was a sad
case. Who could have foreseen it?

Michimasa has had a son and daughter by the daughter of Korenaka, the late Governor-General Middle Counselor. The son, a monk,
appears to be living in Bishop Meison's cloister. For some unaccount-
able reason, Korenaka's daughter has run off and entered the service

[26] *Myōbu*, a card listing the individual's office, rank, name, and age. Its presentation was a symbolic act, pledging unlimited service in return for patronage.

of Grand Empress Kenshi, where she is known as Yamato no senji. A man can't trust a wife just because she has been with him a long time; such women are the very ones who make fools of their husbands and expose them to ridicule. I'd shave my wife's gray head and claw off her nose if she tried anything like that, but I suppose a member of the upper classes, with an illustrious name to protect, can't afford such behavior. Still, Michimasa is anything but a fool; he is a very clever fellow.

Korechika wrote the preface for the poems composed on the Seventh Night after the present sovereign's birth[27]—an affair that showed how indiscreet he could be. By making an appearance at a function from which he ought to have absented himself, he had everyone staring and asking, "What is he thinking of? Why is he here?" It was an awkward situation, don't you agree? But Michinaga was his usual tactful, cordial self, and in the end Korechika produced an enviable composition. He turned into the star of the occasion, praised to the skies by the whole company.

Akogimi was the childhood name of Korechika's full brother Takaie, a Middle Counselor at the age of seventeen, who was reputed to be the wildest youth at Court. Because of his involvement in Korechika's problems, he became provisional governor of Izumo and stayed in Tajima.[28] He came back when Korechika did, regained his old office of Middle Counselor, and was also named War Minister. People considered him exceptionally able.

Takaie could not help resenting the reverses he had suffered. A number of gentlemen, for instance, had risen above him.[29] But he continued to appear at Court. It so happened that he accompanied Michinaga when the latter made a pilgrimage to Kamo Shrine. Feeling it a pity for him to have to take his place so far in the rear, His Lordship invited him to ride in his own carriage, where he engaged him in friendly conversation. "Everyone says I was the person who proposed your exile and pushed it through," Michinaga said presently in a serious voice. "You probably think the same thing. But that wasn't what hap-

---

[27] Noble families held formal celebratory banquets (*ubuyashinai*), with music and poetry, on the third, fifth, seventh, and ninth nights after a child's birth. McCullough and McCullough 1980, s.n. 8.

[28] The appointment was a form of exile. Before he reached Izumo, a second Imperial edict gave him permission to stay in Tajima, which was much closer to the capital. Appendix A, Korechika; Appendix D; McCullough and McCullough 1980, Chapter 5.

[29] Five of his former juniors had moved ahead of him during his absence: Michitsuna, Korenaka, Tokimitsu, Kintō, and Tadanobu.

pened. Do you believe I could visit Kamo Shrine like this if I had added a word to what His Majesty said? The gods have their eyes on us: it is frightening to contemplate." "I was too embarrassed to look at him," Takaie said later. "I didn't know what to do." It was because Michinaga was talking to Takaie that he said what he did. I am sure he would not have gone that far for Korechika.

Except for such events, which were almost compulsory, Takaie gave up his old active social life. On one occasion, Michinaga sent him a special invitation to join a group of gentlemen who were drinking and singing at the Tsuchimikado Mansion. "Parties like this are never the same without the Middle Counselor," he said. Meanwhile the wine bowl kept circulating, and the tipsy guests unfastened their collars. Upon Takaie's arrival, they all tidied themselves and sat erect. "Hurry up and unfasten your collar," Michinaga said to his nephew. "You're spoiling the fun." As Takaie hesitated uncomfortably, Kinnobu approached him from the rear. "I'll do it," he said. Takaie scowled and flared up. "I may have had some bad luck, but I don't have to take anything from the likes of you," he said. Everybody looked shocked, and Toshikata gazed in alarm from one face to another, fearing an ugly scene. But Michinaga burst out laughing. "Let's get along without jokes like that today. I'll untie it for you." He went over to Takaie and opened his collar wide. Takaie's face cleared. "That's the way it ought to be," he said. He took up the bowl in front of him, drank several draughts, and entered into the spirit of things with even more zest than usual, just as anyone would have wished. Michinaga showered him with hospitable attentions.

Meanwhile Takaie was biding his time, still convinced that Prince Atsuyasu was bound to be named Crown Prince. But then Emperor Ichijō's illness took a grave turn;[30] and His Majesty made a private confession when Takaie called at the Palace. "In the end, it was beyond my power to arrange that matter." "I felt like asking him what kind of man he was," Takaie said later. He went home, sank down at the top of the main steps, and beat his fists against the floor. People used to predict governmental reforms if Prince Atsuyasu were to become Emperor with Takaie as his mentor, but I suppose Michinaga's prosperity was not fated to be shared.

Takaie's dazzling attire at Emperor Sanjō's Purification made him a more conspicuous figure than usual, possibly because he wanted to show people that he was not as dejected as they thought. There is a

---

[30] The Emperor appears to have fallen ill in the Fifth Month of 1011. He abdicated on the Thirteenth of the Sixth Month and died nine days later.

proud side to his character. He wore a red glossed-silk under-jacket (quite unorthodox for a banquet or Imperial journey), and an unlined green inner robe, which gave the effect of an autumn-leaf combination; and his outer trousers were of brown double-patterned silk lined with green—a spectacularly elegant and beautiful costume.[31]

Most unfortunately, Takaie began to have trouble with his eyes. Nothing he tried helped, and he stopped going out. Then a vacancy in the office of Senior Assistant Governor-General[32] set off a rush of eager applicants. Recalling stories of a Chinese doctor in Tsukushi who treated eye problems, Takaie conceived the notion of consulting him. "Just in case it might do some good, I would be grateful for the appointment," he told the Court. I suppose Emperor Sanjō, the reigning monarch, must have sympathized with him, because he gave him the post without further discussion.[33]

Takaie's principal wife is a daughter of Kanemoto, the governor of Iyo. One of his two daughters by her has married Prince Atsunori, Emperor Sanjō's son, and the other is the wife of Kanetsune, Michitsuna's son. He seems to look after his two sons-in-law with great solicitude.

Thanks to the support of the local people, who admired his conduct of the government and did whatever he asked, Takaie accomplished as much as ten ordinary Senior Assistants by the time he returned to the capital. While he was in Tsukushi, a Jurchen force suddenly launched an invasion from the sea, apparently hoping to conquer our country.[34] With the Dazaifu unprepared and the Senior Assistant unable to tell one end of a bow or arrow from the other,[35] it was a great crisis, but Takaie knew how to get things done. Of course, he called up the inhabitants of Chikugo, Hizen, Higo, and the rest of the nine provinces, and he even turned the Dazaifu staff into a battle unit. Those rascals lost plenty of men, I can tell you.

When it comes right down to it, Takaie's high birth was what gave him the power to end the Jurchen threat. It would have been natural

---

[31] The Purification took place in the Tenth Month. Robes of the type known as autumn-leaf combinations (*momijigasane*) were red with green linings. For double-patterned silk (*futaeorimono*), a brocaded damask, see McCullough and McCullough 1980, Chapter 20, n. 13.

[32] Of the Kyūshū Government Office (Dazaifu).

[33] Emperor Sanjō suffered from a disease of the eyes.

[34] The Jurchen were Tungusic tribes, natives of the Amur River area, who ruled China as the Chin dynasty from 1122 to 1234. They raided western Japan in 1019. *Nihon kiryaku*, 2.251.

[35] Hyperbole to make Takaie sound even better. He had actually held military posts.

for the Court to reward him with a ministerial appointment or major counselorship, but he still holds the same old office, probably because he lives in retirement. As a result of his recommendations, the men who played the main parts in the fighting were all rewarded. Taneki was named governor of Iki, and his son became a Dazaifu Inspector.[36]

Taneki's family is descended from the Ōkura who attacked Sumitomo, the man who conspired with Masakado to perpetrate dreadful deeds.[37] "I'm going to kill the Emperor," Masakado announced. "I'm going to be the Regent," Sumitomo chimed in. And they pledged to work together so that one of them could run the government as he pleased while the other enjoyed an Emperor's life. Masakado mustered troops in the east, and Sumitomo assembled vast numbers of huge rafts on the western seas. The rafts were permanent habitations, covered with earth, planted with trees, and dotted with rice fields. No ordinary army could have made a dent in them, but they were defeated by the punitive force's strategy—a most impressive accomplishment. I don't suppose the commanders deserve all the credit, though. How could a scheme like that have succeeded in the face of the Court's authority?

A lot of people from Iki and Tsushima Provinces had been captured and carried off to the land of the Jurchen, so the Korean sovereign dispatched an army to get them all back. Then he sent them to those islands,[38] together with an envoy whom Takaie rewarded with 300 *ryō* of gold. Takaie's skillful handling of the Jurchen affair has made Michinaga consider him indispensable, which may explain why he is still so popular. There are always three or four horses and carriages in front of his gate, and sometimes the whole street is blocked.

I believe Takaie's sons include the present Chamberlain Lesser Captain Yoshiyori, Middle Controller of the Right Tsunesuke, and Ceremonials Clerk Suesada.

That's right—I had almost forgotten about Takaie's wager with Retired Emperor Kazan in the days when he was still riding high. That was an outlandish business. "I'll bet not even you can get past my gate," the former sovereign said to him. "What makes you think so?" Takaie answered. On the appointed date, Takaie arrived in a stout-wheeled carriage drawn by a fine ox. He was wearing a beautiful new informal cloak and cap, and his grape-colored bombycine[39] trousers

---

[36] Inspector translates *gen*, a position at the third level of the Dazaifu hierarchy. Appointees seem to have functioned primarily as police officers. Wada 1953, p. 139.

[37] Although the rebellions of Sumitomo and Masakado coincided (938-940), there is no evidence to support the conspiracy theory.

[38] Iki and Tsushima.

[39] *Orimono*, a term of uncertain meaning. It seems to have been used most often

billowed over the front board, their cords trailing to the ground like those of the gentlemen who dash across Murasakino on the day of the Kamo Return. The carriage moved ahead with its blinds high, while fifty or sixty attendants cleared the way with barrages of shouts. Needless to say, the Retired Emperor had mustered men of his own—seventy or eighty valiant monks, temple pages, and others, armed with big rocks and five- and six-foot staves, whom he had stationed in an unbroken line outside his north and south gates and walls, and also on both sides of Higashinotōin Avenue in front of the Koichijō Mansion.[40] An elite corps of husky young attendants and monks was poised for battle inside the gates. All the Retired Emperor's men loved a fight, so you can imagine how they must have looked that day. Both sides had limited their weapons to sticks and stones.

After a brief pause, Takaie took his carriage north from Kadenokōji to a point near the gate, only to be forced back again. The former Emperor's vigilant battalions roared with laughter. Was there ever such a sight? The power of the throne is simply too great; it was hopeless for Takaie to try to get by. He laughed about it later. "I was foolish to talk that way. What a humiliation!" Even though it was all in fun, the Retired Emperor seemed to consider his victory a great accomplishment.

Michitaka probably had a number of other sons. The ones I know about have died one after another—Director of the Palace Storehouse Bureau Yorichika, Director of the Carpentry Bureau Chikayori, and so forth—leaving only Senior Assistant Minister of War Chikaie, who is a rather obscure figure. Chikaie's wife is the nurse of Koichijōin's sons, and he himself acts as an attendant for Koichijōin, which is a great comedown. I think another son, Yoshichika (the one who used to be called the Ide Lesser Captain), is said to have taken religious vows.

Michitaka was punctilious and refined, but his descendants have failed to prosper. They also seem to have been short-lived. As far as I know, Princess Shūshi and Takaie are his sole survivors.

MINISTER OF THE RIGHT MICHIKANE

Kaneie's third son, Michikane, was known as the Awata Lord. He received an Imperial decree naming him Regent on the Second of the

---

to designate a rich changeable damask. McCullough and McCullough 1980, Chapter 3, n. 26.

[40] The Retired Emperor's residence, the Kazan'in, occupied an area south of Konoe and east of Higashinotōin.

Michikane
| Lady Nijō | Sonshi (Kurabeya) | Kanetsuna | Kanetaka | Fukutarigimi |

Fifth Month in the first year of Chōtoku [995], and died on the Eighth of the same month. He was a minister of state for five years and a Regent for only seven days. Many gentlemen of his family have failed to attain the regency, but there has probably never been another who has won the prize and then lost it as though in a dream.

Michikane received the Imperial decree just after he had gone to stay in a house owned by Sukeyuki, the governor of Izumo. We may imagine Sukeyuki's joy! Since the premises were too cramped for the ceremonies, Michikane decided to go home. He went to the Palace to offer thanks on the day of his departure, escorted by a splendid group of outriders who had been selected to exclude all but the most superior. His wife was accompanied back to Nijō by innumerable gentlemen of every status, some in unfigured hunting robes.[41] I must leave you to visualize the scene when Sukeyuki's people saw Michikane off, and also the bustle and excitement inside the mansion after the lady's return. There were those who found the commotion excessive.

Although Michikane had not been feeling well that day, he had forced himself to go to the Palace. It would be unlucky, he thought, to postpone his expressions of gratitude because of a minor indisposition. Once there, he began to suffer such terrible pain that he was incapable of leaving through the Courtiers' Hall. To the amazement of the onlookers, he summoned his outriders to the door in the pantry passageway and made his way out through Sakuheimon Gate, supporting himself on the shoulders of others. Meanwhile the people at the Nijō Mansion awaited his return, busy with all kinds of special preparations. When they saw him struggle out of the carriage, leaning on his companions' shoulders, with his cap askew and his collar unfastened, their feelings were certainly not the same as when he left Sukeyuki's house! But they concealed their misgivings behind cheerful faces, saying to one another in confidential tones, "Oh, but surely. . . ." There was nothing to suggest to outsiders that his life might be in danger.

Sanesuke, our present Ononomiya Minister of the Right, came to offer his congratulations. Michikane had the blinds of the main apart-

---

[41] A sign of low status.

ment lowered before calling him in, and he conducted the interview on his back.[42] "I must speak to you like this because I don't feel up to going outside. I have appreciated the things you have done for me all through the years—even the most trifling—but my status has been too low to permit me to express my thanks. Now that I am Regent, I intend to repay you, both officially and in private. I also hope to consult you in everything, which is why I have been rude enough to bring you to this untidy place." The cordial speech was delivered so haltingly that Sanesuke could only guess what he was trying to say. "He was gasping for breath," Sanesuke said later. "I felt that he must be in very bad shape. Then the wind blew up one of the blinds, so that I caught a glimpse of the interior. He had lost his natural color and looked desperately ill. Nobody would have taken him for a powerful man. He seemed, indeed, to be barely conscious. It was pitiful to hear him talking about the future."

Michikane had three sons, the oldest of whom was called Fukutarigimi. Even assuming that all children are more or less alike, Fukutarigimi was shockingly naughty and perverse. It had been decided that he should perform a dance at the longevity celebration for Kaneie.[43] Although he fretted and rebelled while he was being taught, they managed to make him learn by coaxing him along in every conceivable way (they even offered prayers); and on the day of the celebration he mounted the dance platform arrayed in a beautiful costume. But what a child he was! When the musicians struck up the tune, he tore his coiffure to pieces and ripped his costume, shrieking, "I won't dance!" His ashen-faced father was paralyzed with horror,[44] and the rest of the company watched helplessly, reflecting that it was only to have been expected. Then Michitaka went down and mounted the platform steps. Did he hope to wheedle the boy into performing, or was he going to chase him off? As the others looked on, he drew Fukutarigimi to his side and began to tread the measures with the utmost elegance. The music acquired new interest, Fukutarigimi's disgrace was smoothed over, and the occasion became far more enjoyable than usual. Kaneie was delighted. Michikane felt the warmest admira-

[42] Sanesuke has waited at the middle gate to be called to the house. Michikane puts the blinds between them to avoid meeting him face to face.

[43] Held in 988 to celebrate Kaneie's sixtieth year. Longevity celebrations among the Heian nobility usually took the form of decennial observances held from the individual's fortieth year on. The festivities always included a banquet, dances, and the recitation of poems. McCullough and McCullough 1980, s.n. 49.

[44] Kaneie's displeasure could have had far-reaching consequences, both for the boy and for Michikane.

tion and gratitude, and the others were also much impressed. Anyone who remembers Michitaka's considerate ways must wonder why his line has come to nothing.

Fukutarigimi died after he made the mistake of tormenting a snake, which cursed him and made a tumor grow on his head.

Tōkazu's daughter was the mother of Michikane's second son, Kanetaka, who is now Commander of the Left Gate Guards. Kanetaka has a good many sons and daughters. I believe it was in the Second Month of this year that he took Emperor Sanjō's third son, Prince Atsuhira, as a husband for his oldest daughter, a match that appears to have been very successful. There are four other daughters.

Michikane's third son is Kanetsuna, the former Head Chamberlain Middle Captain. Kanetsuna once ordered a remarkably interesting cypress wickerwork carriage for the Kamo Festival. The wheels were painted to resemble colored targets, and the horizontal and vertical members of the window frames were shaped like bows and arrows—a most entertaining sight. Izumi Shikibu composed a poem about it:

Tōtsura no	You are not the Ten Racers,
Uma naranedomo	Yet when you mount—
Kimi noreba	Carriage though it be—
Kuruma mo mato ni	We gaze, it seems,
Miyuru mono ka na.	On targets and horses ten.[45]

It seemed a splendid conceit, but some people are always ready to pick things to pieces. "The carriage has been hit by the Kamo god's arrows," they announced. Matters thus took an awkward turn, and that was the end of Kanetsuna's inspiration.

It was a shame Kanetsuna had to give up his post as Head Chamberlain. That he should have received it in the first place was natural enough—nothing to occasion joyous surprise; but the odd thing was that he lost it because of gossip. "Michikane tricked Emperor Kazan into stepping down, and Kanetaka did the same with Koichijōin," people said. "That family ought not to be allowed too close access to Emperors and Crown Princes."[46]

[45] *Tōtsura* can mean either ten horses raced at a shrine by each of two teams of guardsmen dancers after the festival dances, or the dancer-riders themselves. Although mounted archery was a separate event at Kamo, held after the races (or race; it is not known whether there was a single race involving twenty horses or ten two-man contests), Shikibu associates the two in her poem, which puns on *mato* ("targets" and "horses ten").

[46] The reason for Kanetsuna's loss of his position is unknown, as is his brother Kanetaka's role in Koichijōin's resignation. Hosaka 1974, 3.165.

So much for Michikane's sons; all of you must know those stories. Now as regards daughters, there was one who was called the Kurabeya Consort in Emperor Ichijō's reign. (Her mother was the Emperor's nurse, Tōsanmi.) She later became the principal wife of Michitō, our present Treasury Minister, and then died. Another—the one whom Michikane's principal wife conceived after prayers to the buddhas and gods—has entered the service of Empress Ishi, where she appears to be known as Lady Nijō. Her father had petitioned the deities to grant him a daughter, but he died without seeing her face. Such sad things happen, alas, in this world of ours. I have heard that Michikane's widow has been the principal wife of Kanemichi's son Akimitsu, the present Minister of the Left, for the past several years. She is the daughter of Morosuke's son, Treasury Minister Tōkazu. So the Awata house has proved fleeting indeed! To be quite truthful, Michikane was a hard, forbidding man, greatly feared by others. It is odd that he left no descendants of consequence.

Instead of staying in an earthen-floored room during the mourning for his father, Michikane used the heat as an excuse for rolling up all his blinds. He did not even bother to recite Buddha-invocations, but called in his friends, read the *Collection of Early and Modern Times* and the *Later Selection*, and cracked jokes with no show of grief at all. The reason was that he was nursing a grievance against Kaneie. "I was the one who persuaded Emperor Kazan to abdicate," he thought, "so my father ought to have handed the regency over to me."[47] That was absurd, wasn't it? There were a number of other unpleasant rumors, too. But I understand that Michitsuna and Michinaga held the prescribed services.

[47] Instead of to Michitaka.

CHAPTER FIVE

Chancellor Michinaga: Part One

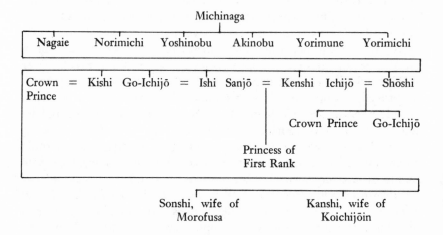

Michinaga is Kaneie's fifth son. His mother was a daughter of Fuji-wara Nakamasa of Junior Fourth Upper Rank, the governor of Settsu and Master of the Right Capital Office. Nakamasa was the seventh son of Middle Counselor Yamakage of Junior Second Rank.

Michinaga is our present Novice Excellency, the father-in-law of former Emperors Ichijō and Sanjō and the grandfather of the Emperor and the Crown Prince. He became a Provisional Middle Counselor in his twenty-third year, without passing through the office of Consultant. It was in that year that Jōtōmon'in was born. On the Twenty-Seventh of the Fourth Month [of 992], at the age of twenty-seven, he received Junior Second Rank. That was the year in which the Regent Yorimichi was born. He received the additional title of Major Captain of the Left on the Twenty-Seventh of the Fourth Month in the first year of Chōtoku [995].

A terrible pestilence struck before the Kamo Festival that year [995], and the disease exacted an even heavier toll during the following year. Ministers of state and senior nobles perished in great numbers, to say nothing of gentlemen of Fourth and Fifth Rank. Of the dignitaries whose lives ended in that year [995], the Kan'in Major Counselor Asateru died on the Twenty-Eighth of the Third Month and the Middle Regent Michitaka on the Tenth of the Fourth. (Michitaka was not carried off by the pestilence; he merely died at the same time.) The Koichijō Major Captain Naritoki succumbed on the Twenty-Third of the Fourth Month, and three others on the Eighth of the Fifth Month—the Rokujō Minister of the Left Shigenobu, the Awata Minister of the Right Michikane and the Momozono Middle Counselor Yasumitsu. The Yamanoi Major Counselor Michiyori died on the Eleventh of the Sixth Month. It is unlikely that seven or eight ministers of state and senior nobles have ever perished so extraordinarily within the space of two or three months, even in antiquity.

In my opinion, the explanation for all those deaths is simply that Michinaga is a supremely lucky man. He would never have risen so high if others had kept the offices to which they were entitled by seniority.

If Korechika had had better sense, it would have been natural for him to inherit the regency, because the Emperor had already commanded him to head the government during his father's illness. But the Court chose Michikane after Michitaka's death, unwilling to entrust affairs of state to someone with the mind of a child. Michikane's appointment conformed to the correct order of precedence and was entirely proper. It was astonishing that he died so suddenly—like something in a dream! Ought such a thing to have happened?

Michinaga held the offices of Major Counselor and Master of the Empress's Household then. On the Eleventh of the Fifth Month, at the age of thirty—a time when he was still very young and could look forward to a long career—he received the Imperial decree naming him Regent, and thereafter he began to prosper in earnest. The regency has never left his house, and we may assume that it never will.

Michinaga has two wives. Rinshi, the mother of the Imperial consorts, is the daughter of the Tsuchimikado Minister of the Left, Minamoto Masanobu. (Masanobu's mother was Tokihira's daughter, and his father was Prince Atsumi, the Minister of Ceremonial of First Rank, a son of Emperor Uda.) As Michinaga's principal consort, she has given birth to four daughters and two sons. All of you must know about those children, who are our own contemporaries, but I shall go on with my story anyway.

The first daughter, Shōshi, became an Imperial bride at the age of twelve, during the reign of Emperor Ichijō. She was granted Imperial status at the age of thirteen, on the Twenty-Fifth of the Second Month in the following year, the second of the Chōhō era [1000]. While she was Empress, she gave birth to the two Princes who are our present Emperor and Crown Prince. As Senior Grand Empress and

Imperial mother of those two personages, she is the foremost mother of the realm.

The second daughter, Kenshi, was a Principal Handmaid. She married Emperor Sanjō while he was still Crown Prince, and became his *chūgū* at the age of nineteen when he ascended the throne. A Princess was born to her on the Twenty-Sixth of the Seventh Month in the following year, the second of the Chōwa era [1013]. That daughter, who was granted First Rank in her third or fourth year, is still alive. Nowadays her mother lives in the Biwa Mansion with the title of Grand Empress. The Princess enjoys equality with the three Empresses and receives the income from 1,000 households, so it is quite as though two Empresses lived there.

The third daughter, Ishi, also served as Principal Handmaid. She married the present Emperor in the Second Month of the second year of Kannin [1018], shortly after His Majesty performed the capping ceremony at the age of eleven on the Second of the First Month; and she became Empress on the Sixteenth of the Tenth Month in the same year. She is our present *chūgū*, living in the Imperial Palace.

The fourth daughter, Kishi, also served as Principal Handmaid. In her fifteenth year she became Junior Consort to the present Crown Prince, who was thirteen. She went to him as Yorimichi's daughter because Michinaga, her real father, had already taken religious vows. She turned nineteen this year, and is now in the seventh or eighth month of a pregnancy. With Michinaga's luck, the baby is bound to be a boy. I can't possibly be mistaken! *(He flourished his uplifted fan with an amusing air of complacency.)*

So much for Rinshi's daughters. The first of her two sons, Yorimichi, is the Regent and Minister of the Left, governing the country as he pleases. I think it may have been when he was twenty-six that he became Palace Minister and *sesshō*. At present he is *kanpaku*, because the Emperor has reached maturity. It used to be considered remarkable when a gentleman in his twenties became a Counselor, but this is the way things go for Michinaga's family. Yorimichi's childhood name was Tazugimi.

Rinshi's other son, Norimichi, is the Palace Minister and Major Captain of the Left. He can be called the second most important man in the country. His childhood name was Seyagimi.

Nobody could possibly be better off than this consort of Michinaga's. Although she is a subject, she is the grandmother of the Emperor and the Crown Prince, and she enjoys the same status as the three Empresses, with annual ranks and offices. She is perfectly free to go about as she pleases in her Chinese carriage—much more so than if

she were an Empress. Whenever she wants to witness a public spectacle or Buddhist ceremony, she watches it from her carriage or viewing stand. The Emperor, the Crown Prince, and the consorts all have
their own beautiful residences, but she sits right inside with the master
or mistress, no matter which one she visits. Today, as mother of the
three Empresses, the Crown Prince's consort, the Regent, and the
Palace Minister (to say nothing of her being the grandmother of the
Emperor and the Crown Prince), she is certainly the parent of the nation. And it is the same with Michinaga, of course. The two of them
must be earthly manifestations of great buddhas or gods.

I think Michinaga and Rinshi have probably been married for about
forty years. How inadequate it seems merely to say that he cares for
her with love and respect! From antiquity until the present, our sovereigns and ministers of state have sprung from the house of Fujiwara,
but this richly blessed lady is a Minamoto. Although everyone knows
about her sixtieth birthday celebration two years ago, I must say again
that it was something to marvel at.

Michinaga's other consort, Meishi, is also a Minamoto. Prince Takaakira, one of Emperor Daigo's sons, was Minister of the Left, but he
was obliged to become Governor-General of the Dazaifu because of
an unexpected occurrence—a most unpleasant affair. Meishi is his
daughter. She was still very young when her father went to Tsukushi,
so she was reared with great care by her paternal uncle, the Fifteenth
Prince, who lacked a daughter of his own. After Takaakira and the
Prince were both gone, she became the adopted daughter of the late
Imperial Lady Senshi, who was an Imperial consort at the time. Senshi
installed her in the east wing of the Higashisanjō Mansion, with a curtain-dais,[1] partitions, and other furnishings that were all quite as splendid as her own belongings. She also gave her some of her ladies-in-waiting, male attendants, stewards, and servants, and reared her with as
much affection and care as though she had been an Imperial Princess.
Impressed by the consort's solicitude, her brothers deluged Meishi with
letters, but Senshi fended them off with great severity. Only Michinaga
was allowed to visit the girl. And so it happened that Meishi bore
Michinaga two daughters and four sons.

One of the daughters is Koichijōin's consort; and Michinaga has
taken Morofusa, the Middle Captain of Third Rank, as a husband for
the other. Morofusa's father was Emperor Murakami's seventh son, the
late Minister of Central Affairs Prince Tomohira. Outsiders proclaimed

---

[1] *Chōdai*, a raised, curtained area in the principal apartment of an upper-class
dwelling. It served the master or mistress as both private sitting room and bedchamber. McCullough and McCullough 1980, s.n. 65.

themselves at a loss to understand why Michinaga failed to pick someone whose office and rank were higher, and members of the family
felt the same way, but I imagine His Lordship's reason was that he
expected great things of Morofusa.

One of Meishi's sons is Major Counselor Yorimune, the Master of
the Crown Prince's Household, who was called Iwagimi as a child.
Another is Major Counselor Yoshinobu, the Provisional Master of the
Empress's Household. Another is Middle Counselor Nagaie, whose
childhood name was Kowakagimi. There was also Akinobu, the Director of the Imperial Stables of the Right (called Kokegimi in his childhood), but he became a monk on the Nineteenth of the First Month
in the ninth year of Kankō [1012], and has lived the life of a buddha
for more than ten years.

Akinobu's renunciation of the world was most unexpected and affecting. It was a fine thing for his own enlightenment, and also for his
father, who had not felt quite comfortable without a son in holy
orders. Michinaga is supposed to have vowed afterward to make the
boy an Archbishop without delay, which does give one pause.

According to what I have heard, Akinobu received splendid ceremonial vestments from the Imperial ladies and a linen robe from Michinaga. He seems to have caused his father great bewilderment by an-
nouncing that he had no use for such finery.

When Akinobu was getting ready to leave home, he spoke to his
nurse about his red glossed-silk inner robes. "I would rather not bother
with so many layers," he said. "Please put the padding from all of them
into one so I won't need anything else."

"It would be a nuisance to pick it all out. I'll just make you a thick
new one," she said.

"That would take too long," he replied. "I want it right away."

"Well," said the nurse to herself, "he must have some reason. . . ."
She combined all the padding in one robe and gave it to him to put on,
and it was on that very night that he went away. Needless to say, the
poor nurse was heartbroken. "Why did I give it to him when he was
acting like that?" she sobbed. "What a careless fool I was, not to suspect anything." As if the lack of a robe would have stopped him!
When she heard he was a monk, she fell into a deathly swoon.

"Akinobu will be upset if he finds out how you are carrying on. He
won't be able to concentrate on holy subjects," people told her. "It is
too late to do anything about it now. You really ought to be pleased,
because you will benefit if he achieves buddhahood. Nothing is as important as happiness in the next life."

"I won't be happy if he does become a buddha," she wailed. "What do I care about the life to come? Today's sorrow is all that matters to me. It's all very well for Her Ladyship—she has plenty of other children. I'm the only miserable one." Her behavior was natural enough. We cannot expect people to understand about the afterlife unless their hearts are consecrated to the Way.

Meishi had had a dream in which she had seen the hair on the left side of Akinobu's head cut off halfway. After he became a monk, she was sure it had been a warning. "If only I had tried to change it—if only I had offered prayers," she said.

Akinobu had his head shaved at the Kawadō. On the same night, he set out to climb Mount Hiei. "The water seemed like ice when I crossed the Kamo River," he said later. "I felt a little depressed, even though I reminded myself that I was now the kind of person who did such things."

Sanenari, the present Commander of the Gate Guards of the Right, always used to say that Akinobu had the face of someone who was going to become a monk. That was why he had refused to let Akinobu marry his daughter, with whom the youth had been corresponding, and accepted Yoshinobu as a son-in-law instead. Once during the First Month, he happened to see Akinobu as he was leaving the Imperial Palace.

"Judging from Akinobu's face when he looked out through the carriage window, I should say he will be taking religious vows very soon," he said to his son Kinnari. "How old is he?"

"He must be nineteen," Kinnari answered.

"Then he will probably do it this year," said his father.

When Sanenari heard that Akinobu had taken the tonsure, he said, "Just as I thought!" A man of insight can predict such things without being a physiognomist.

Michinaga treated Akinobu as an ordinary monk, bound by all the usual rules. "Nothing can be done about it now," he said. "It will be sad for him if his thoughts are led astray; we must not let him hear that anybody is unhappy. None of our other sons has entered holy orders, so we must make the best of it. Actually, I would have given him to the church in his childhood if he had not opposed the notion." He ascended Mount Hiei for Akinobu's commandments, accompanied by throngs of friends who turned his party into a gorgeous and imposing procession. Exalted prelates had been selected to officiate as Masters of Deportment, and eminent members of the two orders made up Akinobu's vanguard.[2] Michinaga was too overcome to watch as his son

[2] Masters of Deportment ([*dai*]*igishi*, *igisō*) stood in front of the ordinary monks at a Buddhist convocation and guided their conduct. "Two orders" trans-

mounted the ordination platform, heralded by warning shouts from temple officers and His Lordship's Escorts. Akinobu considered his show of emotion unseemly. When the abbot appeared, riding in his litter with its white silk parasol, and proceeded to ascend the platform, it seemed that no other preceptor could possibly equal a Tendai abbot.[3] That is what I have been told by a neighbor who happened to be there to see it.

"When his brothers Yorimune and Yoshinobu became Major Counselors, I thought the news would interest Akinobu," Lord Michitō said, "but he showed no emotion as I described the banquet and the way the two of them had been seated side by side. 'Such things are fleeting,' he said, without interrupting his buddha invocations. I found his conduct most praiseworthy and impressive."

Michinaga is the father of twelve children. None has died, and all of them, whether sons or daughters, are quite certain to get whatever offices and ranks they want. There is not one who is at all inadequate or open to criticism in disposition or character, or who lacks accomplishments and elegance. I am sure it is due solely to His Lordship's boundless good fortune that this should be so. Although his predecessors produced children, were all of them so perfect? By no means! Regardless of sex, some were good and some were bad—that is only natural.

Since both of Michinaga's wives belong to the house of Minamoto, we can say that the future of the Genji is assured. So that is how it is with those ladies.

Michinaga was named *kanpaku* in his thirtieth year. After governing as he pleased during the reigns of Emperors Ichijō and Sanjō, he became the present Emperor's *sesshō* when His Majesty ascended the

---

lates *sōgō* and *ushiki*. *Sōgō* was a general term for monks who held the three highest Court-bestowed titles in the ecclesiastical hierarchy: Archbishop (*sōjō*), Bishop (*sōzu*), and Master of Discipline (*risshi*). As a group, the *sōgō* constituted a governing body that exercised broad authority over all Buddhist establishments in the Home Provinces. See McCullough and McCullough 1980, s.n. 41. *Ushiki* referred similarly to another group of three, second in status to the *sōgō*: Past Lecturers (*ikō*, men who had preached at the so-called Three Services—the Vimalakīrti Service at the Kōfukuji, the Suvarṇaprabhāsa Service at the Imperial Palace, and the Suvarṇaprabhāsa Service at the Yakushiji); Palace Chaplains (*naigu[busō]*, ten monks who performed religious functions, such as night duty, at the Imperial Palace, and who played leading roles in the Suvarṇaprabhāsa Service); and Holy Teachers (*ajari*, experts in the performance of healing rituals and other esoteric rites).

[3] The preceptor (*kaiwajō*) was the principal administrant of the commandments at an ordination ceremony.

throne at the age of nine. He was then fifty-one. During that same year, he assumed the office of Chancellor, ceding the regency to Yori-michi. He took Buddhist vows on the Twenty-First of the Third Month in the third year of Kannin [1019], when he was fifty-four.[16] On the Eighth of the Fifth Month, the Court made him equivalent to the three Empresses in status, with annual ranks and offices, even though he was a monk. He is the grandfather of the Emperor and the Crown Prince, and the father of three Empresses, of the Regent Minister of the Left, of the Palace Minister, and of many Counselors; and he has governed the realm for approximately thirty-one years. Since this year is his sixtieth, people say there will be a celebration for him after the birth of Kishi's child. What a magnificent affair that will be, with so many great personages present!

No other minister of state has ever been able to make three of his daughters Empresses at the same time. It must be counted a rare bless-ing that Michinaga's house has produced three Imperial ladies—Senior Grand Empress Shōshi, Grand Empress Kenshi, and Empress Ishi. Our other Empress, Seishi, was the only one who belonged to a different house, but she was also descended from Tadahira, so we certainly can't think of her as an outsider. We may indeed call Michinaga the supreme ruler of the land, particularly since Empress Seishi's death this spring has left his three daughters as the sole surviving Empresses.

The Chinese and Japanese poems Michinaga has composed on various occasions are so ingenious that I am sure not even Po Chü-i, Hitomaro, Mitsune, or Tsurayuki could have thought of them. For example, there was the Imperial visit to Kasuga Shrine, a custom inaugurated in the reign of Emperor Ichijō. Since Emperor Ichijō's precedent was consid-ered inviolable, our present sovereign made the journey in spite of his youth, with Senior Grand Empress Shōshi accompanying him in his litter. To call the spectacle brilliant would be trite. Above all, what can I say about the bearing and appearance of Michinaga, the Emperor's grandfather, as he rode in the Imperial train? It might have been disap-pointing if he had looked anything like an ordinary man. The crowds of country folk along the way must have been spellbound. Even sophisticated city dwellers, dazzled by a resplendence like that of the Wheel-Turning Sacred Monarchs,[4] found themselves, in perfectly natural confusion, raising their hands to their foreheads as though gazing on a buddha.

Shōshi concealed her face behind a red fan, allowing the spectators

---

[4] *Tenrinjōō.* In Buddhism, supernaturally endowed kings who rule the world by turning the wheel of righteous political power bestowed by heaven.

a glimpse of her shoulders. Ladies of her elevated status always stop up every crack in their curtains and blinds, and worry, even then, about not being properly hidden, but there is a limit to everything, and she may have thought it would do no harm to let people witness a little of the day's splendor. We may easily guess that both she and Michinaga were incomparably happy. Michinaga presented her with a poem:

Sono kami ya	That now we follow
Inoriokiken	The selfsame road
Kasugano no	To the plain of Kasuga—
Onaji michi ni mo	May it be because he[5] prayed
Tazuneyuku ka na.	On a bygone day?

Her reply:

Kumori naki	That now we follow
Yo no hikari ni ya	The selfsame road
Kasugano no	To the plain of Kasuga—
Onaji michi ni mo	May it be due to the brilliance
Tazuneyukuran.	Of a cloudless reign?

They continued to exchange poems that struck everyone as exceedingly apt. For instance, Shōshi composed this:

Mikasayama	Toward Parasol Mountain
Sashite zo kitsuru	We have come,
Isonokami	Tracing the path
Furuki miyuki no	Of an Imperial journey
Ato o tazunete.	Old as Isonokami.

I could never conceive of such a poem. It would surprise me to find its equal even in antiquity.[6] In view of the circumstances, I suspect that the Kasuga god was speaking through Her Majesty. We might even

---

[5] Kaneie, who had accompanied Emperor Ichijō, and who had presumably prayed for the continuation of his family's preeminence.

[6] Yotsugi admires the poem because it contains a number of word plays and associated words (*engo*). *Sashite* can mean either holding up (here, a parasol) or heading toward; *furuki* (old) suggests *furu* (fall, as in falling snow); *miyuki* can mean both snow and Imperial journey; *ato* (trace) is conventionally associated with snow, etc. See also Appendix A, Mikasayama and Isonokami. "Old Imperial journey" is an allusion to Emperor Ichijō's trip.

go so far as to wonder if Kaneie, who arranged Emperor Ichijō's visit, was not anticipating the composition of just such poems to enhance the splendor of a later occasion.

No matter how fortunate a man may be, there is something lacking if he is incapable of putting together a decent poem. Michinaga adds to the interest of every event with a notable composition. For the celebration in honor of Rinshi's sixtieth year, which was held a couple of years ago, he wrote:

Arinareshi	Why should it be that now,
Chigiri wa taete	When the old familiar tie
Imasara ni	Is severed,
Kokoro kegashi ni	I defile my heart again:
Chiyo to iuran.	"May she live a thousand years"?[7]

And have you heard the poem he composed for the night on which Shōshi celebrated Princess Teishi's birth? It was most interesting, and the style was quite beyond an ordinary person's capabilities.[8] I have been told that it went something like this:

Otomiya no	How happy I am to see
Ubayashinai o	This birth celebration
Anemiya no	Held by an Imperial elder sister
Shitamau miru zo	To honor the child
Ureshikarikeru.	Of an Imperial younger sister!

(The old man's face was wreathed in smiles.)

As I told you earlier, the Shijō Major Counselor Kintō excels in every accomplishment. "I wonder how he manages it," Kaneie once said. "It makes me jealous. My sons can't even get close enough to tread on his shadow." Speechless with embarrassment, Michitaka and Michikane admitted to themselves that their father's chagrin was natural, but young Michinaga retorted, "I may not tread on his shadow, but I'll walk all over his face."[9] And that seems to be just what

---

[7] "Now that she and I have both entered holy orders, our hearts should be free of worldly attachments. . . ." The transliteration and translation follow Hosaka 1974, 3.255, instead of *Ōkagami*, p. 216, which has *taede* for *taete*. Matsumura 1969-, 4.483-484, 5.465; Hosaka 1974, 3.262.

[8] The poem employs the *Man'yōshū* style of direct statement. Yotsugi probably means that it achieves an effect without the assistance of rhetorical techniques. Hosaka 1974, 3.263.

[9] "I'll rise above him and make him lose face." Michinaga and Kintō were born in the same year, 966.

has happened. Kintō does not even associate on equal terms with Michinaga's son, the Palace Minister.

I believe a man destined for greatness begins very early to reveal a dauntless spirit, and also to enjoy special divine protection. There was a certain dark night late in the Fifth Month during Emperor Kazan's reign. It was still the rainy season, and the downpour was getting on everyone's nerves. The Emperor, who probably felt the need of diversion, went into the Courtiers' Hall to join the gentlemen there, and presently the conversation turned from general topics to stories about frightening occurrences. "As a matter of fact," His Majesty remarked, "we are having an exceptionally eerie sort of night tonight. Even with so many people around, one feels uncomfortable. Imagine being off in some deserted spot! Nobody could possibly go to such a place alone."

Michinaga interrupted a chorus of assent. "I'll go wherever you please," he said.

The Emperor delighted in such amusements. "That sounds most interesting," he said. "Be off with you! Michitaka shall go to the Burakuin, Michikane to the Jijūden storeroom, and Michinaga to the Daigokuden."[10]

Michinaga had put his brothers in an awkward position, the other gentlemen thought. Michitaka and Michikane looked pale and upset, but Michinaga seemed perfectly composed. "I won't take any of my own attendants," he said. "Have a guardsman from this headquarters or a Palace Guard accompany me as far as Shōkeimon Gate.[11] I'll go in alone from there."

"There will be no proof," the Emperor objected.

"That's right," Michinaga said. He asked for a knife from the Imperial handbox and set out.

The other two went off with long faces. The trial had been decreed after the proclamation of the last quarter of the Hour of the Rat [11:00 p.m.-1:00 a.m.], so it must have been the Hour of the Ox [1:00

---

[10] Unlike the Burakuin and the Daigokuden, which were situated in distant, unfrequented locations, the Jijūden faced the Seiryōden across a courtyard. It also seems to have lacked a storeroom. One commentator has suggested that Jijūden may be a mistake for Shinkaden, which is written with somewhat similar graphs, and which is known to have had storerooms. The Shinkaden was the main building in the Chūwain, a special compound used only for occasional Shintō ceremonies. Michikane would probably have been directed to follow a circuitous route past the Shishinden, and to enter the compound via the south gate, Chūwamon, which faced Shōkeimon, the gate through which Michinaga entered the Daigokuden. Hosaka 1974, 3.269.

[11] "This headquarters" refers to the Bodyguards, who maintained posts east and west of the Shishinden. For Palace Guard, see Appendix B, n. 11.

a.m.-3:00 p.m.] by the time they finished talking about it. The Emperor had even specified their routes. "Michitaka is to go out past the Right Gate Guards;[12] Michinaga will use Shōmeimon Gate. . . ."

After the departure, Michitaka kept his courage up as far as the guard post,[13] but the sound of mysterious voices in the vicinity of the Banquet Pine Grove drove him back. The trembling Michikane made his way to a spot next to the dance stage,[14] where he thought he detected a human figure, towering to the eaves from the paving stones east of the Jijūden. "How can I serve His Majesty unless I stay alive?" he said, dizzy with fright. So both men came back, and the Emperor struck his fan and laughed.

There was no sign of Michinaga for an alarmingly long time, but then he came strolling in.

"What happened?" the Emperor asked.

Michinaga calmly presented the Imperial knife and a splinter of wood.

"What's that?" the Emperor said.

"If I had come back empty-handed, there would have been nothing to show I had got there," Michinaga answered in a matter-of-fact voice. "I have brought Your Majesty a splinter from the base of the pillar south of the throne." The Emperor was overcome with admiration.

Still shaken, Michitaka and Michikane listened in silence while the Emperor and others showered their brother with praise—whether from jealousy or from some other reason, I cannot say.

To satisfy a lingering doubt, the Emperor commanded that a Chamberlain be sent to the Daigokuden the next morning to see if the splinter fit the pillar; and it matched perfectly when the man pressed it into position. The scar is still there to inspire us with admiration for Michinaga's bravery.

When the late Imperial Lady Senshi was having some prayers recited, there happened to be a physiognomist among the monks who were assisting the chief officiant, the Iimuro Provisional Archbishop. The ladies-in-waiting called on this expert to read their faces, and one of them took advantage of the opportunity to ask his opinion of Palace Minister Michitaka.

"His is the countenance of a very superior person. There are signs

---

[12] A guard post at Gishūmon, the central gate in the west Middle Enclosure wall.

[13] The one at Gishūmon.

[14] A platform between the Jijūden and the Shishinden.

that he will govern the country," he answered. "But Michinaga, the Master of the Empress's Household, has the really outstanding signs!"

When someone asked about Michikane, he said, "He is another exceptional one. He has the aspect of a future minister of state." But he repeated, "Ah! Lord Michinaga has the really outstanding signs!"

Then they asked about Korechika, and he said, "His lineaments are also distinguished, but he has a thunder face."

"What do you mean by that?" they asked.

"He will make a lot of noise for a while, but it won't last; his future seems precarious. There is no limit at all to the good fortune revealed in Lord Michinaga's face." And thus he brought in a reference to His Lordship the Novice every time they inquired about someone else.

"What kind of face does Michinaga have? Why do you keep mentioning him?" they asked.

"In physiognomy, the best features are those of a tiger cub crossing rugged mountain peaks," he said. "Lord Michinaga's is just such a countenance, which is why I speak as I do. To see him is like looking at the mighty Bishamon.[15] With those lineaments, he is superior to everybody."

What an excellent physiognomist! He made no mistakes at all. Korechika had no trouble in becoming a minister of state, but it was merely the initial good fortune of the prophecy. Because falling thunder may rise again, it might be better to compare the Palace Minister to a falling star that is transformed into a stone. A fallen star never rises.

People say the figure Michinaga has cut on various occasions will be remembered a long time. There was an Imperial pilgrimage to Kamo Shrine during Emperor Sanjō's reign. It was snowing hard that day, and Michinaga let out the sleeve of his inner robe and held his fan over his head. How handsome he looked as he brushed the white flakes away, saying, "A remarkably heavy snow!" I cannot begin to describe the marvelous effect with which the white snow set off the contrast between his black cloak and his red inner robe. He rode a famous high-spirited horse, the name of which I have forgotten, controlling it with admirable skill. The former Emperor himself seems to have remembered the event well, for I have heard that he once said, during his illness, "I shall never forget the snow on the day we visited Kamo Shrine." It was a touching remark.

For some unknown reason, the gods saw fit to impose a year of unhappiness on Michinaga, the shining light of the nation.[16] Just the same,

[15] Also Tamon. Best known as one of the Four Heavenly Kings (*shitennō*), fierce, warlike servants of Indra; also regarded by Buddhists as a victory god.

[16] Michinaga's nephew, Korechika, outranked him from the Eighth Month of

His Lordship refused to abase himself or give way to melancholy. And although he discharged his official duties in a correct and punctual manner, he declined to defer to Korechika in private life. He appeared at the Southern Palace one day while Korechika was holding an archery contest. Surprised by the visit, which he considered suspicious, Michitaka nevertheless welcomed him warmly and let him shoot before Korechika, even though his rank was inferior. Korechika lost by two hits, whereupon Michitaka and some others proposed an extension of the match. "Shoot twice more," they said.

"All right, extend it," Michinaga said, somewhat annoyed. As he prepared to shoot again, he said, "If Emperors and Empresses are to issue from my house, let this arrow hit the mark." And didn't his arrow strike the heart of the target?

Next Korechika prepared to shoot. He was extremely nervous, and it may be that his hands trembled. At any rate, his arrow flew off into the sky without coming near the target. Michitaka turned pale.

Michinaga got ready again. "If I am to serve as Regent, let this arrow find the mark," he said. The arrow hit the very center, striking with such force that the target almost broke. The Regent's cordiality vanished, and he showed his displeasure by ending the match. "Why should you shoot?" he said to Korechika. "Don't shoot! Don't shoot!" A chill pervaded the gathering. Korechika was in no immediate danger of being outstripped by Michinaga, but I suppose he may have been intimidated by his uncle's attitude and language.

Then there was the time when Michinaga and Korechika were both escorting Senshi on a pilgrimage to Ishiyama. Michinaga was on horseback and Korechika was riding in a carriage. Something made Korechika decide to turn back at Awataguchi, and he went over to Senshi's carriage to request permission to leave. When Michinaga saw the Imperial Lady's carriage come to a halt, he rode back to where Korechika was standing with his hand on one of the shafts. "Hurry up!" he said, letting his horse breathe down the back of Korechika's neck. "Can't you see the sun is setting?" Korechika shot an indignant look over his shoulder, but Michinaga stood his ground. "The sun is setting. Hurry up! Hurry up!" What could the furious Korechika do but slowly depart? When he told his father about it, Michitaka said, "A man who insults a minister of state will come to no good end."

There was another incident at the time of the Snake Day purification in the Third Month.[17] After having gone through the ritual, Kore-

---

994, when Korechika became Palace Minister, until the Sixth Month of 995, when Michinaga advanced from Major Counselor to Minister of the Right.

[17] *Mi no hi no harae*, a ritual of Chinese origin performed beside a river on the

chika took a group of friends out onto the river beach for a party, which he held inside a cluster of flat-topped tents, erected by his servants. While he was there, Michinaga arrived to perform his own lustration. Observing that his men were guiding the carriage close to the tents, he told them not to be rude; they must leave more space. "What's His Lordship saying?" grumbled one of his attendants, whose name was Something-or-other-maro. "That kind of talk just invites bad luck." Uttering a disgusted exclamation, he beat the ox and shifted the carriage even closer to the tents.

"The fellow gave me quite a dressing down," Michinaga said later. He was partial to the man afterward, and took a benign interest in his affairs.

Those were the kinds of things that caused bad feeling between Michinaga and Korechika.

Because Michinaga was Senshi's favorite brother, Korechika treated the Imperial Lady with distant formality. He also seized every opportunity to malign her and Michinaga to Emperor Ichijō, whom he saw at all hours because of the Emperor's great affection for Empress Teishi. Senshi naturally heard about his remarks and found them offensive. Meanwhile the Emperor was feeling grave doubts about entrusting the government to Michinaga.

Empress Teishi was concerned about her own position after Michitaka's death, which is why Michikane's appointment was delayed.[18] But Senshi believed in the principle of seniority, and she also disliked Korechika. Although Emperor Ichijō was very hesitant about appointing Michinaga, she pleaded her brother's cause with tireless persistence. "Why do you feel that way?" she asked. "It was bad enough for Michinaga when Korechika became a minister of state ahead of him, but there was nothing you could do about that, because the boy's father was bent on promoting him. If you pass over Michinaga now, after having already appointed Michikane, people will spend more time criticizing you than pitying him."

The Emperor, who may have felt beleaguered, stopped visiting his mother, who then proceeded to take possession of one of the Imperial Apartments. Instead of asking him to call, she invaded the Bedchamber, armed with a new store of tearful expostulations, while Michinaga

---

first Day of the Snake in the Third Month—for capital dwellers, usually, as here, at the Kamo River. The individual's defilements were transferred to a doll, which was sent downstream. McCullough and McCullough 1980, Chapter 21, n. 35; Hosaka 1974, 3.298.

[18] The author implies that she was trying to secure the regency for her brother, Korechika.

waited in the room she had left. After an interval long enough to excite painful misgivings, she opened the door and came out, wearing a triumphant smile on her flushed, tear-stained face. "At last! The decree has been issued!" she told him.

Even the most trivial happenings result from the karma of a previous life, so I need hardly say that such an important event did not come about through the good offices of a single individual. Yet how could Michinaga fail to feel gratitude toward Senshi! He more than repaid the favor, and it was he who carried her ashes to the burial ground after her cremation.

I was both surprised and worried when Michinaga assumed power after the successive deaths of Michitaka and Michikane. How it may have been in remote times I cannot say, but there had been nothing within my memory to compare with Michinaga's long tenure. Indeed, no recent Regent except Tadahira and Saneyori had survived for as long as ten years. So I wondered how it would be with Michinaga—but his fortune could hardly have been more auspicious. I feel sure that his high destiny was responsible for the early deaths of his older brothers. Such prosperity can only be the result of a special karma. But I think people are inclined to believe that all the Fujiwara have been equally blessed, so I had better say a little more about some of the others.

[TALES OF THE FUJIWARA FAMILY]

Aside from the seven divine generations, our first ruler was Emperor Jinmu. And it was during the reign of the thirty-seventh sovereign, Emperor Kōtoku, that ministers of state were first designated. In that reign, Nakatomi Kamako no muraji, a native of Hitachi Province, became the first Palace Minister; and in the reign of the thirty-ninth sovereign, Emperor Tenji, Kamako's surname was changed to Fujiwara. We regard him as the founder of the Fujiwara family—the ancestor of all those Emperors, Empresses, ministers of state, and senior nobles.

Kamatari enjoyed Emperor Tenji's special esteem. The Emperor gave him one of the Imperial consorts, intending that the child she was carrying should be Kamatari's if it were a boy and his own if it were a girl. "If it is a boy, he shall be your son," he promised Kamatari. "If it is a girl, she shall be mine." The baby turned out to be a boy, so they made him Kamatari's son.

Kamatari was already the father of a son and a daughter, and the former consort later bore him two girls and two boys. One after another, the two girls became consorts of Emperor Tenmu—that is, of Emperor Tenji's son, Prince Ōtomo, who became Chancellor and ascended the throne in the course of a single year.[19] Kamatari's oldest son, Nakatomi Omimaro, progressed as far as the office of Consultant, and the first son by Emperor Tenji's consort became a Minister of the Right. That was Fujiwara Fuhito, who was posthumously granted the title of Chancellor. Kamatari's third and fourth sons, Umakai and Maro,[20] got as far as the Consultant level or thereabouts.

Kamatari died during Emperor Tenji's reign, in the year in which he received the Fujiwara surname. He had been Palace Minister for twenty-five years. Although he never became Chancellor, he was given a posthumous name, Tankaikō, in recognition of his illustrious status as founder of the house of Fujiwara.

"It is wrong to call Kamatari Tankaikō,"[21] Shigeki interrupted. "Your eloquence is like the swift flow of the River of Heaven,[22] but an occasional mistake does creep in. Still, who else could talk so well? You remind me of the layman Vimalakīrti, who lived during the Buddha's lifetime."

"Long ago in the land of T'ang," Yotsugi replied, "a sage named Confucius said, 'A wise man is sure to make one mistake in a thousand thoughts.'[23] Everything I have been telling you comes out of my own head, and since I am well over a hundred—closer to two hundred—I think the fact that I have got this far makes me compare rather well with men of earlier times."

"Oh, of course, of course. It is all too entertaining and interesting for words." Shigeki wiped away a tear of emotion. And indeed one could not help feeling that the most extravagant praise would have been inadequate.

[19] As in Chapter 1, the author confuses Emperor Tenji's son with his brother. See Chapter 1, n. 42, and Appendix A.

[20] Actually sons of Fuhito.

[21] Tankaikō was Fuhito's posthumous name. The objection is followed by a sentence, omitted in the translation, which seems to be an inept interpolation: "Kamatari served as a minister of state for twenty-five years and died when he was in his fifty-sixth year."

[22] The Milky Way.

[23] This saying, incorrectly attributed to Confucius by Yotsugi, appears in *Shih chi*, biography of the Marquis of Huai yen. Watson 1961, 1.218.

Kamatari's son Fuhito, the Minister of the Right (*Yotsugi resumed*), was actually Emperor Tenji's child, but he became Kamatari's second son. There was nothing ordinary about him—not even his name, which means "unequaled." He had two sons, of whom the older, Muchimaro, rose to the office of Minister of the Left, and the second, Fusasaki, to that of Consultant. He also had two daughters: Empress Kōmyō, Emperor Shōmu's mother; and the lady who gave birth to a Princess as Emperor Shōmu's Junior Consort.[24] That Princess, placed on the throne by Emperor Shōmu, was called the Takano Empress. She ascended the throne twice.

Each of Fuhito's two sons and two younger brothers established a separate branch of the family. Of the branches, which are called the Four Houses, Muchimaro's is known as the Southern House, Fusasaki's as the Northern House, Umakai's as the Ceremonial House, and Maro's as the Capital House. Those are the Four Houses of the Fujiwara, from which many a sovereign, minister of state, and senior noble has come forth to flourish. Today it is Fusasaki's line that resembles a tree's spreading branches, so I shall confine my remarks to its members, passing over the lines that have ceased to prosper. (Obscure people who bear the Fujiwara surname are probably latter-day descendants of those houses.)

From Kamatari to the present Regent, there have been, I believe, thirteen generations. Please listen while I tell you about them. Some of you may think all the Fujiwara are members of a single family, which is true enough. But it is no easy matter to separate the lines.

Kamatari Palace Minister Kamatari died on the Sixteenth of the Tenth Month in the year during which he was granted the Fujiwara name. He was fifty-six, and had served as a minister of state for twenty-five years.

When a certain member of the Ki family heard that Kamatari had received the name Fujiwara, he said, "A tree [*ki*] dies when a wisteria vine [*fuji*] twines around it. This will be the end of the house of Ki." How right he was!

Kamatari fell ill once. Buddhism had not yet spread throughout the country in those ancient times, and so it must have been hard to find monks to perform healing rituals. (In spite of Shōtoku Taishi's efforts, there are still people today who fail to read the *Lotus Sutra*, which even new-born babes supposedly lisp.) But Kamatari commissioned a

[24] Empress Kōmyō was Shōmu's consort and the Takano Empress's mother. It was another of Fuhito's daughters, Kyūshi (d. 754), who was Shōmu's mother.

Korean nun to celebrate a *Vimalakīrti Sutra* offering, and the single service cured him. He thus became a devout believer in the sutra, which is how we happen to have the Vimalakīrti Service.²⁵

Fuhito   Kamatari's second son, Fuhito, the Minister of the Left of Senior First Rank, was a minister of state for thirteen years and a posthumous Chancellor. He served during the reigns of Empresses Genmei and Genshō.

Fusasaki   Fuhito's second son, Fusasaki, was a Consultant for twenty years. He received the posthumous title of Chancellor on the Seventh of the Eighth Month in the fourth year of Tenpyō hōji [760], during the reign of Emperor Junnin. He served Empress Genshō and Emperor Shōmu.

Matate   Fusasaki's fourth son, Major Counselor Matate, died at the age of fifty-two, on the Sixteenth of the Third Month in the second year of Tenpyō jingo [766], during the reign of Empress Shōtoku. He was a posthumous Chancellor, and a senior noble for seven years.

Uchimaro   Matate's second son was Uchimaro, the Minister of the Right of Junior Second Rank and Major Captain of the Left Bodyguards. He died at the age of fifty-seven. He was a senior noble for twenty years, a minister of state for seven years, and a posthumous Minister of the Left with Junior First Rank. He served during the reigns of Emperors Kanmu and Heizei.

Fuyutsugi   Uchimaro's third son, Fuyutsugi, rose to the office of Minister of the Left and was a posthumous Chancellor. Since I have already told you about him and his successors, I shall not go into detail now.

After having prospered ever since Kamatari's time, the family had gradually begun to lose ground, and by Fuyutsugi's generation its members had found themselves in a shaky position. In those days, it was only the Minamoto who became ministers and senior nobles.²⁶ Then Fuyutsugi built the Nan'endō and enshrined a sixteen-foot Fukū-kensaku Kannon in it.⁽¹⁷⁾

---

²⁵ *Yuimae*, an annual series of lectures delivered at the Kōfukuji, the Fujiwara family temple, from the Tenth to the Sixteenth of the Tenth Month. The topic was the *Vimalakīrti Sutra*, which centers on a discussion of Mahāyāna doctrine in the form of a conversation between Vimalakīrti (J. Yuima, a rich lay disciple of the Buddha) and the bodhisattva Mañjuśrī.

²⁶ While it is true that the Fujiwara were far from enjoying a monopoly on senior Court positions in the Nara and early Heian periods, *Kugyō bunin* shows not a single Minamoto minister of state or senior noble prior to Fuyutsugi's death in 826. The Minamoto surname does not antedate the reign of Emperor Saga (r. 809-823).

Nagara Fuyutsugi's oldest son, Middle Counselor Nagara, became a posthumous Chancellor.

Mototsune Nagara's third son, Mototsune, became a Chancellor.

Tadahira Mototsune's fourth son, Tadahira, became a Chancellor.

Morosuke Tadahira's second son, Morosuke, became a Minister of the Right.

Kaneie Morosuke's third son, Kaneie, became a Chancellor.

Michinaga Kaneie's fifth son, Michinaga, became a Chancellor.

Yorimichi Michinaga's oldest son, Yorimichi, is the present Regent and Minister of the Left.

It is splendid that a son[27] has been born to Yorimichi, who was childless until very recently. Although I have not been telling you about mothers,[28] I must mention that the lady comes of excellent stock. While not himself a prominent figure, her father, Norisada, the late Commander of the Military Guards of the Left, could boast of the highest lineage. It is wonderful for Norisada to have such an important grandson, even though he has not lived to see him.

Michinaga sponsored the Seventh Night celebration.[29] He sent Yorimichi this poem:

Toshi o hete	Spring's green child
Machitsuru matsu no	We have found to our delight
Wakaeda ni	On the young shoot
Ureshiku aeru	Of the pine that has waited
Haru no midorigo.	Year after year.[30]

His Lordship gave the boy the childhood name Osagimi, Leader, because he was his first grandson, except for the Emperor and the Crown Prince.

So now I have shown you which of the Four Houses' many descendants, past and present, have been the ones to survive and prosper.

In recognition of the fact that Hitachi was Kamatari's birthplace, the family enshrined its tutelary god at a place called Kashima in that

---

[27] Michifusa.

[28] Presumably those who, like Michifusa's, were not recognized as wives. Hosaka, 3.346.

[29] Chapter 4, n. 27.

[30] Pine (*matsu*) and young shoot (*wakaeda*) are metaphors for Michinaga and Yorimichi. The last line puns on spring green (*haru no midori*) and infant born in the spring (*haru no midorigo*). The baby was born on the Tenth of the First Month in the second year of Manju (1025), i.e., in what was regarded as the first month of spring.

province; and from Kamatari's time to the present, messengers have been sent there with offerings whenever a new Emperor, Empress, or minister of state has emerged from the house of Fujiwara. After the Court settled at Nara, Kashima was thought to be too distant, so they moved the shrine to Mount Mikasa in Yamato, styling the god the Bright Divinity of Kasuga. Official envoys of both sexes are sent to that god, the present tutelary deity of the house, who is worshipped by Imperial consorts, ministers of state, senior nobles, and other family members. It is a great occasion when all the messengers start out for one of the shrine's festivals, which fall on the first Day of the Monkey in the Second and Eleventh Months.

When the Court moved to the present capital, the god was again transferred to a convenient location, at a place called Ōharano. Two annual festivals are held there, on the first Day of the Hare in the Second Month and the first Day of the Rat in the Eleventh. Imperial messengers attend, and all the Fujiwara nobles present offerings and Ten Racers.[31] The god has also been installed even closer, at Yoshida. It was Middle Counselor Yamakage who enshrined the Bright Divinity of Yoshida, whose festivals take place on the last Day of the Rat in the Fourth Month and the last Day of the Monkey in the Eleventh. "If Emperors and Empresses arise from my family," he vowed, "I shall see that these become official festivals." And so it is that the festivals have been sponsored by the Court ever since Emperor Ichijō's day.[32]

Kamatari's family temple is at Tōnomine in Yamato. His bones are interred in its precincts, and samādhi services are still held there.[33] Fuhito founded Yamashinadera, where prayers are recited on behalf of the family. Whenever there is an unusual or strange occurrence at Yamashina or Tōnomine, or at Kasuga, Ōharano, or Yoshida, the monks or priests report it to the Court. The head of the Fujiwara house instructs diviners to determine its meaning; and, should caution be required, he sees to it that ritual seclusion tags are distributed to family members who are vulnerable that year.

The services that are held two or three times a year probably originated at Yamashinadera.[34] From the Eighth to the Fourteenth of the

[31] See Chapter 4, n. 45.

[32] Emperor Ichijō's grandmother, Tokihime, was Yamakage's granddaughter.

[33] The services, centering on the Lotus Sutra, were designed to expunge the sins of the deceased and ensure his enlightenment.

[34] Service translates [hō]e ([dharma] assembly), a general term for a Buddhist convocation. As the author indicates below, the reference here is to a specific group of great annual events, of which the one with the longest history was the Vimalakīrti Service at the Kōfukuji (also called Yamashinadera; see n. 25).

First Month, Nara monks conduct the Suvarṇaprabhāsa Service at the Court of the Eight Monistries, and the Court and all the Fujiwara gentlemen make offerings.[35] And then there are the Yakushiji Suvarṇaprabhāsa Service, beginning on the Seventeenth of the Third Month and lasting for seven days,[36] and the Yamashinadera Vimalakīrti Service, beginning on the Tenth of the Tenth Month and also lasting for seven days. Imperial messengers are sent with gifts of bedclothes on every such occasion, and Fujiwara gentlemen of Fifth and higher rank also send presents. When Nara monks have lectured at all three of those services, they are called Past Lecturers, and they received the three highest titles in the Buddhist hierarchy,[37] each in his turn. You can see that Yamashinadera is an awesome and holy temple. Even the worst outrage is condoned if the temple is involved; people simply dismiss it as "Yamashina propriety." It merely goes to show what an incomparable position the house of Fujiwara enjoys.

Repetitious as it may seem, I think I probably ought to continue a while longer. Let me tell you about the men who became fathers of Empresses and grandfathers of Emperors.

Kamatari Both of Interior Minister Kamatari's two daughters were presented as brides to Emperor Tenmu. They bore children of both sexes, but neither seems to have produced an Emperor or Crown Prince.

Fuhito One of Posthumous Chancellor Fuhito's two daughters, a Junior Consort during Emperor Monmu's reign, bore the Prince who became Emperor Shōmu. She was called Empress Kōmyō.[38] The other was married to her nephew, Emperor Shōmu, and gave birth to a daughter who ascended the throne—the Princess known as the Takano Empress, who was our forty-sixth sovereign. The Takano Empress abdicated, but she returned to the throne after an intervening reign to act as the forty-eighth sovereign. Her mother is called the Posthumous Empress. Thus both of Fuhito's daughters were Empresses, but the Takano Empress's mother did not receive the title until after her death.

[35] The Suvarṇaprabhāsa Service (*misaie*) at Court consisted of an annual series of lectures on the *Suvarṇaprabhāsa Sutra* (J. Konkōmyōkyō). Dating from the eighth century, it was held at the Daigokuden in the Imperial presence, with the aim of ensuring peaceful conditions and bountiful crops during the coming year. The honor of serving as Lecturer was reserved for monks who had previously expounded the *Vimalakīrti Sutra* at the Kōfukuji. "Nara monks" here means Kōfukuji monks.

[36] Seventeenth should read Seventh. The purpose of the service was to pray for peace and Imperial longevity.

[37] See n. 2. [38] See n. 24.

Fuhito was the father of Empress Kōmyō and the Posthumous Empress, and the grandfather of Emperor Shōmu and the Takano Empress. (According to one book, the Takano Empress's mother was made an Empress before her death, and was called Empress Kōmyō; also, Emperor Shōmu's mother received the title during her lifetime rather than posthumously.)

Fuyutsugi   Posthumous Chancellor Fuyutsugi was the father of Senior Grand Empress Junshi and the grandfather of Emperor Montoku.

Yoshifusa   Chancellor Yoshifusa was the father of Grand Empress Meishi and the grandfather of Emperor Seiwa.

Nagara   Posthumous Chancellor Nagara was the father of Grand Empress Kōshi and the grandfather of Emperor Yōzei.

Fusatsugi   Posthumous Chancellor Fusatsugi was the father of Posthumous Grand Empress Takushi and the grandfather of Emperor Kōkō.

Takafuji   Palace Minister Takafuji was the father of Grand Empress Inshi and the grandfather of Emperor Daigo.

Mototsune   Chancellor Mototsune was the father of Empress Onshi and the grandfather of Emperors Suzaku and Murakami.

Morosuke   Minister of the Right Morosuke was the father of Empress Anshi and the grandfather of Emperors Reizei and En'yū.

Koremasa   Chancellor Koremasa was the father of Posthumous Empress Kaishi and the grandfather of Emperor Kazan.

Kaneie   Chancellor Kaneie was the father of Grand Empress Senshi and Posthumous Empress Chōshi, and the grandfather of Emperors Ichijō and Sanjō.

Michinaga   Chancellor Michinaga is the father of Senior Grand Empress Shōshi, Grand Empress Kenshi, Empress Ishi, and the Crown Prince's consort Kishi, and the grandfather of the present Emperor and Crown Prince.

Of all our many Fujiwara ministers of state, only Michinaga has made three daughters Empresses at the same time. Furthermore, he is the father of a Regent Minister of the Left, a Palace Minister, two Major Counselors, and a Middle Counselor. That is the truth! Compare him with anyone! He stands alone and unrivaled in Japan.

Michinaga's Buddha Hall, the Muryōjuin, is far superior to Kamatari's Tōnomine, Fuhito's Yamashinadera, Mototsune's Gokurakuji, Tadahira's Hōshōji, and Morosuke's Ryōgon'in—and even to Emperor Shōmu's Tōdaiji, in spite of the enormous size of the Tōdaiji buddha. Of course, ordinary temples are not worth mentioning in the same breath! The Daianji is not its equal today, though it is a Japanese sovereign's imitation of the First Cloister of the Hsi ming ssu in China, which is patterned after the Jetavana-vihāra in India, which in turn depicted the First Cloister of the Tusita Heaven.[39] Nor can any of the innumerable other temples in Nara approach it. It surpasses both Tamemitsu's Hōjūji and the Naniwa Tennōji, the latter of which was built by Shōtoku Taishi in return for divine assistance; and when one compares it to the Seven or Fifteen Great Temples of Nara, it is so much more splendid that the Pure Land seems to have manifested itself on earth.[40] Surely such a glorious hall must have been built because of a vow, just as the Jōmyōji was.

People say Michinaga conceived the plan for the Jōmyōji when he went along on the visit of thanks Kaneie made to Kohata after he became a minister of state. "What a shame that no holy bells ring in a place where so many of our ancestors' bones lie," His Lordship thought, looking about him. "I shall make it my business to erect a Samādhi Hall[41] if I have a successful career."

Of numerous similar events in earlier days, probably the most notable were the ones that led to the founding of the Gokurakuji and the Hōshōji. It seems extraordinary to me that Mototsune should have made up his mind to erect a temple when he was only a child. I have not been able to find out exactly who was on the throne at the time, but I think it may have been Emperor Ninmyō. At any rate, Mototsune accompanied the sovereign as a page on an excursion to the Seri River. His Majesty played the seven-stringed koto, and, as was customary, he used special finger picks. To his great distress, he lost one of the picks in the set he had brought along. There was no way of devising a substitute, so he told young Mototsune to find it for him. (I suppose it was fated that he should have thought of asking the boy instead of one of the adults.) Mototsune turned his horse around and headed back. Where should he go? How could he possibly ferret it out? But it was out of the question to return empty-handed. He made a silent vow to build a temple where he found it. The pick came to light, and it is on that very spot that the Gokurakuji now stands! How could such an idea have entered a child's head? It must have

---

[39] The Tusita Heaven (J. *tosotsuten*) is the fourth of six heavens in the realm of desire. Maitreya, the buddha of the future, dwells in its innermost precinct, the First Cloister.

[40] Seven Great Temples of Nara: Tōdaiji, Kōfukuji, Gangōji, Daianji, Yakushiji, Saidaiji, Hōryūji. Fifteen Great Temples of Nara: the preceding plus Shinyakushiji, Ōkisakidera, Futaiji, Hokkemetsuzaiji, Chōshōji, Tōshōdaiji, Sukeiji, and Gufukuji. *Ōkagami uragaki*, item 45, p. 393; *Shūkaishō*, p. 433. Pure Land: Amitābha's paradise.

[41] A mortuary chapel. See n. 33.

been predestined that the pick should get lost, and that the Emperor should command Mototsune to find it.

After Mototsune became a great man, he drove out in a carriage to lay plans for building his temple, taking little Tadahira with him. As they passed the present site of the Hōshōji, Tadahira piped up, "This looks like a good place for a temple, Papa. Build it here." Mototsune wondered what had possessed him. He got out of the carriage, looked around, and saw that it was indeed an excellent site. How could the boy's young eyes have appraised it so well except through the workings of karma? "You are right; it looks like a fine place," he said. "But you had better be the one to build here. I have a reason for going elsewhere." And that was how Tadahira happened to found the Hōshōji.

"What about Morosuke and his Iimuro Hall?" said Shigeki. "I was with him when he climbed Mount Hiei to visit the Yokawa Senior Archbishop's cloister."[42]

"I know of many such cases," Yotsugi answered, "but, after all, Michinaga's is in a class by itself. He is a man who enjoys special protection from the gods of heaven and earth. Winds may rage and rains may fall day after day, but the skies will clear and the ground will dry out two or three days before he plans anything. Some people call him a reincarnation of Shōtoku Taishi; others say he is Kōbō Daishi, reborn to make Buddhism flourish. Even to the censorious eye of old age, he seems not an ordinary mortal but an awesome manifestation of a god or buddha.

"A nation is bound to be perfectly happy with a ruler like Michinaga. In the old days, cattle drivers and horse herders in the employ of noblemen and Princes were always dunning us for coins, paper, and rice, which were needed, they claimed, to pay for festivals and spirit services.[43] They wouldn't even let anyone cut grass in the fields and hills. But now the minor functionaries of the great no longer seize a man's belongings, and there is no more talk of local headmen and village magistrates who pester people to defray the expenses of fire festivals and so forth.[44] Can we ever hope to enjoy such safety and peace

---

[42] It was as a result of that visit that Morosuke decided to build the Iimuro Hall. Hosaka 1974, 3.385.

[43] Spirit services (goryōe) were designed to placate pestilence gods, curse-laying spirits of the dead, and other supernatural troublemakers.

[44] Fire festivals (himatsuri) are conjectured to have been folk events held for the purpose of preventing fires. "The minor functionaries of the great" translates jichō omonomochi. Jichō was a term used of low-ranking men in the service of

again? I unfasten my belt and collar in my cottage, stretch out my legs, and go off to sleep without bothering to lock up. That's how I happen to have preserved my youth and lived so long.

"Look at the beans, cowpeas, melons, and eggplants that people grow at Kitano and the Kamo river beach. There was no way of protecting them not so long ago, but the yields have been wonderful during the past few years. Of course, nobody steals the vegetables, and they aren't even eaten by cattle and horses, so people simply leave them unguarded. It's just like Maitreya's blessed era!"

"People seem to be doing a lot of complaining nowadays about Michinaga's incessant demands for laborers to work on his temple," said the other old man. "Haven't you heard about it?"

"Yes, he does issue a call every two or three days," Yotsugi answered. "But when you go, it's not bad. If a man bears in mind that he is being called on to help build an earthly paradise, he will be glad to go if he can, and he will hope for rebirth as a shrub or tree at the Buddha Hall. Right-thinking people ought to be anxious to contribute their services. I have never evaded a summons, because I know I will never have such an opportunity again. And when a man does go, there is nothing bad about it at all. They are always handing out food and wine, and sometimes we get fruit and other dainties, which have been brought in as offerings. For workers who keep going back, there are even presents of clothing. So it seems that the lower classes scramble to join the levies."

"That's right," Shigeki said. "But I have thought of an even better plan for myself. In all my long life, I have never been forced to wear rags or suffer from lack of food or drink, but if a time should come when I was unable to put my hands on such necessities, I would look for three pieces of paper on which to write Michinaga a petition. And in the petition I would say, 'I was a page in the late Chancellor Tadahira's day. Now that I am old and destitute, I look to you as my lord because you are his descendant. I hope you will grant me a few things.' I know he wouldn't refuse me some trifles, so I feel as secure of them as though they were in my storeroom."

---

the Court, government, and noble houses. The meaning of *omonomochi* is unknown. Hosaka speculates that it may be another name for *shibu*, minor functionaries in the Palace Table Office, where *jichō* are also known to have been employed. He tentatively derives the term from *omono*, food (as in *omonodana*, food shelf, and *omonoyadori*, food repository, two names associated with the Palace Table Office), and *motsu*, hold. The men were presumably supplying the Imperial Table at the expense of the common folk. Hosaka 1974, 3.394.

"I am sure you are right," Yotsugi agreed. "My wife and I have often said we would submit a petition at the temple in case of distress. Well, well, I am so happy to have met you. It has been like taking a bag out of storage, opening it up, and slitting it to let the air in! But tell me, how many times have you visited the famous Muryōjuin?"

"When they dedicated the Great Buddha Hall[45] that year, people said ordinary spectators would be driven off on the day of the ceremony, so I went to the dance rehearsal they held three days in advance."

I have gone a number of times *(Yotsugi said)*. Of course, the splendor of the dedication was beyond description. I went back again the next day, hoping to get a closer view of the images before the decorations were taken away, and I saw the Imperial ladies making a tour of the halls. It seemed to me that I had stayed alive just to witness that spectacle! Never since reaching the age of discretion have I seen the like! There were four ladies in a hand-drawn carriage. Senior Grand Empress Shōshi and Grand Empress Kenshi sat in front, letting a fraction of their sleeves show, and Kenshi's hair trailed the ground in a most marvelous manner. It seemed that only the persons of Empress Ishi and Principal Handmaid Kishi must be inside the carriage at the back, because all their robes were billowing out, and, in fact, trailing to the ground. A gentleman was following along with some garments in his arms, so Princess Teishi may have been seated in the middle. She was probably just wearing an unlined inner robe.[46]

The carriage was being drawn by men of Fourth and Fifth Rank. Behind it walked the Regent Yorimichi, Michinaga's other sons, and other senior nobles and courtiers, all dressed in informal cloaks. What a magnificent sight! The only missing face was that of Yoshinobu, the Provisional Master of the Empress's Household, who was having to observe strict ritual seclusion. He had supplied the Empress's costume, which looked gorgeous. "I had something to tell Her Majesty on the dedication day," he said later. "When I went to see her, I found all five of the ladies seated together. It seemed to me that her costume was quite perfect—but I suppose I may have thought so because I was the one who prepared it."

[45] The Golden Hall of the Hōjōji.

[46] *Hitoe no mizo*, part of a lady's formal costume. Heat and cramped quarters had probably dictated the removal of the Princess's voluminous outer robes. The Golden Hall was dedicated in the Seventh Month of 1022, when she was nine years old.

Though I rattle on with an air of authority, I am really only an ignorant lower-class fellow. The colors of the ladies' costumes have completely left my mind after all this time. Perhaps it is because Empress Ishi looked so splendid that I do seem to recall her wearing a double unlined inner robe of red gossamer. I can't remember her outer robe, but she had on a stunning triple-layered lespedeza bombycine jacket, embroidered or painted with an autumn field design.[47]

People said the other Imperial ladies' costumes were also provided by gentlemen of the family. Shōshi wore quantities of double-patterned silk, and Kenshi was dressed entirely in Chinese stuffs. Yorimichi, who had prepared Kishi's attire, had hastily added a foil design after learning that the other ladies were to wear dresses decorated with pictures. Michinaga laughed when he saw it. "It would make a good costume for a *shushi* actor,"[48] he said.

Michinaga waited for the ladies with the hall doors open. I was overjoyed to witness the scene at all, even from a vantage point as remote as the Great South Gate, but I heard later that three nurses watched from a gallery opening as the ladies descended from the carriage and inched forward respectfully on their knees.[49] They were Ben and Tayū, both in Princess Teishi's service, and a person called Chūjō or something of the sort. All three were trembling with fright, but they told themselves that nobody would give them too severe a scolding on such a day. High as their expectations were, they found each of the Imperial personages so beautiful that it was impossible to prefer one above the others. Shōshi's hair trailed beyond her skirt hems, Ishi's was just a little more than full length, Kenshi's fanned out a foot beyond the edge of her costume, and Kishi's brushed the floor with seven or eight inches to spare. They were hiding their countenances behind fans, held a short distance away.

"Why are you sitting there?" Michinaga asked Princess Teishi.[50]

---

[47] The jacket harmonized with the autumn season, which had begun on the First of the Seventh Month. The lespedeza (*hagi*) fabric weave, named after one of the Seven Plants of Autumn, is thought to have employed a green (*ao*) warp and a reddish brown (*suō*) woof. For bombycine (*orimono*), see Chapter 4, n. 39.

[48] A precursor of the Nō actor. The first *shushi* were Buddhist monks, who used simple dramatic performances to convey the significance of their esoteric rituals. The plays were later presented by professional actors, attached to temples, who wore gorgeous costumes and were accompanied by musical instruments. O'Neill 1956, p. 6.

[49] The ladies had left the carriage at the edge of the veranda.

[50] The Princess, unaccustomed to moving long distances on her knees, was probably stopping to rest.

"Come along." The nurses were quite overcome to see him take her hand and help her over the thresholds.

Although the three were doing their best to stay hidden, Michinaga caught a glimpse of them. Could anything have been more dreadful? Faint with apprehension, they gave up hope of ever serving at Court again. But he spoke to them with a smile and went on, making no attempt to get the ladies out of sight. "Have you seen Their Majesties? How did you like them? They're not so bad, do you think, considering that they are this old monk's daughters? Please don't be too hard on them." They gazed at one another like souls returned from the dead, speechless with joy. Of the three carefully painted faces, the first was as green as a leaf, the second had turned red, and the third was dripping with perspiration. "Even in less exalted circles, it is considered very wrong to spy on people for fun," one of them said later. "We decided that His Lordship must have overlooked it because he was carried away by the extraordinary splendor of the occasion, but we did feel a bit proud."[51]

Sights like that, which fill our minds with the spectacular flowering of Michinaga's fortunes, are likely to multiply our worldly attachments and dampen our impulse toward the religious life. But a certain Buddhist ascetic who lives somewhere in Kawachi Province—a man who ordinarily refuses to leave his hermitage—came to the capital for the Golden Hall dedication, thinking he might be punished in the next life if he failed to attend a sacred event of such magnitude. When he saw the Regent arriving and the people being chased away, he thought, "That must be the greatest personage in the country." Then Yorimichi seated himself in front of Michinaga, and he saw that Michinaga was superior. Next came the Emperor. The music blared, and the monk saw the manner in which Michinaga and Yorimichi waited, and the reverent postures of the gentlemen as they watched the litter approach. "It is the sovereign who is foremost in Japan," he thought. But when His Majesty descended and sat in respectful prayer before the central image of the Amitābha Hall, the holy man realized that it was, after all, the Buddha who was supreme. "I have formed a precious tie at this service," he said. "At last, my faith is unshakable." Do I know all this because he was sitting near me? I find that I don't remember.

Senior Grand Empress Shōshi is to enter religion, it seems, and to become an Imperial Lady with the same status as a Retired Emperor. People say that she will receive the commandments at an ordination

---

[51] The last phrase hints at Michinaga's partiality for the nurses' charge, Princess Teishi, which they take to be the real reason for his leniency.

platform erected at the Hōjōji, and that other nuns are eager to come and receive them with her. When my wife heard the news, she said, "That is when I will crop my white head. Don't try to stop me."

"I won't," I said, "but you must find me a young woman afterward." "I'll have a talk with my niece right away to fix it up," she answered. "There might be problems if we brought in a complete stranger."

"No, it wouldn't work," I said. "At my age, I can't be saddled with someone I'm not used to, whether she's a relative or not."

We went right out after that, and got her a *hiki*[52] or two of good silk to make her a skirt and surplice. (*He was putting on a show of levity, but there was a sad expression on his face—a sign, it seemed to me, of the sorrow his wife's decision must have caused him.*)

Strange celestial phenomena have been frequent this year, and ominous rumors seem to be circulating in a most inauspicious manner. It frightens me to hear talk of Kishi's pregnancy, and also of the illness of Koichijōin's consort Kanshi, who has had no respite this year from her old affliction.[53]

"Well, well," Yotsugi said, "the past seems only yesterday when I go on like this." He exchanged glances with Shigeki, who responded, "I have seen and heard all kinds of splendid things, too, and have often been deeply moved, but there has never been anything to compare with the misery I felt when my dear master died. It was an especially sad time of year, just after the Tenth of the Eighth Month. I couldn't help thinking of the poem 'Any season would have done.' "[54] He blew his nose several times, speechless with grief, looking very much as he must have when Tadahira died. "At the time," he continued, "I had no desire to go on living and mingling in society—no, not for a day or an hour. I think the reason I have lingered so long is probably that Tadahira's spirit wants me to see and praise the constant increase and prosperity of his descendants. Emperor Reizei was born on the Twenty-Fourth of the Fifth Month in the following year. I was terribly sorry that my master had not lived to see the baby, but his birth made me happier than I can say."

[52] A unit of measurement, equivalent to about twenty-one meters.

[53] Kanshi's poor health was attributed to the persecutions of the spirits of Akimitsu and Enshi.

[54] *Kokinshu* 839, composed by Mibu no Tadamine after the death of Ki no Tomonori: "*Toki shi mo are/ aki ya wa hito no/ wakarubeki/ aru o miru dani/ koishiki mono o.* (Any season would have done. Is it right for someone to go in autumn, when the heart aches even to see the living?)"

"I can well believe it," Yotsugi said, beaming with sympathetic pleasure. "And how did you feel when Emperors Suzaku and Murakami were born, one after another?" It was eerie to listen to them.

"I have something on my mind," Yotsugi continued. "It may sound shameless, but who knows whether I will be alive tomorrow? I'm going to speak out. I don't feel ready to die yet because I want to see what the future holds for Princess Teishi. I had a splendid dream before her birth, exactly like my dreams before Senshi and Shōshi were conceived, and so I think we can predict great things for her. I am anxious to let Grand Empress Kenshi know about it, but I have not succeeded in meeting anyone close to her. I mention the matter partly in the hope that there may be some such person in the congregation. People in the future will realize what a good prophet I was."

I felt like coming forward and saying, "Here I am!"

CHAPTER SIX

Chancellor Michinaga: Part Two

[Tales of the Past]

The attendant interrupted this remarkable dialogue. "We are learning some fascinating things," he said. "What are your earliest memories? It would be especially interesting to hear about them. Won't you please give us a few?"

I have a clear recollection of the things I have seen and heard since the age of six or seven *(Yotsugi said)*. There would be no way of proving I was telling the truth about trivial incidents, so let me speak of an important happening when I was nine.

You all know the place where Emperor Kōkō lived while he was a Prince. My father's house was north of Ōinomikado and west of Machijiri, right next door. I always went over there to play, and I knew that the Prince lived a very quiet life.

The first Day of the Horse[1] fell on the Third of the Second Month, which chanced to be the lucky *kinoe uma* day. Everybody made an even greater point of going to the Inari Festival than usual, and my father took me with him. The steep climb was exhausting for a child, so we were not able to go home on the same day. Father arranged for us to spend the night at the lodgings of one of the shrine priests, a man of Fifth Court Rank whom he had often helped out, and whom he knew well. The next day, as we headed north along Higashinotōin on our way home, we were startled by the sight of a noisy mob streaming westward on Ōinomikado. When we got to the intersection, we saw swarms of people milling around our house. Our first fear was of fire, but there was no smoke in the sky, so we wondered if the police might be making a big arrest. Our heads spinning with conjectures, we went along to the neighborhood of the Ononomiya Mansion, and there, to our amazement, we saw senior nobles' carriages, saddled horses, and gentlemen wearing formal caps and Court cloaks. We begged the

---

[1] In the Second Month of Gangyō 8 (884), Yotsugi's ninth year; the regular day of the Inari Festival. A *kinoe uma* day was considered particularly auspicious for visits to shrines. *Shūkaishō*, p. 510; Chapter 1, n. 8.

passersby for an explanation, and someone told us the news before rushing off: "Prince Tokiyasu is to be Emperor. His Lordship[2] and the others are presenting themselves."

There was another thing, which happened, I believe, when I was around seven. It may have been in the second year of Gangyō [878] or thereabouts.[3] The future Emperor Uda, whom we knew as the Gentleman-in-Waiting Son of the Princely Minister of Ceremonial,[4] happened to be addicted to hunting. One day after the Twentieth of the Eleventh Month, I think it was, I ran along behind when he left his father's house on a hawking excursion. While he was pursuing the sport on the bank of the Kamo River, a mist plunged everything into darkness. I found it impossible to tell one direction from another; it was just as though the sun had set. I tumbled into a thicket and lay there, trembling, for as much as an hour. And as I learned later, it was during that very time that the Bright Divinity of Kamo appeared and addressed the Prince.[5] Since the story is well known, I had better not repeat it. You are probably acquainted with it, and it is no subject for idle chatter.

I think it was about six years later that the Kamo Special Festival was inaugurated. I am sure it was the year in which Emperor Uda ascended the throne.[6] That day[7] was a Day of the Cock, so the festival takes place on the last Day of the Cock in the Eleventh Month. Middle Captain Toshiyuki composed the first eastern music song:

Chihayaburu	Not for a myriad ages
Kamo no yashiro no	Will their color change—
Himekomatsu	The fair young pines
Yorozuyo made mo	Of mighty
Iro wa kawaraji.	Kamo Shrine.

Those lines appear in the *Collection of Early and Modern Times*. You all know them—but aren't they splendid? And we can certainly say that Emperor Uda's descendants are still flourishing. Has there ever been another sovereign like him?

[2] Mototsune, the Chancellor.

[3] Since Yotsugi has stated earlier that he was born in 876 (Preface, p. 66, the vulgate texts substitute "the sixth year of Gangyō" (882) here.

[4] The Minister of Ceremonial was Yotsugi's neighbor, Prince Tokiyasu, who later became Emperor Kōkō.

[5] See Appendix B, (4).

[6] Emperor Uda ascended the throne in 887. The first Kamo Special Festival was held in 889.

[7] The day of the oracle. Appendix B, (4).

The Yawata Special Festival began during Emperor Suzaku's reign.[8] Through fear of the Kitano god, the shutters of that Emperor's residence were kept closed for three years after his birth;[9] he was reared inside a curtain-dais in a room where lights burned day and night. There were no such elaborate precautions in Emperor Murakami's case. Emperor Suzaku's birth came at an opportune time. If it had not been for him, the house of Fujiwara would have been less prosperous.[10]

Be that as it may, it was after Emperor Suzaku ascended the throne that Masakado's revolt broke out, and I have heard that the Yawata Special Festival originated with some services at which the Emperor offered prayers for the rebel's defeat. Tsurayuki composed an eastern music song:

Matsu mo oi	Until a young pine grows old
Mata mo koke musu	And wears a robe of moss,
Iwashimizu	Thus far into the future
Yukusue tōku	Shall we serve
Tsukaematsuran.	Mossy-rocked Iwashimizu.

Those lines appear in the poet's collected works.

I won't give you as many details as Yotsugi *(said Shigeki)*, but I must say, at the risk of seeming repetitious, that I have vivid recollections of certain occurrences when Emperors Uda and Daigo abdicated. For instance, there was a poem, scribbled on one of the Kokiden walls by Lady Ise, that everyone found most affecting:

Wakaruredo	I take my leave
Ai mo omowanu	With no thought of return
Momoshiki o	To the Hundred Stones Palace—
Mizaran koto ya	Yet how poignant the grief
Nani ka kanashiki.	Never to see it more.[11]

[8] This paragraph appears twice in the vulgate texts in virtually identical forms, the first time in the annals of Emperor Suzaku. Satō 1929, p. 51.

[9] Until his mother, Anshi, gave birth to a second son, the future Emperor Murakami.

[10] The Fujiwara regency, in abeyance since 890, was reactivated on the day of the eight-year-old Emperor's accession in 930.

[11] Composed when Emperor Uda abdicated. Now that the Emperor is to be gone, Ise has no desire to remain in the Palace, but she feels a pang at leaving familiar surroundings.

The Emperor wrote this in reply:

Mi hitotsu no	All will be the same
Aranu bakari o	Save that I alone am gone:
Oshinabete	Why should you not
Yukikaerite mo	Go to and fro
Nado ka mizaramu.	And see those halls as usual?

("I have heard that it was the Retired Emperor who wrote the first poem, and that Emperor Daigo, catching sight of it later, jotted down the second next to it. I wonder which is right," said someone nearby.)[12]

One Emperor is the same as another as far as the title is concerned, but Emperor Daigo's kindness was a blessing for all who were born in his day, down to the humblest commoners. On snowy, freezing nights around the time of the Greater and Lesser Colds,[13] he would throw his robes outside the Imperial Bedchamber, saying, "How cold the ordinary folk in the provinces must be!" Even fellows like me felt that he cared about us, and we considered ourselves greatly honored.

The events I witnessed during Emperor Daigo's reign will never lose their luster. Listen, everyone! I feel self-conscious about talking this way here, but I am afraid I still haven't overcome my youthful sin of thrilling to the splendor of worldly things. I want to make my confession today in this temple.[14]

Prince Atsumi, the Rokujō Minister of Ceremonial, was Emperor Daigo's full brother. On a certain occasion, the Emperor went out to see some hawking in the countryside. The Prince, who had planned to accompany him, overtook the procession at Katsuranosato after a belated start, and His Majesty halted his litter in order to put his brother at the head of the party. Just then, one of the dog handlers forded the deep river with his dog's two front legs draped over his shoulder.[15] The whole entourage watched with interest, and the Emperor also seemed impressed by the handler's expertise. After they entered the hunting grounds, the Imperial falcon Shirashō came swooping down to the phoenix on top of His Majesty's litter, holding a bird in its talons.

---

[12] The second poem would then mean, "Although you no longer live here, there is no reason why you should not visit." Hosaka 1974, 3.451-452.

[13] Two of the twenty-four points (*nijūshi sekki*) in the old Japanese solar calendar. The Greater Cold fell around January 20; the Lesser, around January 6 or 7. Webb and Ryan 1963, pp. 17-18.

[14] By describing the events responsible for his lapses. A devout Buddhist tries to divorce himself from worldly interests.

[15] The dog was perched on his back. For a picture illustrating the scene, see Hosaka 1974, 3.458.

The sun was sinking toward the rim of the hills, and the autumn leaves on the slopes resembled a brocade mantle in the brilliant shafts of light. The falcon was pure white, the pheasant dark blue. And yes— a light snow sifted down as the raptor stood with outstretched wings. For me the moment captured the full charm of the season, and I was sure there had never been so marvelous a sight. What a karma burden that impression must have created! *(He snapped his fingers.)*[16]

Emperor Daigo almost always wore a smile on his face. "People hesitate to address a solemn man," he explained, "but they talk freely to someone who seems relaxed. I wear a smile because I want to hear everything, no matter how trivial it may be." What he said was quite right. A sour countenance discourages conversation. "I do hope I won't die in the Seventh or Ninth Month," His Majesty once remarked. "It would be such a pity if they cancelled the wrestling matches or the Ninth Day Festival."[17] But he did die in the Ninth Month, and consequently there was no festival. It was touching when his hawks were set free that day in front of the Left Gate Guards post.[18] They waited a while before flying off.

To Emperor Daigo's mind, Controller Kintada was a man who acquitted himself with distinction in everything he undertook. His Majesty especially admired Kintada's skill as a falconer. The moment the Controller finished his official duties, to which he devoted his best efforts every day, he would set out toward Nakayama, riding a horse that he kept tethered in an out-of-the-way place. I expect some of his hawks' droppings are still to be found on the walls of the Controllers' Office at the Council of State.[19] He could tell by a pheasant's taste whether it came from Kuze or from Katano. A skeptical acquaintance once tested him with a dish containing marked pieces of meat from both places, and he identified them all correctly. Someone told Emperor Daigo it was wrong to allow courtier privileges to a man who was virtually a professional falconer. "He would be culpable if he neglected his duties for the hunt," His Majesty answered. "Let him do whatever he pleases as long as he attends to his work first."

And then there was the splendid dance when Emperor Daigo visited

[16] A means of getting rid of trouble or guilt. By snapping his forefinger against his thumb, Shigeki symbolically expels his pleasure in an incident involving the taking of life, making it go off in the direction taken by the finger. *Ōkagami*, p. 485, s.n. 12.

[17] For the wrestling matches, see Chapter 4, n. 2; for the Ninth Day Festival, Chapter 2, n. 18.

[18] Situated at Kenshunmon, the central gate in the eastern Middle Enclosure wall.

[19] In the southeast sector of the Greater Imperial Palace.

the Ōi River—the incomparable performance of the seven-year-old
Prince whose mother was the Tominokōji Lady of the Bedchamber.
Not one of all those people failed to shed tears. The Prince was just
too beautiful; the mountain god fell in love with him and took him
away.[20]

So many interesting things happened during Emperor Daigo's reign
that it would be impossible to describe them all. I shall simply tell you
about them as they occur to me, whether they are in the proper order
or not.

Retired Emperor Uda went to many places on pious journeys and
other excursions. During his visit to Miya Waterfall, which was very
splendid, the Sugawara Minister of State composed this poem:[21]

Mizuhiki no	This cloth
Shiraito haete	Woven of white threads
Oru hata wa	Drawn from water-soaked hemp—
Tabi no koromo ni	Shall I cut a piece
Tachi ya kasanemu.	To wear over my travel garb?

The Retired Emperor also visited the Ōi River.[22] He instructed his
attendants to tell Emperor Daigo that the spot deserved an Imperial
visit, and Tadahira composed a poem by way of a message:

Ogurayama[23]	If you have feelings,
Momiji no iro mo	O autumn colors
Kokoro araba	At Ogura Mountain,
Ima hitotabi no	Pray tarry for another
Miyuki matanan.	Imperial journey.

It was an elegant gesture.

Numerous topics were set for the Japanese poems composed during

[20] The Prince died at the age of nine (ten *sai*) in 929, three years after the
Ōigawa excursion.

[21] Sugawara Michizane was a Provisional Major Counselor and Major Captain
at the time. His poem alludes indirectly to the season, which was winter. "Cloth
woven of white threads" is a metaphor for the waterfall.

[22] On the Tenth of the Ninth Month in 907. The occasion produced sixty-three
poems, composed by leading poets on topics set by the Retired Emperor, as well
as a famous preface by Tsurayuki. Ceadel 1953.

[23] Emended from Ōharayama. Ogurayama occurs in versions of the poem recorded in other *Ōkagami* texts, *Yamato monogatari*, and *Shūishū*. *Ōkagami*, p. 485,
n. 19.

the Imperial excursion.[24] Mitsune wrote one on the theme "Monkeys Crying in the Valleys":

Wabishira ni	Cease, monkeys,
Mashira na naki so	Your forlorn cries.
Ashihiki no	Does not today
Yama no kai aru	Bring honor
Kyō ni ya wa aranu.	To every mountain valley?

Tsurayuki composed the preface for the day while the party was still at the river.

Emperor Suzaku was also considered most elegant, but Masakado's revolt caused him great anxiety; and then he suddenly stepped down from the throne. It was all very strange. He paid a visit to his mother, who told him how happy she was to see him Emperor. "My next desire," she went on, "is to have the Crown Prince enjoy the same good fortune." He concluded that she must be impatient for the Crown Prince's accession, and he abdicated soon afterward. "That was not at all what I meant," she protested, greatly upset. "I was thinking of something far in the future."

After Emperor Suzaku relinquished the throne, the grief of those about him prompted him to compose this poem, which he sent to his mother on the day of his abdication:

Hi no hikari	Where may it be—
Idesou kyō no	That mountain
Shigururu wa	Wet with wintry showers
Izure no kata no	Today when the sun's radiance
Yamabe naruran.	Bursts forth in new glory?[25]

I have heard that she replied:

Shirakumo no	Although the mountains
Oriiru kata ya	Share a common sun,
Shigururamu	It must be showering

---

[24] The author is apparently confusing Uda's visit with Daigo's, which seems to have taken place on the following day. Mitsune's poem was composed on the Tenth, as was Tsurayuki's preface. Hosaka 1974, 3.473.

[25] Mountain, showers, and sun are metaphors for Suzaku, his tears, and his brother. According to the headnote accompanying the poem in the Retired Emperor's personal collection, it was raining at the time. Hosaka 1974, 3.480.

| Onaji miyama no | There where the white clouds |
| Yukari nagara ni. | Have come down to rest.[26] |

The Retired Emperor stayed in the Ryōkiden for several months.[27] I wonder if it is true that later regrets led him to pray for a return to the throne. He was a man of the utmost refinement. The sight of his young daughter[28] cost him many tears during his last illness. He composed this poem:

Kuretake no	Though I may go
Waga yo wa koto ni	To a world
Narinu tomo	Different from hers,
Ne wa taesezu zo	I shall not cease
Nao nakarubeki.	To weep aloud.[29]

I felt very sad and sympathetic when I heard about it.

Emperor Murakami was another admirable sovereign. It was said of him that he was even more approachable and urbane than Emperor Daigo. Once he asked what kind of reputation he had. "They call you liberal," someone answered. "Then they praise me. How can people bear a ruler who makes severity a habit?" he said.

I remember one interesting and affecting incident from that reign. A plum tree in front of the Seiryōden had died, and His Majesty was looking for a replacement. He entrusted the matter to a certain gentleman who was serving as a Chamberlain at the time. "Young people can't recognize a good tree," the Chamberlain said to me. "You find one for us." After walking all over the capital without success, I located a beautiful specimen, covered with deep red blossoms, at a house in the western sector. As I was digging it up, the owner sent someone out with a message. "Attach this to it before you carry it away." I supposed there was some reason behind it, so I took the paper along. The Emperor saw it and said, "What's that?" It was a poem in a woman's hand:

26 Here mountains and sun are metaphors for the brothers and their father, Emperor Daigo. "White clouds" is introduced to permit a pun on *oriiru*, a form of *oru* (descend, abdicate).

27 Suzaku had apparently been living there before his abdication. Hosaka 1974, 3.481.

28 Princess Shōshi, his only child.

29 The poem contains a number of rhetorical devices and wordplays. The last two lines can be interpreted as "my roots will endure forever"—i.e., as a prediction that the Princess will perpetuate his line.

Choku nareba	I tremble and obey
Ito mo kashikoshi	The Imperial command—
Uguisu no	Yet how shall I answer
Yado wa to towaba	If the warbler, asks,
Ikaga kotaen.	"Where is my home?"

Somewhat taken aback, the Emperor had inquiries made about the owner, and she turned out to be Tsurayuki's daughter. "I wish we hadn't done it," he said uncomfortably. It was the most embarrassing thing that ever happened to me. What me feel even worse (*he added with a smile*) was that they made me a present of a robe— because, they said, the tree was just what they wanted.

Another event during Emperor Murakami's reign impressed me as very moving and elegant. It concerned the Shōkyōden Consort, the one who was sometimes called the Virgin Consort. According to the *Collection*,[30] it happened on an autumn evening, when the Emperor had not visited the lady for a long time. She began to play the koto with a brilliance that brought the Emperor hurrying over to her apartments. As though unaware of his arrival, she drew fresh cascades of melody from the instrument, and presently he heard her murmur a touching poem:

Aki no hi no	At dusk on an autumn day
Ayashiki hodo no	When I marvel that longing
Yūgure ni	Can cause such pain,
Ogi fuku kaze no	There is only the sound of wind
Oto zo kikoyuru.	Rustling through the reeds.

That was true refinement. (*He really had no business discussing such things.*)

"Have you ever visited the provinces?" a voice asked.

"Not the distant ones," Shigeki answered, "but I accompanied Tsurayuki when he was posted to Izumi. I also went along on the journey during which Tsurayuki recited, 'How might one know of the presence of stars?'[31] What a downpour that was!" The incident had seemed

---

[30] Probably the lady's. Tachibana 1974, p. 388, n. 5.

[31] According to a note in Tsurayuki's collection, the poet was riding back to the capital from Kii Province when his horse suddenly fell ill. A passerby said, "This is probably the doing of the god who lives here. His shrine disappeared

very remote when I read about it in an old book, but Shigeki made me feel as though I had stepped back into the past.

The attendant was quite carried away. "I am sure Shigeki's wife can tell some delightful stories," he said.

"I don't come from the capital," the old woman answered, "and I have never been in service in a great house. I have been married to Shigeki ever since my girlhood. So I'm afraid I haven't had any interesting experiences."

"What province are you from?" the attendant asked.

"Asakanonuma in Michinokuni."

"How did you happen to come to the capital?"

"I travelled with a retiring governor. I don't know his name, but his wife was a poet." That would have been Nakatsukasa, I thought, pricking up my ears.

"How splendid!" said the attendant. "Who *was* the governor's wife? Do you remember any of her poems?"

"Well, that's not in my line; I can't say that I do. But I might be able to piece together the one she composed at Ōsaka Barrier on the way to the capital":

Miyako ni wa	I should like to send word
Matsuramu mono o	To those who wait
Ōsaka no	In the capital,
Seki made kinu to	Telling them we have come
Tsuge ya yaramashi.	To Meeting Hill Barrier.

She faltered out the lines with a lack of assurance that was a far cry from Shigeki's fluency.

"Do you mean you can't remember who she was?" said Shigeki. "How could anyone forget a thing like that? Her one redeeming feature is that she has a wonderful head for practical matters. That's why I can't divorce her."

"My wife's memory is excellent," said Yotsugi. "She is twelve years older than I am, so she knows about things that happened before my

---

years ago, but he is a fearsome deity, and others in the past have had the same kind of trouble. You had better offer a prayer." Tsurayuki cleansed his hands, knelt, and, having ascertained that the god was called the Aridōshi deity, recited this poem: "*Kakikumori/ ayame mo shiranu/ ōzora ni/ ari to hoshi o ba/ omou-beshi ya wa.* (How might one know of the presence of stars in heavens where all is concealed by clouds?)" A pun on *ari to hoshi* and *aridōshi* permits the substitution of Aridōshi for stars. The horse recovered. Hosaka 1974, 3.496; *Makura no sōshi*, sec. 244, p. 264; Morris 1967, 1.202.

time. She was the Somedono Empress's bath maid. Thanks to her mother, who was a head pantrymaid, she also had access to the Empress's house while she was growing up. She even saw Yoshifusa. I suppose she wasn't a bad-looking girl, because a number of important gentlemen noticed her. She has love letters from people like Middle Counselor Kanesuke and the Consultant Yoshimine Moroki. The Middle Counselor wrote on Michinokuni paper and the Consultant on light brown paper.

"That Consultant, by the way, had no career to speak of until he was fifty years old. The Court seemed to ignore his existence. Then he made a pilgrimage to Yawata, toiling up the Iwashimizu Hill in the pouring rain. When he reached the shrine, he noticed a withering orange tree in front of the sanctuary. He went over to it and recited a poem:

Chihayaburu	We have both
Kami no mimae no	Grown old and useless—
Tachibana mo	Moroki and the orange tree
Moroki mo tomo ni	Standing in the presence
Oinikeru ka na.	Of the mighty god.

"People say the god heard and was moved to compassion. The tree revived, and Moroki was astonished to find himself a Head Chamberlain."

"I seem to remember hearing that old story in the streets," said the attendant. "It is supposed to have happened at Kamo Shrine."

"I won't argue the point," Yotsugi answered. "It was a long time ago; I may be mistaken. I did know Moroki by sight, but I learned of the incident by making inquiries after I grew up."

"It is true about Moroki's career," said the attendant. "He became a Consultant at the age of fifty-six, and held the additional office of Middle Captain of the Left."

"At the time, I didn't see anything odd about my marriage," said Yotsugi, "but it shocks me when I look back now."[32]

"How did an ordinary young fellow like you happen to capture such a prize?" said the attendant.

"Well, I'll tell you," Yotsugi said. "She didn't think I was good enough for her when she landed in my house with her head still full of romantic notions. We had our share of arguments, but I didn't let her fool around after she was mine. She finally settled down, and since then

---

[32] Because his bride was so much older?

she hasn't let me look at another woman, not even for a night." After this droll speech, delivered with a grin, he went on. "I think the two of us must have been joined by ties from another life. She is around two hundred years old now. What would have become of her if she had cast her lot with Middle Counselor Kanesuke or Consultant Moroki, who don't even have any descendants living today? I am not going to be swept off my feet by some young thing, either."

"It would have been a shame if two such long-lived people had not managed to get together," said Shigeki with a cheerful laugh. True enough, I thought in amusement—but was I really hearing all this?

"If only I could have brought her today, she could have told you ladies some things you might have found more interesting," Yotsugi resumed. "Her private patron was Hyōe no naishi's father, so she used to visit Naishi occasionally."

"Who was the father?" someone asked.

"Why, the famous lute player. He once played 'Waves of the Blue Sea' on Genjō at a wrestling-match banquet in the Imperial presence.[33] It was splendid, I can assure you. Even somebody like Hakuga of Third Rank used to have trouble with Genjō, but you could hear Naishi's father all the way to Shōmeimon Gate. I went to the Left musicians' stand[34] and listened.

"But such events lost their brilliance after Emperor Murakami's reign, and less attention was paid to doing things correctly. It must be admitted that a pall seemed to settle over the Court when Emperor Reizei ascended the throne. His was also the reign in which the government's authority began to decline. Regent or not, Saneyori was an outsider, so he left everything to the Emperor's powerful young father-in-law[35] and his family—and, needless to say, the Emperor did the same.

"A sad thing happened in the year following Emperor Murakami's death. There was a gathering at the Ononomiya Mansion—not a Special Reception or anything like that, but people were humming 'Joyous

[33] Genjō was the name of an heirloom lute (*biwa*), reputedly imported from China, which had become the property of the throne in Emperor Murakami's day. "Waves of the Sea" was a Chinese dance piece. It was said that Genjō refused to produce sounds for an incompetent performer. Hosaka 1974, 3.511.

[34] Presumably a reference to the professional orchestra that provided musical accompaniment for dance performances. Why it should be identified as Left is not known. It has been conjectured that there may be some connection with the distinction known to have been made between two types of Court dance music: Chinese (*tōgaku*), known also as Music of the Right; and Korean (*komagaku*), Music of the Left. See n. 51; also Hosaka 1974, 3.511.

[35] Koremasa.

Time, Felicitous Season,'[36] and so forth. Then Masanobu and Shigenobu began to sing 'Mushiroda,'[37] beating time with their batons. 'Ah, if only Emperor Murakami were here,' a voice said. Masanobu and Shigenobu put down their batons, and the whole party, including the host, cast prudence to the winds and wept until their cloak sleeves were drenched.[38] It was natural enough. Anything seems worth doing if there is someone to appreciate it, but what's the point otherwise? You, sir, are such a discriminating listener that it makes me feel like continuing a while longer." The attendant looked embarrassed.

I have been talking about the Fujiwara so far, but now I intend to switch to the Minamoto *(Yotsugi said)*. Masanobu and Shigenobu were the sons of Prince Atsumi, the Rokujō Minister of Ceremonial of First Rank. Besides being Emperor Uda's grandsons, they were outstanding men in their own right, and both were favored by Emperor Murakami, Shigenobu perhaps especially so. Masanobu, the older one, was so correct that he never relaxed or talked about anything but business. Shigenobu, though a poor hand with the ladies, did possess a certain youthful charm and superior amiability, which probably accounted for the Emperor's preference—or so people said.

[36] "Joyous time, felicitous season, happiness without end; a myriad years, a thousand autumns, pleasures not half exhausted." The song is a *rōei*, a type of vocal music popular at the time. *Rōei* lyrics, sung to the accompaniment of Chinese musical instruments, consist of short excerpts from Chinese poems, usually two seven-word lines—or, less often, of *waka*. This one makes use of a couplet from a poem by the early T'ang literatus Hsieh Yeh. *Wakan rōeishū*, no. 774, p. 250; Tanabe 1963, p. 110.

[37] A *saibara*.

Mushiroda no ya	The cranes that dwell,
Mushiroda no	The cranes that dwell,
Itsunukikawa ni ya	The cranes that dwell
Sumu tsuru no	By the Itsunuki River
Sumu tsuru no ya	In Mushiroda,
Sumu tsuru no	In Mushiroda,
Chitose o kanete zo	Will frolic together
Asobiaeru	For a thousand years,
Yorozuyo kanete	Will frolic together
Asobiaeru.	For ten thousand years.

The *saibara*, like the *rōei*, was a major Heian vocal genre. The lyrics were for the most part Nara-period folk songs, set to Chinese music. The place names in this one are associated with the area that is now Gifu Prefecture. Hosaka 1974, 3.515.

[38] It was considered inauspicious to weep on a festive occasion.

While Shigenobu was Master of the Palace Repairs Office, he used to inspect the Imperial Palace whenever he visited his father, who had taken religious vows and gone to live at the Ninnaji. On the way to the temple, he would travel east on Higashinoōmiya and west on Ichijō; on the return, south on Nishinoōmiya and east on Nijō. In that way, he could note damaged places and arrange to have them fixed. It was ingenious of him, wasn't it?

"Having grown up among Princes," Masanobu once said, "I knew nothing of what the world was like or how to live in it, so 1 learned by being the first to arrive at every important official function and the last to leave." He used to offer a horse at the Yawata Release of Living Things Festival.[39] Possibly it was because he gave his messenger purified robes, and also purified himself, but there would always be a dove perched in a tree near the sanctuary. The bird would take to the air when the horse was led in, and the delighted Masanobu would interpret its flight as a sign that the gift had been received with favor.[40] I am sure his extreme piety and rectitude were what made his offerings acceptable to the bodhisattva. One year, he accompanied Kaneie when the latter went to Kamo to pray for rain. No minister of state had ever formed part of the retinue on a regental visit to the shrine, but Masanobu regarded the drought as a national emergency. (Instead of appearing at the starting point, he drove out in his carriage to join the procession as it passed his house.) He never in his life used prayer beads. Every day he intoned, "I put my faith in the Great Bodhisattva Hachiman! I put my faith in Kinbusen Kongō Zaō! I put my faith in the *Heart Sutra*," repeating each invocation 100 times, while he kept count with the ribs of his cypress fan.[41] Those were his only religious exercises. When someone told the Shijō Empress Junshi about it, she said, "What grim divinities he worships!"[42]

Masanobu had an unusual way of singing "Growing in the Untilled Rice Paddies."[43] I heard him during Emperor Ichijō's reign. It was

[39] *Hōjōe*, held annually at Iwashimizu Hachiman Shrine on the Fifteenth of the Eighth Month. McCullough and McCullough 1980, s.n. 46.

[40] Doves were thought to be messengers of Hachiman, a Shintō god who was also worshipped as a bodhisattva.

[41] The number of ribs differed according to the user's rank, ranging from twenty-five for holders of Third or higher rank, like Masanobu, to twelve for men of Sixth or lower rank.

[42] Hachiman, the god of war, was the special divinity worshipped by the Minamoto family. Kongō Zaō, the principal object of worship at Kinbusen, was a deity of fierce aspect, said to be a manifestation of Śākyamuni.

[43] A *fuzokuuta* (folk song): "Let us pick the ears of the rice growing in the untilled paddies and go to the shrine, to the middle shrine." *Fuzokuuta*, in the

after the end of the Kamo Special Festival ceremonies in the Imperial presence, when the senior nobles were going out to watch the procession. They were just passing the Secretariat corner,[44] and Masanobu was singing under his breath in a manner that seemed the more elegant for its casualness. It sounded to me as though he introduced an unusual twist somewhere around "Let us pick the ears of the rice and go to the shrine." I thought my old ears must be deceiving me, especially since I was so far away, but somebody told me later that Major Counselor Kintō, the great connoisseur, had noticed the same thing. "I was only a courtier then, so I was too far away to hear very well," Kintō said. "I wonder if it was because the singer was Masanobu that his variation struck me as so fresh and novel. I was anxious to hear it again, but I never did, and I regret it to this day."

The younger brother of Masanobu and Shigenobu—the Major Counselor[45]—also had refined tastes. In fact, all of Prince Atsumi's sons were splendid men. The ones who became monks were none other than the Hirosawa Archbishop Kanchō and the Kanjuji Archbishop Gakei. Ah, those were days when there were great figures in every walk of life!

(*"But nobody can say we don't have such men nowadays, too," said the attendant.*)

We do have the Four Major Counselors. Of course, Tadanobu, Kintō, Yukinari, and Toshikata are very distinguished.

Of the many spectacles I have witnessed, the most interesting was Retired Emperor En'yū's viewing of the Iwashimizu Special Festival procession during Emperor Kazan's reign. Minister of the Right Sanesuke was a Head Chamberlain then. Guessing that time might be hanging heavy on the former sovereign's hands, he paid him a visit after the ceremonies in the Imperial presence.[46] There proved to be no gentlemen of consequence at the palace. His Majesty, looking most forlorn, was all alone except for his Chamberlains and Secretaries, and he seemed pathetically happy to see Sanesuke.

---

narrow sense, was a term used of a few dozen specific folk songs from the provinces, taken up at Court during or before the Heian period, and sung primarily at banquets. They differed from *saibara* (n. 37) in that both the lyrics and the music were of folk origin. Tsuchihashi and Konishi 1960, p. 439.

[44] The Secretariat (*gekichō*) occupied offices just outside Kenshunmon Gate. For its functions, see McCullough and McCullough 1980, Appendix A.

[45] Of Prince Atsumi's sons, only Masanobu and Shigenobu rose high enough in the bureaucracy to serve as Major Counselors. The author may be thinking of Masanobu's son, Major Counselor Tokinaka, who was an expert musician. *Sonpi bunmyaku*, 3.379.

[46] It was something over half a year since En'yū's abdication.

"Why don't you go to watch the procession?" Sanesuke suggested. "Just on the spur of the moment? How could I?" En'yū asked.

"You have me," Sanesuke urged. "You don't need anybody else except the people from your Courtiers' Hall."

The Retired Emperor ordered horses from the stables. His gentlemen prepared to serve as mounted outriders, and Chamberlain Middle Captain Sanesuke joined the party in his formal Court attire. Since the Imperial residence was in the Horikawain, they soon approached the throng of sightseeing carriages at the Nijō-Ōmiya intersection. The spectators were consumed with curiosity as the carriage moved closer, its path cleared with an extraordinary show of authority by outriders in unfigured hunting costumes and informal Court garb. Then Sanesuke came into view, seated on a Chinese saddle, with his jacket tail tucked into his belt, and everyone realized that Retired Emperor En'yū must be inside. What a stir it caused among the assembled pedestrians and carriages! Proceeding to a point a little north of Nijō, the Imperial vehicle came to rest beside the tile-capped wall of the Reizeiin, and the outriders, dismounting, formed a line.

Meanwhile, the senior nobles were streaming out of the Palace to watch the parade. To their astonishment, they found the avenue in an uproar. "What's going on?" they asked. "They say it's the Retired Emperor," people told them. Strange as it seemed, Sanesuke's presence attested to the truth of the rumor, and all of them piled out of their carriages to pay their respects. Masanobu and Kaneie, who were the Ministers of the Left and Right, stood at the left and right wheels with their hands steadying the axles, and the Counselors and others stationed themselves near the shafts. It was even more splendid than an elaborate formal ceremony.

The dancers, singers, and musicians went riding by. The Messenger was the Minamoto Major Counselor Tokinaka, who was still Treasury Minister at the time. He rode over close to the Imperial carriage, dismounted, sketched the motions of "Motomeko" with his sleeves, and knelt with one sleeve pressed to his face.[47] The former sovereign traced the words "Make haste" with his outthrust red fan, and Tokinaka left, wiping away a tear. It was incomparably elegant. The pathos of the scene was reflected in the spectators' countenance, and I heard later that there were tears in His Majesty's eyes. I saw the whole thing from inside the fence at the northeast corner of the Shinsen'en.

Even in my youth, I was not greatly interested in Buddhism—cer-

[47] A sign of emotion. "Motomeko" was an eastern music piece (Appendix B, n. 3).

tainly not enough to attend any but the biggest and most popular services—and I am even less willing to go out for such things now that I am old. But I did hear Dharma Bridge Seishō's sermon at the farewell service before the Mikawa Novice's departure for China, and I must say that a real sensation of piety touched my irreverent heart for the first time. Seishō began by reciting the *Heart Sutra* to summon the protective deities. Then he announced the purpose of the gathering and rang the bell, and everyone in the huge congregation choked up. It was natural enough.

Somebody once asked Master of Discipline Seihan to deliver a memorial sermon for a dog. Seishō went to the service with his head muffled up, curious to learn how a rival would meet the challenge, and he was much impressed to hear Seihan say, "We may be sure the spirit of the deceased is barking on a lotus pedestal at this very moment." "He didn't disappoint me!" Seishō said. "Nobody else would have thought of that. Not many preachers can equal him in resourcefulness." I heard the sermon myself and found it highly diverting; and the congregation went out laughing. The dog must have turned into a jolly buddha! The story is silly, but I thought it was worth telling because Seihan's wit and resourcefulness seemed so interesting and admirable.

Wasn't it in the Twelfth Month that they dedicated the Hall of the Five Great Mystic Kings at the Hōjōji?[48] Anyway, it was a very cold time of year. The service was a hundred-monk ritual, with the title chanters seated in a northern eavechamber which had been built for such occasions.[49] Instead of serving the monks a meal on individual dining tables, Michinaga gave them cooked rice in hot water.[50] There were two officials in charge of the affair, each responsible for fifty men. The rice was added to the hot water, which was kept steaming in a three-legged cauldron south of the hall, and they served it straight off the fire. When the monks began to bolt it down, expecting it to be

[48] The Hall of the Five Great Mystic Kings at the Hōjōji was dedicated at the same time as the Golden Hall (Kondō)—i.e., in mid-summer, on the Fourteenth of the Seventh Month in 1022. The author has probably confused the building with another of the same name at the Hōshōji, dedicated by Michinaga on the Twenty-Sixth of the Twelfth Month in 1006. Hosaka 1974, 3.547. For the Five Great Mystic Kings (*godai myōō*), fierce Buddhist divinities worshiped in esoteric rites, see McCullough and McCullough 1980, s.n. 12.

[49] A hundred-monk ritual required the services of seven major officiants and approximately 100 lesser clerics. One of the functions of the latter was to repeat sutra titles after the Reader (*tokushi*).

[50] *Yuzuke*, a winter dish similar to the modern *chazuke*, which is a combination of rice with tea.

lukewarm, they were amazed to find it boiling hot, but the frigid north wind made it bearable, and some of them consumed prodigious quantities. Asked later by Michinaga if it had not been very cold in the north room, they said, "The food warmed us up so much that we forgot the cold." His Lordship concluded that the officials had done a good job. Nobody would have been critical if the food had been tepid, but the supervisors' resourcefulness won praise from Michinaga and the others, and it will probably be cited on future occasions, so what they did was much better than simply carrying out their duties in a routine way.

And then there were the wonderful dances at Senshi's longevity celebration, when Yorimichi and Yorimune performed "Ranryōō" and "Nassori."[51] Yorimichi's "Ranryōō" was noble and aristocratic, and it seemed to me that nothing could equal the charm and elegance with which he finished his dance and entered the music pavilion, paying no attention to the present he had received. But "Nassori" was splendidly impressive, too, and when Yorimune danced a final dazzling measure, with his gift robe draped majestically over his shoulder, the gesture seemed perfect. Anticipating that Yorimichi would ignore his reward, Yorimune's teacher had contrived a novel effect by coaching his pupil to do something different, which everyone considered most resourceful.

Senshi arranged for Yorimune's teacher to receive Junior Fifth Lower Rank—the reason being, people said, that she was partial to his charge. Yorimichi's teacher was disgruntled at being passed over, and Rinshi also felt put out, but the man must have been promoted later. Neither of the boys was old enough to be criticized for failure to improve on the standard level of performance, and I am sure there would have been no disposition to look for flaws. As a matter of fact, though,

[51] The occasion marked Senshi's fortieth year. "Nassori" and "Ranryōō" belonged to the category of Court music known as *bugaku* (dance music, essentially a Heian modification of instrumental dance music imported earlier from China and Korea). *Bugaku* compositions were divided into two categories: Left (*sahō*), mostly of Chinese origin, and Right (*uhō*), mostly of Korean origin, with the Left considered superior. The dances were performed by two, four, or six persons, or, less often, by eight or by one, as here. "Ranryōō" was presented by an elaborately costumed dancer, who held a golden baton and wore a fierce gold mask surmounted by a dragon. According to one tradition, the dance celebrated the bravery of a sixth-century Chinese king, Kao Ch'ang-kung, who was said to have hidden his mild features behind a mask and led 500 men to victory against an enemy army. As a Left piece, it was presumably considered suitable for Yorimichi, the son of Michinaga's principal wife. "Nassori," usually performed as a sequel to "Ranryōō," was a Right piece, in which the dancer bounded energetically about the stage, wearing a blue mask and flourishing a six-inch stick.

neither of them seemed like an ordinary mortal. I could have mistaken them for divine children descended from heaven.

Shoshi's visit to Ōharano was another grand event. It was a pity it had to rain. The dancers were young gentlemen from good families, including Yorimichi, who performed the first number. On the day of the rehearsal, Yorimichi wore a red glossed-silk under-jacket and a black sleeveless tunic, which was most unusual. I had never seen anyone wear a tunic with a divided cloak before.[52] Michinaga rode a horse named Something-or-other during the journey, and he and his four Escorts[53] went dashing gaily about. Kintada[54] kept reining in his mount and holding back, apparently unable to discard his scruples, even after Michinaga had told him not to be foolish. Fortunately, the rain held off while the procession was passing through the city. Kinsue annoyed Michinaga by turning back at Nishishichijō, but Akimitsu went all the way to the shrine and was rewarded with a horse.[55] Kenshi and Ishi traveled in a gold-trimmed carriage, accompanied by outriders who were all courtiers from the best families. Kenshi's nurse (Koretsune's mother) and Ishi's nurse (the mother of Kaneyasu and Sanetō) acted as attendants, sitting in the rear of the carriage. Those of Michinaga's sons who had not performed the capping ceremony went along with their hair done up in boys' loops.

Now let me change the subject and tell you about a bizarre incident that ended without troublesome consequences. On the day of Emperor Ichijō's accession audience, the people who went to decorate the Dai-gokuden were amazed to find a furry creature's gory head lying on the throne. Afraid to hush the matter up, the officials in charge per-suaded a certain nobleman to inform Kaneie. The Regent heard him in silence, looking sleepy, and when the gentleman repeated his request for instructions, thinking that he might not have been understood, he kept his eyes closed and said nothing. His behavior was most odd, the visitor thought. Could he really be asleep? He stood there a while, and suddenly Kaneie's eyes popped open. "Is everything ready?" he asked.

[52] Divided cloaks (*wakiage no ue no kinu*), worn on formal occasions by mili-tary officers of Fourth or lower rank, were split at the sides, as opposed to *nuiake no ue no kinu*, which were sewn. Since etiquette books prescribed the wearing of the tunic (*hanpi*) with the *wakiage* variety, commentators surmise that the old forms were no longer being observed in Emperor Ichijō's day. Yorimichi was a Lesser Captain of Senior Fourth Rank at the time (1005). Hosaka 1974, 3.559.

[53] As a minister of state, he was entitled to eight. The occasion apparently did not call for rigid adherence to form.

[54] One of the Escorts.

[55] Kinsue and Akimitsu were the other two ministers of state in 1005. The office of Chancellor was vacant.

Then the gentleman understood that he wanted it to seem as if he had
not heard the report. He took his leave, and his role in the affair cost
him many later regrets. The Regent had been right, he realized. It
would have been inauspicious to cancel such a great celebration on the
very day when it was to take place. They should have disposed of the
head in silence. What must His Lordship have thought of the way he
had blurted the story out? In my opinion, it was natural for him to
feel that way. Kaneie's action produced no ill results—indeed, quite
the contrary.

When Senior Grand Empress Shōshi was still young, her mother
took her on a pilgrimage to Kasuga. A whirlwind came out of nowhere, caught up the offerings the two had deposited in front of the
sanctuary, and dropped them at the Great Buddha Hall of the Tōdaiji.
People wondered at the time whether it was not an ill omen for things
to be taken away from Kasuga by the Minamoto family temple,[56] but
the Fujiwara have prospered for so long that it must have been auspicious. Dreams and other portents that we consider lucky sometimes
fail to amount to anything, and suspicious occurrences may presage
good fortune.

Are you thinking that we old fellows must have accumulated an in-
exhaustible store of interesting tales, both sad and happy? We may
seem guilty of an important omission, since we have said nothing about
the high-born ladies and other women who live out their lives behind
the blinds we menfolk see. But don't you suppose ladies-in-waiting
and page girls spread the news whenever there is a noteworthy event
inside an Imperial, noble, or lesser household? Whether you might
have expected it or not, we know all about such stories. It is just that
there is no point in repeating them. When I see the stares some people
favor us with, I have the feeling that they consider it foolish even to
talk about past events of public interest, which certainly ought to be
worth their attention; so if I have rambled on today, it was only because you, sir,[57] have seemed to find our conversation unusual and interesting, and because you have joined us to such splendid effect. Much
more might be said; indeed, I could go on and on. But please send a
pack horse for me if you should really want to hear it all. I'll scramble
onto his back and pay you a visit. As a matter of fact, I would like
very much to call on you and receive the benefit of your learning, be-

[56] The Tōdaiji, founded by Emperor Shōmu as an act of national policy, was
not the official Minamoto family temple. As Hosaka suggests, it may have been
linked to the family in the public mind through Hachiman, the Minamoto god,
who was the temple's guardian deity. Hosaka 1974, 3.568.

[57] He addresses the attendant.

cause I have never in all my years met anyone capable of answering me as you do. Although you look young enough to be my grandson's grandson, your comments show how much you know. I think you must be in the habit of reading ancient diaries, which is a most refined pursuit, far beyond the education of a humble fellow like me, who simply manages to chatter away with an air of authority by drawing on his memories. It is embarrassing to meet someone with a formal education, because I feel he must be finding all kinds of things wrong with what he hears. Old as I am to be a pupil, I would be very pleased if I might resolve some of my doubts by asking you questions.

("That's right," Shigeki added eagerly. "I feel exactly the same way. Be sure and let me know when you're going. I'll join you, even if I have to hobble along with a cane." The two exchanged nods.)

Young people who lack this gentleman's discernment may call me an old liar, but if you think I have intentionally added a single falsehood, may the buddhas of this temple bear witness on my behalf, and also the buddhas and bodhisattvas invoked by the preceptor at today's service. Of all the ten commandments, the prohibition against falsehood is the one I have observed most carefully ever since my youth, which is precisely why I have been able to live so long. I certainly would not come and violate that commandment today at the site of a service where a special point is to be made of administering it.

The human life span, which was 80,000 years at the beginning of the world, gradually decreased to 100 years by the time of Śākyamuni Buddha's appearance. The Buddha wished to teach mankind that life and death are uncertain and transient, so he entered nirvana at the age of eighty, thus reducing the span by another twenty years. It has been 1,973 years from that time to this. In view of the example he set, it is proper to think of eighty years as the normal limit of a life. We sometimes hear nowadays of people who live to ninety or a hundred, possibly because the Buddha wants us to see that human existence is uncertain; but ages like mine and Shigeki's are rare indeed! Such phrases as "fraught with significance" and "rarity of rarities" seem made to describe our lives.[58] There were others of our kind in remote antiquity (including approximately ten sovereigns, all of whom lived to be a hundred or more, during the first twenty or so reigns beginning with Emperor Jinmu), but in recent generations we have been the only preternaturally aged people.[59] I believe this shows that we obeyed the

---

[58] Both phrases appear frequently in Buddhist scriptures, notably the *Lotus Sutra*. See, e.g., Sakamoto and Iwamoto 1964-1968, 2.218; Hurvitz 1976, p. 199.

[59] The translation follows Satō 1929, p. 660, rather than *Ōkagami*, p. 278, which reads "There were no others of our kind. . . ."

commandments in previous lives, and I mean to return to the other
world without violating them in this one. May I be heard by the gods
and buddhas who manifest themselves at this hall today! (*He exchanged glances with Shigeki, fanning himself smugly, as well he
might have. I could only envy his great knowledge of public and private affairs.*)

"Please calculate my age for me," Shigeki said. "I have never paid
much attention to it before, but after what Yotsugi has said I feel anxious to know it."

"Well, then," said the attendant, counting on his fingers, "you say
you entered Tadahira's service at the age of thirteen, which makes you
about ten when Emperor Yōzei abdicated. Judging from that, and
since you seem to be a dozen or so years younger than Yotsugi, you
must be over 170—almost 180. Tell me, have you remarkable old people been examined by physiognomists?"

I have never been seen by a professional (*said Shigeki*). The two of
us[60] went to a Korean once, and he did say we would both have long
lives, but we never dreamed of anything like this. Lord Mototsune's
three sons[61] came in just as we were getting ready to ask some other
questions, so we couldn't say anything more. When the Korean told
Tokihira's fortune, he said, "His splendid person and great resourcefulness are more than Japan needs; it would be a shame if he became
nothing more than a national leader." Of Nakahira, he said, "He is too
upright and honest to fit into a little country full of flatterers and dis-
simulators." Of Tadahira, "Ah, he will lead Japan! His is the line that
will survive and flourish." "You embarrass me," Tadahira told him. "I
seem to be the stupid, sycophantic one."

I was much impressed when I saw that Tadahira's line did expand
and prosper, just as the Korean had predicted. I went to the man's
house again, but Saneyori was there, so I couldn't talk to him. Saneyori had put on shabby attire and taken a back seat among the lower
orders, but the Korean craned his neck, picked him out of the crowd,
pointed a finger, and uttered a remark I would have liked to hear.
Someone told me later that he had said, "There is an exalted personage." Saneyori was still very young at the time.

My stories may seem frivolous, but we old men have our virtues.
Why shouldn't people indulge us? Please keep on listening—tell your-
selves those simple fellows have seen and heard things worth noticing.

[60] Presumably Shigeki and his wife.   [61] Tokihira, Nakahira, and Tadahira.

When Retired Emperor Uda went to Kawajiri, he summoned an entertainer named Shirome, watched her perform a dance, and ordered her to compose a poem on the topic "Serving Afar in a Remote Seat." She recited these lines:

Hamachidori	The beach plover's flight is limited,
Tobiyuku kagiri	And thus it sees but indistinctly
Arikereba	The mountain
Kumo tatsu yama o	Where clouds hover:
Awa to koso mire.	"Might it be Awa?"[62]

Well pleased, His Majesty rewarded her with a robe.

Shirome was also the author of the poem that runs, "If only our lives might last as long as our hearts desired."[63]

When the former sovereign visited the Torikainoin, the usual entertainers flocked to the villa, including one who was a daughter of Ōe Tamabuchi.[64] Attracted by the girl's pleasant voice and pretty face, he called her up into the room. "Tamabuchi was an excellent poet, versed in the art of literature," he said. "I will think you a true child of his if you join us in composing on the topic 'Torikai.'" She recited promptly:

Fukamidori	Though not a mist,
Kai aru haru ni	I have ascended
Au toki wa	In this season
Kasumi naranedo	When we greet the spring
Tachinoborikeri.	With its fruitful green.[65]

[62] *Yamato monogatari*, sec. 145, p. 310 (Tahara 1970, p. 303), explains that Shirome, the beach plover, is separated from the Retired Emperor, the mountain, by a crowd of important people. A pun, involving the place name Awa and the demonstrative pronoun *a*, makes it possible to interpret the poem in three ways: because the bird's powers of flight are limited, (a) it achieves only an indistinct view of the mountain where clouds hover; (b) it thinks the mountain must be in Awa; (c) it thinks, looking at the mountain, "What is that [splendid thing]? Is it a cloud?"

[63] *Kokinshū* 387. "*Inochi dani/ kokoro ni kanau/ mono naraba/ nani ka wakare no/ kanashikarubeki.* (If only our lives might last as long as our hearts desired, what cause for sorrow would parting bring?)"

[64] She is possibly to be identified with Shirome, listed in *Sonpi bunmyaku*, 4.92, as Tamabuchi's only daughter.

[65] The place-name topic, Torikai, is concealed in the end of line 1 and the beginning of line 2. Spring is a metaphor for the Retired Emperor. A pun on *kai aru* (fruitful, worthwhile; here, worth looking at) suggests green valleys (*kai*). Valley is a conventional association (*engo*) with mist, as is ascend.

*(He went on with a detailed account of how greatly everyone admired
the poem, how the Retired Emperor and others gave the girl presents,
and how Nan'in shichirō no kimi was commanded to look after her.)*

When poems were selected for the *Collection of Early and Modern
Times* during Emperor Daigo's reign, Tsurayuki and the other compilers—Tadamine, Mitsune, and so forth—were commanded to work
in the Palace Library. It was only the Second of the Fourth Month, a
time when the cuckoos are just beginning to utter a few subdued notes,
so the Emperor was most intrigued when he heard a bird in full song.
He called Tsurayuki in and told him to compose a poem. Tsurayuki
recited:

Kotonatsu wa	How might the cuckoo have sung
Ikaga nakiken	In other summers?
Hototogisu	Surely he has never
Kono yoi bakari	Held us in thrall
Ayashiki zo naki.	As he does tonight.

As though that were not memorable enough, there was another incident of the same kind during His Majesty's reign. It was a night on
which there had been a concert. The Emperor called Mitsune near his
front steps and said, "Compose a poem explaining the term 'drawn
bow,'[66] which people use of the moon." Mitsune recited:

Teru tsuki o	That men should call the shining moon
Yumihari to shi mo	A drawn bow
Iu koto wa	Must be because
Yamabe o sashite	It shoots toward the mountains
Ireba narikeri.	When it sets.

The Emperor signified his approbation by giving him an oversized
lined robe. Mitsune draped it over his shoulder, reciting:

Shirakumo no	That the white cloud
Kono kata ni shi mo	Should have descended
Oriiru wa	To my shoulder
Amatsukaze koso	Must be thanks to a wind
Fukite kinurashi.	Blowing from heaven.

Wasn't that splendid? It was not quite the thing for the Emperor to
call someone like that close and give him a present, but nobody offered

[66] *Yumihari*, a name for the crescent moon.

a word of criticism. (I supposed it was because the Emperor's personality inspired respect; also, everyone recognized Mitsune as a master poet.) It was all right for Retired Emperor Uda to praise the entertainer's poem, because he had already abdicated and the place was remote from the capital. (*He was really acting a bit too authoritative.*)

"Tell us about that business with Sone no Yoshitada during Retired Emperor En'yū's Rat Day excursion to Murasakino,"[67] said the attendant. "What actually happened?"

"Well," said Shigeki, "that was very interesting. It was natural enough to want to be a part of such an affair, seeing that they were going to appraise poems without regard to social status, but it would have been a terrible breach of etiquette even to hide somewhere on the premises and come out with a good composition. To sit right down with the invited guests was shocking! Sanesuke and Asateru were the ones who issued the orders for Yoshitada to be marched off. What a contrast with Mitsune, a man whom an Emperor deigned to reward! Even the best poet has to know when and where to compose. Yoshitada was talented enough, but his judgment left a lot to be desired."[68]

The attendant gave him a warm smile. "I don't know about the great events of antiquity," he said, "but my own most remarkable experience was seeing the ladies' carriages Shōshi and Kenshi sent out for Emperor Sanjō's Purification.[69] Nijō Avenue was enveloped in a marvelous cloud of incense from a silver censer, which hung suspended below the entrance eaves of Shōshi's first carriage. There has never been a spectacle to equal it."

"That's right," said Yotsugi. "The Imperial sisters must have been trying their best to outdo one another. And then some of Kenshi's conceited ladies spoiled Her Majesty's plans by keeping their blinds closed. Can you imagine that! I heard that they did it because they had been assigned to the back of the carriage, instead of to the front, where they thought they belonged. I can understand their being upset, but

---

[67] In 985. Chapter 3, n. 9.

[68] The fullest version of this famous anecdote appears in *Konjaku monogatarishū*, 5.56-58 (28.3), where Yoshitada is quoted as replying, when asked why he had crashed the party, "I came because I was told that poets were to attend. Why shouldn't I come? I'm as good a poet as anybody here."

[69] On the Twenty-Seventh of the intercalary Tenth Month in 1012. The carriages served as escorts for the Acting Consort (*nyōgodai*, the principal feminine participant in the Purification procession), who was Ishi, the thirteen-year-old sister of the two Imperial ladies. For Imperial Purification, see Chapter 1, n. 33.

still, to ignore their mistress's wishes. . . . No man could have brought himself to do such a thing.

"Willful ladies seem to be the rule at Kenshi's palace. When Princess Teishi performed the Putting On of the Train, Michinaga sent over a beautiful new beaded train and jacket, decorated with rock and stream designs. After the Princess had worn them, he said, they could be given to one of her favorite attendants. A certain person made up her mind that she would be the lucky recipient, and when it turned out otherwise, she took to her bed and died seven days later. Why did she have to be so stubborn? As though obstinacy were not a bad enough sin, she must have been consumed by jealousy, too." It was amazing, and a little frightening, to listen to him. Was there anything he didn't know? And how had he found out about things that had happened behind blinds?

It is usually tedious and annoying to be forced to listen while old crones and graybeards spin their yarns about the past, but Yotsugi and Shigeki made me feel as though I had stepped back into a bygone age. If only they would go on and on, I thought; if only I might have a chance to bring up all my comments and questions. What a blow it was when people began to shout that the preacher had arrived! I consoled myself by planning to have men follow the old people home after the service, but a sudden disturbance, erupting halfway through the sermon, sent the packed congregation surging outside, and I was dismayed to find that I had lost sight of all three in the crush.[70] My heart had been set on hearing more about that dream[71]—which was, in fact, why I had wanted to find out where they lived. But not one of them was to be seen.[72]

[70] The disturbance may have been caused by a fight, Hosaka suggests. Hosaka 1974, 3.609.

[71] Yotsugo's dream about Princess Teishi (p. 214).

[72] All *kohon* versions contain the following appended paragraph, which is conjectured to have been set down for later insertion elsewhere in the text: "Oh, yes, that reminds me. It was in the reign of Emperor Ninmyō, we are told, that they began the custom of bringing up the Imperial litter when a sovereign visited his mother. The previous practice had been for the Emperor to enter the litter after descending the steps, but Empress Kachiko said, 'I want to watch you get in. Have it brought right up to the hall.' The Emperor complied, and now it is the custom."

Persons and Places Mentioned in the Text

Listings are by personal names; the surname for laymen is Fujiwara unless otherwise specified. M. indicates Minamoto. Western years listed are those corresponding in general to lunar years. Thus 1027 is given as the year of Michinaga's death, which occurred on the Fourth of the Twelfth Month in the fourth year of Manju (January 3, 1028). Only pertinent offices are included. Tenure in a major central office was usually for life unless the incumbent received a promotion or became a monk. For further information concerning the Greater Imperial Palace and its buildings, see McCullough and McCullough 1980, Appendix B.

Aimiya Daughter of Morosuke; wife of M. Takaakira.

Akashi Post Station Said to have been situated in what is now Ōkuradani, Akashi City, Hyōgo Prefecture. Hosaka 1974, 2.235.

Akimasa Identity uncertain. Possibly a son of M. Shigemitsu. For theories, see Hosaka 1974, 2.538.

Akimitsu (944-1021) Son of Kanemichi. Mother: Emperor Murakami's fifth daughter. Consultant (975-977), Minister of the Right (996), Minister of the Left (1017). Father of Genshi (consort of Ichijō) and Enshi (consort of Koichijōin). Figurehead minister; unable to compete with Michinaga for power. Called Horikawa Minister of the Left or Hirohata Minister of the Left, the latter presumably from a property that had belonged to his mother's family.

Akimitsu, principal wife of, see Tōkazu, daughter of

Akimoto, M. (1000-1047) Son of Toshikata; adoptive son of Fujiwara Yorimichi. Provisional Middle Counselor (1035-1036); took religious vows in 1036.

Akinobu

1. Takashina (d. 1009?). Son of Naritada; uncle of Empress Teishi. Governor of Harima. Matsumura 1969-, 2.536.

2. (994-1027). Son of Michinaga and Meishi. Childhood name: Kokegimi. Became a monk in 1012.

Akitada (898-965) Son of Tokihira. Minister of the Right (960). Called Tominokōji Minister of State, presumably because of the location of his house.

Akogimi, *see* Takaie

Amitābha Hall, *see* Hōjōji

Anrakuji   Burial place of Sugawara Michizane. A Buddhist temple on the site of what is now Tenmangū, a shrine dedicated to Michizane in the town of Dazaifu in Fukuoka Prefecture. The shrine dates from around 919, when Emperor Daigo erected a building for Michizane's worship inside the temple compound. This shrine and the one at Kitano have traditionally been regarded as the most important of the many dedicated to the minister. As of 1941, the only remaining vestige of the Anrakuji was the Lecture Hall, which had been converted into a purification site. Shimonaka 1941, 2.437.

Anshi (927-964)   Daughter of Morosuke; consort of Emperor Murakami. Married Murakami while he was a Prince; dominated the Imperial harem until her death twenty-four years later. Junior Consort (946), Empress (958), Grand Empress (967), Senior Grand Empress (969). Mother of three of Murakami's nine sons, including his two immediate successors on the throne, and of four of his ten daughters.

Arashiyama   Storm Mountain. A hill facing Ogurayama and Kameyama across the Ōi River in Saga, Ukyō-ku, Kyōto. Famous for cherry blossoms and autumn foliage.

Ariakira, Prince   Son of Emperor Daigo. War Minister.

Arihira (892-970)   Grandson of Middle Counselor Yamakage; son of Bishop Nyomu. Major Counselor under Murakami. Became Minister of the Right in 969 as a result of the Anna incident; named Minister of the Left in 970.

Ariwara Middle Captain, *see* Narihira

Asahira (917-974)   Son of Minister of the Right Sadakata. Head Chamberlain (955), Consultant (958), Provisional Middle Counselor (970), Middle Counselor (971). Called Sanjō Middle Counselor.

Asakanonuma   Said to have been a marshy area at the foot of Mount Asaka in what is now Asaka-machi, Kōriyama City, Fukushima Prefecture. Well known from references in classical poetry.

Asateru (951-995)   Son of Kanemichi, who regarded him as his heir. Rapid promotions; rose above older brother Akimitsu. Middle Counselor (975), Provisional Major Counselor (977), Major Counselor (987). Died in the epidemic of 995. Called Kan'in Major Captain, from the name of his house.

Asateru, daughter of, *see* Shinshi

Asatsune (973-1029)   Son of Asateru. Provisional Middle Counselor (1023).

Atsuakira, Prince (994-1051)   Son of Emperor Sanjō and Seishi. Named Crown Prince in 1016; resigned under pressure from Michinaga in 1017. Assumed style of Retired Emperor with title Koichijōin. Principal consorts: Enshi (daughter of Akimitsu) and Kanshi (daughter of Michinaga).

Atsuhira, Prince

    1. (999 or 1000-1050). Son of Emperor Sanjō and Seishi. Minister of Central Affairs, Minister of Ceremonial, War Minister.

    2. *See* Go-Ichijō

Atsumi, Prince (893-967) Son of Emperor Uda; grandfather of Michinaga's wife Rinshi. Known as a musician.

Atsumichi, Prince (981-1007) Son of Emperor Reizei. Succeeded his brother Tametaka as Governor-General of the Dazaifu and as Izumi Shikibu's lover.

Atsunaga, Prince, *see* Go-Suzaku

Atsunori, Prince (997-1054) Son of Emperor Sanjō and Seishi. Minister of Ceremonial, Minister of Central Affairs.

Atsutada (906-943) Son of Tokihira. Provisional Major Counselor (942).

Atsutada, daughter of Wife of M. Nobumitsu; later married Asateru.

Atsutoshi (912-947) Son of Saneyori. Lesser Captain of the Left, Junior Fifth Lower Rank.

Atsuyasu, Prince (999-1018) Son of Emperor Ichijō and Teishi. Governor-General of the Dazaifu; Minister of Ceremonial (1016). Prevented by Michinaga from becoming Crown Prince in 1016, when he was passed over in favor of the future Koichijōin, and again in 1017, when the appointment went to his younger half-brother, Shōshi's son Atsunaga.

Awa A province corresponding to Tokushima Prefecture in Shikoku.

Awata An area on the far side of the Kamo River from the capital, probably in the general vicinity of the present Shōgoin, Yoshida Shrine, and Shishigatani.

Awataguchi An area extending eastward from Sanjō to the base of the Higashiyama hills. Point of departure for travelers heading from the capital toward Ōtsu.

Awata Lord, *see* Michikane

Banquet Pine Grove En no Matsubara. An open wooded area in the Greater Imperial Palace, north of the Burakuin.

Ben Nurse of Princess Teishi. Thought by some scholars to have been a daughter of Masatoki, a provincial governor, but the identification is uncertain. McCullough and McCullough 1980, Chapter 5, n. 38.

Bingo A province corresponding to eastern Hiroshima Prefecture.

Bishi, Princess (1000-1008)   Daughter of Emperor Ichijō and Teishi.

Bitchū   A province corresponding to western Okayama Prefecture.

Biwa Major Counselor, *see* Nobumitsu

Biwa Mansion   Probably located south of Konoe and east of Muro-machi; named for the loquat trees (*biwa*) in its grounds. Successively owned by Fuyutsugi, Nagara, Mototsune, Kanehira, Nakahira, Atsutada, Atsutada's daughter, and Michinaga. During Michinaga's ownership, it was used from time to time as a residence by Emperors Ichijō and Sanjō, and by Sanjō's widow, Kenshi. It burned in 1028. Tsunoda 1963, pp. 68-69, 111-112.

Biwa Minister of the Left, *see* Nakahira

Biwa Minister of State, *see* Nagara

Bizen   A province corresponding to part of Okayama Prefecture.

Black Chamber   A name for the north corridor of the Seiryōden, the Emperor's private residence in the Imperial Residential Compound.

Burakuin   A large enclosure in the Greater Imperial Palace; site of important banquets.

Central Hall   Chūdō. The building housing a temple's principal image. Particularly, the Enryakuji Central Hall.

Chikaie   Son of Michitaka. Minor posts, Junior Fourth Lower Rank.

Chikayori   Son of Michitaka. Minor posts, Junior Fourth Lower Rank.

Chikugo   A province corresponding to southern Fukuoka Prefecture.

Chisatonohama   A coastal strip in the area now called Iwashiro, Hidaka District, Wakayama Prefecture.

Chishō, Great Teacher (814-891)   Posthumous title of Enchin, a leading Tendai monk who spent six years in China, served as Tendai abbot, and founded the Jimon subsect with headquarters at the Onjō-ji. Administered commandments to members of the Imperial family and other personages; much in demand for prayers.

Chōgen (d. 1050)   Son of Tōnori; grandson of Morosuke. Master of Discipline (1027), Lesser Bishop. *Sonpi bunmyaku*, 1.57; Hosaka 1974, 2.454.

Chōshi (d. 982)   Daughter of Kaneie. Junior Consort of Emperor Reizei (968); mother of Emperor Sanjō, Princes Tametaka and Atsumichi, Princess Kōshi; posthumous Grand Empress (1011).

Chūgikō, *see* Kanemichi

Chūjinkō, *see* Yoshifusa

Chūjō   Nurse of Princess Teishi (daughter of Emperor Sanjō and Kenshi). Identified by some commentators as a daughter of a former provincial official, Takakata. Tachibana 1974, p. 365, n. 29; McCullough and McCullough 1980, Chapter 11, n. 15.

Chūjō no miyasudokoro   In commenting on a lady with this sobriquet in Tokihira's biography, the *Ōkagami* author seems to be confusing two of Tadahira's daughters. The elder, Kishi (904?-962), is listed in *Sonpi bunmyaku*, 1.50, and elsewhere as one of Prince Yasuakira's consorts, but there is no known evidence that she remarried after the Prince's death in 923. Two sources, *Ichidai yōki*, p. 138, and *Sanjūrokunin kasen den*, p. 712, attest to the fact that the Virgin Consort's parents were Prince Shigeakira and a daughter of Tadahira, but neither identifies the mother with Kishi, and the second specifies that she was Tadahira's second daughter, who is shown in *Sonpi bunmyaku* as Shigeakira's wife. For quotations of relevant sources, none of which refers to either lady as Chūjō no miyasudokoro, see Satō 1929, p. 137.

Courtiers' Hall   Tenjō no Ma. A room in the Seiryōden, or in the residence of another Imperial personage.

Court of the Eight Ministries   Hasshōin. Also Court of Government (Chōdōin). A major compound in the south central portion of the Greater Imperial Palace; site of the Great Hall of State (Daigokuden).

Daianji   Situated in what is now Daianji-chō, Nara. Founded by Shōtoku Taishi; rebuilt by Emperor Shōmu in imitation of the Chinese Hsi ming ssu. The present buildings date from the Meiji period.

Daigo, Emperor (885-930, r. 897-930)   60th sovereign. Oldest son of Uda. Mother: Inshi, daughter of Takafuji. Admired as a statesman and as a patron of learning and the arts. Called Engi Emperor, after an era name (901-923). The name Daigo derives from the Daigoji in Fushimi-ku, Kyōto, the site of his tomb.

Daigokuden   The Great Hall of State at the Greater Imperial Palace, used for accession audiences and other occasions of supreme importance. Situated in the south center of the Palace Compound.

Dairi   The Imperial Residential Compound in the Greater Imperial Palace. Situated inside the Nakanoe, from which the main entrances were Genkimon on the north, Sen'yōmon on the east, Shōmeimon on the south, and Inmeimon on the west.

Daytime Chamber   Hi no Omashi. A room in the Seiryōden.

Dazaifu   The Court's Kyūshū Government Office, with headquarters in Chikuzen, a province corresponding to part of Fukuoka Prefecture. For its functions and personnel, see McCullough and McCullough 1979, Appendix A.

Demon Room   Oni no Ma. A room in the Seiryōden.

Dining Room Court. Asagarei no Tsubo. A courtyard between the Kōrōden and the Seiryōden.

Eighth Prince, *see* Nagahira

Empress Mother   *Haha kisaki.* Employer of the young Yotsugi. Probably Princess Hanshi (833-900), consort of Emperor Kōkō (r. 884-887) and mother of Emperor Uda (r. 887-897). According to another theory, she is to be identified with Inshi (d. 896, daughter of Takafuji), consort of Emperor Uda and mother of Emperor Daigo (r. 897-930). Inshi was given the posthumous title Senior Empress in 897. Hosaka 1974, 2.21.

En'en   A noted painter. Son of Yoshichika, with whom he took Buddhist vows in 986. Associated with the Onjōji. Called Painter Holy Teacher (*eajari*).

Engi Emperor, *see* Daigo

En no Matsubara, *see* Banquet Pine Grove

Enryakuji   The great headquarters of the Tendai sect on Mount Hiei near the capital; founded by Saichō in 788. Its first Central Hall (Konpon Chūdō) was a small structure erected in 788 by Saichō to house an image of Yakushi, the Healing Buddha; a much larger building replaced it in 938.

Enshi

   1. (d. 1019). Daughter of Akimitsu; first wife of Prince Atsuakira (Koichijōin). Called Horikawa Consort, from the name of her home.

   2. Princess (972-998). Daughter of Prince Tamehira. Married Emperor Kazan in 985; later married Sanesuke.

En'yū, Emperor (959-991, r. 969-984)   64th sovereign. Son of Murakami. Mother: Anshi, daughter of Morosuke. Name: Morihira.

Eshin Bishop, *see* Genshin

Fifteenth Prince, *see* Moriakira
Fire Princess, *see* Sonshi
First Princess, *see* Sōshi
Former Crown Prince, *see* Yasuakira
Former Crown Prince, mother of, *see* Onshi
Former Lesser Captain, *see* Takakata
Fourth Princess, *see* Kōshi
Fuhito (659-720)   Son of Kamatari. Minister of the Right (708), posthumous Chancellor (720). Succeeded his father as an architect of the

new Chinese-style government; consolidated the position of the Fujiwara family. Posthumous name: Tankaikō.

Fujisashi, *see* Fuyutsugi

Fujitsubo   A building in the Imperial Residential Compound, usually occupied by a leading consort. Situated northwest of the Seiryōden, to which it was connected by a gallery.

Fujitsubo Imperial Apartment   A room in the northernmost part of the Seiryōden, used primarily by Imperial consorts and concubines who were visiting the Emperor from quarters elsewhere in the Palace.

Fukakusa   An old name for the region at the southwest base of Inariyama, extending to the Kamo River on the west. Many aristocrats from the capital owned villas there, and the name appears in numerous classical poems, often in conjunction with references to quail and the autumn moon. A number of Emperors and other prominent figures were buried in the area.

Fukakusa Emperor, *see* Ninmyō

Fukakusayama   A general term for the hills in Fushimi-ku, Kyōto, between Inariyama on the north and Fushimiyama (Momoyama) on the south.

Fukō   Son of Shigesuke. Provisional Major Bishop (1021). Kōfukuji provisional abbot. Matsumura 1969-, 4.222.

Fukutarigimi (d. 989)   Son of Michikane. Died in childhood.

Fuminori (909-996)   Minister of Civil Affairs (970-996), Provisional and regular Middle Counselor (971-988).

Funado, Prince (d. 757)   Grandson of Emperor Tenmu; son of Prince Niitabe. Named Crown Prince of Empress Kōken by direction of Retired Emperor Shōmu in 756; deposed in following year on grounds of disrespectful conduct toward the late sovereign, apparently at the instigation of the powerful Nakamaro. Put to death in the same year for joining Tachibana Naramaro's conspiracy against Nakamaro.

Furu, *see* Isonokami

Fusasaki (681-737)   Son of Fuhito; founder of the Northern House of the Fujiwara. Consultant (717), posthumous Minister of the Left (760). Died in the epidemic of 737. *Sonpi bunmyaku*, 1.17.

Fusatsugi (773-843)   Grandson of Palace Minister Uona. A provincial governor in life, he received the posthumous title of Chancellor with Senior First Rank after the accession in 884 of his grandson, Emperor Kōkō.

Fuyutsugi (775-826)   Also Fuyutsugu. Son of Minister of the Right

Uchimaro. In 825 he became the first Minister of the Left since 782. He married his daughter Junshi to the future Emperor Ninmyō, son of his patron, Retired Emperor Saga, and received the posthumous title of Chancellor during the reign of his grandson, Montoku. His sobriquet, Fujisashi, combines syllables from his surname and his official title (*sadaijin*, Minister of the Left) in a manner that is not understood. Hosaka 1974, 2.191.

Fuyutsugu, *see* Fuyutsugi

Gaen Unidentified. Apparently an Enryakuji Holy Teacher (*ajari*). Hosaka 1974, 2.507.

Gakei (932?-1012) Son of Prince Atsumi. Abbot of Tōji, Tōdaiji, Kanjuji; Archbishop.

Genji Sino-Japanese equivalent of the Minamoto surname.

Genmei, Empress (661-721, r. 707-715) 43rd sovereign. Daughter of Tenji.

Genmyō, Empress, *see* Genmei

Genshi

1. (891?-1002) Daughter of Michitaka and Kishi; consort of Crown Prince (future Emperor Sanjō), 995-1002. Called Shigeisha. Kawakita 1968, pp. 181-183.
2. Daughter of Kanemichi. Principal Handmaid (976).
3. Daughter of Akimitsu; Junior Consort of Emperor Ichijō (996). Called Shōkyōden Consort. Began affair with M. Yorisada around 1012, after Ichijō's death.

Genshin (942-1017) Pure Land teacher; author of *Ōjō yōshū*, a famous handbook for Pure Land believers. Called Eshin Bishop, from the name of the Eshin'in at Yokawa, his residence on Mount Hiei. For *Ōjō yōshū*, see Andrews 1973.

Genshō, Empress (680-748, r. 715-724) 44th sovereign. Daughter of Empress Genmei.

Gentleman-in-Waiting Novice, *see* Suketō

Gishi (974-1053) Daughter of Kinsue; Junior Consort of Emperor Ichijō (996). Called Kokiden Consort. Became a nun in 1026.

Go-Ichijō, Emperor (1008-1036, r. 1016-1036) 68th sovereign. Second son of Ichijō. Mother: Shōshi. Grandson and son-in-law of Michinaga. Name: Atsuhira.

Gojō Empress, *see* Junshi

Gojō Mansion Location unknown.

Gokurakuji A temple founded by Mototsune in what is now the Fukakusa Gokurakuji-chō area of Fushimi-ku, Kyōto. It has not survived.

Go-Suzaku, Emperor (1009-1045, r. 1036-1045) 69th sovereign. Third son of Ichijō. Mother: Shōshi. Succeeded Koichijōin as Crown Prince in 1017. Name: Atsunaga.

Grand Empress, *see* Kenshi

Great Kamo Virgin, *see* Senshi

Gyōganji Popularly called Kawandō (Skin Hall). Founded around the beginning of the eleventh century by Gyōen, one of a class of wandering ascetics and popular preachers (*hijiri*) who often carried horn-tipped staffs, used berries for rosary beads, and dressed in deerskins. It was situated north of Ichijō and east of Machijiri. Now located at Nishikōdō-machi, Nakakyō-ku, Kyōto.

Hachijō Major Captain, *see* Yasutada

Hachiman, *see* Yawata

Hakuga, *see* Hiromasa

Hanayama, *see* Hanayamadera

Hanayamadera Also Kazanji. Another name for the Gangyōji, a Tendai temple founded in 877 by Archbishop Henjō at what is now Kitakazan, Yamashina, Higashiyama-ku, Kyōto.

Hanshi

  1. Princess (833-900). Daughter of Prince Nakano. Junior Consort of Emperor Kōkō; mother of Emperor Uda. Imperial Dame (887), Grand Empress (898). Called Tōin Empress, presumably in allusion to a residence in the vicinity of Higashinotōin or Nishinotōin.

  2. Daughter of Morosuke. Liaison with Michikane; Assistant Handmaid. Called Tō Naishi no suke and Tōsanmi.

Harima A province corresponding to parts of Hyōgo Prefecture.

Harukami (856-933) Son of Middle Counselor Morokuzu, who helped Mototsune put Emperor Kōkō on the throne. Consultant (919).

Heizei, Emperor (774-824, r. 806-809) 51st sovereign. Son of Kanmu.

Hiei, Mount A high mountain northeast of the capital on the old Yamashiro-Ōmi provincial boundary. Site of the Enryakuji.

Higashigojō Mansion Listed in *kohon* texts as birthplace of Emperor Kōkō. The vulgate texts and *Sandai jitsuroku* have Higashirokujō, which is probably correct. *See* Higashirokujō Mansion

Higashirokujō Mansion Listed in *Sandai jitsuroku* and *Ōkagami* vulgate texts as birthplace of Emperor Kōkō. Said to have been located north of Rokujō and east of Higashinotōin.

Higashisanjō Imperial Lady, *see* Senshi

Higashisanjō Mansion Originally built by Yoshifusa, probably on a single block west of Machijiri and south of Nijō. After passing through the hands of Mototsune, Onshi (daughter of Mototsune), Tadahira (brother of Onshi), Kanshi (daughter of Tadahira), and Kanemichi (grandson of Tadahira), it went to Kaneie, who is believed to have enlarged it by acquiring the adjacent block on the east as a site for additional structures, notably the Higashisanjō Minaminoin. It later belonged in succession to Kaneie's sons Michitaka and Michinaga, to Michinaga's son Yorimichi, and to Yorimichi's descendants for several generations. Emperor Ichijō, born in the house in 980, used it from time to time as a temporary residence after his accession. Tsunoda 1963, pp. 65-66.

Higashisanjō Minaminoin   A residential compound southeast of Kaneie's great Higashisanjō estate. Michitaka appears to have built or rebuilt structures there in 992 in order to provide a suitable residence for his daughter, Empress Teishi. *See* Nijō Mansion

Higashisanjō Minister of State, *see* Kaneie

High Hat Raisei, *see* Raisei

Higo   A province corresponding to Kumamoto Prefecture.

Hine   In Izumi Province. Now Hineno, Izumi Sano City, Ōsaka.

Hirohata   Conjectured to have been an area east of Kyōgoku and south of Konoe. McCullough and McCullough 1980, Chapter 1, n. 29.

Hirohata Lady of the Bedchamber, *see* Keishi

Hiromasa, M. (922-980)   Son of Prince Katsuakira; grandson of Emperor Daigo; famous as a musician. Held Third Rank without serving as a member of the Council of State. Often called Hakuga no sanmi.

Hirosawa   A pond in eastern Saga (Ukyō-ku, Kyōto).

Hirotaka, Kose (fl. late 10th-early 11th century)   Head of the Office of Painting. Famous artist; subject of numerous anecdotes. Hosaka 1974, 2.638.

His Lordship the Novice, *see* Michinaga

Hitachi   A province corresponding to part of Ibaragi Prefecture.

Hitomaro, Kakinomoto (fl. ca. 680-700)   Great poet, admired especially for his mastery of the *chōka* (long poem).

Hitoyoshiko   Daughter of Tokihira. Wife of Crown Prince Yasuakira; mother of Crown Prince Yoshiyori.

Hizen   A province in Kyūshū, now incorporated in Saga and Nagasaki Prefectures.

Hōjōji   A great temple built by Michinaga on a site immediately east of the Tsuchimikado Mansion. Its first major building, the Amitābha Hall (also called Muryōjuin, Nakagawa Midō, Midō), which housed nine statues of Amitābha, was dedicated in 1020. Meanwhile, the grounds had been beautified by the addition of a lake and an artificial hill, and Michinaga had moved into modest residential quarters east of the hall. A number of structures were added later—notably the Golden Hall (Kondō), dedicated with immense pomp in 1022. See McCullough and McCullough 1980, Chapter 17 and passim.

Hōjūji   A major temple of the Heian period, founded late in his lifetime by Tamemitsu, probably in memory of his daughter Kishi. It was situated southeast of the present Sanjūsangendō in Kyōto.

Hōjūji Bishop   Jinkō (971-1038), a son of Tamemitsu. Later an Archbishop. For the identification, see Hagitani 1971-1973, 1.50-51.

Hōjūji Minister of State, *see* Tamemitsu

Hōki   A province corresponding to what is now western Tottori Prefecture.

Hokoin   Also Hōkōin. The Buddhist name given to Kaneie's subsidiary residence, the [Higashi]nijō Mansion, when it was converted into a temple shortly before his death. It was situated north of Nijō and east of Kyōgoku.

Hon'in Mansion   Residence of Tokihira, north of Tsuchimikado and east of Horikawa.

Hon'in Minister of State, *see* Tokihira

Hōrai, *see* Peng lai

Horikawa Consort, *see* Enshi

Horikawa Empress, *see* Kōshi

Horikawain, *see* Horikawa Mansion

Horikawa Mansion   A great estate south of Nijō and east of Horikawa, near the east bank of the Horikawa River (a small stream in the old main bed of the Kamo, flowing parallel to Horikawa Avenue). Successively owned and/or used by Mototsune, Kanemichi, Kanemichi's daughter Kōshi and her husband (Emperor En'yū), Akimitsu, and Akimitsu's daughters (Enshi and Genshi). Later sold to a rich provincial official; eventually passed into the hands of Michinaga's descendants. McCullough and McCullough 1980, s.n. 24.

Horikawa Minister of State, *see* Mototsune

Horikawa Palace, *see* Horikawa Mansion

Horikawa Regent, *see* Kanemichi

Hōshi

1. Daughter of Tokihira; Junior Consort of Emperor Uda. Mother of Prince Masaakira (920-929). Called Kyōgoku no miyasudokoro (Kyōgoku Lady of the Bedchamber) and Tominokōji no miyasudokoro.

2. (d. 967) Daughter of Morotada; a favorite Junior Consort of Emperor Murakami. Called Sen'yōden Consort.

Hōshōji   Also Hosshōji. A great Tendai temple south of Kujō.

Founded by Tadahira in 925 and patronized by successive generations of Fujiwara leaders.

Hsi ming ssu   A temple in Ch'ang an, founded ca. 650 by T'ang Kao
Tsu.

Hyōe no naishi   Unidentified. For speculations, see Hosaka 1974, 3.510.

I ai Temple   I ai ssu. A temple on the north side of Incense Burner
Peak in Kiukiang, Kiangsi, southern China.

Ichijō, Emperor (980-1011, r. 986-1011)   66th sovereign. Son of En'yū.
Mother: Senshi, daughter of Kaneie.

Ichijō Mansion   South of Ichijō and east of Ōmiya. Owned at various
times by Morosuke, Koremasa, Tamemitsu, Tamemitsu's daughter
(Shinden no onkata), Senshi, and Michinaga. Used as a residence by
Emperor Ichijō. McCullough and McCullough 1980, s.n. 19.

Ichijō Minister of the Left, *see* Masanobu

Ichijō, oldest son of, *see* Atsuyasu

Ichijō Regent, *see* Koremasa

Ide   A place in the delta of the Tama River, a tributary of the Kizu,
in southern Kyōto Prefecture. Famous in classical poetry for *yama-
buki* flowers (*Kerria japonica*) and singing frogs.

Iga   A province corresponding to part of Mie Prefecture.

Iimuro   One of the Six Valleys in the Yokawa area of Mount Hiei.
See Yokawa, Ryōgon'in

Iimuro Bishop, *see* Jin'en

Iimuro Provisional Archbishop, *see* Jinzen

Iki   A province consisting of an island situated between Kyūshū and
the Korean peninsula. Now Iki District, Nagasaki Prefecture. Captured by the Jurchen in 1019.

Imperial Apartment, *see* Kokiden Imperial Apartment and Fujitsubo
Imperial Apartment

Imperial Bedchamber   Yon no Otodo. In the Seiryōden, north of the
Daytime Chamber.

Inari Hill, *see* Inari Shrine

Inari Shrine   Fushimi Inari Taisha. Situated in northern Fushimi-ku,
Kyōto. A major place of worship for people of all classes; one of the
Twenty-Two Shrines. Prior to 1438, when it was moved to its
present location at the western base of Inariyama (the southernmost
of the thirty-six Higashiyama peaks), it consisted of three separate
establishments, one on each of that mountain's highest points. The
cryptomeria trees on the mountain were revered as symbolic of the
divine spirit, and small branches were given to worshippers at the

annual festival on the first Day of the Horse in the Second Month. Hosaka 1974, 2.290.

Incense Burner Peak Hsiang lu feng. A mountain in Kiangsi, China. Po Chü-i occupied a cottage nearby. Waley 1949, p. 118.

Ingen (954-1028) A prominent Tendai monk who was on close terms with Michinaga. He rose ultimately to the offices of Archbishop (1023) and Enryakuji abbot (1020). Hosaka 1974, 3.246.

Inshi (d. 896) Daughter of Takafuji. Junior Consort of Uda; mother of Daigo. Posthumous Grand Empress (897).

Inspector Major Counselor, *see* Asateru

Ise

1. A province corresponding to part of Mie Prefecture.
2. Daughter of Tsugikaze, a governor of Ise. Bore a son to Emperor Uda. Retired from Court after Uda's abdication; later gave birth to the poet Nakatsukasa as a result of an affair with Prince Atsuyoshi, Uda's son. A leading *Kokinshū* poet.

Ise, Grand Shrine of The foremost shrine in Japan, dedicated to the Sun Goddess Amaterasu, progenitrix of the Imperial family. At the beginning of each reign, a new Virgin (*saigū*) was selected by divination from among unmarried Imperial or princely offspring to serve as its high priestess and Imperial surrogate. McCullough and McCullough 1980, s.n. 25.

Ishi (999-1036) Daughter of Michinaga and Rinshi. Principal Handmaid, consort of Go-Ichijō (1018), Empress (*chūgū*, 1018). Mother of Princesses Shōshi and Keishi, who became the Empresses of Go-Reizei and Go-Sanjō. Nine years older than Go-Ichijō. Died of smallpox.

Ishikawamaro, Soga no [Kura] Yamada (d. 649) One of the Taika reformers. Minister of the Right under Emperor Kōtoku until forced to commit suicide after having been slandered by his half-brother.

Ishiyama[dera] Famous old Shingon temple in what is now Ōtsu City, Shiga Prefecture. Its image of Kannon, to which miraculous powers were ascribed, was a cult object for people of all classes.

Isonokami In the present Tenri City, Nara Prefecture. Appears frequently in poetry as a *makura kotoba* (pillow word) for *furu*, grow old. Furu was a place name in the general area known as Isonokami.

Iwagimi, *see* Yorimune

Iwakura Another name for the Daiunji, a temple founded by vow of Emperor En'yū in 971. Its reconstructed main hall survives at Ononosato Iwakura, Sakyō-ku, Kyōto.

Iwashimizu, *see* Yawata

Iyo   A province in Shikoku corresponding to Ehime Prefecture.

Iyo Novice, *see* Tametō

Izumi   A province corresponding to part of Ōsaka Prefecture.

Izumi Shikibu (fl. ca. 1000)   Married Tachibana Michisada, governor of Izumi (thus her sobriquet); liaisons with Princes Tametaka and Atsumichi and others; lady-in-waiting of Empress Shōshi after Prince Atsumichi's death in 1007. A major poet. See Cranston 1969, pp. 3-24.

Izumo   A province corresponding to eastern Shimane Prefecture.

Jetavana-vihāra   J. Gion shōja. Traditionally regarded as the first Buddhist monastery; said to have been built for Śākyamuni and his disciples by Sudatta (J. Sudatsu), a wealthy merchant in the central Indian state of Kośala, and to have been situated south of the city of Śravastī in a park called Jetavanānāthapiṇḍadārāma (J. Giju-gikko-kudoku-on, usually contracted to Gikkoon or Gion).

Jijūden   A building in the Imperial Residential Compound, directly north of the Shishinden. It had been the Imperial residence in the early Heian period, but in Michinaga's day was used for occasional religious services, banquets, and other entertainments.

Jin'en   Son of Yoshichika. Eventually a Major Archbishop at the Enryakuji. Called Iimuro Bishop in *Ōkagami*.

Jingikō, *see* Kinsue

Jinkaku (955-1043)   Son of Morosuke. Archbishop, Tōji abbot.

Jinkū (d. 1035)   Grandson of Morosuke; son of Tōnori. Master of Discipline, Lesser Bishop.

Jinmu, Emperor   Quasi-historical first Emperor. Said to have died in 585 B.C.

Jinsei (d. 1051)   Grandson of Kanemichi; son of Tōmitsu. Tōdaiji abbot, 17th Kōya abbot, Ninnaji Bishop. According to Hosaka 1974, 2.616, he did not become Ninnaji abbot until 1041, sixteen years after the *Ōkagami* narrative present.

Jinzen (943-990)   Son of Morosuke. Iimuro Archbishop, 19th Tendai abbot. Posthumous name: Jinin.

Jitō, Empress (645-702, r. 686-697)   41st sovereign. Daughter of Tenji; widow of Tenmu.

Jōganden   A building in the Emperor's residential compound. It housed the Wardrobe (*mikushigedono*), where sewing was done, and apparently also served as a residence at times.

Jōganden Principal Handmaid, *see* Tōshi

Jōki (977-1033)   Master of Discipline. Later Bishop, Tennōji abbot. Hosaka 1974, 3.246.

Jōmyōji Founded by Michinaga in 1005 at what is now the city of Uji, near the Fujiwara burial ground at Kohata.

Jōtōmon Gate, *see* Tsuchimikado Gate

Jōtōmon'in, *see* Shōshi

Jōzō (891-964) A prominent Tendai monk. As Satō 1929, p. 107, points out, *Ōkagami* is in error in listing him as a prayer monk for Yoshimi, who died before he was born.

Junna, Emperor (786-840, r. 823-833) 53rd sovereign. Third son of Kanmu.

Junnin, Emperor (733-765, r. 758-764) 47th sovereign. Son of Prince Toneri.

Junshi
  1. (809-871) Daughter of Fuyutsugi. Consort of Ninmyō; mother of Montoku. Junior Consort (833), Imperial Dame (*kōtai fujin*, 850), Grand Empress (854), Senior Grand Empress (864, after having taken Buddhist vows in 861). Called Gojō Empress from the location of her residence, the Higashigojōin, in the Gojō area of the eastern half of the capital. Satō 1929, p. 24; Tachibana 1974, p. 43.
  2. (957-1017) Daughter of Yoritada; sister of Kintō. Married Emperor En'yū (978). Empress (982), Grand Empress (1000), Senior Grand Empress (1012). Called Barren Empress or Shijō Empress.

Jusshi (933-947) Third daughter of Saneyori; Junior Consort of Emperor Murakami. Contracted smallpox while pregnant, miscarried, and died.

Kachiko, Tachibana (786-850) Daughter of posthumous Chancellor Kiyotomo; Empress of Emperor Saga; mother of Emperor Ninmyō.

Kaishi (945-975) Daughter of Koremasa. Junior Consort (967) of Emperor Reizei, whom she married before he ascended the throne. Mother of Emperor Kazan. Posthumously named Grand Empress (984) during her son's reign.

Kamako, Nakatomi (or Ōnakatomi), *see* Kamatari

Kamatari (614-669) Ally of Prince Naka no Ōe (Emperor Tenji) in the overthrow of the Soga family and the institution of the Taika reforms. His personal name was originally Kamako; his surname, Nakatomi (or, with an honorific prefix, Ōnakatomi). Named Interior Minister (*naishin*) after the accession of Emperor Kōtoku; with Prince Naka no Ōe, wielded real power. Received the Fujiwara surname and the title Palace Minister (*naidaijin*) shortly before his death in 669. Called Taishokkan from the supreme Court rank of that name, which he held.

Appendices

Kamo River   A short stream that rises in the hills north of the Kyōto basin and flows through eastern Kyōto to its confluence with the Katsura. It bordered the eastern edge of Heiankyō.

Kamo Shrine   Properly two shrines, an upper and a lower sanctuary, situated northeast of the old capital on the bank of the Kamo River, in what is now Sakyō-ku, Kyōto. Venerated by the Heian nobility; site of two great annual festivals. McCullough and McCullough 1980, s.n. 50.

Kamo Virgin, *see* Senshi

Kanchō (936-998)   Son of Prince Atsumi. Became a monk at the age of twelve. Abbot of Ninnaji and Tōdaiji; first Shingon Major Archbishop (986). Known as a preacher and chanter; founded the Hirosawa school of the Shingon sect. In 989 he founded and took up residence at the Hanjōji, northwest of Hirosawa.

Kanehira (875-935)   Son of Mototsune. His claim to prominence seems to have rested on his skill as a lute (*biwa*) player. He never progressed beyond such modest offices as Imperial Household Minister and Provisional Master of the Grand Empress's Household.

Kaneie (929-990)   Son of Morosuke. Chancellor (989), Regent (986). Father-in-law of Emperor En'yū; grandfather of Emperor Ichijō. Called Higashisanjō Minister of State.

Kanemichi (925-977)   Son of Morosuke. Competed with his brother Kaneie for power. Acquired regental authority while a Provisional Middle Counselor by producing a statement of support from the late Empress Anshi (972). Palace Minister (972), Chancellor (974). Handed on the regency to his cousin, Yoritada, to block Kaneie's succession. Posthumous name: Chūgikō. Called Horikawa Regent from the name of his residence.

Kanemoto, M.   Son of Consultant Koremasa. A provincial governor.

Kanesada   Son of Masamitsu; grandson of Kanemichi. A provincial official.

Kanesuke (877-933)   Son of Toshimoto. Provisional Middle Counselor (927), Middle Counselor (930). Known as a poet.

Kanetaka (985-1053)   Son of Michikane; adopted by Kaneie. Consultant (1008), Provisional Middle Counselor (1019), Middle Counselor (1023-1035), Commander of Left Gate Guards (1021-1029).

Kanetsuna (988-1058)   Son of Michikane. Middle Captain, Senior Fourth Lower Rank.

Kanetsune (1000-1043)   Son of Michitsuna. Consultant (1023).

Kaneyasu   Possibly the obscure figure of that name listed by *Sonpi bunmyaku*, 2.303, among the great-grandsons of Yasuchika (932?-

996). His grand-aunt was Michinaga's mother, Tokihime. *Ōkagami* appears to be mistaken in calling Sanetō his brother.

Kan'in Situated south of Nijō, north of Sanjōbōmon, and west of Nishinotōin; adjacent to the Horikawain. It was Fuyutsugi's principal residence, and is said in *Ōkagami* to have been used later by Mototsune. Translation, p. 94. After having apparently passed into obscure hands at some point, it returned to the family and served as a residence for Kanemichi (who is believed to have acquired it in 976), Asateru, Kinsue, and Yoshinobu. Hosaka 1974, 2.376, 645; *Sonpi bunmyaku*, 1.9; Tsunoda 1963, p. 26; Takamure 1966, 1.373.

Kan'in Major Captain, *see* Asateru

Kan'in Minister of State, *see* Fuyutsugi, Kinsue

Kanjuji Also Kajuji, Kajūji. Founded in 900 by vow of Emperor Daigo's mother, Inshi, at what is now Kanjuji-chō, Higashiyama-ku, Kyōto. Patronized by successive Emperors.

Kanmu, Emperor (737-806, r. 781-806) 50th sovereign. Son of Kōnin.

Kannonji Also Kanzeonji. Said to have been founded during the reign of Empress Saimei (r. 654-661), and to have been completed in 723 by command of Empress Genshō. Situated approximately 200 meters east of the old Dazaifu, at what is now Dazaifu Town in Fukuoka Prefecture. The present buildings date from the Tokugawa period, but the bell, a national treasure presented to the temple by Emperor Tenji, is reputed to be the one Michizane heard. Hosaka 1974, 2.241; Tachibana 1974, p. 95, n. 10.

Kanshi (ca. 999-1025) Daughter of Michinaga and Meishi. Consort of Koichijōin; Mistress of the Wardrobe (*mikushigedono*).

Kanzan Or Gajō. Said to have been an Enryakuji monk during the reign of Emperor Daigo, and to have persecuted successive sovereigns after his death because of dissatisfaction with the ecclesiastical rank he had received from the Court. Hosaka 1974, 2.158.

Kashima The area of the present Kashima District, Ibaragi Prefecture.

Kasuga Shrine Located at the base of Mount Mikasa in the present Kasugano, Nara. During the Heian period, it enjoyed enormous prestige as the Fujiwara family shrine. The central role in its festivals, which were held twice annually on the first Day of the Monkey in the Second and Eleventh Months, was played by an Imperial Messenger, usually a Fujiwara Middle Captain, who journeyed to Nara with offerings, accompanied by dancers and courtiers.

Katano An old district on the left bank of the Yodo River in the northernmost part of Kawachi Province (now incorporated into

Katano City and Hirakata City, Ōsaka Prefecture). Famous as an Imperial hunting preserve.

Katsuranosato   A general name for the Kamikatsura and Shimokatsura areas in the present Ukyō-ku, Kyōto, near the Katsura River.

Kawachi   A province corresponding to part of Ōsaka Prefecture.

Kawadō   Usually Kawandō; also Kōdō. Another name for the Gyō-ganji.

Kawajiri   A name for the mouth of the Yodo River (known in its upper reaches as the Seta, and in its middle course as the Uji), a stream that rises in Lake Biwa and empties into Ōsaka Bay. Site of a busy port, used by travelers to and from the Heian capital.

Kayain   South of Nakamikado, north of Ōimikado, west of Nishino-tōin, and east of Horikawa—i.e., north of the Horikawa Mansion, and, like it, bordering the east bank of the Horikawa River. In 1021 it had become the principal residence of Michinaga's son Yorimichi, who had made it, according to a contemporary diarist, a place of "incomparable magnificence." See McCullough and McCullough 1980, Chapter 23, n. 1 and passim.

Kazan, Emperor (968-1008, r. 984-986)   65th sovereign. Son of Reizei. Mother: Kaishi, daughter of Koremasa. Mentally ill.

Kazan'in   Residence of Retired Emperor Kazan. South of Konoe and east of Higashinotōin.

Keihōbō   A building in the extreme north of the Emperor's residential compound. Little is known of the uses to which it was put during successive reigns, but scattered mentions indicate that it functioned variously as a medical facility, a dormitory for female servants, a residence for at least one Crown Prince, a storage area, and the site of an appointments ceremony. Hosaka 1974, 2.111; McCullough and McCullough 1980, Appendix B.

Keishi, M.   Daughter of Middle Counselor Moroaki; consort of Emperor Murakami. Called Hirohata Lady of the Bedchamber from the location of her family home.

Kenshi (994-1027)   Second daughter of Michinaga and Rinshi. Principal Handmaid (1004), consort of Crown Prince (Emperor Sanjō, 1010), Junior Consort (1011), Empress (*chūgū*, 1012), Grand Empress (1018). Gave birth to only one child, Princess Teishi; thus not an influential figure.

Kenshunmon   The main east gate leading into the Nakanoe.

Kentokukō, *see* Koremasa

Kinbusen   A sacred mountain in the Yoshino range in Nara Prefecture. Michinaga visited it in 1007.

Kinnari (999-1043) Son of Sanenari; adopted by his grandfather Kinsue. Provisional Middle Counselor (1043).

Kinnobu (977-1026) Also Kiminobu. Son of Tamemitsu. Commander of Military Guards of the Left (1021), Provisional Major Counselor (1023).

Kinsue (959-1029) Son of Morosuke by Princess Kōshi, a daughter of Daigo. Childhood name: Miyaogimi. Palace Minister (997), Minister of the Right (1017), Chancellor (1021). Called Kan'in Minister of State. Posthumous name: Jingikō.

Kintada, M. (889-948) Grandson of Emperor Kōkō. Held minor positions. Known as a poet; friend of Tsurayuki.

Kintō (966-1041) Son of Yoritada. As scholar, musician, poet in Chinese and Japanese, arbiter of taste, and the foremost literary critic of the day, Kintō was a leader in the Court's cultural life during the first two decades of the eleventh century, but his official career languished after the death of his father in 989. In 1024, he resigned as Provisional Major Counselor, after having stagnated in the position for fifteen years; and two years later he became a monk, relinquishing his remaining title of Inspector, which he had held since 1021. See McCullough and McCullough 1980, Chapter 27.

Kintō, wife of Daughter of Prince Akihira (954-1013); mother of Noriyori's wife and Sadayori.

Kishi
1. Princess (929-985) Daughter of Prince Shigeakira by one of Tadahira's daughters. Entered Emperor Murakami's harem (949), but was unable to compete with strong rivals like Anshi and Hōshi. Spent most of her time at home, where she held poetry contests and created a salon frequented by some of the leading literary figures of the day. Known as Shōkyōden Consort and as Virgin Consort, the latter in reference to her childhood service as Ise Virgin.
2. Daughter of Tadahira *See* Chūjō no miyasudokoro
3. (d. 985) Daughter of Tamemitsu; Junior Consort (984) of Kazan. The Emperor's grief after her death is said to have led to his abdication. Called Kokiden Consort.
4. (1007-1025) Daughter of Michinaga and Rinshi. Principal Handmaid (1018), consort of Crown Prince (Go-Suzaku, 1021). Died shortly after giving birth to future Emperor Go-Reizei. Posthumously named Senior Grand Empress (1045).
5. Takashina Daughter of Naritada; principal consort of Michitaka. Called Kō no naishi (Takashina Handmaid). See Kawakita 1968, pp. 159-169.

Kitano   An area corresponding to the northwestern part of Kamikyō-
ku, Kyōto; the wide plain north of the Greater Imperial Palace.
Kitano god, *see* Kitano Shrine, Michizane
Kitano no sanmi, *see* Tōnori
Kitano Shrine   Situated in what is now Bakuro-chō, Kamikyō-knw,
Kyōto. Founded around 947 for the worship of Sugawara Michizane;
known as Kitano Tenmangū after Morosuke enlarged the sanctuary
in 959. Michizane, initially dreaded as a thunder god, later came to
be revered as a patron of letters, and the shrine developed into a
major religious institution, enjoying Court patronage and sending
out many branches.
Kiyohito, Prince (ca. 998-1030)   Sixth and favorite son of Retired
Emperor Kazan, born after the latter had taken Buddhist vows. To
make it possible for the boy to be named an Imperial Prince, Kazan
arranged for his adoption by Retired Emperor Reizei, who was still
a layman. President of the Board of Censors.
Kōbō Daishi, *see* Kūkai
Kōbun, Emperor (648-672, r. 671-672)   Prince Ōtomo. 39th sovereign.
Son of Emperor Tenji, who made him the first Chancellor in the
First Month of 671. Crown Prince Ōama, Tenji's brother, resigned
when the Emperor was facing death later in the same year, thus
clearing the way for Prince Ōtomo's succession. There is no proof
that Prince Ōtomo formally became Emperor, but he is treated by
modern historians as having done so in the Twelfth Month of 671.
He was forced to commit suicide when Prince Ōama mounted a successful challenge to his rule.
Kochiyo, *see* Korechika
Kōfukuji   The Fujiwara family temple in Nara, one of the great religious institutions of the Heian period. Also called Yamashinadera,
from the location of the family's first temple, built by Kamatari's
wife in 669 at Yamashina in Yamashiro Province (Kyōto Prefecture). The temple was moved to the Asuka area in Yamato (Nara
Prefecture) when Emperor Tenmu ascended the throne in 673, and
there was a third and final move to Nara, accomplished by Fuhito,
when the Court was established there in 710.
Kohata   A Fujiwara burial ground in what is now the northernmost
part of Uji City, Kyōto; final resting place of many family heads and
Imperial consorts.
Koichijō Chancellor, *see* Tadahira
Koichijōin, *see* Atsuakira
Koichijōin, consorts of, *see* Kanshi, Enshi
Koichijō Mansion   Probably located south of Konoe and west of Hi-

gashinotōin. A famous Fujiwara residence, owned successively by Fuyutsugi, Yoshifusa, Mototsune, Tadahira, Morotada—and, in Michinaga's day, by Morotada's son, Naritoki, by Naritoki's daughter, Empress Seishi, and by Seishi's son, Koichijōin (Prince Atsuakira). See Tsunoda 1963, p. 164.

Koichijō Minister of State, *see* Morotada

Kokegimi, *see* Akinobu

Kōken, Empress (718-770, r. 749-758, and, as Empress Shōtoku, 764-770) 46th and 48th sovereign. Daughter of Emperor Shōmu and Empress Kōmyō. Called Takano Empress.

Kokiden A building in the Imperial Residential Compound. Ordinarily occupied by a principal Imperial consort.

Kokiden Consort, *see* Gishi, Kishi

Kokiden Imperial Apartment A room in the northernmost part of the Seiryōden, used primarily by Imperial consorts and concubines visiting the Emperor from quarters elsewhere in the Imperial Palace compound.

Kōkō, Emperor (830-887, r. 884-887) 58th sovereign. Prince Tokiyasu, third son of Ninmyō. Mother: Takushi, daughter of Fusatsugi. Dominated by Mototsune. Known as Komatsu Emperor, from the Komatsu Mansion, his earlier residence (said to have been situated north of Ōimikado and east of Machijiri), and from the site of his grave near the Ninnaji, which seems to have been named Komatsu in reference to the sobriquet he had borne during his lifetime. Hosaka 1974, 2.80-81.

Kōkō, mother of, *see* Takushi

Komatsu Emperor, *see* Kōkō

Kōmyō, Empress (701-760) Asukahime, a daughter of Fuhito. Empress of Shōmu; mother of Empress Kōken. Named Empress in 729.

Kō nii, *see* Naritada

Kō no naishi, *see* Kishi (Takashina)

Korechika (973-1010) Son of Michitaka. Childhood name: Kochiyo. Rose rapidly from Consultant (991) to Palace Minister (994-996). Briefly in charge of the government during and after his father's final illness (995), but was prevented by Senshi from becoming Regent. Exiled in 996 on a number of charges, the most serious of which was disrespectful treatment of Retired Emperor Kazan, a fancied rival in love, whom he and Takaie had attempted to discourage by having arrows shot at him under cover of darkness. Recalled to capital in 997. Later acquired Senior Second Rank, but remained outside the bureaucracy. See Kawakita 1968, pp. 168-175; McCullough and McCullough 1980, Chapters 4 and 5.

Korehira (876-938)   Third son of the *Kokinshū* poet Toshiyuki. Became Provisional Middle Captain of the Right in 924; eventually
rose as high as Consultant (934). A leading poet of his day.

Koremasa (924-972)   Also Koretada. Oldest son of Morosuke. Regent
(970-972), Chancellor (971-972). Called Ichijō Regent from the
name of his residence. Posthumous name: Kentokukō.

Koremasa, daughters of
   1. *See* Kaishi
   2. Married Tamemitsu; died.
   3. Succeeded her older sister as Tamemitsu's wife; died.
   4. (Or 6?) Wife of Tadagimi and, later, of Munekata.
   9. Married Emperor Reizei's son, Prince Tametaka.

Korenaka, Taira (944-1005)   Son of Yoshiki. On close terms with
Kaneie. Provisional Middle Counselor (996), Middle Counselor
(998).

Koreshige (953-989)   Also Korenari. The offspring of a poor but
gifted family, Koreshige appears in contemporary sources as a poet,
scholar, and bureaucrat of exceptional verve. A protégé of Koremasa, he became a scholar (*gakushi*) in the household of Crown
Prince Morosada (Emperor Kazan), after whose accession he joined
with Yoshichika in the institution of a number of political reforms,
exercising a de facto authority substantial enough to win him the
nickname Regent of Fifth Rank.

Koretada, *see* Koremasa

Koretaka, Prince (844-897)   Favorite son of Emperor Montoku, who,
however, was obliged to make Yoshifusa's grandson his heir apparent. The Prince, whose mother was a daughter of Ki no Natora,
took religious vows in 872 and retired to Ono. A good poet; friend
and patron of Ariwara Narihira.

Koretsune   Son of Yasumichi, whose mother had been Michinaga's
nurse. Both father and son were members of the provincial governor
class, and both served as stewards in Michinaga's household. Koretsune's mother, a daughter of a vice-governor of Hitachi, seems to
have nursed both Kenshi and Kishi. Hosaka 1974, 3.561.

Kōrōden   A building adjacent to the Seiryōden on the west. It housed
the Imperial kitchens and was also sometimes used as a residence.

Kōshi
   1. (842-910) Called Takaiko. Daughter of Nagara; sister of Mototsune. Junior Consort of Seiwa; mother of Yōzei. Named Imperial
Dame (*kōtai fujin*) after accession of Yōzei (877). Became Grand
Empress (882); stripped of title for alleged sexual improprie-

ties (896), but regained it posthumously (943). Said to have been abducted by Narihira prior to her marriage to the then Crown Prince (Seiwa). Called Nijō Empress. McCullough 1968, pp. 45-46.

2. Princess Fourteenth daughter of Emperor Daigo, (rather than fourth, as *Ōkagami* has it). Consort of Morosuke; mother of Kinsue. Hosaka 1974, 2.646-647.

3. (947-979) Daughter of Kanemichi; consort of Emperor En'yū. Junior Consort (Fourth Month, 973), Empress (Seventh Month, 973). Called Horikawa Empress from the name of her family home.

4. Daughter of Masamitsu. One of Grand Empress Kenshi's principal attendants; wife of Kinnobu. Called Tsuchimikado Mistress of the Wardrobe.

Koshiro   Another name for Karasumarukōji. See Figure 1.

Kōtoku, Emperor (597-654, r. 645-654)   36th sovereign.

Kōtokukō, *see* Tamemitsu

Kowakagimi, *see* Nagaie

Kōzuke   A province corresponding to Gunma Prefecture.

Kubira, *see* Kumbhīra

Kujō Lord, *see* Morosuke

Kujō Mansion   Residence of Morosuke, situated south of Kujōbōmon and east of Machijiri.

Kūkai (774-835)   Founder of the Shingon sect in Japan; also a calligrapher and literatus. One of the great figures of the Heian period. Posthumous name: Kōbō Daishi.

Kumano   A general term for three shrines in what is now Higashimuro District, Wakayama Prefecture: Hongū, or Kumanonimasu, in Hongū Town; Shingū, or Kumanohayatama, in Shingū City; and Nachi, or Kumanonachi, in Nachikatsura Town. Although separated geographically, they were unified by the Kumano faith, a hybrid Buddhist-Shintō cult, devoted to the prolongation of life and rebirth in paradise, which developed toward the end of the Heian period. As one of the great religious centers of the Heian and Kamakura periods, Kumano was frequently visited by Retired Emperors and other notables, as well as by wandering ascetics and ordinary pilgrims.

Kumbhīra   One of the Twelve Divine Commanders who protect worshipers of Yakushi, the Healing Buddha.

Kunitsune (ca. 828-908)   Oldest son of Nagara; brother of Mototsune. Major Counselor (902).

Kurabeya Consort, *see* Sonshi

Kurahashimaro, Abe (d. 649) Minister of the Left under Emperor Kōtoku.

Kuze A plain used as a hunting ground, situated on the west bank of the Katsura River in what is now Minami-ku, Kyōto.

Kyōmei (965-1038) Named Major Bishop in 1014. Served as abbot of leading temples; on close terms with Michinaga. Matsumura 1969-, 4.223.

Later Lesser Captain, *see* Yoshitaka

Machiosa[gimi], *see* Takamitsu

Maro (695-737) Son of Fuhito; founder of the Capital House of the Fujiwara family. His career, primarily military, was cut short by his death in the smallpox epidemic of 737.

Masabun Son of Major Counselor Michiakira; held provincial governorships.

Masakado, Taira (d. 940) Member of an influential family in eastern Japan. After serving the Fujiwara Regent Tadahira in his youth, he returned to the east with frustrated ambitions and began a series of bloody quarrels with relatives and neighbors. By 939, he was in rebellion against the Court, styling himself New Emperor and controlling the chief Kantō provinces. In 940, as he was moving against Izu and Suruga Provinces, he was killed by forces under Taira Sadamori (his cousin) and Fujiwara Hidesato, a government police officer in Shimotsuke Province.

Masamitsu (957-1014) Son of Kanemichi. Treasury Minister (998), Consultant (1004).

Masamitsu, daughter of, *see* Kōshi

Masanari, M. (d. 1082?) Son of Tsunetō; like his father, a minor official known as a poet. *Sonpi bunmyaku*, 3.369; Hosaka 1974, 2.409.

Masanobu, M. (920-993) Son of Prince Atsumi; father of Rinshi. Minister of the Left (978). Known as a connoisseur of music. Called Ichijō Minister of the Left from the name of his house, which was south of Ichijō and east of Takakura.

Matate (715-766) Son of Fusasaki. Junior Third Rank (760), Major Counselor (766), posthumous Chancellor. Known as a poet.

Meishi

1. (829-900) Called Akirakeiko. Daughter of Yoshifusa; consort of Montoku; mother of Seiwa. Imperial Dame (858), Grand Empress (864), Senior Grand Empress (882). Called Somedono Empress.

2. M. Daughter of Takaakira, after whose exile she was adopted by

her uncle, Prince Moriakira (928-986), a brother of Emperor Murakami. After the Prince's death, she became the protégée of Michinaga's sister Senshi. Michinaga made her his secondary wife, and she gave birth to Yorimune, Akinobu, Yoshinobu, Nagaie, Kanshi, and Sonshi. Called Lady Takamatsu from the name of her residence.

Meison (971-1063)　Son of Ono no Mototoki; grandson of the calligrapher Michikaze. Eminent Tendai monk; served as abbot of both Onjōji and Enryakuji. Major Archbishop (1038).

Michifusa (1024-1044)　Son of Yorimichi. Childhood name: Osagimi. Provisional Major Counselor (1042).

Michikane (961-995)　Son of Kaneie. Palace Minister (991), Minister of the Right (994), Regent (995). Called Awata Lord from the location of his villa; also Machijiri Lord from his principal residence at Nijō Machijiri.

Michikane, wife of, *see* Tōkazu, daughter of

Michimasa (933?-1054)　Son of Korechika. Childhood name: Matsugimi. Middle Captain; Third Rank (1016). Remembered for his affair with the former Ise Virgin, Princess Tōshi, and as a poet.

Michinaga (966-1027)　Fifth son of Kaneie. Provisional Middle Counselor (988), Provisional Major Counselor (991), Minister of the Right with *nairan* powers (995), Minister of the Left (996-1016), Regent (1016-1017), Chancellor (1017-1018). Took religious vows in 1019. Father-in-law of three Emperors, one Retired Emperor, and one Crown Prince; grandfather of two Emperors; father of two Regents.

Michinaga, wife of, *see* Rinshi, Meishi

Michinobu (972-994)　Son of Tamemitsu; adoptive son of Kaneie. Known as a poet. Matsumura 1969-, 1.489.

Michinokuni　Also Michinoku or Mutsu. An old province in northeastern Honshū, corresponding to Fukushima, Miyagi, Iwate, and Aomori Prefectures.

Michitaka (953-995)　Son of Kaneie and Tokihime. Provisional Major Counselor (986), Palace Minister (989-991), Regent (990-995). Called Middle Regent (*naka no kanpaku*), probably because he was preceded by Kaneie and followed by Michinaga. Hosaka 1974, 2.299.

Michitaka, third daughter of, *see* San no kimi

Michitō (974-1039)　Son of Naritoki. Treasury Minister (1020), Provisional Middle Counselor (1035).

Michitsuna (955-1020)　Son of Kaneie by *Kagerō nikki* author. Major Counselor (997).

Michitsuna, mother of (d. ca. 995)   Daughter of Tomoyasu. Subsidiary wife of Kaneie; *Kagerō nikki* author.

Michiyori (971-995)   Son of Michitaka; adopted by Kaneie. Childhood name: Ōchiyo. Provisional Major Counselor (994). Called Yamanoi Major Counselor.

Michiyoshi   Son of Kaneie. Junior Assistant Minister of Civil Affairs.

Michizane, Sugawara (845-903)   Son of Koreyoshi; member of a family of scholars and literati. Admired for his poetic skill in Chinese and Japanese. Named Minister of the Right in 899, the first scholar to receive such an appointment since the Nara period. His patron, Retired Emperor Uda, had hoped to use him to counter Fujiwara influence, but Tokihira and others persuaded Emperor Daigo that the minister was plotting to replace him with his own son-in-law, Uda's son Prince Tokiyo, and he was exiled to Kyūshū with the nominal title of Provisional Governor-General of the Dazaifu (901). After his death, misfortunes suffered by the Fujiwara were attributed to his vengeful spirit. He was reinstated as Minister of the Right in 923 and named Chancellor in 993. Borgen 1978. *See* also Kitano Shrine

Middle Enclosure, *see* Nakanoe

Miidera, *see* Onjōji

Mikasayama   Parasol Mountain. A hill (283 meters) on the eastern edge of the Kasuga Shrine precincts in Nara. Thought to resemble a parasol (*kinugasa*, [*mi*]*kasa*).

Mikawa   A province corresponding to part of Aichi Prefecture.

Mikawa Novice, *see* Sadamoto

Mikushigedono

1. *See* Kanshi

2. (983-1002) Daughter of Michitaka and Kishi; concubine of Emperor Ichijō. Died during pregnancy.

Minaminoin, *see* Southern Palace

Mineo, Kantsuke   Said by *Ōkagami uragaki*, item 17, p. 317, to have flourished around the Jōwa era (834-847), but otherwise unknown. Conjectured to have been in Mototsune's employ. Hosaka 1974, 2.218.

Mishima   A shrine at what is now Ōmishima, Ochi District, Ehime Prefecture, on the Inland Sea. Called Mishima Myōjin or Ōyamatsumi Shrine, the latter from the name of the deity worshipped. The plaque in Sukemasa's hand is still among its treasures.

Mitsuhiro, Ōkura   Son of Taneki. Fought with valor during the Jurchen invasion of 1019; named Dazaifu Inspector.

Mitsuko   Listed in *Sonpi bunmyaku*, 1.43, as an Imperial Handmaid of posthumous Senior First Rank, daughter of the provincial governor Sanesaku and mother of Yoshifusa, Nagara, and Yoshimi.

Mitsune, Ōshikōchi   A minor bureaucrat and major *Kokinshū* poet.

Miyaogimi, *see* Kinsue

Miya Waterfall Miyadaki   On the upper Yoshino River in Nara Prefecture, near the sites of the old Yoshino pleasure palaces; actually a stretch of white water rather than a waterfall. Hosaka 1974, 3.472, 474.

Mizunoo   Site of Emperor Seiwa's grave. Southwest of Atagoyama near the old Yamashiro-Tanba provincial border, in Saga, Ukyō-ku, Kyōto. A mountainous area, to which the former Emperor retired after taking religious vows.

Mizunoo Emperor, *see* Seiwa

Momozono Mansion   North of Ichijō and west of Ōmiya. Used successively by a number of Imperial Princes and Kamo Virgins, by several Fujiwara, including Morosuke and Koremasa, by Minamoto Yasumitsu, etc. Converted into a temple, the Sesonji, by Yukinari, grandson of both Koremasa and Yasumitsu, in 995.

Monkei (968-1047)   Also Monkyō. Grandson of Tokihira; son of Sukemasa. Bishop; abbot of the Daiunji at Iwakura.

Monmu, Emperor (683-707, r. 697-707)   42nd sovereign. Grandson of Tenmu; son of Prince Kusakabe and Empress Genmei.

Montoku, Emperor (827-858, r. 850-858)   55th sovereign. First son of Ninmyō; grandson of Fuyutsugi. Called Tamura Emperor from the location of his grave at what is now Uzumasa, Ukyō-ku, Kyōto.

Montoku, mother of, *see* Junshi

Moriakira, Prince (928-986)   Fifteenth son of Emperor Daigo; brother of M. Takaakira. Adopted Takaakira's daughter Meishi, who later married Michinaga.

Morihito   Son of Yasuchika. A provincial official.

Morimasa (fl. ca. 945)   Son of Middle Counselor Kanesuke (d. 933). Minor official; Junior Fifth Lower Rank.

Moroakira, Prince (1004?-1085)   Son of Emperor Sanjō and Seishi. Entered Ninnaji as monk Shōshin. Highly regarded as a ritualist.

Morofusa, M. (1008-1077)   Son of Prince Tomohira; husband of Sonshi (daughter of Michinaga and Meishi). Childhood name: Masumiya. Adopted by his brother-in-law, Yorimichi. Minister of the Right (1069); scholar and literatus.

Morofusa, wife of, *see* Sonshi

Moroki, Yoshimine (862-920)   Nephew of the poet Henjō. Head Chamberlain (915), Consultant (917).

Morosuke (908-960)   Son of Tadahira. Minister of the Right under

Emperor Murakami; grandfather of Murakami's two immediate successors, Reizei and En'yū. Grandfather of Michinaga. Called Kujōdono (Kujō Lord) from the name of his house.

Morotada (920-969)   Also Moromasa. Provisional Major Counselor (960) and Major Counselor (966) under Emperor Murakami; advanced to Minister of the Right late in 967, shortly after the accession of Emperor Reizei. Early in 969, operating in the near power vacuum created by the death of Morosuke and the advanced age of Saneyori, he secured the exile of the Minister of the Left, M. Takaakira, whose position he inherited. His death seven months later was attributed by contemporaries to divine retribution. Called Koichijō Minister of State from the name of his house.

Morouji (913?-970)   Son of Tadahira. Provisional Major Counselor (969). A poet of some repute, he does not appear to have been politically influential. Called Momozono Major Counselor from the name of his house.

Motohira, Prince (d. 958)   Son of Emperor Yōzei. Shown in *Honchō kōin shōunroku*, p. 417, as Present of the Board of Censors, rather than as Minister of Ceremonial, a post held by his brother, Prince Motonaga.

Motokata (888-953)   Son of Consultant Sugane. Middle Counselor (941), Major Counselor (951), Minister of Popular Affairs (947). His daughter, Sukehime, was the mother of Emperor Murakami's first son, Prince Hirohira, who failed to become Crown Prince because the Emperor's second son, the future Emperor Reizei, enjoyed the support of the leading Fujiwara faction. Motokata's angry spirit and that of his daughter were blamed for many later Fujiwara misfortunes, including Reizei's insanity. The *Ōkagami* author suggests that Motokata was involved in Koichijōin's resignation because Koichijōin's father, Emperor Sanjō, was Reizei's son.

Mototsune (836-891)   Son of Nagara; adopted by Yoshifusa. Regent of Emperors Seiwa, Yōzei, Kōkō, and Uda, 872-890. Minister of the Right (872-880), Chancellor (880-891). Called Horikawa Minister of State. Posthumous name: Shōsenkō.

Mototsune, daughter of, *see* Onshi

Mototsune, mother of, *see* Otoharu

Muchimaro (680-737)   Son of Fuhito; founder of the Southern House of the Fujiwara. Minister of the Right (734), Minister of the Left (737). Died in the epidemic of 737.

Munekata, M. (951-989)   Son of Shigenobu. Major Controller of the Right. *Sonpi bunmyaku*, 3.380.

Murakami, Emperor (926-967, r. 946-967)   62nd sovereign. Fourteenth son of Daigo. Mother: Onshi, daughter of Mototsune. His reign and that of his father, Daigo, have traditionally been bracketed together as "the glorious reigns of Engi and Tenryaku," periods during which the arts flourished, Court life was brilliant, and the Emperor played a relatively prominent political role. Called Tenryaku Emperor after an era name (947-957).

Murakami, fifth daughter of, *see* Seishi

Murakami, mother of, *see* Onshi

Murasakino Also Murasaino. An area immediately north of the capital (now Murasakino, Kita-ku, Kyōto). Site of the Kamo Virgin's residence, of the Urin'in, etc.

Muryōjuin An early name for the Hōjōji. *See* Hōjōji

Musashi A province corresponding to Tōkyō Prefecture, Saitama Prefecture, and part of Kanagawa Prefecture.

Mutsu, *see* Michinokuni

Nagahira, Prince (965-988) Eighth son of Emperor Murakami. Mother: Hōshi, daughter of Morotada. War Minister. Mentally retarded. Reared by his uncle, Naritoki, after Hōshi's death.

Nagaie (1005-1064) Son of Michinaga and Meishi. Childhood name: Kowakagimi. Provisional Middle Counselor (1023), Provisional Major Counselor (1028). Adopted by Rinshi.

Nagaie, wife of (1007-1021) Daughter of Yukinari. Name unknown.

Nagara (802-856) Son of Fuyutsugi. Provisional Middle Counselor; posthumously named Chancellor (879) during the reign of his grandson, Emperor Yōzei. Called Biwa Minister of State.

Nagara, daughter of, *see* Kōshi

Naishi, Ki Daughter of Tsurayuki. Said to have been a good poet, but *Choku nareba* (*Shūishū* 531) is the only surviving composition attributed to her.

Nakahira (875-945) Son of Mototsune. Eventually became Minister of the Right (933) and Minister of the Left (937), but was far less influential than his younger brother, Tadahira. Called Biwa Minister of the Left after the name of his house.

Nakamasa Seventh son of Middle Counselor Yamakage; father of Kaneie's principal consort, Tokihime. A minor courtier. Master of the Left Capital Office, Governor of Settsu. Junior Fourth Rank.

Nakano, Prince (792-867) Twelfth son of Emperor Kanmu. Became Minister of Ceremonial during reign of Ninmyō; posthumously named Chancellor on accession of Suzaku. Hosaka 1974, 1.87.

Nakanoe Middle Enclosure. A buffer zone in the Greater Imperial Palace, leading into the Inner Enclosure (Uchinoe or Dairi) where the Emperor lived. Its principal gates were Sakuheimon on the north, Kenshunmon on the east, Kenreimon on the south, and Gishūmon on the west.

Naka no kimi   Daughter of Naritoki; adopted by her paternal grandmother. Married Prince Atsumichi, from whom she was later divorced.

Naka no Ōe, *see* Tenji

Nakatsukasa

1. Daughter of the poet Ise and Prince Atsuyoshi; wife of the poet M. Nobuakira, who was named governor of Mutsu in 961, and who probably returned to the capital with his family about five years later, at the expiration of his term. A poet. Hosaka 1974, 3.496.
2. Identified by commentators with the nurse of that name (a daughter of Takakata, an obscure provincial official) who helped rear Princess Teishi, the daughter of Emperor Sanjō.

Nakayama   An area east of the Kamo River, between Kaguragaoka and Kurodani. A hunting ground during the Heian period.

Nan'endō   A hall inside the precincts of the Kōfukuji. Built by Fuyutsugi in 813, with a statue of Fukūkensaku Kannon as its main image. One of the Thirty-Three Sacred Places of the western provinces. Fukūkensaku Kannon, one of the Six Kannon, holds a net and trident with which to convey deva and human fish from the sea of illusion to the shore of enlightenment.

Nan'in, *see* Southern Palace

Nan'in shichirō no kimi   Seventh Son from the Southern Palace. Conjectured to have been Retired Emperor Uda's nephew, M. Kiyohira (877-945), who was the seventh son of Prince Koretada, a son of Emperor Kōkō. The Prince's residence was called the Southern Palace. Hosaka 1974, 3.588.

Naniwa   An old name for the Ōsaka area.

Naniwazu   Naniwa harbor. Now reclaimed land in Ōsaka.

Narifusa   Son of Korechika. A minor bureaucrat.

Narihira, Ariwara (825-880)   Son of Prince Abo; grandson of Emperors Heizei and Kanmu. Middle Captain (875). One of the great classical poets. McCullough 1968, pp. 41-55.

Naritada, Takashina (926-998)   Father-in-law of Michitaka. A minor scholar-official who achieved high Court rank through Michitaka. Called Kō nii (Takashina of Second Rank).

Naritō, Takashina (d. 1010)   Son of Atsutada; nephew of Naritada. Governor of Tanba. He appears to have been one of Kanemichi's stewards.

Naritoki (941-995)   Son of Morotada; brother of Emperor Mura-kami's Junior Consort Hōshi. Though less influential than the members of Morosuke's family, he was a prominent figure until his death in the great epidemic of 995. Known as the Koichijō Major Captain; held the concurrent office of Major Counselor. Posthumously named Minister of the Right when his daughter Seishi became Empress (1012).

Natomaro, Asukabe   Father-in-law of Fuyutsugi. Conjectured to have been of Korean ancestry. It is thought that one of his daughters may have borne a child to Emperor Kanmu. Hosaka 1974, 2.195.

Nijō Empress, *see* Kōshi

Nijō Lady (b. 995)   Posthumous daughter of Michikane. Entered service of Empress Ishi.

Nijō Mansion · A non-specific name for a house in the vicinity of Nijō Avenue. During Michinaga's lifetime, it was used of all the establishments listed below.

1. Michikane's residence north of Nijō and west of Muromachi. Also called Machijiri Mansion.

2. A house owned by Sanesuke north of Nijō and west of Higashino-tōin.

3. The one-time residence of Kōshi, consort of Emperor Seiwa, which was owned successively by Koremasa, Michinaga, and Norimichi. Location uncertain; possibly to be identified with the Yōzeiin, where Emperor Yōzei lived after his abdication. Hosaka 1974, 2.68.

4. Michitaka's establishment south of Nijō and east of Machijiri, adjacent to the Higashisanjōin. It had a northern portion, called Kitanoie or Nijō Kitanomiya, and a southern, called Minaminoie or (Higashisanjō) Minaminoin, the latter of which burned in 995. Used from time to time by Korechika and Teishi; called Nijōno-miya, Nijōtei, Konijō. (The prefix Ko usually indicated that a house was being distinguished from a more imposing establishment in the same area.)

5. Kaneie's subsidiary residence north of Nijō and east of Kyōgoku, later the Hokoin.

Nijō Palace   Nijōnoin, Nijōnomiya. A name for any residence in the Nijō area occupied by a member of the Imperial family. *See* Nijō Mansion

Ninmyō, Emperor (810-850, r. 833-850)   54th sovereign. Son of Saga. Called Fukakusa Emperor from his burial site at what is now Fukakusa, Higashidate-chō, Fushimi-ku, Kyōto.

Ninnaji   A major Shingon temple, founded by Emperor Kōkō and dedicated by Emperor Uda in the fourth year of Ninna (888). Situated in what is now Omuro, Ukyō-ku, Kyōto.

Ninnaji abbot, *see* Jinsei

Ninnaji Archbishop   Saishin (954-1030). Son of M. Masanobu; half-brother of Michinaga's wife Rinshi. Abbot of Ninnaji and Tōji; Major Archbishop (1017). A leading monk of the period.

Nishinomiya   Residence of M. Takaakira, north of Shijō and west of Suzaku.

Nishinomiya Minister of the Left, *see* Takaakira

Nishisanjō Mansion   Residence of Yoshimi. Said to have been situated north of Sanjō and west of Suzaku. Hosaka 1974, 2.206.

Nishisanjō Minister of State, *see* Yoshimi

Noboru, M. (849-918)   Son of Minister of the Left Tōru. Major Counselor (914).

Nobumasa   Son of Consultant Yasuchika. A minor bureaucrat.

Nobumitsu, M. (927-976)   Son of Prince Yoakira; grandson of Emperor Daigo. Provisional Major Counselor (975). Called Biwa Major Counselor after the name of the house where he lived with his wife, Atsutada's daughter.

Norimichi (996-1075)   Second son of Michinaga and Rinshi. Childhood name: Seyagimi. Married Kintō's daughter (d. 1024) in 1012. Palace Minister (1021), Minister of the Right (1047), Minister of the Left (1060-1069), Chancellor (1070-1071), Regent (1068-1075).

Norisada, M. (d. 1017)   Son of Prince Tamehira by a sister of M. Takaakira. Commander of the Military Guards of the Right.

Novice Middle Captain, *see* Narifusa

Novice Princess of First Rank, *see* Shūshi

Nun Princess of First Rank, *see* Shishi

Nyogen (977-1021)   Son of Kinsue. Called Samādhi Bishop after his residence, the Samādhi Hall in the Western Compound (Saitō) on Mount Hiei.

Ōchiyo, *see* Michiyori

Ogurayama   Situated across the Ōi River from Arashiyama in Saga, Ukyō-ku, Kyōto. Famous for autumn color.

Ōharano   A shrine at the foot of Mount Oshio in what is now Ukyō-ku, Kyōto. Dedicated to the Fujiwara tutelary deities, the Kasuga gods; visited at least once by every Imperial consort of Fujiwara birth. McCullough and McCullough 1980, s.n. 45.

Ōinumaro, *see* Shigeki

Ōi River   A stream at the foot of Arashiyama in what is now Ukyō-ku, Kyōto; called the Hozu in its upper reaches and the Katsura in its lower. Site of many elegant entertainments during the Heian period.

Ōmi   A province corresponding to Shiga Prefecture.

Omimaro, Nakatomi (d. 714)   Either Kamatari's grandson or a more distant relative; possibly his adopted son. According to *Kugyō bunin*, 1.11, he became a Middle Counselor in 708 without having served as Consultant. On the question of his parentage, see *Sonpi bunmyaku*, 1.24, 29; Satō 1929, p. 543; Hosaka 1974, 3.317.

Onjōji   Also Miidera. A Tendai temple in Ōtsu City, Shiga Prefecture. Neighbor and ancient rival of the Enryakuji.

Ononomiya Mansion   One of the showplaces of the Heian period, situated at Ōimikado Karasumaru. It had been the residence of an Imperial Prince who had later moved to Ono at the foot of Mount Hiei—thus its name. Owned by Saneyori and, in Michinaga's day, by Sanesuke.

Ononomiya Minister of the Right, *see* Sanesuke

Ononomiya Minister of State, *see* Saneyori, Sanesuke

Onshi (885-954)   Fourth daughter of Mototsune; consort of Daigo. Junior Consort (901), Empress (*kōgō*, 923), Grand Empress (931), Senior Grand Empress (946).

Osabe, Prince (d. 775?)   Son of Emperor Kōnin, who named him Crown Prince in 771. Deposed in 772 after his mother was stripped of the title of Empress for using magic in an attempt to kill the Emperor.

Osagimi, *see* Michifusa

Ōsaka Barrier   A checkpoint in the mountains between the Yamashiro and Ōmi basins, within the area of the present city of Ōtsu. Situated on the main route from the capital to the east. Often mentioned in poetry because of the orthographic identity of its initial syllable with *au*, meet.

Otoharu   Probably a daughter of Fusatsugi. Mother of Mototsune. Hosaka 1974, 2.215.

Ōtomo, Prince, *see* Kōbun

Owari   A province corresponding to part of Aichi Prefecture.

Palace Library   Goshodokoro, Mifumidokoro. Situated in the eastern eavechamber of the Shōkyōden.

Pantry   Oyudono, a room in the north part of the western eavechamber of the Seiryōden. Used for the preparation of hot water (for drinking and other purposes), and for the temporary storage of fish, birds, vegetables, etc.

Parasol Mountain, *see* Mikasayama
P'eng lai   J. Hōrai. In Chinese legend, a fairy mountain in the eastern
seas. Its immortal inhabitants live in palaces of silver and gold.
Po Chü-i (772-846)   T'ang poet. Widely read, admired, and imitated
in the Heian period.
Posthumous Empress, *see* Kōmyō
Posthumously Appointed Retired Emperor, *see* Sawara
President of the Board of Censors, *see* Tametaka
Priestly Crown Prince, *see* Sawara
Pure Land   Jōdo. A paradise presided over by a buddha. In Japanese
literature, usually Amitābha's Western Paradise.

Raisei   Unidentified. Conjectured to have been a roughneck monk in
the Retired Emperor's service. His nickname, High Hat, was presumably inspired by unorthodox headgear.
Reizei, Emperor (950-1011, r. 967-969)   63rd sovereign. Second son of
Murakami. Mother: Anshi. Suffered from mental illness, which was
ascribed to the angry spirits of Motokata and others.
Reizeiin   Bounded by four avenues: Ōimikado, Nijō, Horikawa, and
Ōmiya. A palatial establishment built by Emperor Saga in the ninth
century; served for 200 or more years as an interim residence for
reigning and retired sovereigns, and as a repository for books and
other Imperial possessions. It was destroyed by fire in 949, rebuilt in
960, and burnt again in 970, after which it was not rebuilt until 1008.
Reizei Palace, *see* Reizeiin
Rengikō, *see* Yoritada
Rinshi, M. (964-1053)   Daughter of Masanobu; principal wife of
Michinaga. Mother of Yorimichi, Norimichi, Shōshi, Kenshi, Ishi,
and Kishi.
River of Crossings   Watarigawa, Sanzunokawa. A river in hell, forded
by the soul on the seventh day after death. The worst sinners were
required to use the deepest of its three crossings.
Rokuharamitsuji   A prominent temple in the outskirts of the capital,
situated in what is now Yamato-ōji, Matsubaradōri, Higashiyama-ku,
Kyōto. Said to have been founded in 951 by Kūya Shōnin.
Rokujō Mansion   Residence of M. Shigenobu. Probably located near
the intersection of Rokujō and Nishinotōin. Satō 1929, p. 181.
Rokujō Minister of the Left, *see* Shigenobu
Ryōen   Son of Sanesuke. Provisional Lesser Bishop.
Ryōgen (912-985)   18th Hiei abbot (966); said to have transformed
the appearance of the mountain by an ambitious building program.
Called Yokawa Senior Archbishop. Posthumous name: Jie.

Ryōgon'in   The central hall at Yokawa on Mount Hiei, founded in 848 by Jikaku Daishi. "Morosuke's Ryōgon'in" was probably the Samādhi Hall (Sanmaidō) built at Iimuro by Morosuke around 954. Satō 1929, p. 567.

Ryōkiden   A building in the Imperial Residential Compound, situated north of the Giyōden, east of the Jijūden, and south of the Reikeiden. The Emperor went there to bathe and to put on the purified garments worn during periods of ritual seclusion. It was also used from time to time as an Imperial residence.

Ryūen (980?-1015)   Son of Michitaka and Kishi; Enryakuji monk. Called Komatsu Bishop.

Sadamoto, Ōe (959?-1035)   Son of Consultant Narimitsu. Served as governor of Mikawa before becoming a monk in 986. In 1003 went to China, where he died. Known as a poet.

Sadatsune, Ōe   Son of Kiyomichi. A provincial governor.

Sadayori (995?-1045?)   Son of Kintō. Major Controller of the Left (1021), Provisional Middle Counselor (1030-1044). Poet and calligrapher.

Sakuheimon Gate   One of the Nakanoe gates leading into the Imperial Residential Compound; situated in the center of the north wall.

Samādhi Bishop, *see* Nyogen

Sanenari (975-1044)   Son of Kinsue. Provisional Middle Counselor (1015), Middle Counselor (1023-1038).

Sanenobu (964-1001)   Son of Tamemitsu. Consultant (988).

Sanesuke (957-1046)   Son of Tadatoshi; adopted son of his grandfather, Saneyori. A major figure of the mid-Heian period, admired by his contemporaries both for his mastery of scholarship and the arts and for a courage and probity that were rare at the Imperial Court. Promoted slowly by members of Kaneie's branch of the family, he became a Provisional Major Counselor in 1001, a Major Counselor in 1009, and Minister of the Right in 1021. His diary, *Shōyūki*, is a valuable resource for the historian. Called Ononomiya Minister of State from the name of his residence.

Sanetō   A minor official, son of Moronaga by a lady known as Kii no naishi, the daughter of Michimasa, a governor of Ise. He does not appear to have been the brother of Kaneyasu, and it is not clear whether Ishi's nurse was Kii no naishi or Kaneyasu's mother. *Sonpi bunmyaku*, 2.443; Hosaka 1974, 3.561.

Sanetsune (d. 1045)   Son of Yukinari. Failed to advance beyond Fourth Rank.

Saneyasu, Prince (831-872)   Fourth son of Emperor Ninmyō. Mother: Takushi, daughter of Fusatsugi. President of the Board of Censors.

Saneyori (900-970) Childhood name: Ushikai. First son of Tadahira, whom he succeeded in 949 as head of the house of Fujiwara, after having become Minister of the Right (944) and Minister of the Left (947). As Minister of the Left, he was the senior bureaucrat throughout Emperor Murakami's reign, although a number of factors combined to diminish his influence, notably the death of his daughter Jusshi, the success of Anshi in the Imperial harem, and Morosuke's more genial personality. As a result of Morosuke's early death, it was Saneyori who became Regent and Chancellor upon the accession of Morosuke's minor grandson, Reizei (r. 967-969)—offices he retained until his death at the age of seventy under Reizei's successor, En'yū. Called Ononomiya Minister of State after the name of his residence. Posthumous name: Seishinkō.

Saneyori, daughter of, *see* Jusshi

Saneyori, mother of Said by *Ōkagami* to have been a daughter of Emperor Uda—presumably M. Junshi (or Keishi, according to *Uragaki*, item 34, p. 325), who is shown in *Honchō kōin shōunroku*, p. 425, as Tadahira's wife. *Sonpi bunmyaku*, 2.1, however, lists M. Shōshi, a daughter of Minister of the Right Yoshiari (845-897).

Sanjō, Emperor (976-1017, r. 1011-1016) 67th sovereign. Son of Reizei. Mother: Chōshi, daughter of Kaneie. Afflicted by poor health, he retired under pressure from Michinaga, whose grandson, Go-Ichijō, succeeded him.

Sanjō, daughters of, *see* Tōshi, Shishi, Teishi

Sanjōin Emperor Sanjō's post-retirement residence, probably located in the vicinity of the Sanjō-Machijiri intersection. It had been the property of a grandson of Emperor Daigo, and later of Princess Shishi, Emperor Murakami's ninth daughter. Soon after the Princess's death in 1015, it was acquired by the vice-governor of Kōzuke, Sadasuke, who presented it to the then Emperor as a future retirement palace. Sanjō lived there from the Eleventh Month of 1016 until his death on the Ninth of the Fifth Month in 1017. Tsunoda 1963, p. 162, n. 77.

Sanjō Palace, *see* Sanjōin

San no kimi Daughter of Michitaka and Kishi. Mentally disturbed. Dropped out of sight after termination of her marriage to Prince Atsumichi.

Sanuki A province in Shikoku, corresponding to Kagawa Prefecture.

Sanzunokawa, *see* River of Crossings

Sawara, Prince (d. 785) Son of Emperor Kōnin; uterine brother and

Crown Prince of Emperor Kanmu. Died en route to exile after having been implicated in the assassination of Fujiwara Tanetsugu by a political rival. Subsequent visitations of disease were attributed to his angry spirit. A tomb was built for him at Awaji, his place of exile; he was given the title Emperor Sudō (800); and his grave was moved to Yamato (Nara Prefecture). Called the Priestly Crown Prince because he had lived at the Tōdaiji as a monk before his recall to lay life by his father.

Second Prince, *see* Go-Ichijō

Second Princess, *see* Sonshi

Seihan (962-999) Kōfukuji and Kiyomizudera monk from Harima; Provisional Master of Discipline (998). Famous as a preacher; called an incarnation of the bodhisattva Mañjuśrī. Hosaka 1974, 3.543.

Seimei, Abe (921-1005) One of the two leading diviners of his period, the other being Kamo no Mitsuyoshi (939-1015). He lived north of Tsuchimikado and east of Nishinotōin. Hosaka 1974, 2.139.

Seiryōden The Emperor's private residential structure in the Imperial Palace.

Seishi
  1. Princess (d. 998) Daughter of Emperor Murakami and the Hirohata Lady of the Bedchamber (M. Keishi). Married Akimitsu; mother of Genshi, Enshi, and Shigeie.
  2. (972-1025) Daughter of Naritoki; consort of Emperor Sanjō. Junior Consort (1011), Empress (*kōgō*, 1012). Mother of six children, including Prince Atsuakira (Koichijōin), who was Crown Prince until pressure from Michinaga forced him to resign. Called Sen'yōden Consort.

Seishinkō, *see* Saneyori

Seishō Son of Takashina Naritada. Known as a preacher and poet.

Seiwa, Emperor (850-880, r. 858-876) 56th sovereign. Fourth son of Montoku; grandson of Yoshifusa, who served as his Regent. Called Mizunoo Emperor, from the name of his burial place at what is now Saga Mizunoo Seiwa, Ukyō-ku, Kyōto.

Senji Daughter of Kaneie; so called because she had been granted the honor of transmitting the decree (*senji*) elevating Senshi to Imperial status.

Senshi
  1. Princess (964-1035) Tenth daughter of Emperor Murakami. Mother: Anshi. Kamo Virgin under five Emperors, from 975 until 1031, when she retired and became a Buddhist nun. Presided over a literary salon; a poet.
  2. (962-1001) Daughter of Kaneie; consort of Emperor En'yū;

mother of Emperor Ichijō. Junior Consort (978), Grand Empress (986), first Imperial Lady (*nyōin*, 991). Called Umetsubo Consort, Higashisanjō Imperial Lady, etc. A major political figure after her son's accession in 986.

Sen'yōden Consort, *see* Hōshi, Seishi

Seri River A small stream traversing part of Kii District in Yamashiro (now Shimotoba, Fushimi-ku, Kyōto). It flowed near the Seinan Shrine—i.e., in the vicinity of the famous Toba Palace built late in the Heian period. The adjacent plain was a favorite spot for Imperial excursions.

Sesonji Originally a private residence, the Momozono Mansion. Converted into a temple by Yukinari in 995. *See* Momozono Mansion

Settsu A province corresponding to parts of Ōsaka and Hyōgo Prefectures.

Seyagimi, *see* Norimichi

Shakuzenji A building inside the precincts of the Hokoin, dedicated by Michitaka in 994. For Sei Shōnagon's brilliant description of the dedication, see Morris 1967, 1.219-233.

Shigeakira, Prince (906-954) Son of Emperor Daigo. Minister of Ceremonial. Known for his learning, polite accomplishments, and luxurious tastes. His daughter, Princess Kishi, was one of the consorts of his half-brother, Emperor Murakami. In 948, after the death of the Princess's mother, he married Anshi's sister Tōshi, who eventually became another of Murakami's consorts.

Shigeie Son of Akimitsu. Known as Radiant Lesser Captain (*hikaru shōshō*) because of his beauty. Became a monk in 1001. McCullough and McCullough 1980, Chapter 1, n. 45.

Shigeisha
1. *See* Genshi
2. A building in the Imperial Residential Compound; also called Kiritsubo. It served as a residence for consorts and Crown Princes.

Shigeki, Natsuyama Childhood name: Ōinumaro. One of the two old *Ōkagami* raconteurs, aged 180 (*sai*). The literal meaning of Natsuyama is summer mountains; that of Shigeki, luxuriant trees.

Shigemitsu, M. (923-998) Son of Prince Yoakira. Provisional Major Counselor (991-992).

Shigenobu, M. (922-995) Son of Prince Atsumi, a uterine brother of Emperor Daigo; uterine brother of Rinshi's father, Masanobu. Minister of the Right (991), Minister of the Left (994). Called Rokujō Minister of the Left.

Shigesuke Son of Akitada. Assistant Commander of the Military

Guards (of the Left, according to *Sonpi bunmyaku*, 1.46; of the Right, according to *Ōkagami*, p. 79).

Shijō Empress, *see* Junshi

Shijō Palace   Shijōnomiya. South of Shijō and east of Nishinotōin. Used as a residence by Yoritada, and by his children Kintō and Junshi. Called a palace because Junshi was an Empress (982-1017).

Shinden no onkata, *see* Takatsukasa, Lady

Shin'e   Unidentified.

Shin no naishi   Unidentified. For a list of women by that name, see *Ōkagami*, p. 451, s.n. 41.

Shinsen'en   A large park with a lake, across Nijō Avenue from the southeast corner of the Greater Imperial Palace. Visited by Emperors from Kanmu on; also the site of prayers for rain.

Shinshi   Also Chōshi. Daughter of Asateru. Presented to Emperor Kazan (984); briefly his favorite consort.

Shin'yo (941?-1029?)   Son of Fujiwara Shigesuke; grandson of Minister of the Right Akitada. A prominent Tendai monk. Bishop, Archbishop (1028), Onjōji abbot (1025). Matsumura 1969-, 2.412, 4.374.

Shirakawa
1. A tributary of the Kamo River, rising in what is now Higashiyama-ku, Kyōto.
2. The area between the Kamo River and the mountains on the east, now a part of Sakyō-ku, Kyōto. Yoshifusa maintained a subsidiary residence there.

Shirakawa Minister of State, *see* Yoshifusa

Shirome, Ōe   A female entertainer, said to have lived at the port of Eguchi; daughter of a minor bureaucrat, Ōe Tamabuchi; sister of the early Heian literatus and calligrapher Asatsuna (886-957). *Kokinshū* 387 is attributed to her.

Shishi
1. Princess (955-1015)   Daughter of Emperor Murakami. Mother: Anshi. Prominent at Emperor En'yū's Court as Princess of First Rank. Took Buddhist vows in 986.
2. Princess (1003?-1048)   Daughter of Emperor Sanjō. Mother: Seishi. Married Michinaga's son Norimichi.
3. (d. 1035)   Daughter of Yoritada. After a rather unsuccessful career as a Junior Consort during Emperor Kazan's brief reign, she lived quietly in the family mansion at Shijō.

Shishinden   The main ceremonial building of the Imperial Residential Compound (Dairi) inside the Greater Imperial Palace.

Shōen (ca. 827-901)   Bishop. Parentage uncertain. Said by a Ki family genealogy to have been a monk-poet who was the son of Ki no

Yukihiro, a governor of Yamato. *Ōkagami uragaki*, item 16, p. 317; Hosaka 1974, 2.217.

Shōkeimon Gate   The main north gate of the Court of Government (Chōdōin), the compound within which the Daigokuden was situated.

Shōkyōden   A building in the Imperial Residential Compound. It housed the Imperial Library and was also used as a consorts' residence. Situated immediately behind the Jijūden.

Shōkyōden Consort, *see* Kishi, Genshi

Shōmeimon Gate   The south gate of the Imperial Residential Compound.

Shōmu, Emperor (701-756, r. 724-749)   45th sovereign. Son of Emperor Monmu. Mother: Kyūshi, daughter of Fuhito. Founder of Tōdaiji.

Shōsenkō, *see* Mototsune

Shōshi

1. Princess (950-999)   Only child of Emperor Suzaku. Married the future Emperor Reizei in 963. Empress (967), Grand Empress (973), Senior Grand Empress (986).
2. (988-1074)   Oldest daughter of Michinaga. Mother: Rinshi. Fujitsubo Consort of Emperor Ichijō; mother of Emperors Go-Ichijō and Go-Suzaku. Junior Consort (999), Empress (*chūgū*, 1000), Grand Empress (1012), Senior Grand Empress (1018). Became a nun in 1026; granted name Jōtōmon'in on same day. A leading Court figure during the peak of Michinaga's prosperity.

Shōtoku, Empress, *see* Kōken

Shōtoku Taishi (574-622)   Son of Emperor Yōmei; Regent of his aunt, Empress Suiko (r. 592-628). Famous as a political figure and as a sponsor of Buddhism.

Shun   A mythical model Chinese Emperor.

Shūshi, Princess (996-1049)   Daughter of Emperor Ichijō and Fujiwara Teishi. Isolated after deaths of influential relatives; became a nun in 1024. Called Novice Princess of First Rank.

Sixth Prince, *see* Kiyohito

Sochi, Lady   Also Naka no kimi. Second daughter of Korechika. Entered service of Michinaga's daughter Shōshi.

Somedono Empress, *see* Meishi

Somedono Minister of State, *see* Yoshifusa

Somedono Palace   Principal residence of Yoshifusa, and of his daughter Meishi, Emperor Seiwa's mother. Situated south of Ōgimachi and west of Kyōgoku. Hosaka 1974, 2.201.

Sonshi

1. Princess (966-985) Second daughter of Emperor Reizei and Kaishi. Left home at the age of two to serve as Kamo Virgin; retired after her mother's death in 975. Entered the Imperial Palace as a consort of Emperor En'yū in 980; became a nun soon afterward. Called Fire Princess.

2. (984-1022) Daughter of Michikane. Married Emperor Ichijō (998). Junior Consort (1000). Married Naritoki's son Michitō after Ichijō's death. Called Kurabeya Consort. For theories concerning the meaning of her sobriquet, see Matsumura 1969-, 1.548.

3. Daughter of Michinaga and Meishi; wife of Morofusa.

Sosei (d. ca. 909?) Son of Henjō; lay name Yoshimine Harutoshi. A leading *Kokinshū* poet.

Sōshi, Princess (964-986) Older daughter of Emperor Reizei and Kaishi.

Southern Palace Nan'in, Minaminoin.

1. Residence of Prince Koretada, a son of Emperor Kōkō. North of Shijō and west of Mibu.

2. A residence associated with the names of Emperor Reizei and his sons, Princes Okisada (Emperor Sanjō), Atsumichi, and Tametaka. It is thought by some commentators to have been part of Kaneie's Higashisanjō Mansion; by others, to have belonged to the Reizeiin. The fire mentioned in *Ōkagami* was probably the one recorded in Michinaga's diary, *Midō kanpakuki*, on the Third of the Tenth Month in the third year of Kankō (1006). Matsumura 1969-, 1.469; Cranston 1969, p. 294, n. 369; *Nihon rekishi daijiten*, 19.177; Hosaka 1974, 2.557.

3. Michitaka's residence. *See* Nijō Mansion

Storm Mountain, *see* Arashiyama

Suesada Son of Takaie. Held provincial governorships.

Sugawara Minister of State, *see* Michizane

Suishi (974-1004) Daughter of Kaneie by a minor consort. Principal Handmaid (987), consort of future Emperor Sanjō (989). Marriage ended when she became involved in a liaison with M. Yorisada.

Sukehira (986-1067) Son of Yasuhira; adopted by Sanesuke. Consultant (1017), Provisional Middle Counselor (1029), Provisional Major Counselor (1061), Major Counselor (1065). A favorite of Emperor Sanjō, but career was blocked by Michinaga.

Sukekuni Son of Yoshimasa; grandson of Morimasa. A minor official.

He became governor of Iga in 1043, after the *Ōkagami* narrative present. *Ōkagami*, p. 454, s.n. 3.

Sukemasa

1. Son of Atsutada; grandson of Tokihira. Assistant Commander of the Military Guards of the Right, Senior Fifth Lower Rank. Became a monk.

2. (944-998) Son of Atsutoshi; grandson of Saneyori. Best calligrapher of his day; one of the Three Experts (*sanseki*) of calligraphy in the Japanese style, the others being Ono no Michikaze (894-966) and Fujiwara Yukinari (972-1028). Consultant (978-991, Senior Assistant Governor-General of the Dazaifu (991-995), War Minister (998).

Sukemasa, daughter of   Daughter of Sukemasa (944-998); known as a calligrapher. Wife of Yasuhira; mother of Tsunetō.

Sukenobu   Son of Atsutada; grandson of Tokihira. Held middle-ranking offices, the most important of which was Middle Captain of the Right.

Suketō (b. 971?)   Son of Naritoki. Childhood name: Chōmeigimi. Took Buddhist vows in 986. Called Gentleman-in-Waiting Novice.

Sukeyori   Son of Sanesuke. According to *Sonpi bunmyaku*, 2.9, his true father was Sanesuke's brother Yashuhira; his mother, a daughter of the provincial governor Tsunetane. He does not appear to have risen above the provincial governor level. Hosaka 1974, 2.310.

Sukeyuki (d. 995)   Son of Sukenobu; great-grandson of Tokihira. A poet and provincial official.

Sumitomo (d. 941)   An ex-official who stayed in Iyo Province (Ehime Prefecture) as a local chieftain after the expiration of his term in 936. As the leader of the powerful families ("pirates") in the area, he virtually controlled the Inland Sea for a period of about five years. After becoming an open rebel in 939, he was finally suppressed by a punitive force in 941.

Suzaku, Emperor (923-952, r. 930-946)   61st sovereign. Son of Daigo. Mother: Onshi, daughter of Mototsune.

Suzakuin   A large Imperial family residence, situated in the area bounded by Sanjō on the north, Shijō on the south, Suzaku on the east, and Kōkamon on the west. Imazumi et al. 1968-1976, vol. 1, appended map.

Suzakumon Gate   The south central gate of the Greater Imperial Palace; an imposing two-story structure with a tiled roof, designed to function as the formal entrance to the Palace. It stood at the north end of Suzaku Avenue.

Suzaku Palace, *see* Suzakuin

Table Room Daibandokoro. A room in the Seiryōden. It contained storage facilities for dining tables and served as an office for Imperial ladies-in-waiting who were authorized to enter the Courtiers' Hall. The term was also used of similar rooms in the houses of prominent persons.

Tadagimi (d. 968) Son of Morosuke; adopted by Tadahira. Guards Commander.

Tadahira (880-949) Son of Mototsune. Controlled the Court for the last thirty-five years of his life. Minister of the Right (914), Minister of the Left (924), Chancellor (936), Regent for his two nephews, Suzaku and Murakami (930-949). Called Koichijō Chancellor from the name of his residence. Posthumous name: Teishinkō.

Tadahira, daughter of, *see* Chūjō no miyasudokoro

Tadamine, Mibu (fl. ca. 900) A *Kokinshū* compiler and leading poet; minor bureaucrat.

Tadanobu (967-1035) Son of Tamemitsu. Provisional Middle Counselor (1001), Provisional Major Counselor (1009), Major Counselor (1020). A prominent Court figure in Michinaga's day, admired for his literary ability and knowledge of ceremonial.

Tadatoshi (928-973) Son of Saneyori. Consultant (967).

Tadayoshi, Prince Son of Emperor Saga. Minister of Ceremonial.

Tajima A province corresponding to the northern part of Hyōgo Prefecture.

Takaakira, Prince, *see* Takaakira, M.

Takaakira, M. (914-982) Son of Emperor Daigo; took Minamoto surname in 923. Consultant (939), Middle Counselor (948), Major Counselor (953), Minister of the Right (966), Minister of the Left (967-969). In the second year of Anna (969), members of the Fujiwara family, disturbed by his growing influence, accused him of plotting to replace Crown Prince Morihira (Emperor En'yū) with his own son-in-law, Prince Tamehira, and he was exiled to Kyūshū. He returned to the capital in 972. Author of *Saikyūki*, a work on Court usages and ceremonies. Called Nishinomiya Minister of the Left from the name of his residence.

Takafuji (838-900) Son of Yoshikado; grandson of Minister of the Left Fuyutsugi. Became a Middle Counselor in 897 after the birth of his grandson, the future Emperor Daigo. After Daigo's accession, served as Major Counselor (899) and Palace Minister (900).

Takaie (979-1044) Son of Michitaka. Childhood name: Akogimi. Middle Counselor (995-996). In exile, 996-997 (*see* Korechika). Reentered government; served as Provisional Middle Counselor (1002), Middle Counselor (1009-1023), and, with distinction, as Provisional

Governor-General of the Dazaifu (1014-1019). Kawakita 1968, pp. 190-203.

Takakata (953-974) Son of Koremasa. Called Former Lesser Captain to distinguish him from his brother Yoshitaka, who had been appointed to the same office after him. Died in the smallpox epidemic of 974.

Takakuni, M. (1004-1077) Son of Toshikata; brother of Akimoto. Known as a poet and as putative author of the lost *Uji dainagon monogatari*, a collection of brief tales and anecdotes. Provisional Major Counselor (1067-1074). Called Uji Major Counselor from the location of his villa.

Takamatsu, Lady, *see* Meishi

Takamatsu Mansion South of Sanjōbōmon, east of Nishinotōin, north of Anenokōji, and west of Machijiri; adjacent to the Higashisanjō Mansion on the south. Long-time residence of Michinaga's secondary wife, Meishi, to whom it had come from her father, M. Takaakira. Refurbished by Michinaga for the use of Kanshi and Koichijōin after their marriage. It burned in 1021, was rebuilt, and eventually served as an Imperial residence. Tsunoda 1963, p. 102; Hosaka 1974, 2.371.

Takamitsu (939-994) Son of Morosuke. Childhood name: Machiosagimi. Known as a poet and as the protagonist of a tale called *Tōnomine shōshō monogatari*, thought to have been compiled by someone in his service, which describes his renunciation of the world in the Twelfth Month of 961. As a monk, he stayed for a time on Mount Hiei and then settled at Tōnomine. Called Tōnomine Novice.

Takano Empress, *see* Kōken

Takaoka, Prince Son of Emperor Heizei. Named Crown Prince under Emperor Saga in 809; deposed in 810 as a result of Fujiwara Kusuko's unsuccessful plot to restore Retired Emperor Heizei to the throne. Later became a monk and went to China; believed to have died in Laos at an advanced age.

Takatō (949-1013) Son of Tadatoshi; grandson of Saneyori. Senior Assistant Governor-General of the Dazaifu (1004).

Takatsukasa, Lady Also San no kimi, Shinden no onkata. Third daughter of Tamemitsu; occupant of the main apartments (*shinden*) in the Takatsukasa Mansion, the home of Tamemitsu's daughters by Koremasa's daughter. (The location of the mansion is uncertain.) Remembered for her liaison with Korechika; not recorded elsewhere as having become a nun. Hosaka 1974, 2.639.

Takechi, Prince (654-696) Son of Emperor Tenmu. Named Chancellor in 690 by Empress Jitō; held post until his death.

Takushi (d. 839) Daughter of Fusatsugi; Junior Consort of Ninmyō; mother of Kōkō. Posthumously named Grand Empress after accession of Kōkō.

Tamabuchi, Ōe Son of Consultant Otondo (811-877). Governor of Hyūga.

Tamehira, Prince (952-1010) Son of Murakami. Mother: Anshi. Lost chance at succession when he became son-in-law of M. Takaakira. Minister of Ceremonial.

Tamemasa Son of Middle Counselor Fuminori. A provincial governor whose daughter was one of Korechika's wives.

Tamemitsu (942-992) Son of Morosuke. Minister of the Right (986), Chancellor (991). Called Hōjūji Minister of State, from the name of the temple built under his sponsorship. Posthumous name: Kōtokukō.

Tamemitsu, daughters of
1. Married Yoshichika.
2. *See* Kishi
3. *See* Takatsukasa, Lady
4. Shi no kimi One of Retired Emperor Kazan's mistresses.
5. Go no kimi One of Kenshi's ladies-in-waiting.

Tametaka, Prince (977-1002) Son of Emperor Reizei and Chōshi. President of the Board of Censors, Governor-General of the Dazaifu. One of Izumi Shikibu's lovers. Cranston 1969, pp. 8-9.

Tametō Son of Naritoki. Served as governor of Iyo.

Tamiko (fl. ca. 870) Second daughter of Yoshimi; one of Emperor Seiwa's numerous Junior Consorts. Hosaka 1974, 2.207; *Sonpi bunmyaku*, 1.44.

Tamura Emperor, *see* Montoku

Tanba A province corresponding to parts of Kyōto and Hyōgo Prefectures.

Taneki, Ōkura Grandson of Haruzane, a subordinate commander and hero of the punitive force that ended Sumitomo's rebellion. Third-level official in the Dazaifu. He was named governor of Iki after his predecessor in the office was killed by the Jurchen (1019). Hosaka 1974, 3.130; Kawakami 1926, pp. 555-557.

Taneki, son of, *see* Mitsuhiro

Tankaikō, *see* Fuhito

Tayū
1. *See* Tayū no kimi
2. Nurse of Princess Teishi (daughter of Emperor Sanjō and Kenshi). Daughter of M. Kanezumi (ca. 986-1013); wife of Chikayori, son of Michitaka.

Tayū no kimi Said to have been a daughter of a provincial governor,

M. Tasuku. Nurse of Crown Prince Yasuakira, son of Emperor Daigo. A prominent *Gosenshū* poet.

Tazugimi, *see* Yorimichi

Teiji Emperor, *see* Uda

Teishi

1. (976?-1000) Daughter of Michitaka and Kishi. Consort of Emperor Ichijō; mother of Prince Atsuyasu and Princesses Shūshi and Bishi. Junior Consort (990), Empress (*chūgū*, 990; *kōgō*, 1000). Overshadowed by Michinaga's daughter Shōshi after Michitaka's death. Kawakita 1968, pp. 175-180.

2. Princess (1013-1094) Daughter of Emperor Sanjō and Kenshi. Consort of Emperor Go-Suzaku; mother of Emperor Go-Sanjō. Empress (1037), Grand Empress (1052), Senior Grand Empress (1068); retired as Yōmeimon'in (1069). Many poems in Imperial anthologies.

Teishi, daughters of, *see* Shūshi, Bishi

Teishinkō, *see* Tadahira

Tenji, Emperor (626-671, r. 661-671) Prince Naka no Ōe. 38th sovereign. Son of Emperor Jōmei and Empress Kōgyoku. Leader of Taika reforms; controlled government as Crown Prince under Emperor Kōtoku and Empress Saimei (Kōgyoku).

Tenmu, Emperor (631-686, r. 673-686) Prince Ōama. 40th sovereign. Son of Emperor Jōmei and Empress Kōgyoku; uterine brother of Tenji. Named Crown Prince under Tenji in 668. Resigned in 671 and took Buddhist vows when it became apparent that the Emperor wanted to replace him with his (Tenji's) son, Prince Ōtomo, but gained the throne in a brief succession war after Tenji's death.

Tennōji Also Shitennōji. A temple situated in what is now Tennōji-ku, Ōsaka. Said to have been founded in the sixth century by Shōtoku Taishi, in recognition of divine assistance rendered by the Four Heavenly Kings (*shitennō*) during a battle against Mononobe Moriya. See Aston 1956, Part Two, pp. 113-115.

Tenryaku, *see* Murakami

Tenth Princess, *see* Senshi

Third Prince, *see* Go-Suzaku

Tōchi An old district in Yamato Province. Apparently a place name with elegant or romantic connotations, since Sei Shōnagon lists it in her "Villages" category. Tanaka 1972-1975, 1.477, sec. 66. It survives in the name Tōichi-chō, Kashiwara City, which is fifteen or twenty kilometers south of Nara—i.e., far off the route between Nara and Kyōto. In the *Ōkagami* exchange between Koremasa and the lady, the name is presumably introduced for the sake of the pun on the first syllable of *tōshi* (distant).

Tōdaiji Great Nara temple founded by Emperor Shōmu in 749, famous for its immense statue of Vairocana Buddha, which was about twenty-two meters tall. The present smaller statue dates from the early Edo period.

Tōin Empress, *see* Hanshi

Tōkaden A building behind the Kokiden in the Imperial Residential Compound. Used as a residence for consorts.

Tōkazu Son of Morosuke. Treasury Minister.

Tōkazu, daughter of Principal wife of Michikane; mother of Fukutarigimi, Kanetaka, Kanetsuna, and Lady Nijō. Later married Akimitsu. Hosaka 1974, 2.454.

Tokihime (fl. ca. 965) Daughter of a minor noble, Nakamasa. Principal consort of Kaneie; mother of Michitaka, Michikane, Michinaga, Chōshi, and Senshi.

Tokihira (871-909) Oldest son of Mototsune. Minister of the Left (899). Controlled government after engineering the exile of Sugawara Michizane in 901. Called Hon'in Minister of State after the name of his house, located north of Tsuchimikado and east of Horikawa.

Tokihira, daughter of, *see* Hōshi, Hitoyoshiko

Tokihira, grandson of, *see* Yoshiyori

Tokimitsu (948-1015) Son of Kanemichi. Middle Counselor (997). Called North-Facing Middle Counselor, probably because his house was oriented toward the north, rather than toward the south, as was usual. Hosaka 1974, 2.615.

Tokinaka, M. (943-1001) Oldest son of Masanobu. Like his father, a renowned flautist. Major Counselor (996).

Tokitsura (836-875) Oldest son of Yoshimi. Major Counselor (872).

Tokitsura, sons of According to *Sonpi bunmyaku*, 1.44, Tokitsura fathered four sons. The two mentioned in *Ōkagami* are presumably to be identified with the oldest, Natsugu, who served as Assistant Director of the Bureau of Medicine, and the third, Sukekuni, who was Director of the Bureau of Grounds.

Tokiyasu, Prince, *see* Kōkō

Tominokōji Lady of the Bedchamber, *see* Hōshi

Tominokōji Minister of State, *see* Akitada

Tōmitsu Son of Kanemichi. No official career of consequence.

Tomohira, Prince (964-1007) Son of Emperor Murakami and Princess Sōshi. Minister of Central Affairs. Scholar, poet, calligrapher, musician. Ancestor of the Murakami Genji.

Tomoyasu (ca. 905-977) Son of Koreoka. Father of Michitsuna's mother, the *Kagerō nikki* author. Held provincial posts.

Tōnomine A hill inside the boundaries of the present Sakurai City, Shiki District, Nara Prefecture. Site of a Buddhist temple; burial place of Kamatari, founder of the Fujiwara family.

Tōnomine Novice, *see* Takamitsu

Tōnori (d. 989) Son of Morosuke. Junior Third Rank; minor (non-*kugyō*) offices. Called Kitano no sanmi (Kitano Lord of Third Rank), presumably because he lived in the Kitano area.

Torikainoin An Imperial villa at Torikai, on the bank of the Yodo River near the port of Eguchi in Settsu Province (Ōsaka Prefecture). Eguchi was situated where a smaller river, the Kanzakigawa, branched off from the Yodo.

Tōru, M. (822-895) Son of Emperor Saga. Minister of the Left (872). Remembered for the Kawaranoin, his magnificent house and grounds in the capital, and for his elegant Uji villa, which later became the Byōdōin.

Tōsanmi, *see* Hanshi

Tōshi
1. Princess (1001?-1023) Oldest daughter of Emperor Sanjō. Mother: Seishi. Ise Virgin (1012-1016); later involved in affair with Fujiwara Michimasa. Late in 1017, several months after her father's death, she became a nun as the result of a severe illness.
2. (d. 975) Daughter of Morosuke. Wife of Prince Shigeakira; later a consort of Emperor Murakami. Known as Jōganden Principal Handmaid.

Toshikata, M. (960-1027) Son of Takaakira and Morosuke's third daughter; brother of Michinaga's wife Meishi. Provisional Major Counselor (1017-1018), Minister of Popular Affairs (1020). For many years, an official in the successive households of Michinaga's daughter Shōshi.

Toshiyuki (d. 901?) Son of Fujimaro. Head Chamberlain (895), Middle Captain. A *Kokinshū* poet.

Tsuchimikado Gate Another name for Jōtōmon Gate, the Greater Imperial Palace entrance fronting on Tsuchimikado Avenue.

Tsuchimikado Mansion Michinaga's great estate south of Tsuchimikado and west of Kyōgoku, which had come to him through Rinshi from his father-in-law, Masanobu, and which was his principal residence during most of his adult life. Known also as the Kyōgoku Mansion and as the Jōtōmon'in, the latter because of its proximity to Jōtōmon Gate. During Michinaga's lifetime, it was the birthplace of three Empresses (Shōshi, Kenshi, and Ishi), a Crown Prince's consort and posthumous Senior Grand Empress (Kishi), and three Emperors (Go-Ichijō, Go-Suzaku, and Go-Reizei). It burned on several occasions, the first in 1016, but continued to play an important role in Court life after Michinaga's death.

Tsukushi A general term for the provinces of Chikuzen and Chikugo, and, by extension, for Kyūshū.

Tsunekuni A minor Fujiwara of the provincial governor class. Maternal grandfather of Empress Anshi.

Tsunemichi (982-1051) Son of Yasuhira. Commander of Military Guards of the Right (1021), Provisional Middle Counselor (1029).

Tsunesada, Prince (825-884) Son of Emperor Junna. Named Crown Prince after accession of Emperor Ninmyō in 833; deposed on charges of conspiracy in 842. See Appendix D.

Tsunesuke (1006-1081) Son of Takaie. Provisional Major Counselor (1065-1069).

Tsunetō

1. (1000-1066) Son of Yasuhira. Provisional Major Counselor (1065).
2. M. Son of Masatsune. A minor official, known as a poet.

Tsuneyori, M. (986-1039) Son of Sukeyoshi. Consultant (1030). Author of diary *Sakeiki*.

Tsurayuki, Ki (868-945?) A minor bureaucrat who was the leading poet of his day. Principal *Kokinshū* compiler.

Tsushima A province corresponding to part of Nagasaki Prefecture. A group of islands between Kyūshū and the Korean peninsula.

Two-Bay Room Futama. A room in the Seiryōden. Used as a Buddhist chapel.

Uchimaro (756-812) Son of Major Counselor Matate. Consultant (794), Minister of the Right (806), posthumous Chancellor.

Uda, Emperor (867-931, r. 887-897) 59th sovereign. Son of Emperor Kōkō. Became a monk in 899. Called Teiji[in] Emperor, from the name of his retirement residence, and Kanpyō Priestly Retired Emperor, from an era name (889-898).

Umakai (694-737) Son of Fuhito; founder of the Ceremonial House of the Fujiwara family. Consultant (731); important political figure until his death in the epidemic of 737.

Umetsubo A Palace building used as a residence for Imperil consorts.

Umetsubo Consort, *see* Senshi

Urin'in Also Uryūin, Unrin'in, Unryūin. A prominent Tendai temple in the outskirts of the capital, situated at what is now Murasakino, Kita-ku, Kyōto. Famous for its enlightenment sermons. Mentioned in *Kokinshū, Genji monogatari*, and *Makura no sōshi*. It had been a subsidiary residence of Emperor Junna before its conversion into a temple. A small temple of the same name survives in its approximate location.

Usa   Usa Hachiman Shrine, in Usa, Ōita Prefecture. Parent shrine of the great Iwashimizu Hachiman Shrine near the capital, and of other Hachiman shrines throughout the country. From 833 on, Imperial messengers were sent to announce events of major national importance to its deities, of whom the most important were Emperor Ōjin (identified with the war god Hachiman) and Empress Jingū.

Ushikai, *see* Saneyori

Uzumasa   Also Uzumasadera, Kōryūji. A Shingon temple west of the capital, in what is now Sakyō-ku, Kyōto. Its principal object of worship was an image of Yakushi, the Healing Buddha.

Vimalakīrti   J. Yuima. A rich lay disciple of Śākyamuni. Said to have been an eloquent exponent of Buddhist doctrines.

Virgin Consort, *see* Kishi

Watarigawa, *see* River of Crossings

Wing Chamber, Lady in the   Minor wife of Kaneie; mother of Suishi. She also bore Michitaka a daughter. Probably to be identified with the Ōmi of *Kagerō nikki*. Hosaka 1974, 3.78.

Yakushiji   A major Buddhist temple in what is now Nishinokyō-machi, Nara. Founded in 680 by Emperor Tenmu.

Yamakage (824-888)   Son of Takafusa. Middle Counselor (886), Junior Third Rank (rather than Second as in *Ōkagami*). Hosaka 1974, 3.177.

Yamanoi Mansion   North of Sanjōbōmon and west of Kyōgoku. Residence of Michiyori.

Yamashinadera, *see* Kōfukuji

Yamato   A province corresponding to Nara Prefecture.

Yamato no senji   A daughter of Korenaka; wife of Michimasa. In service with Kenshi.

Yamazaki   A town on the right bank of the Yodo River at the Settsu-Yamashiro provincial boundary (now Ōyamashiro Village, Otokuni District, Kyōto). During the Heian period, travelers heading west from the capital embarked there for the boat trip down the Yodo.

Yao   A mythical model Chinese Emperor.

Yasuakira, Prince (903-923)   Son of Emperor Daigo and Fujiwara

Onshi. Named Crown Prince (904), but died before ascending throne.

Yasuhira (953-1017) Son of Tadatoshi; grandson of Saneyori; uterine brother of Sanesuke. Consultant (998), Commander of the Right Gate Guards (1009-1016), Provisional Middle Counselor (1013).

Yasukiyo, M. (936-999) Son of Prince Ariakira. Treasury Minister, Junior Third Rank.

Yasumitsu, M. (924-995) Son of Prince Yoakira. Provisional Middle Counselor (978), Middle Counselor (988). Called Momozono Middle Counselor from the name of his house.

Yasutada (890-936) Son of Tokihira. Major Counselor, Major Captain. Called Hachijō Major Captain.

Yawata Another name for Iwashimizu Hachiman Shrine, situated on Mount Otoko near the capital, in what is now Yawata Town, Tsuzuki District, Kyōto, and dedicated primarily to the god Hachiman. Its Special Festival (*rinjisai*), held on the second Day of the Horse in the Third Month, was one of the highlights of the Court year; its Release of Living Things Festival (*hōjōe*), celebrated on the Fifteenth of the Eighth Month, was a hybrid Buddhist-Shintō event during which birds and fish were set free, as recommended in the *Saishōō Sutra*. McCullough and McCullough 1980, s.n. 46.

Yoakira, Prince (904-937) Son of Emperor Daigo. Minister of Central Affairs. Father of three Minamoto senior nobles (Shigemitsu, Yasumitsu, and Nobumitsu) and of three Princesses (Genshi, consort of Yoritada; Keishi, consort of Koremasa; and Sōshi, consort of Emperor Murakami).

Yokawa One of three Buddhist centers in three main valleys on Mount Hiei, each consisting of a principal hall and many lesser buildings, and together comprising most of the Enryakuji. The Eastern Compound (Tōtō) was the temple's central area, the Western Compound (Saitō) lay to the northwest, and Yokawa was on the north.

Yokawa Senior Archbishop, *see* Ryōgen

Yorichika (972-1010) Son of Michitaka. Middle Captain.

Yorimichi (992-1074) Oldest son of Michinaga and Rinshi. Childhood name: Tazugimi. Palace Minister (1017), Minister of the Left (1021-1060), Chancellor (1061-1062), Regent (1017-1067). Titular Regent at age twenty-five; inherited power after Michinaga's death.

Yorimune (993-1065) Oldest son of Michinaga and Meishi. Childhood name: Iwagimi. Provisional Major Counselor (1021), Palace Minister (1047), Minister of the Right (1060).

Yorisada, M. (977-1020)   Son of Prince Tamehira; brother of Princess Enshi. Consultant (1009). Lover of Crown Prince's consort Suishi; married daughter of Tachibana Sukemasa soon after Suishi's death; began affair with Akimitsu's daughter Genshi at about age thirty-five.

Yoritada (924-989)   Son of Saneyori. Minister of the Right (971), Minister of the Left (977), Chancellor (978), Regent (977-986). Called Sanjō Lord from his residence at Sanjō Horikawa. Posthumous name: Rengikō.

Yoshiari, M. (845-897)   Son of Emperor Montoku. Minister of the Right (896).

Yoshichika

1. (957-1008)   Son of Koremasa. Consultant (984), Provisional Middle Counselor (985-986). Took religious vows after the abdication of his nephew, Emperor Kazan, during whose reign he and a colleague, Koreshige, held the real power.

2. Son of Michitaka. Lesser Captain, Junior Fourth Lower Rank. Called Ide Novice Lesser Captain, presumably from the location of a villa or hermitage.

Yoshida Shrine   At the foot of Yoshidayama in what is now Yoshida Kaguraoka, Sakyō-ku, Kyōto.

Yoshifusa (804-872)   Son of Fuyutsugi. The first subject to serve as Regent (858-872), and, except for the monk Dōkyō (d. 772), the first to bear the title of Chancellor during his lifetime (served 857-872). Father-in-law of Emperor Seiwa. Called Shirakawa Minister of State, Somedono Minister of State. Posthumous name: Chūjinkō.

Yoshimi (817-867)   Also Yoshisuke, Yoshiwaka. Son of Fuyutsugi. Minister of the Right (857). Called Nishisanjō Minister of State.

Yoshimi, daughter of, *see* Tamiko

Yoshimi, mother of, *see* Mitsuko

Yoshimitsu   Son of Tamemitsu; Hiei monk. Holy Teacher (*ajari*), later Master of Discipline.

Yoshinobu (995-1065)   Son of Michinaga and Meishi; brother of Kanshi. Provisional Major Counselor (1021), posthumous Chancellor. Instrumental in accession of Emperor Go-Sanjō. Adoptive maternal grandfather of Go-Sanjō's son Shirakawa, who gave him the posthumous title.

Yoshino Mountains   A range of high, wild mountains in Yoshino District, Nara Prefecture. Famous for cherry blossoms and snow, and as a religious retreat.

Yoshitada, Sone   An eccentric and innovative poet; eighty-nine compositions in Imperial anthologies. Conjectured to have been in his fifties at the time of the Day of the Rat excursion in 985. Hosaka 1974, 3.598.

Yoshitaka (954-974)   Son of Koremasa. Called Later Lesser Captain to distinguish him from his brother Takakata, who had been appointed to the same office earlier. Died in the smallpox epidemic of 974.

Yoshitoshi, Tachibana (fl. ca. 900)   A native of Hizen Province, where he served as a provincial official. Famous in the Heian period as a champion at the game of *go*. He took religious vows with Retired Emperor Uda, at whose Court he had served, and assumed the name Kanren.

Yoshitsune (d. 1058)   Son of Yukinari. Failed to advance beyond Fourth Rank.

Yoshiyori

1. Prince (921-925)   Son of Prince Yasuakira, whom he succeeded as heir apparent. Mother: daughter of Tokihira. Named Crown Prince in 923; died two years later.
2. (1002-1048)   Son of Takaie. Consultant (1036), Provisional Middle Counselor (1045).

Yotsugi, Ōyake   Chief *Ōkagami* raconteur, aged 190 (*sai*). Ōyake can be taken to mean Court; Yotsugi, chronicle.

Yōzei, Emperor (868-949, r. 876-884)   57th sovereign. First son of Emperor Seiwa. Mother: Kōshi, daughter of Nagara. Criminally insane.

Yōzeiin   Residence of Retired Emperor Yōzei. Said to have been situated south of Ōimikado, west of Nishinotōin, and north of Nijō.

Yubadono   Another name for the Butokuden, a building in the Greater Imperial Palace compound from which the Emperor watched horse races, archery contests, etc.

Yukinari (972-1027)   Son of Yoshitaka. Provisional Major Counselor (1020). Ancestor of the Sesonji family and author of the diary *Gonki*. Celebrated as a calligrapher.

Yukitsune (1012-1050)   Son of Yukinari by a younger sister of the latter's first wife, the daughter of M. Yasukiyo. Consultant (1045). Known as a calligrapher.

Zenrinji   A Shingon temple north of the present Nanzenji at the foot of the Higashiyama hills in Kyōto. Now the Eikandō, a Pure Land temple.

Zenrinji Archbishop, *see* Jinkaku

Translations from Other Ōkagami Textual Lines

This appendix contains passages, absent from the *kohon* texts, which have seemed sufficiently lengthy, well-known, and/or pertinent to the original author's purpose to warrant translation. Unless otherwise specified, they are taken from the vulgate line.

(1) Emperor Ninmyō deposed the former Crown Prince and gave the title to this Emperor on the Fourth of the Eighth Month in the ninth year of Jōwa [842]. We can imagine how resentful the former Crown Prince must have felt.[1] [Hosaka 1974, 2.47; translation, p. 70.]

(2) One wonders why Chishō, a veritable buddha, found it impossible to overcome the terrible spirit by which the Empress was afflicted. I suppose Her Majesty was fated to suffer the visitations because of something that had happened in a previous existence.[2] [Hiunkakubon, an *ihon* text. Hosaka 1974, 2.64; translation, p. 71.]

(3) While he was a courtier, known as the Princely Gentleman-in-Waiting, he got into a wrestling match with Narihira in front of the Imperial chair in the Courtiers' Hall. The two collided with the chair, and one of the handrails broke. People say the fracture still shows. [Hosaka 1974, 2.84; translation, p. 74.]

(4) Before the Emperor ascended the throne, the Bright Divinity of Kamo spoke to him as he was hawking in the vicinity of Kamo Shrine. It was a few days after the Twentieth of the Eleventh Month.

"I am an old man who lives near here. We have plenty of spring festivals, but the winters are terribly boring. Please arrange for a winter festival."

The future sovereign realized that the speaker was a god. "I have no

---

[1] See Appendix D, p. 337.

[2] As the source of the final paragraph in Emperor Seiwa's annals, Hosaka postulates an early reader, dissatisfied with the brevity of the treatment, and wishing, perhaps, to call attention to the strain of insanity in the Fujiwara and Imperial families, inherited by Emperors Yōzei, Reizei, and Kazan, by Emperor Murakami's eighth son, and by Michitaka's third daughter. He surmises that the addition was later excised by someone who inadvertently spared the introductory sentence, and that the present final sentence represents a subsequent attempt to flesh out the reference to Chishō.

authority in such matters," he answered. "You had better address the Emperor."

"It is because you will have authority that I mention it," said the god. "From now on you had better give up frivolous amusements. There is a reason for what I say; something is going to happen very soon." He disappeared in an instant.

While the Prince was wondering what to make of it, the Imperial succession fell to him. And thus it was that he inaugurated the Kamo Special Festival. Because the divine command had been uttered on the Day of the Cock, he selected the last Day of the Cock in the Eleventh Month as the festival date. Lord Toshiyuki composed a song for the eastern music:[3]

Chihayaburu	Not for a myriad ages
Kamo no yashiro no	Will their color change—
Himekomatsu	The fair young pines
Yorozuyo made mo	Of mighty
Iro wa kawaraji.	Kamo Shrine.

Those lines appear in the *Collection of Early and Modern Times*. You all know them—but aren't they splendid! And we can certainly say that Emperor Uda's descendants are still flourishing. Has there ever been another sovereign like him?

The first Special Festival was held two years after the Emperor's accession. Lord Tokihira, the Middle Captain of the Right, served as messenger. [Tachibana 1974, pp. 51-52; translation, p. 75. Omitted by Hosaka 1974 because it partially duplicates a later passage. See translation, p. 216.]

(5) Yoritada established some excellent customs. He was the one who first ordered the Imperial Police to follow the carriage during regental visits to Kamo Shrine; and he also arranged for the Regent to have four mounted Escorts, one pair on the left and one on the right.[4]

---

[3] Eastern music (*azuma asobi*), a feature of several major Shintō festivals, was a combination of singing, instrumental music, and dancing, so called because it was based on folk music from the eastern provinces. Hosaka 1974, 3.442; McCullough and McCullough 1980, s.n. 46.

[4] A Regent was entitled to ten Escorts (*zuijin*), who were normally drawn chiefly from among the lowest-ranking members (*konoe*) of the Imperial Bodyguards. When Yoritada received his appointment, he was assigned four *konoe* from each of the two Bodyguards divisions, plus two *udoneri* (guards under the jurisdiction of the Central Affairs Ministry). The text implies that two of the eight *konoe* were *banchō*, functionaries who rode horseback when serving as Escorts. In order to obtain two more mounted men, Yoritada petitioned success-

In the old days, people could not recognize the Regent's carriage, because there were no *fushō*—only one rider on the left and one on the right for important events. It was a change that needed to be made.

Yoritada carried good management too far. Early each morning, one of his attendants had to take a jar and make the rounds of the mansion, including the ladies' apartments,[5] to collect oil left over from the night before and mix it with the new day's supply. Really! [Hosaka 1974, 2.312; translation, p. 111.]

(6) On the Twenty-Third of that month, they brought him the sword Tsubokiri[6] from the Imperial Palace. By rights, the sword ought to have been delivered to Crown Prince Atsuakira when the present sovereign ascended the throne, but there had been a problem of some kind (possibly because this had all been ordained), and it had stayed in the Palace Storeroom. [Hosaka 1974, 2.358; translation, p. 118.]

(7) I am afraid Yotsugi is mistaken about the sword Tsubokiri. The late Retired Emperor Sanjō seems to have brought the matter up several times, but somebody always found an excuse for not delivering it. At last the Retired Emperor said, "Very well, never mind about it. Sword or no sword, he will still be the Crown Prince." Michinaga's friends made it seem accidental by saying things like, "It must have been fated." [Hosaka 1974, 2.374; translation, p. 120.]

(8) Because he was aware that Toshikata had spoken up for him, Yukinari always refused to sit above him after he outranked him. I think that probably happened when Yukinari achieved Junior Second Rank. He would stay home, pleading illness, on days when Toshikata was supposed to report for duty, or, if both happened to be present at the same time, he would sit across from him. When Toshikata later rose to Senior Second Rank, Yukinari went back to sitting below him. [Hosaka 1974, 2.521; translation, p. 145.]

(9) It was he who began the practice of linking principal building, wings, and galleries into a single whole, with a continuous cypress-bark

---

fully to replace the *udoneri* (foot Escorts, as were ordinary *konoe*) by two *fushō* (*konoe* who, like *banchō*, were entitled to ride on horseback). Virtually nothing is known about the criteria that distinguished *banchō* and *fushō* from one another, or from ordinary *konoe*. Hosaka 1974, 2.315; Wada 1953, pp. 57, 113-115.

[5] According to one commentator, this was an especially petty economy because it deprived the women of hair oil. Hosaka 1974, 2.316.

[6] The Crown Prince's symbol of office. Originally owned by Fujiwara Nagara, the weapon had been presented by Mototsune to Emperor Uda, by that Emperor to his designated successor, the future Emperor Daigo, and by all subsequent sovereigns to their Crown Princes.

roof. In the old days, buildings stood apart from one another, with gutters in between, just as they do to this day at the Imperial Palace. [Hosaka 1974, 2.567; translation, p. 152.]

(10) He became a Consultant on the Seventh of the First Month in the second year of Anna [969], and was appointed Imperial Household Minister on the Twenty-First of the intercalary Fifth Month in the same year. He became a Middle Counselor on the Twenty-Ninth of the intercalary Second Month in the third year of Tenroku [972]. On the Twenty-Seventh of the Eleventh Month in the same year, he accomplished the remarkable feat of becoming Palace Minister without having passed through the office of Major Counselor. It had been very painful for him to languish as a Consultant while his younger brother Kaneie was already a Middle Counselor, and so he found the promotion immensely gratifying. He attained Junior Second Rank on the Seventh of the First Month in the second year of Ten'en [974], and became Chancellor on the Twenty-Eighth of the Second Month, with Senior Second Rank and permission to enter the Imperial Palace in a hand-drawn carriage. On the Twenty-Sixth of the Third Month, he was named Regent.[7] That was how far he had risen in the sixth year after his appointment as Consultant. He was promoted to First Rank on the Seventh of the First Month in the third year of Ten'en [975], and died on the Eighth of the Eleventh Month in the second year of Jōgen [977], at the age of fifty-three. On the Twentieth of the latter month, he was posthumously elevated to Senior First Rank by Imperial decree. He received the posthumous name Chūgikō. Considering the brilliance of his career, it was too bad there was no vacant major captaincy for him to fill.[8] But it was only his swift elevation to the regency that denied him the title, so please believe me when I say that everything worked out for the best. [Hosaka 1974, 2.573; translation, p. 153.]

(11) Emperor En'yū's mother, Empress Anshi, was Kanemichi's sister. She died during Emperor Murakami's reign, on the Twenty-Ninth of the Fourth Month in the first year of Kōhō [964], but not before Kanemichi, for reasons of his own, had persuaded her to write, "Let each of my brothers become Regent in the order of his birth."

---

[7] *Kanpaku. Nihon kiryaku*, 2.124, entry of the Twenty-Sixth of the Third Month, Ten'en 2, confirms this statement, but *Kugyō bunin*, 1.211, gives the date as 972. As Hosaka 1974 surmises, 2.579, he probably received *nairan* (private inspection) powers on the earlier date and the formal regental title on the later. The holder of *nairan* powers was, in effect, the Regent, since he controlled the destinies of all official documents.

[8] Major Captain was a coveted office in the Imperial Bodyguards. McCullough and McCullough 1980, Appendix A.

He kept the paper through the years, wearing it suspended from his neck like an amulet. Meanwhile, during Emperor Reizei's reign, Kaneie became a Head Chamberlain, achieved Third Rank ahead of his brother, and rose to the dignity of Middle Counselor while Kanemichi was barely managing to secure a consultancy.[9] Kanemichi found it so disagreeable to show his face in public that he rarely appeared at Court, and the Emperor[10] felt as though he scarcely knew him.

Upon the death of his older brother, Regent Koremasa, which occurred during the Tenth Month in the third year of Tenroku [972], Kanemichi took his paper to the Palace for the Emperor to read. His Majesty happened to be in the Demon Room—a stroke of luck from Kanemichi's point of view—but he started to leave when he saw that the newcomer was his uncle, with whom he was on very distant terms. Kanemichi moved to his side. "I have something to report," he said. The Emperor turned back, took the paper, and examined it. It was a sheet of violet tissue, bearing in the late Empress's handwriting the words, "Let each of my brothers become Regent in the order of his birth. Let there be no exception whatever."

His Majesty seemed deeply moved. "It is undoubtedly the Empress's writing," he said, and went inside with the paper—or so I have heard. And I have also been told that Kanemichi left the Palace as head of the government.

Kanemichi had shown great foresight. I suppose, too, that he must have been destined for greatness. But there is still something very impressive about the extreme filial piety that made Emperor En'yū appoint him rather than disobey his mother's last testament.

"As Minister of the Right, Lord Yoritada was the one in line for the regency," people said. "Things happened as they did because of the Empress's note." To be sure, Kaneie himself outranked Kanemichi. Kanemichi was exceedingly clever about the whole affair. [Hosaka 1974, 2.573-574; translation, p. 153.]

(12) She has turned into a frightful spirit, haunting people in concert with her father. Her persecution of Koichijōin's wife never ceases. [Hosaka 1974, 2.594; translation, p. 156.]

(13) Asateru later left the mother of his sons for Major Counselor Nobumitsu's widow, an aging woman whom people had always tended to ignore, possibly because she was ugly. People said he had married the widow because she was rich, and thought less of him for it. His beautiful, high-born first wife was too poor to suit him, so he

[9] Kaneie became a Middle Counselor on the Seventh of the Second Month in 969, about two weeks after Kanemichi had become a Consultant.

[10] Emperor En'yū, who had ascended the throne in the Eighth Month of 969.

took up with the widow and abandoned her. At his new wife's house, there were rows of ladies-in-waiting—at least thirty, gorgeously attired in trains and formal jackets. All the furnishings and arrangements were perfect, and nothing was too good for the master. When Asateru came home during one of the winter months, his wife made up a hot fire, added some big, freshly compounded incense balls to the ashes, put a wickerwork basket over the top, and warmed his house clothes. She used to set out as many as twenty silver pitchers on the hearth, all filled with healthful decoctions. She also saw to it that his bed matting was padded, and ordered three or four ladies to heat it with large flat-irons before he retired. Her solicitude bordered on the excessive.

Although everything was handsomely managed, and although the ladies-in-waiting were exquisitely turned out, the widow limited her own dress to a pair of white trousers and two pale yellow padded robes. She was past forty, old enough to be Asateru's mother. She may have believed that her costume suited her swarthy skin, pock-marked forehead, and frizzled hair, as in fact it did. One would not have thought her the sort of wife for a prominent man.

Asateru's former wife, the daughter of Prince Shigeakira and Lady Tōshi, was well-born and beautiful. It is hard to understand how he could have left her for a woman like Nobumitsu's widow, unless he was blinded by the widow's wealth, and by the way she pampered him. Those of high rank are not immune to such temptations.

Common as men like me may be, I don't think one of us could bring himself to desert a wife after many years of marriage, no matter how extravagantly some other woman might be willing to shower treasures and attentions on him—and poverty is far more grim for us than for members of the nobility. Asateru's remarriage made others look down on him, and he seemed much less popular than before. It was all very unfortunate. He must have known what he was doing. An ordinary old man isn't likely to be smarter than he was. But I have told you about it because it was such a terrible way to act. (*He smiled with an impressive air of dignity.*) When a man in his position behaves that way, it would be only natural to expect anything at all from lesser folk. I think it is rather praiseworthy for a couple to endure poverty together year after year in a shack, as my wife and I have done. (*An amusingly smug expression stole over his face.*)

Asateru sometimes told his ox drivers and carriage men to head to-ward his former wife's house, but they always ignored him. Of course, the widow made presents of clothing to his attendants, underservants, Escorts, and carriage men, and she also supplied them with daily wine rations and looked after them in other ways, all of which may explain their refusal to listen to him. Just the same, his behavior was odd. He couldn't visit his first wife because his servants and ox drivers didn't want him to? Who ever heard of such a crazy thing! And yet nobody equalled him in beauty and disposition. [Hosaka 1974, 2.607-608; translation, p. 156.]

(14) When Kanemichi was dying, he transferred the regency to his cousin Yoritada. Everybody called it a shocking act.

(*The attendant interrupted.*) According to my information (*he said*), Kaneie's demotion was only natural. I have the details from the lips of my grandfather, who served for years in Kanemichi's mansion. Because of rivalry over ranks and offices, the two brothers had been on bad terms for a long time before Kanemichi was stricken by his fatal illness. As the crisis drew near, the Regent's people heard outriders off to the east, and someone reported that Kaneie was approaching.

"Even though we have been estranged all these years, he wants to see me before I die," Kanemichi thought. He saw to it that the unsightly objects near him were cleared away, ordered his bed to be tidied, and waited expectantly for his brother's arrival, only to learn that Kaneie had gone on past toward the Imperial Palace. He was speechless with mortification, and his attendants must have felt foolish, too.

"I was going to talk to him about resigning in his favor," Kanemichi said to himself. "It is just because he is that kind of person that I have never been able to get along with him. I won't put up with such behavior." On the point of death though he was, he told his dumbfounded people to lift him up, and had them prepare a carriage and muster some outriders. They wondered if a spirit might have possessed him; if not, he must be delirious. He called for his cap, put on his Court robes, and drove to the Palace. Supporting himself on his sons' shoulders beyond the guard post, he proceeded by way of the Palace Guards headquarters to the K'un ming partition in the Seiryoden.[11]

Kaneie was in the Daytime Chamber with the Emperor. A rumor had reached him of Kanemichi's death, and so he had gone past his brother's gate to the Palace to ask for the regency. Just as he was

---

[11] Members of the guards units (*hyōe, emon*) maintained posts (*jin*) at entrances to the Middle Enclosure (Nakanoe). Kanemichi probably rode in a hand-drawn carriage as far as the Inner Enclosure (Uchinoe) gate, after which it would have been necessary for him to walk. The Palace Guards (*takiguchi*) were a special group under the jurisdiction of the Chamberlains' Office (*kurōdodokoro*), with headquarters north of the Seiryōden. The K'un ming partition, situated in front of the Kokiden Imperial Apartment, was decorated with a picture of the lake of that name created west of Ch'ang an for naval maneuvers by Han Wu Ti (156-87 B.C.).

stating his request, he and the Emperor were astonished to see Kane-michi himself appear, popeyed with rage. Kaneie retreated to the De-mon Room, and Kanemichi knelt scowling. "I have come to make my last appointments," he said. Calling the Head Chamberlain, he handed down an Imperial decree appointing Yoritada Regent and making Middle Counselor Naritoki a Major Captain in place of Kaneie. He then conferred the inferior title of Minister of Civil Affairs on Kaneie and took his leave. He died soon afterward.

Kanemichi had a stubborn disposition. Although he was dying, his anger kept him alive all the way to the Palace and through the appoint-ments. It was not the sort of thing an ordinary person could have done. So you see Kaneie was not relieved of his office through pure malice. That was how it happened.

When we come to think about it, only a man of frightening deter-mination could have prevailed on Empress Anshi to give him the note, or could have kept himself alive at the very last to accomplish that final series of acts. [Here the attendant's comments end.] [Hosaka 1974, 2.621-622; translation, p. 157.]

(15) That Emperor was called Ichijō. After his mother took Bud-dhist vows, her status was equal to that of a Retired Emperor, and she bore the title Imperial Lady. She did as she pleased with the nation. [Hosaka 1974, 3.38; translation, p. 166.]

(16) His chest had begun to hurt around midnight on the Eighteenth. There was no great danger, but it must have set him to thinking. Dur-ing the Hour of the Sheep [1:00 p.m.-3:00 p.m.] on the Twenty-First, he suddenly sat up in bed, put on a cap, a glossed-silk under-jacket, and all the rest of a full Court costume, except for the formal outer trous-ers, and washed his hands. Next, while Yorimichi and the other sons gaped, he went out to the west corridor and bowed to the south, ask-ing leave of the Kasuga god to renounce the world. And then he told Bishop Kyōmei and Master of Discipline Jōki to cut off his hair. Yori-michi, his brothers, and the other gentlemen were horrified, but it all happened too fast for them to interfere, especially since they were stupefied with astonishment. What can I say!

Dharma Sign[12] Ingen administered the commandments, and His Lordship put on Bishop Shin'e's surplice and robe. I suppose he may not have had anything ready, since it was so sudden. He took the name Gyōkan, which he later changed to Gyōkaku.

---

[12] *Hōin*, the highest of three Court-awarded ecclesiastical ranks, as distinguished from offices. The other two, in descending order of importance, were Dharma Eye (*hōgen*) and Dharma Bridge (*hokkyō*). McCullough and McCullough 1980, s.n. 41.

After everything was over, word was sent to the Emperor, the Crown Prince, and the consorts. I shall not be so foolish as to try to describe the amazement and agitation of the Imperial ladies. Koichijōin called at about the Hour of the Monkey [3:00 p.m.-5:00 p.m.], unhitching his ox outside the main gate, and directing his men to pull the carriage as far as the middle gate, where he alighted. It was most impressive and admirable of him to respectfully decline to ride all the way. The Imperial ladies arrived that night, with Ishi and Kenshi in the same carriage. In view of the suddenness of the affair, they dispensed with the usual forms for such journeys.

His Lordship received the commandments again at Nara on the Twenty-Seventh of the Ninth Month in that year. All sorts of splendid things happened then, too, but you must know about them, so I shall not trouble you with the details. [Hosaka 1974, 3.242; translation, p. 191.]

(17) At the same time, he made a 1,000-scroll offering of the *Fukū-kensaku Sutra*.[13] The scrolls still survive, and various members of the Fujiwara family have taken them to serve as household guardians. That the Fujiwara have risen again, and that they continue to this day to act as protectors of the throne, must be due to the merit Fuyutsugi acquired when he copied the sutra and made the sacred image. Many senior nobles from other families died on the very day of the dedication, and there are people who claim, rightly or not, that the same explanation applies. [Hosaka 1974, 3.338; translation, p. 202.]

[13] Presumably about thirty-five copies. The sutra, which describes the virtues of Fukūkensaku Kannon, normally consists of thirty scrolls.

Chronology of the Ōkagami Period

Unless otherwise identified, holders of ministerial and
regental posts are Fujiwara

A. D.	Era		Emperor	Retired Emperor	Regent K- kanpaku S- sesshō
850	Kashō	3	Montoku 3.21		
851	Ninju 4.28	1			
852		2			
853		3			
854	Saikō 11.30	1			
855		2			
856		3			
857	Ten'an 2.21	1			
858		2	Seiwa 8.27	8.27	Yoshifusa (S) 11.7
859	Jōgan 4.15	1			
860		2			
861		3			
862		4			

Principal source: Nishioka 1955

Chancellor	Minister of the Left	Minister of the Right	Notes
	(M. Tokiwa)	(Yoshifusa)	Future Emperor Seiwa becomes Crown Prince.
	6.13		
Yoshifusa 2.19	M. Makoto 2.19	Yoshimi 2.19	Yoshifusa becomes first subject to serve as Chancellor.
			Yoshifusa becomes first subject to serve as Regent. Start of regental government.

A. D.	Era		Emperor	Retired Emperor	Regent
863	(Jōgan)	5	(Seiwa)		(Yoshifusa)
864		6			
865		7			
866		8			Yoshifusa (S) 8.19
867		9			
868		10			
869		11			
870		12			
871		13			
872		14			9.2 Mototsune (S) 11.29
873		15			
874		16			
875		17			

Chancellor	Minister of the Left	Minister of the Right	Notes
(Yoshifusa)	(Makoto)	(Yoshimi)	
			Ōtenmon incident.
		10.10	
	intercal. 12.28		
		Ujimune 1.13	
9.2	M. Tōru 8.25	Mototsune 8.25 2.7	Prince Koretaka becomes a monk.

A. D.	Era		Emperor		Retired Emperor	Regent
876	(Jōgan)	18	Yōzei (Seiwa) 11.29 11.29		Seiwa 11.29	(Mototsune)
877	Gangyō 4.16	1				
878		2				
879		3				
880		4			12.4	11.8 (K)
881		5				
882		6				
883		7				
884		8	2.4 Kōkō 2.5		Yōzei 2.4	
885	Ninna 2.21	1				
886		2				
887		3	Uda 8.26 8.26			
888		4				

Chancellor	Minister of the Left	Minister of the Right	Notes
	(Tōru)	(Mototsune)	Yotsugi is born.
Mototsune 12.4		12.4	
		M. Masaru 1.10	
			Akō controversy begins.
		10.17	

A.D.	Era		Emperor		Retired Emperor	Regent
889	Kanpyō 4.27	1	(Uda)		(Yōzei)	(Mototsune)
890		2				12.14
891		3				
892		4				
893		5				
894		6				
895		7				
896		8				
897		9	Daigo 7.3	7.3	Uda 7.3	
898	Shōtai 4.26	1				
899		2				
900		3				
901	Engi 7.15	1				

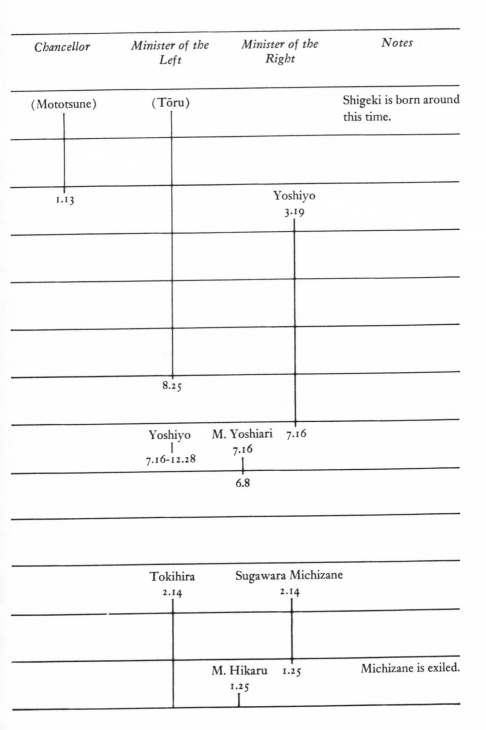

Chancellor	Minister of the Left	Minister of the Right	Notes
(Mototsune)	(Tōru)		Shigeki is born around this time.
1.13		Yoshiyo 3.19	
	8.25		
	Yoshiyo 7.16-12.28	M. Yoshiari 7.16 7.16 6.8	
	Tokihira 2.14	Sugawara Michizane 2.14	
		M. Hikaru 1.25 1.25	Michizane is exiled.

A.D.	Era		Emperor	Retired Emperor	Regent
902	(Engi)	2	(Daigo)	(Yōzei) (Uda)	
903		3			
904		4			
905		5			
906		6			
907		7			
908		8			
909		9			
910		10			
911		11			
912		12			
913		13			
914		14			

Chancellor	Minister of the Left	Minister of the Right	Notes
	(Tokihira)	(Hikaru)	
			Retired Emperor Uda visits the Ōi River.
	4.4		
		3.12	
		Tadahira 8.25	

A.D.	Era		Emperor	Retired Emperor	Regent
915	(Engi)	15	(Daigo)	(Yōzei) (Uda)	
916		16			
917		17			
918		18			
919		19			
920		20			
921		21			
922		22			
923	Enchō 4.11	1			
924		2			
925		3			
926		4			
927		5			

Chancellor	Minister of the Left	Minister of the Right	Notes
		(Tadahira)	
	Tadahira 1.22	Sadakata 1.22	1.22

A. D.	Era		Emperor	Retired Emperor	Regent
928	(Enchō)	6	(Daigo)	(Yōzei) (Uda)	
929		7			
930		8	Suzaku 9.22 9.22		Daigo Tadahira (S) 9.22-9.29 9.22
931	Jōhei 4.26	1		7.19	
932		2			
933		3			
934		4			
935		5			
936		6			
937		7			
938	Tengyō 5.22	1			
939		2			
940		3			

Chancellor	Minister of the Left	Minister of the Right	Notes
	(Tadahira)	(Sadakata)	
		8.4	
		Nakahira 2.13	
			Taira Masakado stirs up trouble in the eastern provinces.
(Tadahira) 8.19	8.19		
	Nakahira 1.22	Tsunesuke 1.22 · 1.22	Masakado revolts.
		5.5	
			Fujiwara Sumitomo revolts in the west.
			Masakado is put down.

A. D.	Era	Emperor	Retired Emperor	Regent
941	(Tengyō) 4	(Suzaku)	(Yōzei)	(Tadahira) 11.8 (K)
942	5			
943	6			
944	7			
945	8			
946	9	Murakami 4.20 4.20	Suzaku 4.20	
947	Tenryaku 1 4.22			
948	2			
949	3		9.29	8.14
950	4			
951	5			
952	6		8.15	
953	7			

Chancellor	Minister of the Left	Minister of the Right	Notes
(Tadahira)	(Nakahira)		Sumitomo is put down.
		Saneyori 4.9	
	9.1		
	Saneyori 4.26	Morosuke 4.26 4.26	
8.14			

A. D.	Era		Emperor	Retired Emperor	Regent
954	(Tenryaku)	8	(Murakami)		
955		9			
956		10			
957	Tentoku 10.27	1			
958		2			
959		3			
960		4			
961	Ōwa 2.16	1			
962		2			
963		3			
964	Kōhō 7.10	1			
965		2			
966		3			

Chancellor	Minister of the Left	Minister of the Right	Notes
	(Saneyori)	(Morosuke)	
		Akitada 8.22 5.4	
			Prince Tamehira's Day of the Rat outing.
	4.24		
		M. Takaakira 1.16	

A.D.	Era		Emperor	Retired Emperor	Regent
967	(Kōhō)	4	Reizei (Murakami) 5.25 5.25		Saneyori 6.22
968	Anna 8.13	1			
969		2	8.13 En'yū 8.13	Reizei 8.13	
970	Tenroku 3.25	1			Koremasa (S) 5.18 5.20
971		2			
972		3			10.23 Kanemichi (K) 11.27
973	Ten'en 12.20	1			
974		2			
975		3			
976	Jōgen 7.13	1			
977		2			Yoritada (K) 10.11 10.11
978	Tengen 11.29	1			
979		2			

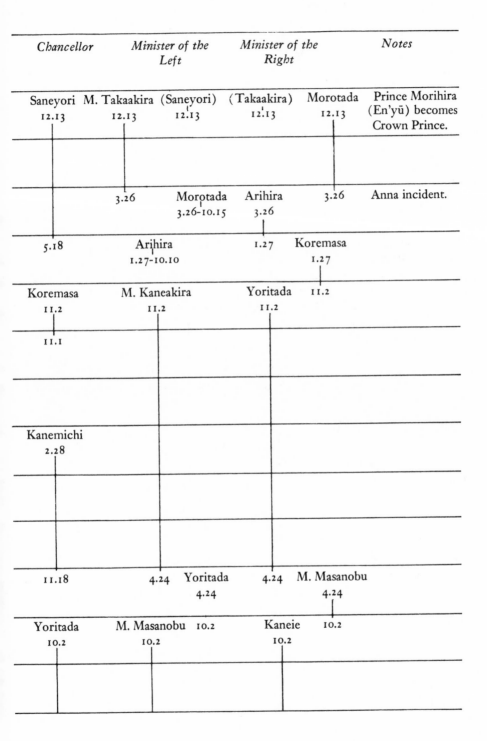

Chancellor	Minister of the Left		Minister of the Right		Notes
Saneyori 12.13	M. Takaakira 12.13	(Saneyori) 12.13	(Takaakira) 12.13	Morotada 12.13	Prince Morihira (En'yū) becomes Crown Prince.
	3.26	Morotada 3.26–10.15	Arihira 3.26	3.26	Anna incident.
5.18		Arihira 1.27–10.10	1.27	Koremasa 1.27	
Koremasa 11.2	M. Kaneakira 11.2		Yoritada 11.2	11.2	
11.1					
Kanemichi 2.28					
11.18	4.24	Yoritada 4.24	4.24	M. Masanobu 4.24	
Yoritada 10.2	M. Masanobu 10.2	10.2	Kaneie 10.2	10.2	

A.D.	*Era*		*Emperor*	*Retired Emperor*	*Regent*
980	(Tengen)	3	(En'yū)	(Reizei)	(Yoritada)
981		4			
982		5			
983	Eikan 4.15	1			
984		2	Kazan 8.27 / 8.27	En'yū 8.27	
985	Kanna 4.27	1			
986		2	6.23 Ichijō 6.23	Kazan 6.23	6.23 Kaneie (S) 6.24
987	Eien 4.5	1			
988		2			
989	Eiso 8.8	1			
990	Shōryaku 11.7	1		Michitaka (K) 5.8 / 5.26 (S)	5.5 (K) 5.8
991		2		2.12	
992		3			

Chancellor	Minister of the Left	Minister of the Right	Notes
(Yoritada)	(Masanobu)	(Kaneie)	
			En'yū's Day of the Rat outing.
		Tamemitsu 7.20 7.20	
			Kaneie's longevity celebration (60).
Kaneie 6.26 12.20 5.5			
Tamemitsu 9.7 6.16		9.7 M. Shigenobu 9.7	

A. D.	Era		Emperor	Retired Emperor		Regent
993	(Shōryaku)	4	(Ichijō)	(Reizei)	(Kazan)	(Michitaka) 4.22 (K)
994		5				
995	Chōtoku 2.22	1				Michikane (K) 4.3 4.27-5.8
996		2				
997		3				
998		4				
999	Chōhō 1.13	1				
1000		2				
1001		3				
1002		4				
1003		5				
1004	Kankō 7.20	1				
1005		2				

Chancellor	Minister of the Left	Minister of the Right	Notes
	(Masanobu) 7.26	(Shigenobu)	
	M. Shigenobu 8.28	Michikane 8.28 8.28	
	5.8	Michinaga 5.8 6.19	Great epidemic.
	Michinaga 7.20	7.20 Akimitsu 7.20	Banishment of Korechika and Takaie.
			Pardon of Korechika and Takaie.
			Senshi's lengevity celebration (40).

A. D.	Era	Emperor	Retired Emperor	Regent
1006	(Kankō) 3 .	(Ichijō)	(Reizei) (Kazan)	
1007	4			
1008	5		2.8	
1009	6			
1010	7			
1011	8	Sanjō 6.13 / 6.13	Ichijō 10.24 / 6.13-6.22	
1012	Chōwa 1 / 12.25			
1013	2			
1014	3			
1015	4			Michinaga [S]* 10.27
1016	5	1.29 Go-Ichijō 1.29	Sanjō 1.29	1.29 (S)
1017	Kannin 1 / 4.23		5.9	Yorimichi (S) 3.16 / 3.16
1018	2			

* De facto regental powers

Chancellor	Minister of the Left	Minister of the Right	Notes
	(Michinaga)	(Akimitsu)	
			Michinaga visits Kinbusen.
	11.7		
Michinaga 12.4	Akimitsu 3.4	Kinsue 3.4	Kinsue 3.4 Prince Atsuakira (Koichijōin) resigns as Crown Prince.
2.9			

A. D.	Era		Emperor	Retired Emperor	Regent
1019	(Kannin)	3	(Go-Ichijō)		(Yorimichi) 12.22 (K)
1020		4			
1021	Jian 2.2	1			
1022		2			
1023		3			
1024	Manju	1			
1025		2			

Chancellor	Minister of the Left	Minister of the Right	Notes
	(Akimitsu)	(Kinsue)	Michinaga takes Buddhist vows.
Kinsue 7.25	Yorimichi 5.25 7.25	Sanesuke 7.25 7.25	
			Hōjōji Golden Hall is dedicated.
			Rinshi's longevity celebration (60).

The Fujiwara Role in Japanese Court History from Kamatari to Michinaga

(Principal source: Kawakami 1926)

Early Leaders   The first person to bear the Fujiwara surname was Kamatari (614-669, also Kamako), one of the major figures of early Japanese history. He was born into the Nakatomi, a once powerful family of hereditary Shintō priests, which had receded into the background after the introduction of Buddhism in the sixth century. When the time came for him to assume his priestly duties, the low prestige of the Nakatomi, and of Shintō in general, made him decide to live in retirement as a scholar, but in 645 he joined an Imperial Prince, Naka no Ōe, in a successful attempt to overthrow the Soga clan, which had dominated the Court since the death of Prince Shōtoku in 622. With a new Emperor on the throne, Kamatari and Prince Naka no Ōe assumed control of the government as chief minister and heir apparent, respectively, and Kamatari became the principal architect of the Taika reforms of 645-646, which were designed to transform Japan from an unstable coalition of semi-autonomous clans into a centralized state with Chinese administrative, land tenure, and taxation systems. During his last illness in 669, he was granted the surname Fujiwara as a mark of Imperial favor.

Kamatari's son Fuhito (659-720) became Minister of the Right, married two daughters to Emperors, and produced four successful sons. Fuhito is remembered particularly for his contribution to the compilation of the Taihō Code of 701 and its successor, the Yōrō Code of 718. A general amnesty was declared when he fell ill in 720, and he was posthumously honored with Senior First Rank and the title of Chancellor.

Of Fuhito's four sons, the oldest, Muchimaro (680-737), was a Minister of the Right; the second, Fusasaki (681-737), served as an Imperial adviser and expert on local government; the third, Umakai (694-737), became Minister of Ceremonial after having travelled to China as one of the leaders of an official mission in 716; and the fourth, Maro (695-737), was Master of the Left Capital Office. All four were carried off by smallpox in 737.

The epidemic of 737 dealt a severe blow to the house of Fujiwara. Men from other families replaced its dead leaders and withstood challenges from sons of Umakai and Muchimaro in 740 and 764, respectively. Muchimaro's line, known as the Southern House, gradually declined after 764. Since Maro's line, the Capital Branch, had never prospered, the family's future rested with the Northern and Ceremonial houses, founded by Fusasaki and Umakai.

Umakai's son Momokawa (732-779), known as a prudent, upright man, was largely responsible for the accession of Emperor Kōnin (r. 770-781) and the selection of the future Emperor Kanmu (r. 781-806) as Kōnin's Crown Prince. Momokawa's son Otsugu and his nephew Tanetsugu were influential during Kanmu's reign, but the Ceremonial House receded into the background after two of Tanetsugu's children attempted an unsuccessful coup d'état in 810.

At the time of the abortive plot, which had been intended to depose the reigning Emperor—Kanmu's son Saga (r. 809-823)—in favor of Saga's abdicated brother Heizei (r. 806-809), the Minister of the Right was Uchimaro (756-812), a grandson of Fusasaki, and thus a member of the Northern House. Uchimaro and his son Fuyutsugi (775-826) played the chief role in the suppression of the revolt, a fact which established them in Saga's favor. Uchimaro died two years later, but Fuyutsugi lived to lay the foundations of a new era of Fujiwara power.

As a young man, Fuyutsugi was a popular Court figure, highly regarded by Emperor Saga, who gave him the important post of Head Chamberlain in the new personal secretariat he had created in 810. He later held a series of responsible positions, culminating in 825 with his appointment as Minister of the Left, a post that had been vacant since 782. Meanwhile, his son Yoshifusa (804-872) had been betrothed to one of Saga's daughters at the age of ten, and his daughter Junshi (809-871) had married the Crown Prince. Junshi bore a son, the future Emperor Montoku, in the year following her father's death. The Northern House, which had no more than held its own against other powerful families during the first years of the Heian period, was thus well launched on its upward journey.

Yoshifusa Yoshifusa, the second of Fuyutsugi's three sons by his principal wife, began his official career in 826 as a member of Emperor Junna's personal secretariat, and passed through the usual subordinate offices in the next several years. He became extremely influential after 833, when Junna's abdication cleared the way for the accession of Emperor Ninmyō (r. 833-850), who was Yoshifusa's brother-in-law, and whose oldest son was Yoshifusa's nephew. His career as a high-ranking official began in 834 with an appointment as Consultant. In 835, he was promoted over the heads of seven men to the office of Provisional Middle Counselor.

The year 840 saw the death of Retired Emperor Junna (r. 823-833), whose son, Prince Tsunesada, had been named heir apparent at the time of Ninmyō's accession, in repayment of an obligation incurred when Junna (Saga's brother) had chosen Ninmyō (Saga's son) as his successor. When Saga died two years later, Tsunesada, a youth of seventeen, found himself in an uncomfortable position. Not only was he blocking the aspirations of Yoshifusa's nephew, Prince Michiyasu, but his mother was not even a Fujiwara. Two days after Saga's death, it was announced to the Emperor that a faction headed by Ban no Kowamine and Tachibana Hayanari was conspiring to put the Crown Prince on the throne. The alleged ringleaders were taken into custody, and a week later the Prince was stripped of his title, after initial reluctance on the Emperor's part. No firm evidence of conspiracy was obtained; on the contrary, the Prince seems to have been uncomfortable in his position and desirous of relinquishing it. It is assumed by historians that the incident was contrived by the Fujiwara, who used it to overthrow two rival families, the Ban and the Tachibana, and to secure the succession of Fuyutsugi's grandson. Prince Michiyasu became Crown Prince, Yoshifusa was promoted to the office of Major Counselor, and Yoshifusa's daughter Meishi (829-900) married the new heir apparent.

Yoshifusa was made Minister of the Right in 848, second in status but superior in power to the Minister of the Left, his brother-in-law Minamoto Tokiwa (812-854), who appears to have been an unassertive man.

Prince Michiyasu (Emperor Montoku) came to the throne in 850 as a result of the death of his father, Emperor Ninmyō. Then twenty-three, he is said to have been able and conscientious, but his physical infirmities, which were to claim his life after a reign of eight years, made it difficult for him to withstand pressure from Yoshifusa. When Meishi gave birth to a son, Prince Korehito (850-880), her father immediately began to seek the infant's nomination as Crown Prince. Montoku's personal preference was for his six-year-old son Koretaka (844-897), whose mother was a lady from the ancient house of Ki, and who was thought by many to have a better claim to the throne than Meishi's child. The Emperor wavered briefly, while the temples resounded with prayers commissioned by the Fujiwara and the Ki, but Prince Korehito was nominated before the end of 850.

Yoshifusa headed the government after Tokiwa's death in 854. Three years later, without passing through the office of Minister of the Left, he achieved the unprecedented honor of being named Chancellor. His junior colleagues were his younger brother Yoshimi (817-867) as Minister of the Right, and a brother-in-law, Minamoto Makoto (810-868), as Minister of the Left. When his eight-year-old grandson, Emperor Seiwa (r. 858-876), ascended the throne, he was named Regent in another precedent-shattering decree, "because he was His Majesty's maternal grandfather."

Thus far in his career, Yoshifusa had dealt heavy blows to three families, the Tachibana, the Tomo (Ban), and the Ki. The year 866 saw the banishment of the last prominent Tomo, Major Counselor Yoshio (809-868), who was found responsible for a fire at Ōtenmon, one of the Palace gates.

During the settlement of the Ōtenmon affair, Emperor Seiwa reconfirmed Yoshifusa as Regent, an even more startling break with tradition than the original appointment. The decree was particularly surprising because Seiwa had come of age two years earlier, and so might have been expected to proclaim his intention of assuming control of the government. From Yoshifusa's point of view, it came at an opportune juncture. He had just placed the Minister of the Left, Minamoto Makoto, under obligation by defending him against Yoshio, who had blamed him for the fire; and almost all the other positions of consequence were occupied by his relatives. The revolutionary decree met with no opposition, and Yoshifusa ruled until his death in 872.

Since Meishi was his only child, Yoshifusa adopted two of his brother Nagara's offspring, a son and a daughter. The son, Mototsune (836-891), succeeded him as head of the family. The daughter, Kōshi (842-910), bore a son to Emperor Seiwa in 869, and the boy, Emperor Yōzei, succeeded to the throne in 876, in spite of the fact that he was criminally insane.

Mototsune   After his capping ceremony, which is said to have taken place in the Imperial presence, Mototsune passed through a series of official posts to become a Head Chamberlain in 858, the year of Emperor Seiwa's accession. In 864 he became a Consultant; in 866 he was promoted over the heads of seven others to the office of Middle Counselor—a result of Yoshifusa's appointment as Regent and his own contribution to the settlement of the Ōtenmon affair, which had been to interrogate Makoto and establish his innocence—and in 870 he became a Major Counselor. In 872 he and Minamoto Tōru (822-895), a son of Emperor Saga, were named Minister of the Right and Minister of the Left.

Yoshifusa died a few days after Mototsune attained ministerial rank. Emperor Seiwa, who was twenty-two at the time, named Mototsune Regent, and in 876 he abdicated, giving as his reasons poor health and ill omens implying loss of the mandate of heaven. He was the first Emperor in Japanese history to voluntarily cede the throne to a child while still a young man. On his abdication day, he named Mototsune Regent of his eight-year-old son and successor, Yōzei, an act that caused the Minister of the Left, Tōru, to retire in displeasure to his private residence, where he remained throughout the new Emperor's eight-year reign (876-884).

The mad Emperor Yōzei seems to have become wholly intractable after his capping ceremony in 882. Unable to resign as Regent in spite of repeated requests, Mototsune went into retirement in 883, and his Horikawa Mansion became the informal seat of the government, since no official business could be transacted without him.

Toward the end of 883, a courtier was murdered at the Imperial Palace under circumstances incriminatory to the Emperor. There appears to have been no objection when Mototsune, roused to action, went to the Palace, evicted a number of Yōzei's hangers on, and set the machinery in motion for the selection of a new Emperor. Instead of recommending a close relative of his own who was still a minor—Seiwa's second son by Kōshi, for instance, or Seiwa's son by Mototsune's own daughter—he proposed Prince Tsunesada, the son of Junna who had been removed as Crown Prince to make way for the future Emperor Montoku. When the Prince declined, on the grounds that he was fifty-nine years old and a monk, Mototsune transferred his support to one of Emperor Ninmyō's sons, Prince Tokiyasu, who was then fifty-four; and he succeeded in winning approval of his choice at a council of nobles, in spite of an attempt by Tōru to press his own claim to the throne. Some Japanese historians have praised Mototsune's conduct as public-spirited and statesmanlike, but there seems to have been little danger that either of his candidates would embark on a lengthy period of personal rule, since both were well along in years, and Tokiyasu, in particular, was related to him by blood and marriage.[1]

Yōzei was taken from the Palace by a group of courtiers who pretended to be escorting him to a racing meet. The Emperor, inordinately fond of horses, had stabled thirty animals in the Palace and made inti-

[1] Tokiyasu's mother was Mototsune's aunt; Mototsune's wife, Tokiyasu's niece.

mates of two skilled riders of questionable character, both of whom seem to have been involved in the murder.[2]

The new Emperor, Kōkō (r. 884-887), took a personal interest in affairs of state, seeking to curb ostentation and to reform local government, but it was Mototsune who exercised ultimate authority. In spite of the fact that Kōkō was capable of ruling, he issued a decree authorizing Mototsune to supervise the bureaucracy and approve reports to the throne. Although the term *kanpaku* was not used, Mototsune became, in effect, the Regent.[3]

Appointment of a Crown Prince became an urgent necessity when Emperor Kōkō fell seriously ill in 887, three years after his accession. Since none of Kōkō's sons was the offspring of a Fujiwara lady, Mototsune found it necessary either to choose an heir unrelated to himself or to seek a candidate among the descendants of earlier rulers. He decided on Minamoto Sadami, Kōkō's favorite son, who was a young man of twenty. The dying Emperor is said to have summoned Sadami after the decision was reached, joined his son's hand to Mototsune's, and tearfully adjured him never to forget the minister's loyal conduct.

The new Emperor, Uda (r. 887-897), acceded on the day of Kōkō's death, the Twenty-Sixth of the Eighth Month of 887, and was formally enthroned on the Seventeenth of the Eleventh Month. Four days after the enthronement ceremony, he issued a decree investing Mototsune with the office of *kanpaku*. As was required by etiquette, Mototsune went through the form of refusing the honor. Also according to the rules, the Emperor issued a routine repetition of his command. At that point, there occurred an unscheduled incident, known to historians as the *akō* controversy, which provides a commentary on the nature and extent of Fujiwara influence.

Uda had named Mototsune Regent against his will. He would have liked to rule personally, but Mototsune had achieved such a commanding position that the Emperor could do no more than seek to diminish Fujiwara power by entrusting as much responsibility as possible to a

---

[2] Yōzei lived to the age of eighty-one. Stories tell of his riding to Minamoto Tōru's famous Uji Villa and destroying the brushwood fences; riding into commoners' houses and chasing women and children; ordering a servant to tie up a girl and throw her into a pond, etc.

[3] A *kanpaku* was the Regent of a grown male sovereign of sound mind and body, as distinguished from a *sesshō*, the Regent of an Emperor incapacitated by sex, youth, or disability. Since the office of *kanpaku* had been unheard of in earlier times, the word did not come into use in this sense until the reign of Kōkō's son Uda, who made the first formal appointment, as noted below. (In this Appendix, as elsewhere in the book, both *sesshō* and *kanpaku* are rendered as Regent.)

member of another family. The person selected for that role was Tachibana Hiromi (837-890), a leading Confucian scholar, who had been the Emperor's tutor before his accession, and whose daughter had borne His Majesty two sons. Hiromi, named a Consultant by Kōkō, quickly became Uda's most trusted adviser. It was he who composed the answer to Mototsune's memorial declining the regental appointment.

The Imperial reply, couched in the flowery language considered suitable, contained the phrase, "Let Mototsune serve as Our *akō*." Fujiwara Sukeyo, another Confucian scholar, told Mototsune that *akō* (Chinese *a heng*) was a word used by the Chinese to denote a nominal office, and that its use in the Imperial communication was a subtle way of informing Mototsune that his services were not required. Mototsune seems to have been aware of the new Emperor's desire for independence, and to have welcomed an opportunity to destroy Hiromi. Professing to accept Sukeyo's views, he retired to his mansion, where he refused to see official callers or concern himself with state affairs until a new writ of appointment was issued.

Meanwhile, eminent Confucianists were asked to study the Chinese use of *akō*. It appears that the term had generally been used as a synonym for Prime Minister, although it had been an empty title during one comparatively brief period. Hiromi's position was defensible, but most of the Court scholars refused to support him, either through jealousy or through fear of Mototsune. After protracted wrangling, during which some of the learned disputants exchanged blows, the Emperor ordered Hiromi and Sukeyo to present their cases before him, but found himself unable to render a judgment. By that time the struggle had dragged on for over six months, with increasing numbers of nobles absenting themselves from Court on one pretext or another. On the Second of the Sixth Month in 888, the day after his failure to reach a decision, the Emperor finally issued a new command to Mototsune—a humiliating document, begging Mototsune to serve as Regent. "In the end, unable to make Our will prevail, We were constrained to yield to a subject's demand," Uda wrote in his diary. "Such is the degeneracy of the times."[4]

The *akō* controversy disposed of Hiromi, who lived in retirement until his death two years later, and of the Tachibana family. On the surface, at least, Uda accepted defeat gracefully. He took Mototsune's daughter Onshi as a consort within a few months after the settlement, personally bestowed the cap of manhood on Mototsune's son Nakahira

---

[4] *Uda tennō gyoki*, p. 4.

two years later, and declared a general amnesty when Mototsune fell ill in 890.

Mototsune's position was unchallenged during his last years.[5] He asked to resign as Regent and Chancellor when he fell ill in 890, but only the first half of the rquest was granted. He died in 891 at the age of fifty-five.

MOTOTSUNE'S SONS

Tokihira Mototsune's oldest son, Tokihira (871-909), was too young to inherit his father's full power at once, and the highest ministers of state, Minamoto Tōru and Fujiwara Yoshiyo (823-900), were old and decrepit. Left with a relatively free hand, Emperor Uda brought a number of new faces into the government, including a Confucian scholar, Sugawara Michizane (845-903), who became, in a sense, Hiromi's successor.[6] Michizane began a rapid rise after Mototsune's death. A Head Chamberlain in 890, he had become a Provisional Major Counselor by 897, with a daughter who was an Imperial consort. Since all the ministerial posts had meanwhile fallen vacant, Michizane, Tokihira (named a Major Counselor in 897), and Minamoto Hikaru (a Provisional Major Counselor) were the highest-ranking officials in the bureaucracy. Hikaru was a figurehead and Tokihira was not always consulted in matters of importance. It was Michizane alone who advised the Emperor when a Crown Prince was being selected, and Michizane alone who received advance notification of the Emperor's intention to abdicate.

Uda was an energetic sovereign who reformed the police, reorganized the civil administration, and took steps to correct abuses in the provinces. Yet in 897, only six years after Mototsune's death, he turned over the throne to his twelve-year-old son, Crown Prince Atsuhito (Emperor Daigo, r. 897-930).[7] His reasons for abdicating are not clear. He may have wished to govern through his young successor, free of the ceremonial restraints imposed on a reigning sovereign, or he may have been subjected to pressure by the Crown Prince's relatives, or by other Fujiwara resentful of the preferment given to Sugawara Michi-

---

[5] His only associate of ministerial rank after 888 was Minamoto Tōru, who had recognized the futility of opposition. It was Tōru who persuaded Uda to capitulate in the *akō* controversy.

[6] Michizane seems to have attracted Imperial notice at the time of the *akō* controversy, when he wrote Mototsune a letter in defense of Hiromi.

[7] Prince Atsuhito, the grandson of Fujiwara Takafuji, owed his position to the failure of Mototsune's daughter Onshi to produce a son.

zane. At any rate, he abdicated in the middle of 897, commanding Michizane and Tokihira to advise his son, and instructing Daigo to value the counsels of both.

In 899 Tokihira was named Minister of the Left and Michizane Minister of the Right. The disparity in age between Mototsune's twenty-eight-year-old son and his fifty-four-year-old junior colleague was in itself sufficient to impose a strain on their relationship, even if they had not been temperamentally unsuited to collaboration. Tokihira was a practical man who saw a need for sweeping governmental reforms and was anxious to proceed with an active program; Michizane was a conservative literatus. As time passed, they found themselves frequently at odds. With his father's encouragement, Emperor Daigo conceived the plan of ending the conflict by making Michizane Regent, but Michizane declined in horror when summoned to hear the news, and went so far as to present His Majesty with a Chinese poem to prevent speculation about the audience. His apprehension was natural. As Minister of the Right, occupying a position to which only one other scholar in Japanese history had attained;[8] he outranked the senior Minamoto and the Emperor's Fujiwara grandfather, and the nobility and the jealous scholarly community were united against him.

In spite of Michizane's precautions, news of the Imperial offer spread, and a coalition headed by Tokihira, Minamoto Hikaru, Fujiwara Sadakuni (an uncle of the Emperor), and Fujiwara Sugane (a disgruntled scholar) persuaded Emperor Daigo that Michizane had secured Retired Emperor Uda's approval of a scheme to dethrone the sovereign in favor of Prince Tokiyo, who was Daigo's younger brother, Michizane's son-in-law, and a grandson of Tachibana Hiromi. Refusing to see Uda, who went to the Palace to intercede for his favorite, Daigo exiled Michizane to Kyūshū, where he soon died. Uda ceased to be active politically, although he lived until 931.

Michizane's political ability does not seem to have equaled his skill as a poet. It was not until after his departure that Tokihira was able to move ahead with a reform program designed to destroy the power of local families, put the government's provincial authority on a firm footing, increase revenues, and revive the dying system of public land distribution. The success of Tokihira's measures was ephemeral, chiefly because local officials failed to enforce them, but his policies reflected a degree of statesmanship which was unique in his day, and which no later Fujiwara autocrat approached.

[8] The other was Kibi no Makibi (695-775), Minister of the Right from 766 to 771.

Tadahira   After Tokihira's death in 909, the only remaining minister of state was the ineffectual Minamoto Hikaru, who had succeeded Michizane as Minister of the Right. With no powerful subject to over-shadow him, the twenty-four-year-old Emperor Daigo made his own decisions. He attempted to force local governors to go to the provinces, stop tax embezzlements, prevent falsification of acreage reports, and encourage development of new lands. His efforts met with no important success, but his reign has traditionally been regarded as a glorious era—primarily, it would seem, because he was a great patron of learning and the arts. He occupied the throne for thirty-three years, until shortly before his death in 930.

Meanwhile Tadahira (880-949), Mototsune's fourth son, was being given responsible positions. After the elderly Hikaru was killed in a hunting accident, Tadahira replaced him as Minister of the Right, and ten years later, in 924, he was appointed to the office of Minister of the Left, which had remained vacant after Tokihira's death. Easy-going and genial, Tadahira exhibited no particular capacity for leadership, but his economic resources and social prestige as head of the Fujiwara family,[9] combined with a talent for making friends, compensated for his deficiencies. When Emperor Daigo decided to abdicate in the Ninth Month of 930, he commanded Tadahira to act as Regent for the seven-year-old future Emperor, Prince Hiroakira.

The new Emperor Suzaku (r. 930-946) was Daigo's son by Empress Onshi, Mototsune's fourth daughter.[10] During the first two years of his life, he had been kept closely confined behind curtains as a protection against Sugawara Michizane's spirit, which was blamed for the prema-ture deaths of his two predecessors as Crown Prince. Perhaps for that reason, he was a frail child and, later, a sickly young man who died at the age of twenty-nine. As an Emperor, he appears to have been an amiable non-entity.

In 933 Tadahira's older brother, Nakahira (875-945), became Min-ister of the Right. Nakahira, described by some chroniclers as generous and honorable and by others as avaricious and miserly, was no more of a statesman than Tadahira. Under the aegis of the two brothers the government drifted, while robber gangs pillaged the provinces, mur-dered local officials, and invaded the Imperial Palace. Between 935 and

[9] A position he had inherited upon Tokihira's death. The Fujiwara wealth came from their extensive holdings of private lands, acquired by gift, reclamation, com-mendation, and other methods.

[10] Not to be confused with Uda's consort of the same name (in Sino-Japanese reading), who was Mototsune's second daughter.

941 there were two revolts against the central authority, one in eastern Japan by Taira Masakado and one in the west by Fujiwara Sumitomo. The Court cut a particularly sorry figure in the east, where it was rescued from its difficulties not by its own arms, but by local adversaries of Masakado.

Tadahira became Chancellor in 936 and continued in that office and the regency until his death in 949.

Tadahira's Sons Emperor Suzaku, who sired no sons, appointed his eighteen-year-old younger brother, Nariakira (Emperor Murakami, r. 946-967), to the heir apparency. He abdicated two years later.

After the death of Tadahira, Emperor Murakami had no Regent. The Emperor interested himself in such matters as curbing extravagance and promoting able men, but failed to solve the basic political problems of lawlessness, tax evasion, falsification of land records, and incendiarism. Robbers roved the capital, most of the Imperial Palace was destroyed by fire in 960, and delayed tax deliveries forced the Emperor to set an example of frugal living.

Tadahira's oldest and second sons, Saneyori (900-970) and Morosuke (908-960), were the Fujiwara leaders of the day. Saneyori, as Minister of the Left, served as titular head of the government from 947 to the end of Murakami's reign, and Morosuke acted as Minister of the Right from 947 until his death in 960. Saneyori was a mild, punctilious man, whose encyclopedic knowledge of precedents and ancient usages was a valuable asset in a traditional society, but Morosuke was the more influential of the two.

One of the main reasons for Morosuke's prestige was his success as a father-in-law. At one time or another, three of Tadahira's sons—Saneyori, Morosuke, and Morotada (920-969)—introduced daughters into Murakami's palace. Saneyori's daughter Jusshi (933-947), a pathetic sacrifice to political expediency, conceived a child in 947 at the age of fourteen, contracted smallpox, and died. Morosuke's daughter Anshi (927-964) was more fortunate. Although she died at the relatively early age of thirty-seven, she was probably the single most influential person at Court for more than twenty years.

Anshi entered Murakami's household in 940, while he was still a Prince. She became a Junior Consort in 946, the year of the Emperor's accession, and was named Empress in 958. She gave birth to three of Murakami's nine sons—Norihira (Emperor Reizei), Tamehira, and Morihira (Emperor En'yū)—and to four daughters. Not only did she greatly increase Morosuke's prestige, but she saw to it that the Fujiwara power ultimately passed into the hands of her brothers, Koremasa, Kanemichi, and Kaneie.

Morotada's daughter Hōshi (d. 967) gave birth to two sons (of whom only one survived beyond infancy), but never displaced Anshi from her preeminent position in the Imperial harem.

Emperor Murakami's death in 967 brought his son Reizei to the throne at the age of seventeen. The boy, Anshi's first son, had been named Crown Prince in 950 at the age of two months. He was subject to periodic fits of insanity, an affliction attributed to the angry spirits of his half-brother and disappointed rival, Murakami's oldest son, and of the mother and grandfather of the unsuccessful Prince, all of whom had died when Reizei was about three years old. The new Emperor's brief two-year reign (967-969) is often called the start of the period of complete Fujiwara domination. He was unable even to go to the Great Hall of State for the enthronement ceremony, and all political matters were left to Saneyori, who became Regent and Chancellor in the year of his accession.

Emperor Reizei's incapacity made it expedient to select a Crown Prince as soon as possible. Anshi's second son, Tamehira (952-1010), was regarded as the logical choice. An attractive youth, he had been a favorite with both his parents, and both had wanted him to succeed the ailing Norihira (Reizei). In 966, however, Tamehira had married the daughter of Minamoto Takaakira, the Minister of the Right, whose wife was Anshi's sister. The Fujiwara leaders refused to agree to the nomination of an heir apparent whose father-in-law belonged to another family, and Murakami was forced to bow to their will. Shortly before his death, the Emperor is said to have told Saneyori to arrange the appointment of Anshi's third son, Morihira (Emperor En'yū).

Soon after Reizei's accession, Minamoto Takaakira had become Minister of the Left and Morotada Minister of the Right. Unlike earlier Minamoto ministers, who had looked to Fujiwara patronage for advancement, Takaakira was able and experienced enough to threaten Fujiwara interests. In the Third Month of 969, with his supporters Anshi, Morosuke, and Murakami safely dead, he was exiled to Kyūshū, charged with participation in a plot to dethrone Emperor Reizei in favor of Prince Tamehira. His sensational removal from office, and the sentencing of various conspirators, created a commotion in the capital unparalleled since Masakado's revolt. There is evidence that some of Prince Tamehira's supporters had actually planned a coup d'état, but

Takaakira's alleged complicity seems to have been a Fujiwara fabrication.[11]

The destruction of this last potential external rival, followed by Morotada's death in 969 and Saneyori's in 970, set the stage for an internal power struggle among members of the next Fujiwara generation.

TADAHIRA'S GRANDSONS

Koremasa In 969, before the deaths of Morotada and Saneyori, Emperor Reizei abdicated in favor of his ten-year-old brother, Morihira (Emperor En'yū, r. 969-984), apparently at the instigation of his uncle and father-in-law, Koremasa (924-972), who was Morosuke's oldest son. Koremasa's daughter Kaishi (945-975), who had entered Reizei's household before his accession, had given birth to a son in 968, and the grandfather was eager to establish the child as heir apparent before a son was produced by Kaishi's rival Chōshi (d. 982), a daughter of Koremasa's younger brother Kaneie (929-990). On the day of Reizei's abdication (Thirteenth Day, Eighth Month, 969), Kaishi's infant son, Morosada, was named Crown Prince.

Koremasa had shared much of the Regent Saneyori's power during Reizei's reign. He became Minister of the Right a few months after En'yū's accession, and the successive deaths of Morotada, Saneyori, and Arihira (the Minister of the Left) placed him in an unassailable position by the end of 970. Assuming the regency, he quickly promoted himself from Minister of the Right to Chancellor, but he lived to enjoy his power for only two years.

Kanemichi Koremasa was succeeded as Regent by his brother Kanemichi (925-977), Morosuke's second son. That event, unremarkable on the surface, was actually a shock to Court society. Kanemichi, described by chroniclers as a neurotic, boorish man of mediocre attainments, had been dismissed from two different positions a decade or so earlier, in the first instance by Murakami and in the second by Reizei. His younger brother Kaneie had replaced him in both offices, and had then consistently won preferment over him. Kaneie became a Provisional Middle Counselor in 969, the year of Emperor En'yū's accession,

---

[11] Apparently by Morotada, who aspired to Takaakira's office. The affair is known as the Anna incident, after the era name.

and Kanemichi, forced to be content with the inferior office of Consultant, alienated the Emperor by refusing to go to Court, where he would have been obliged to yield precedence to Kaneie.

In the Tenth Month of 972 it became known that Koremasa was dying. Kanemichi hurried to the Palace, obtained an interview with the reluctant Emperor, and produced a note in the handwriting of the late Empress Anshi, in which she recommended that her brothers be appointed to the regency successively in the order of their births. The Emperor had intended to name Kaneie, with whom he was on friendly terms, but he dutifully decided to appoint Kanemichi instead; and, as a first step, commanded him to assume control of the government during Koremasa's illness. Koremasa died on the first day of the following (Eleventh) month. Shortly afterward, Kanemichi became Palace Minister, and on the Twenty-Seventh of the Eleventh Month he was named Regent. Kaneie, a confident, aggressive man, is said to have been infuriated.

Early in 973, Kanemichi arranged a match between his twenty-six-year-old daughter Kōshi (947-979) and the fourteen-year-old Emperor; and within a matter of months he succeeded in elevating Kōshi to Imperial status. Meanwhile, in order to diminish Kaneie's influence, he turned to his cousin, Saneyori's son Yoritada (924-989), for help in administering the government.

During the next few years, the ill feeling between the brothers was nourished by mutual suspicion, and by rumors that Kaneie was planning to marry his daughter Senshi (962-1001) to the Emperor as Kōshi's rival. Just before his death in 977, Kanemichi demoted Kaneie and transferred the regency to Yoritada.

Yoritada The new Regent, like his father, was conscientious, painstaking in his observance of forms, discreet, and frugal. He had got along well with Kanemichi, and his relations with Kaneie were also amicable. On his recommendation, Kaneie was made Minister of the Right in 978, the year in which Yoritada became Chancellor. Around the same time, Kaneie presented Senshi as an Imperial bride. Yoritada's daughter Junshi (957-1017) also entered the Palace in 978. Two years later, Senshi gave birth to the Emperor's first son, the future Emperor Ichijō.

Meanwhile Chōshi, another of Kaneie's daughters, had borne three sons to Retired Emperor Reizei. Kaneie's future looked bright, especially since Empress Kōshi (Kanemichi's daughter) had died in 979 and Junshi was becoming known as the Barren Consort. In the First Month of 982, however, Chōshi died suddenly, and in the Third Month of the same year the Emperor elevated Junshi to Imperial status. Both events were bitter blows to Kaneie—particularly, it would seem, the latter. He retired to his Higashisanjō Mansion with Senshi and the baby, refusing to respond to summonses to Court.

Demoralized, apparently, by such behavior on the part of the powerful Minister of the Right, Emperor En'yū informed Kaneie in the Seventh Month of 984 of his intention to abdicate and make Senshi's child the new Crown Prince. Kaneie and his faction returned to Court, and the Emperor made good his commitment in the following month, at the age of twenty-five.

En'yū's successor was Emperor Kazan, the sixteen-year-old son of Reizei and Kaishi (Koremasa's daughter). His ministers were the same as En'yū's: Yoritada as Regent and Chancellor, Minamoto Masanobu as Minister of the Left, and Kaneie as Minister of the Right. Neither Yoritada nor Kaneie was directly related to the sovereign, a circumstance which made it possible for Kazan's twenty-seven-year-old uncle, Yoshichika (957-1008, Koremasa's fifth son), to acquire a voice in affairs of state. Yoshichika's power appears, indeed, to have exceeded the Regent's, even though his highest office during his nephew's reign was that of Provisional Middle Counselor.

Yoshichika is said to have been a shrewd and vigorous administrator. He and an able colleague, Koreshige, attempted to deal with some of the evils of the day, such as the growth of illegal private estates, but with little success.

Late in 984 Yoshichika's sister-in-law, Fujiwara Kishi (a daughter of Morosuke's ninth son, Tamemitsu), became an Imperial consort. Her death in the Seventh Month of 985 during the course of a pregnancy seems to have been a devastating shock to Emperor Kazan, who had inherited his father's mental instability, and who is described in *Eiga monogatari* as morbidly obsessed by the belief that a pregnant woman could not be reborn in the Pure Land. Kaneie, impatient for his grandson's accession, encouraged his son Michikane (961-995), who was Kazan's friend, to try to persuade the grieving Emperor to become a monk, and Michikane succeeded in doing so in the Sixth Month of 986.

Kaneie With the accession of his six-year-old grandson, Emperor Ichijō (r. 986-1011), Kaneie became Regent. His daughter Senshi, who had been living in her own home, returned to the Palace as the Emperor's mother, his grandson Prince Okisada (one of Reizei's sons by

Chōshi) was made heir apparent, and his daughter Suishi (974-1004) was presented to the new Crown Prince at the age of thirteen.

In the Seventh Month of 986, Kaneie turned over the office of Minister of the Right to his brother Tamemitsu, the father of the ill-fated Kishi. Yoritada and Minamoto Masanobu continued as Chancellor and Minister of the Left, but they were dominated by the Regent, who is reported to have treated the child sovereign with casual rudeness, to have allowed members of his family to insult important personages, and to have handled matters of state as though they were the private concerns of the Fujiwara family.

Kaneie established a reputation for ostentation and extravagance toward the end of his life. As part of the observances commemorating his sixtieth year, Imperial messengers were sent to commission sutra readings at sixty temples, and a banquet was held at the Palace, during which two of the Regent's grandsons danced in the Imperial presence. In 988 there was another great celebration, attended by the Minister of the Left and lesser dignitaries, to mark the completion of Kaneie's luxurious new Nijō Mansion. On that occasion, we are told, wine was poured by a troupe of courtesans, and thirty valuable horses were presented as gifts to the chief guests.

Kaneie assumed the office of Chancellor after Yoritada's death in 989. In the middle of 990 he fell ill, resigned as Regent, took religious vows, and converted the Nijō Mansion into a Buddhist hall, the Hōkōin (Hokoin). He died in his Higashisanjō residence in the Seventh Month of 990, at the age of sixty-one.

MICHINAGA AND HIS CONTEMPORARIES

In addition to his serviceable daughters, Kaneie had possessed numerous sons to bolster his position. The most prominent were three full brothers of Chōshi and Senshi: Michitaka (953-995), Michikane (961-995), and Michinaga (966-1027), all of whom rose rapidly after Emperor Ichijō's accession in 986. By 989 Michitaka, the oldest, was Palace Minister, Michikane was a Provisional Major Counselor, and Michinaga was a Provisional Middle Counselor. When Kaneie took Buddhist vows in 990, Michitaka succeeded him as Regent.

Michitaka is said to have cut an imposing and elegant figure as Regent, and to have been meticulous in his conduct of state affairs. During his five-year tenure he promoted his relatives even more rapidly than Kaneie had done. A few days after he assumed office his oldest son, Michiyori (971-995), was made a Consultant. In the following year, 991, his second and favorite son, Korechika (973-1010), became a Consultant at the age of eighteen. In the Ninth Month of the same year Michitaka turned over the office of Palace Minister to his brother Michikane, in spite of the prior claims of two other men. His brother Michinaga was made a Provisional Major Counselor and his son Michiyori a Provisional Middle Counselor, in each case over the heads of four men with greater seniority. At about the same time, Korechika became a Provisional Middle Counselor, and in the following year he moved ahead of Michiyori to become a Provisional Major Counselor.

Korechika's two promotions were merely a start. Michitaka was intent on grooming him for the regency, not only for the boy's sake but also to thwart the aspirations of Michikane, who had alienated the rest of the family by claiming exclusive credit for Emperor Kazan's abdication. In 994 he made him Palace Minister, brushing aside the claims of Tomomitsu (a son of Kanemichi), Naritoki (a son of Koremasa), and Korechika's uncle, Michinaga; and in 995, when he himself fell ill, he secured his appointment as interim head of the government.

The failing Michitaka pressed Emperor Ichijō to transfer the regency to Korechika. He was seconded by his daughter Teishi (976?-1000), who had become Ichijō's Empress in 990. But Ichijō's mother, Senshi, insisted that the appointment should go not to Korechika, whom she disliked, but to Michikane, the next of Kaneie's sons. Michitaka died in the Fourth Month of 995, while the Emperor was still trying to reach a decision.

In the end the mandate went to Michikane, who is described as a cold man, feared and disliked. Meanwhile, however, Michikane had contracted an epidemic disease, which claimed his life a week after the issuance of the edict, causing him to go down in history as the Seven-Day Regent.

Handsome, popular, favored by the Emperor and championed by the Empress, Korechika expected to be named the new Regent, but the formidable Senshi prevailed on His Majesty to order that all state affairs were to pass through Michinaga's hands. Although the word *kanpaku* did not appear in the edict, the powers granted were regental in scope, and Michinaga was the most powerful man in Japan from that date on (Eighth Day, Fifth Month, 995).

In the early days of Michinaga's rule the ambitious Korechika remained a threat, backed by Empress Teishi and their brother Takaie (979-1044), who was already showing signs of ability at the age of sixteen. On one occasion Korechika and Michinaga quarreled in a Palace apartment while a crowd of courtiers listened outside. A few days later, servants of the two engaged in a pitched battle. It was even rumored that Korechika had hired a soothsayer to curse his uncle. But Korechika made a fatal misstep early in 996. He was in the habit of visiting a lady known as Shinden no onkata, a sister of Retired Emperor Kazan's late consort Kishi. At the same time, the Retired Emperor, undaunted by his clerical status, was surreptitiously courting Shinden no onkata's younger sister, who lived with her. When Korechika learned of the Imperial visits, he concluded that Kazan must be competing with him for the favors of Shinden no onkata, a celebrated beauty. Takaie volunteered to frighten the former sovereign off, but when he waylaid him one of his companions shot an arrow through the Imperial sleeve. Kazan tried to cover up this act of lese majesty for obvious reasons, but the story became known, and the Court was compelled to take cognizance of it. To save Kazan's face, the official accusation against Korechika and Takaie refrained from naming the Retired Emperor, merely stating that some of the brothers' men had started a brawl with members of Kazan's entourage.

Since Emperor Ichijō was inclined to hush the matter up for Kazan's sake, it appeared for a time that Korechika would not be seriously affected. Soon, however, the Palace Minister was accused of having concealed a doll, with presumably hostile intent, in the main building of the Higashisanjō Mansion, where Senshi was lying ill; and a few days later the Court was informed by Hōrinji monks that Korechika had gone to their temple to perform a special esoteric rite, prohibited to all but members of the Imperial family. It is not clear whether or not Michinaga trumped up the last two charges. In any case, Korechika and Takaie were exiled on the Twenty-Fourth of the Fourth Month in 996. Although a general amnesty permitted their return in less than a year, Korechika's influence had been destroyed forever.

Empress Teishi fell on hard times after the disgrace of her brothers, who had been her only backers at Court. Through fear of Michinaga, Emperor Ichijō did not go in person to see his first child, a girl, to whom the Empress gave birth late in 996, but secretly sent a Court lady instead. For a time it seemed that Teishi would never appear in the Imperial Palace again, since she had taken religious vows on the day of Korechika's departure, but she finally went back in the middle of 997. Two years later, she prepared to leave the Palace to await the birth of her second child. Early on the day of her formal departure, Michinaga set out for Uji with a huge retinue, and the few remaining courtiers were afraid to assist in the departure ceremonies. After that public humiliation, Teishi lived quietly in the capital until the Eleventh Month of 999, when she gave birth to the Emperor's first son, Prince Atsuyasu (999-1018).

Although Michinaga prevented the birth from being celebrated as an event of great magnitude, he appears to have regarded the Empress as enough of a threat to necessitate his putting his own eldest daughter, Shōshi (988-1074), into the Palace, even though she was only eleven years old. Shōshi became a Junior Consort on the day of Prince Atsu-yasu's birth.

Eiga monogatari contains an enthusiastic description of the splendor of Shōshi's presentation. Courtiers streamed in and out of Michinaga's Tsuchimikado Mansion on the great day, and the highest nobles accompanied the bride's magnificent procession through the city streets. Her Palace apartments, luxuriously furnished by Michinaga, were filled with rare and tasteful objects. Among the things she brought with her was a folding screen decorated with poems, which had been composed for the occasion by the most important personages of the day, including—to the disgust of straitlaced observers—Retired Emperor Kazan, who had supposedly renounced the world and its vanities.

During the weeks after Prince Atsuyasu's birth, Teishi lived in seclusion with her two children, while Korechika busied himself with petitions to shrines and temples calculated to secure the succession for his nephew. In the Second Month of 1000, when Shōshi went home for a brief stay, Teishi returned to the Palace.

In the following month Teishi, who had previously borne the title *chūgū*, was named *kōgō*, and Shōshi became *chūgū*.[12] Shōshi's return to the Palace as a consort of Imperial rank was an even more glittering event than her original arrival, but Teishi was not there to witness it. Pregnant again, she had slipped away to the city, where she lived in neglect, except for the visits of Korechika and Takeie. Her pregnancy was a difficult one. We are told that Korechika begged famous monks to come and offer prayers, and that all refused. She gave birth to a daughter on the Fifteenth of the Twelfth Month and died on the Sixteenth.

Eight years later Shōshi bore her first child, Prince Atsuhira (1008-1036). The birth, which was commemorated by lavish celebrations (including an Imperial visit to the Tsuchimikado Mansion), extinguished Korechika's last hopes. The former Palace Minister died in 1010.

In 1009 Shōshi gave birth to a second son, Prince Atsunaga (1009-1045).

Emperor Ichijō fell seriously ill in 1011, by which time Teishi's son, Prince Atsuyasu, had become a bright twelve-year-old. His father would have liked to nominate the Prince for the succession, but Michinaga's opposition made it impossible. When the dying Emperor abdi-

---

[12] *Kōgō* and *chūgū*, both translatable as Empress, were originally interchangeable terms for the single consort of Imperial rank to whom an Emperor was entitled under the provisions of the Taihō Code. Emperor Ichijō was the first sovereign to confer the two titles on two different ladies.

cated in the Sixth Month of 1011, Prince Atsuhira became the Crown Prince of the new Emperor Sanjō (r. 1011-1016).

Emperor Sanjō was thirty-five years old, a son of the demented Emperor Reizei by Kaneie's daughter Chōshi. He had been happily married since 991 to a daughter of Morotada's son Naritoki, Seishi (d. 1025), who had presented him with numerous children, including his oldest son, Prince Atsuakira. Even before his accession, however, Michinaga had placed his sixteen-year-old second daughter, Kenshi (994-1027), in his household. Kenshi, a beauty like all of Michinaga's daughters, was a particular favorite with her father, who saw to it that all her costumes and furnishings rivaled those provided for Shōshi's memorable presentation. Both Seishi and Kenshi became Junior Consorts when Sanjō ascended the throne, and Kenshi was named Empress (*chūgū*) a few months later.

A curious episode followed. To the Emperor's surprise, Michinaga recommended that Seishi be given the title *kōgō*, but neither he nor the other two ministers of state appeared at the Palace on the date set for the ceremony. Many lesser notables also absented themselves. Meanwhile a crowd of courtiers had assembled at the apartments of Empress Kenshi, who was to travel from Michinaga's residence to the Palace on the same day. When messengers were sent to summon them, the gentlemen merely laughed, or, in some cases, pelted the envoys with stones. Sanjō commanded two or three loyal men to prepare the decree, held a makeshift ceremony, and appointed Takaie as head of the new Empress' household, a post that was going begging. Seishi had no influence from the time of her elevation on. She became a nun in 1019, three years after Sanjō's abdication, and died in 1025.

Eager for the accession of his grandson, Crown Prince Atsuhira, Michinaga waged a campaign to force Emperor Sanjō to abdicate. Since Sanjō suffered from failing vision, Michinaga used the disability as an excuse, but his motive seems to have been clear to the Emperor, who is said to have told Takaie that Michinaga had looked disappointed when he noticed a slight improvement in his eyes. Sanjō yielded in 1016, securing the heir apparency for his oldest son, Atsuakira, as the price of surrender. He abdicated late in the First Month and died a little over a year later.

The new Emperor, Go-Ichijō (r. 1016-1036), was eight years old. Michinaga acted as his *sesshō* until the Third Month of 1017, when he turned over the office to his son Yorimichi (992-1074)—the only period during which he held the formal title of Regent. He assumed the office of Chancellor in the Twelfth Month of 1017, after twenty-one years as Minister of the Left, but resigned in the Second Month of 1018.

In the middle of 1016, a great fire destroyed over 500 houses in the capital, including Michinaga's Tsuchimikado Mansion. Michinaga was overwhelmed with visits of sympathy, not only from residents of the city, but also from provincial governors, who hurried back from their posts at the news. The cost of rebuilding was borne by the governors, who were ordered to assign it first priority. Commoners were impressed to haul boulders for the garden, and gifts of every description were presented by members of the upper classes, notably the warrior chieftain Minamoto Yorimitsu (d. 1021), who supplied furnishings for the entire mansion, all in the most exquisite and luxurious taste. The magnificence of the completed house and its grounds is said to have attracted swarms of sightseers.

In the Eighth Month of 1017, pressure from Michinaga, exerted in the manner described in *The Great Mirror*, forced Prince Atsuakira to resign the heir apparency. He was replaced by Prince Atsunaga, Shōshi's second son.

In the First Month of 1018, two years after Go-Ichijō's accession, Michinaga supplied his ten-year-old Imperial grandson with a consort —his third daughter, Ishi (999-1036), who became Empress in the same year, at the age of nineteen. According to *Eiga monogatari*, His Majesty amused himself by playing with Ishi's comb boxes.

There was little left for Michinaga to desire. He had been a singularly fortunate man, as the *Ōkagami* author frequently reminds us, and had capitalized on his opportunities with shrewdness and determination. The epidemic of 995 had not only opened the way to his own advancement, but had also provided empty posts for him to fill with men of his choice. Firmly established early in life, he was able to supply successive Emperors with consorts as his daughters reached suitable ages. Korechika's imprudence, Sanjō's infirmity, and Koichijōin's weak nature were all turned to account.

At the pinnacle of earthly success, Michinaga set about in businesslike fashion to secure a comparable position in the life to come. He took Buddhist vows in 1019, and thereafter devoted much of his time and energy to religious activities, including the construction of the Hōjōji, the wonder of the age, which was dedicated in 1022.[13] In the Fifth Month of 1025, the narrative present of *The Great Mirror*, his family situation left nothing to be desired, his political power was absolute, and his prospects in the next world were as sanguine as money, art, and pious works could make them.

[13] For a voluminous account of Michinaga's Buddhist activities, see McCullough and McCullough 1980, Chapter 15ff.

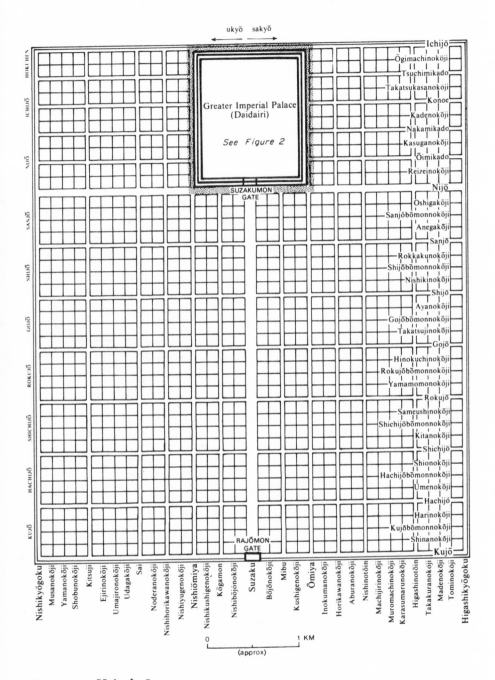

Figure 1. *Heiankyō*

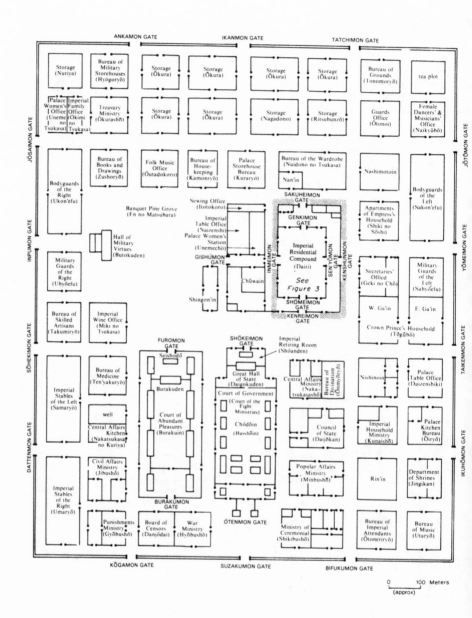

Figure 2. *The Greater Imperial Palace (Daidairi)*

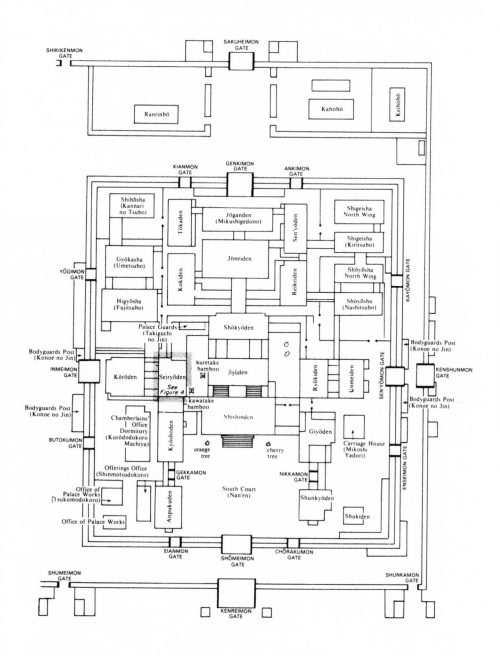

Figure 3. *The Imperial Residential Compound (Dairi)*

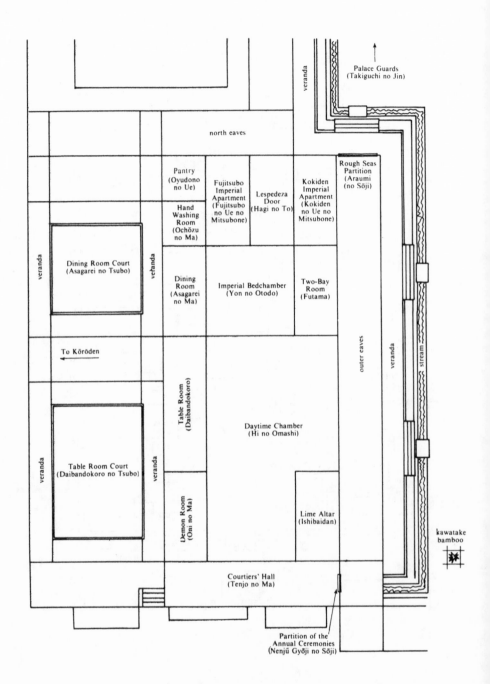

Figure 4. *The Emperor's Residence (Seiryōden)*

Works Cited

(Place of publication is Tōkyō unless otherwise noted.)

Andrews, Allan W. *The Teachings Essential for Rebirth: a Study of Genshin's Ōjōyōshū.* 1973.

Aston, W. G., tr. *Nihongi.* London, 1956.

Borgen, Robert. *Sugawara no Michizane: Ninth-Century Japanese Court Scholar, Poet, and Statesman.* Ph.D. dissertation, University of Michigan, 1978.

Braudy, Leo. *Hume, Fielding, and Gibbon: Narrative Form in History and Fiction.* Princeton, N.J., 1970.

Brower, Robert H. *The Konzyaku monogatarisyū: an Historical and Critical Introduction, with Annotated Translations of Seventy-Eight Tales.* Ph.D. dissertation, University of Michigan, 1952.

Carlyle, Alexander. *Anecdotes and Characters of the Times.* London, 1973.

Ceadel, E. B. "The Ōi River Poems and Preface." *Asia Major,* New Series, 3.1 (1953), pp. 65-106.

Chūgaishō, see Nakahara Moromoto

Chūyūki, see Fujiwara Munetada

Cranston, Edwin A. *The Izumi Shikibu Diary.* Cambridge, Mass., 1969.

Dainihon kokiroku, see Tōkyō Daigaku Shiryō Hensanjo

Dante Alighieri. *The Paradise.* Tr. John Ciardi. Mentor Book. New York and Toronto, 1970.

Eiga monogatari, ed. Matsumura Hiroji and Yamanaka Yutaka, Vols. 75-76 of *Nihon koten bungaku taikei.*

Eoyang, Eugene Chen. *Word of Mouth: Oral Storytelling in the Pien-wen.* Ph.D. dissertation, Indiana University, 1971.

Fujiwara Kintō. *Sanjūrokunin kasenden,* Vol. 3 of *Gunsho ruijū.*

———. *Wakan rōeishū,* ed. Kawaguchi Hisao and Shida Nobuyoshi, Vol. 73 of *Nihon koten bungaku taikei.*

Fujiwara Michinaga. *Midō kanpakuki,* in *Dainihon kokiroku.* 3 vols.

Fujiwara Munetada (1062-1141). *Chūyūki,* Vols. 4-10 of *Shiryō tsūran,* ed. Sasagawa Taneo. 1915-1918.

Fujiwara Sanesuke. *Shōyūki,* in *Dainihon kokiroku.* In progress.

Genji monogatari, see Murasaki Shikibu

Genkō shakusho, see Kokan Shiren

Genshin. *Ōjō yōshū,* Vol. 84 of Takakusu et al.

Gjertson, Donald Edward. *A Study and Translation of the Ming-pao chi: a T'ang Dynasty Collection of Buddhist Tales.* Ph.D. dissertation, Stanford University, 1975.

Gunsho ruijū, see Hanawa Hokiichi

Hagitani Boku. *Murasaki Shikibu nikki zenchūshaku*, in *Nihon koten hyō-shaku zenchūshaku sōsho*. 2 vols. 1971-1973.

Hallberg, Peter. *The Icelandic Saga*. Translated by Paul Schach. Lincoln, Neb., 1962.

Hanan, Patrick. "The Making of *The Pearl Sewn Shirt* and *The Courtesan's Jewel Box*." *Harvard Journal of Asiatic Studies*, 33 (1973), pp. 124-153.

Hanawa Hokiichi, comp. [*Shinkō*] *Gunsho ruijū*, ed. Sakamoto Kōtarō et al. 24 vols. 1938-1939.

────── and Hanawa Tadatomi, comps. *Zoku gunsho ruijū*. 71 vols. 1923-1930.

Honchō kōin shōunroku, Vol. 3 of *Gunsho ruijū*.

Hori Ichirō. "Mysterious Visitors from the Harvest to the New Year." *Studies in Japanese Folklore*, ed. Richard M. Dorson, pp. 76-103. Indiana University Folklore Series No. 17. Bloomington, Ind., 1963.

Hosaka Hiroshi. *Ōkagami shinkō*. 3 vols. 1974.

Hurvitz, Leon, tr. *Scripture of the Lotus Blossom of the Fine Dharma*. New York, 1976.

Ichidai yōki, Vol. 1 of *Shiseki shūran*, ed. Kondō Heijō et al., rev. Kondō Keizō. 1900.

Imazumi Atsuo et al. *Kyōto no rekishi*. 10 vols. 1968-1976.

Ishimura Teikichi. *Yūsoku kojitsu kenkyū*. 3 vols. 1958.

Kanke goshū, see Sugawara Michizane

Kawakami Tasuke. *Heianchō* (1), Vol. 3 of *Sōgō nihonshi taikei*. 1926.

Kawakita Noboru. *Eiga monogatari kenkyū*. 1968.

Keene, Donald. "The Tale of the Bamboo Cutter." *Monumenta Nipponica*, 11 (1956), pp. 1-27.

Ki no Tsurayuki et al., comps. *Kokin wakashū*, ed. Saeki Umetomo, Vol. 8 of *Nihon koten bungaku taikei*.

Kikuchi Ryōichi. "Shōdō bungei," Vol. 4 of *Iwanami Kōza nihon bungakushi*. 1958.

Kitagawa Hiroshi and Bruce T. Tsuchida, trs. *The Tale of the Heike*. 1975.

Koga Motoko. *Genji monogatari no shokubutsu*. 1971.

Kokan Shiren. *Genkō shakusho*, Vol. 31 of *Kokushi taikei*.

Kokinshū, see Ki no Tsurayuki

Kokin wakashū, see Ki no Tsurayuki

Kokushi taikei, see Kuroita Katsumi

Konishi Jin'ichi. "Association and Progression: Principles of Integration in Anthologies and Sequences of Japanese Court Poetry." Tr. Robert H. Brower and Earl Miner. *Harvard Journal of Asiatic Studies*, 21 (1958), pp. 67-127.

Konjaku monogatari, see *Konjaku monogatarishū*

Konjaku monogatarishū, ed. Yamada Yoshio et al., Vols. 22-26 of *Nihon koten bungaku taikei*.

Kugyō bunin, Vols. 53-57 of *Kokushi taikei*.

Kuroita Katsumi, ed. *Kokushi taikei*. Rev. ed. 66 vols. 1929-1964.

Kyōkai. *Nihon ryōiki*, ed. Endō Yoshimoto and Kasuga Kazuo, Vol. 70 of *Nihon koten bungaku taikei.*

Lord, Albert B., ed. *Serbocroatian Heroic Songs*. Vol. 1. Cambridge, Mass., and Belgrade, 1954.

Low, D. H. *The Ballads of Marko Kraljević*. Cambridge, England, 1922.

Makura no sōshi, see Sei Shōnagon

Matsumura Hiroji. *Eiga monogatari zenchūshaku*, in *Nihon koten zenchūshaku sōsho*. In progress. 1969-

———. *Rekishi monogatari.* 1961.

McCullough, Helen Craig, tr. "A Tale of Mutsu." *Harvard Journal of Asiatic Studies*, 25 (1965), pp. 178-211.

———. *Tales of Ise*. Stanford, Calif., 1968.

———. *Yoshitsune, a Fifteenth-Century Japanese Chronicle*. Stanford, Calif., 1966.

McCullough, William H. "Japanese Marriage Institutions in the Heian Period." *Harvard Journal of Asiatic Studies*, 27 (1967), pp. 103-167.

——— and Helen Craig McCullough. *A Tale of Flowering Fortunes*. Stanford, Calif., 1980.

Midō kanpakuki, see Fujiwara Michinaga

Mills, Douglas E. *A Collection of Tales from Uji: a Study and Translation of Uji shūi monogatari*. Cambridge, England, 1970.

Montoku jitsuroku, Vol. 8 of *Rikkokushi.*

Morris, Ivan, tr. *As I Crossed a Bridge of Dreams: Recollections of a Woman in Eleventh-Century Japan*. New York, 1971.

———, tr. *The Pillow Book of Sei Shōnagon*. 2 vols. New York, 1967.

Murasaki Shikibu. *Genji monogatari*, ed. Yamagishi Tokuhei, Vols. 14-18 of *Nihon koten bungaku taikei.*

Nagai Yoshinori. *Nihon bukkyō bungaku kenkyū*. 2 vols. Rev. ed. 1966-1967.

Nagano Jōichi. *Setsuwa bungaku jiten.* 1969.

Nakahara Moromoto. *Chūgaishō*, Vol. 11b of *Zoku gunsho ruijū.*

Nakamura, Kyoko Motomochi. *Miraculous Stories from the Japanese Buddhist Tradition: the Nihon ryōiki of the Monk Kyōkai*. Cambridge, Mass., 1973.

Nihon kiryaku, Vol. 11 of *Kokushi taikei.*

Nihon koten bungaku taikei, see Takagi Ichinosuke

Nihon rekishi daijiten. 22 vols. Kawade Shobō, 1956-1960.

Nihon ryōiki, see Kyōkai

Nishioka Toranosuke. *Shin nihonshi nenpyō*. Chūō Kōronsha, 1955.

Ōjō yōshū, see Genshin

Ōkagami, ed. Matsumura Hiroji, Vol. 21 of *Nihon koten bungaku taikei.*

Ōkagami, ed. Tachibana Kenji, Vol. 20 of *Nihon koten bungaku zenshū.* Shōgakkan, 1974.

O'Neill, P. G. *Early Nō Drama*. London, 1958.

Ovid. *Metamorphoses*. Tr. Rolfe Humphries. Midland paperback. Bloomington, Ind., and London, 1955.

Pai shih chang ch'ing chi. See Po Chü-i

Pálsson, Hermann, and Paul Edwards. *Egil's Saga*. Penguin Books. New York, 1978.

Payne, Robert. *The White Pony*. New York, 1947.

Plutarch's Lives. Ed. T. E. Page et al. The Loeb Classical Library. 11 vols. Cambridge, Mass., and London, 1914.

Po Chü-i. *Pai shih chang ch'ing chi*. Ssu pu ts'ung k'an ed. Shanghai, 1922.

Price, Glanville, ed. *William, Count of Orange: Four Old French Epics*. London and Totawa, N.J., 1975.

Rekisei Fukusō Bijutsu Kenkyūkai. *Nihon no fukusō*, Vol. 1. 1965.

Rikkokushi, see Saeki Ariyoshi

Ryō no gige, Vol. 22 of *Kokushi taikei*.

Saeki Ariyoshi, ed. [*Zōho*] *Rikkokushi*. 11 vols. 1940.

Sakamoto Yukio and Iwamoto Yutaka, eds. *Hokekyō*. Iwanami Bunko. 3 vols. 1964-1968.

Sanjūrokunin kasenden, see Fujiwara Kintō

Sasagawa Tanerō, comp. *Shiryō taisei*, ed. Yano Tarō. 43 vols. 1934-1944.

Satō Kyū. *Ōkagami shōkai*. 1929.

Sei Shōnagon. *Makura no sōshi*, ed. Ikeda Kikan and Kishigami Shinji, Vol. 19 of *Nihon koten bungaku taikei*.

Seidensticker, Edward G., tr. *The Gossamer Years: the Diary of a Noblewoman of Heian Japan*. Tōkyō and Rutland, Vt., 1964.

———, tr. *The Tale of Genji*. New York, 1976.

Shimonaka Yasaburō, ed. *Shintō daijiten*. 3 vols. 1941.

[*Shinkō*] *Gunsho ruijū*, see Hanawa Hokiichi

Shiryō taisei, see Sasagawa Tanerō

Shoku nihongi, Vols. 3-4 of *Rikkokushi*.

Shōyūki, see Fujiwara Sanesuke

Shūkaishō, Vol. 22 of *Kojitsu sōsho*, ed. Kojitsu Sōsho Hensanbu. Rev. ed. 39 vols. 1951-1957.

Sonpi bunmyaku, Vols. 58-60 of *Kokushi taikei*.

Soothill, William Edward, and Lewis Hodous. *A Dictionary of Chinese Buddhist Terms*. London, 1937.

Sugawara Michizane. *Kanke goshū*, Vol. 72 of *Nihon koten bungaku taikei*.

Swan, Charles. *Gesta Romanorum: Entertaining Moral Stories*. London, 1905.

Tachibana Kenji, see *Ōkagami*

Tahara, Mildred Machiko. *A Translation and Study of Yamato monogatari*. Ph.D. dissertation, Columbia University, 1969.

Takagi Ichinosuke et al., eds. *Nihon koten bungaku taikei*. 102 vols. 1957-1968.

Takakusu Junjirō, Watanabe Kaikyoku, and Ono Genmyō, eds. *Taishō shinshū daizōkyō*. 85 vols. 1924-1932.

Takamure Itsue. *Shōseikon no kenkyū*, Vols. 2-3 of *Takamure Itsue zenshū*, ed. Hashimoto Kenzō. 1966.

Tamagami Takuya. *Genji monogatari hyōshaku*. 14 vols. 1974-1976.

Tanabe Hisao. *Nihon ongakushi*. 1963.

Tanaka Jūtarō. *Makura no sōshi zenchūshaku*, in *Nihon koten zenchūshaku sōsho*. 2 vols. 1972-1975.

Thompson, Stith. *The Folktale*. Berkeley, Los Angeles, and London, 1977.

Tōkyō Daigaku Shiryō Hensanjo. *Dainihon kokiroku*. In progress. 1952-

Tomikura Tokujirō. "Biwa hōshi no katarimono," Vol. 5 of *Iwanami Kōza nihon bungakushi*. 1958.

Tsuchihashi Yutaka and Konishi Jun'ichi, eds. *Kodai kayōshū*, Vol. 3 of *Nihon koten bungaku taikei*.

Tsunoda Bun'ei. *Jōkyōden no nyōgo*. 1963.

Tubach, Frederic Christian. *History of the Exemplum in Germany to 1500*. Ph.D. dissertation, University of California (Berkeley), 1957.

Uda, Emperor. *Uda tennō gyoki*, Vol. 20 of *Ressei zenshū*, ed. Ressei Zenshū Hensankai. 1917.

Uji shūi monogatari, ed. Watanabe Tsunaya and Nishio Kōichi, Vol. 27 of *Nihon koten bungaku taikei*.

Ury, Marian. *Genkō shakusho, Japan's First Comprehensive History of Buddhism*. Ph.D. dissertation, University of California (Berkeley), 1970.

Wada Hidematsu. *Kanshoku yōkai*. 1953.

Wakan rōeishū, see Fujiwara Kintō

Waley, Arthur. *The Life and Times of Po Chü-i*. London, 1949.

Watson, Burton. *Records of the Grand Historian of China*. New York and London, 1961.

Webb, Herschel, and Marleigh Ryan. *Research in Japanese Sources: a Guide*. New York, 1963.

Wilson, William Ritchie. "The Way of the Bow and Arrow: the Japanese Warrior in *Konjaku Monogatari*." *Monumenta Nipponica*, 28.2 (Summer 1973), pp. 177-233.

Yamato monogatari, ed. Abe Toshiko and Imai Gen'e, Vol. 9 of *Nihon koten bungaku taikei*.

Yanagita Kunio. "Josei to minken denju," Vol. 8 of *Teihon Yanagita Kunio shū*. 1962-1971.

Zall, P. M., ed. *A Hundred Merry Tales and Other Jestbooks of the Fifteenth and Sixteenth Centuries*. Lincoln, Neb., 1963.

Zeami. *Fushi kaden*, ed. Hisamatsu Sen'ichi and Nishio Minoru, Vol. 65 of *Nihon koten bungaku taikei*.

Zoku gunsho ruijū, see Hanawa Hokiichi and Hanawa Tadatomi

Index

The surname is Fujiwara for persons listed only by given names. See also Appendix A.